SO-BYV-840

THE UTILIZATION OF 1 AND 2 CHRONICLES IN THE RECONSTRUCTION OF ISRAELITE HISTORY IN THE NINETEENTH CENTURY

SOCIETY
OF BIBLICAL
LITERATURE

DISSERTATION SERIES
J. J. M. Roberts, Old Testament Editor
Charles Talbert, New Testament Editor

Number 116

THE UTILIZATION OF 1 AND 2 CHRONICLES
IN THE RECONSTRUCTION OF ISRAELITE
HISTORY IN THE NINETEENTH CENTURY

by
Matt Patrick Graham

Matt Patrick Graham

THE UTILIZATION OF 1 AND 2 CHRONICLES IN THE RECONSTRUCTION OF ISRAELITE HISTORY IN THE NINETEENTH CENTURY

Scholars Press
Atlanta, Georgia

THE UTILIZATION OF 1 AND 2 CHRONICLES IN THE RECONSTRUCTION OF ISRAELITE HISTORY IN THE NINETEENTH CENTURY

BS
1345.2
.G7
1990

Matt Patrick Graham

© 1990
The Society of Biblical Literature

Library of Congress Cataloging in Publication Data

Graham, Matt Patrick.
    The utilization of 1 and 2 Chronicles in the reconstruction of
    Israelite history of the nineteenth century / Matt Patrick Graham.
    p.   cm. -- (Dissertation series / Society of Biblical
    Literature ; no. 116)
    Bibliography: p.
    ISBN 1-55540-354-9. -- ISBN 1-55540-355-7 (pbk.)
    1. Bible. O.T. Chronicles--Criticism, interpretation, etc. -
-History--19th century. 2. Jews--History--To 586 B.C.-
-Historiography. I. Title. II. Series: Dissertation series
(Society of Biblical Literature) ; no. 116.
BS1345.2.G7   1989
222'.6095--dc20   89-6336
                                                   CIP

Printed in the United States of America
on acid-free paper

ACKNOWLEDGMENTS

The present study is a corrected version of my 1983 Emory University doctoral dissertation. Credit for its completion and whatever benefit it offers other researchers must be shared with many. In particular, I want to acknowledge the encouragement of J. Maxwell Miller, Gene M. Tucker, Martin J. Buss, and the other Emory faculty, whose unselfish devotion to scholarship and teaching has placed me and many others in their debt. Most of all, however, thanks are due to John H. Hayes, whose patience, accessibility, and advice sustained and guided my research. Finally, I want to dedicate this work to my wife Doris in acknowledgment of her support and the sacrifices that she made for my education at Emory.

CONTENTS

CHAPTER I

INTRODUCTION: PRE-CRITICAL TRADITIONAL VIEWS OF CHRONICLES

The canonical books of Chronicles have presented their readers with problems since antiquity. This is because there are numerous differences in detail between 1, 2 Chronicles and other books in the Hebrew canon and because the spirit and tone of Chronicles are decidedly different from those in Samuel and Kings. These factors about Chronicles are no modern discovery. On the contrary, they were recognized in antiquity and the fact that Chronicles occupies the last place in the Hebrew canon may perhaps reflect concern about these issues. Josephus and the earliest Christian commentators on Chronicles were well aware of the difficulties associated with Chronicles. De Wette and later biblical critics, who departed from the traditional interpretation of Chronicles, called attention to these problems more clearly and forcefully than formerly and then suggested on the basis of these problems some radically different conclusions about Chronicles' historical reliability. Thus, while earlier generations had detected some of the problems that were raised in the use of Chronicles as a historical source, it was only with de Wette and others in the nineteenth century that serious and widespread scepticism arose concerning the historical credibility of 1, 2 Chronicles.

In this chapter we will quickly survey the pre-nineteenth century attitudes toward Chronicles as a historical source. Practically all the evidence—Josephus, ancient and medieval Christian commentaries, the English historian Prideaux, and the early German critics Eichhorn and Jahn—suggests that Chronicles was trusted as a reliable source for historical information. Therefore, it was used to supplement information in Samuel-Kings, and whenever dissimilarities between the two parallel histories occurred, they were harmonized. Spinoza, Hugh of St. Cher, and a few others diverged somewhat from their contemporaries' confidence in Chronicles, but their views were not systematically presented and did not enjoy much popularity. Finally, it will be shown that in the years just before de Wette's *Beiträge zur Einleitung in das Alte Testament* of 1806 the questions of *Einleitungswissenschaft* were being applied to Chronicles, and the authorship, date, and sources for the books were being explored and discussed more thoroughly than before.

Before the nineteenth century most of those who wrote commentaries on Chronicles or histories of Israel used 1, 2 Chronicles with confidence and accepted their historical testimony about the pre-exilic period largely at face value. In these works Chronicles was generally understood to supplement the contents of other biblical books, especially Samuel-Kings. The Greek title *Paraleipomena* ("omitted things") points to such an understanding of the work at a relatively early date, and Josephus used Chronicles in this way throughout his *Antiquitates Judaicae*. This can be seen, for example, when he included the list of Rehoboam's fortified cities from 2 Chr 11:5-12 and the account of Asa's war with Zerah in 2 Chr 14:8-14.[1] The same use of Chronicles occurred in the fifth and sixth centuries in the works of Theodoret of Cyrrhus (ca. 393-458) and Procopius of Gaza (ca. 475-538). Both of these writers appropriated Chronicles' report that King Joash was assassinated as punishment for his role in the murder of Zechariah the prophet.[2] In the eighteenth century Humphrey Prideaux also used Chronicles as a source for supplementary information about the pre-exilic period. He was following Chronicles, when he wrote that Hezekiah began his reign with a cultic reform (2 Chronicles 29) and organized an extensive Passover celebration (2 Chronicles 30). When he turned to consider Manasseh's reign, he included details about the king's imprisonment in Babylon, his repentance and release. This information about Manasseh is found in 2 Chronicles 33 but not in 2 Kings.[3] Later scholars, such as Johann J. Jahn (1750-1816) and J. G. Eichhorn (1752-

---

[1]Josephus, *Antiquitates Judaicae* VIII 246, 292.

[2]Theodoret, *Quaestiones in libros Regnorum et Paralipomenon* (PG 80.844) and Procopius, *Commentarii in Libros I,II Paralipomenon* (PG 87.1216). Theodoret of Cyrrhus was educated in Antioch of Syria and his works represent some of the best examples of Antiochene exegesis. His work on Chronicles amounts to little more than a simple retelling of the biblical narrative. Occasionally, he adds a moralizing ending to his account of a king's reign. Procopius of Gaza authored a shorter work, reproducing much of what he had read in Theodoret. Cf. Thomas Willi, *Die Chronik als Auslegung* (FRLANT 106; Göttingen: Vandenhoeck & Ruprecht, 1972) 17.

[3]Humphrey Prideaux, *The Old and New Testament Connected in the History of the Jews, and Neighbourina Nations; from the Declension of the Kingdoms of Israel and Judah to the Time of Christ* (15th ed.; New York: Harper & Bros., 1871) 1.70-71, 80. Prideaux (1648-1724) was Dean of Norwich and issued the first volume of his history in 1715. The work begins only with 747 B. C. E. and aimed at correlating the history of Israel with the history of its neighbors. The author used a variety of sources (the Bible, Josephus, the Talmud, early Christian authors, and Herodotus), but he did not accept their testimony without discretion. Whenever he found their information useful, he employed the Books of Chronicles, accepting their reports virtually without question.

1827), also advocated such a use of Chronicles. Jahn regularly incorporated information from Chronicles in his work *The History of the Hebrew Commonwealth*, and he used that information as confidently as that from Samuel-Kings. In his treatment of Rehoboam, for example, he accepted Chronicles' enumeration of Shishak's forces in their attack on Judah, as well as Chronicles' account of Shemaiah's prophecy against Rehoboam and its theological motivation for the Egyptian attack. He also repeated Chronicles' story about Asa's war with Zerah.[4] Eichhorn believed that Chronicles offered reliable historical information about the pre-exilic period since the author of Chronicles faithfully transmitted the information from his sources which were themselves reliable.[5]

Whenever it appeared that Chronicles contradicted statements elsewhere in Scripture, the usual procedure in pre-nineteenth century scholarship was to harmonize the accounts. Since Josephus' apparent purpose in his *Antiquitates Judaicae* was to demonstrate the antiquity of the Jewish race and defend the Jews against the disparagement of their enemies,[6] his treatment of contradictions between Chronicles and Samuel-Kings comes as no surprise. His usual method was not to draw attention to any conflicts among the biblical books, but simply to choose the testimony of one over the other and then to pass silently over the rejected testimony. To have done otherwise would have been to lay the Jewish scriptures open to the very charge that he had made against the Greek historians: the reporting of contradictory accounts.

> Surely, then, it is absurd that the Greeks should be so conceited as to think themselves the sole possessors of a knowledge of antiquity and

---

[4]Johann J. Jahn, *The History of the Hebrew Commonwealth from the Earliest Times to the Destruction of Jerusalem A.D. 72* (London: Hurst, Chance, & Co., 1829) 129-30. Jahn was a Roman Catholic scholar who had served as a pastor and later as professor of oriental languages, biblical archaeology, and dogmatics in Vienna until he was forced to resign his chair at the latter in 1806 because of clerical opposition to his publications. His edition of the Hebrew Bible (*Biblia Hebraica*; 4 vols.; Vienna: F. C. Wappler & Beck, 1806) differed from other editions in that it divided the Books of Chronicles into segments and printed them alongside their parallels elsewhere in the Old Testament. Werner, "Jahn, Johann J.," *ADB* 13 (1881) 665-66; "Jahn, Johann," *Enc Brit* 13 (1889) 542-43.

[5]J. G. Eichhorn, *Einleitung in das Alte Testament* (3d ed.; Leipzig: Weidmann, 1803) 3.591-93. The first edition of Eichhorn's *Einleitung* appeared in 1780-83. The third edition, though, was issued in 1803 and so represents the author's latest thinking on the eve of the publication of de Wette's *Beiträge* (1806-07). Eichhorn (1752-1827) studied at Göttingen under Michaelis and Heyne and returned there in 1788 to teach. He was the "most important exegete of his time" according to Smend, and the science of Old Testament introduction grew up largely out of his work. Cf. Hans-Jürgen Zobel, "Eichhorn, Johann Gottfried, " *TRE* 9 (1982) 369-71.

the only accurate reporters of its history. Anyone can easily discover from the historians themselves that their writings have no basis of sure knowledge, but merely present the facts as conjectured by individual authors. More often than not they confute each other in their works, not hesitating to give the most contradictory accounts of the same events.[7]

Josephus' care to avoid mentioning the contradictions between Chronicles and the other books of the Bible, therefore, was a natural expression of his desire to vindicate the Jewish people. A striking example of his method in this regard can be found in his blending of the accounts of Asa's reign in Chronicles and Kings. The latter work presents the king as a righteous monarch, who nevertheless suffered several reverses (wars with Baasha and disease in his feet), but Chronicles accounts for Asa's setbacks by reporting instances of the king's sin. Josephus attempted to portray Asa as a wholly righteous king, and he did this by reporting items from Kings and Chronicles that would advance this aim, and by omitting items that would detract from it. Thus, he repeated the account of Asa's victory over Baasha, but he omitted Hanani's condemnation of Asa for faithlessness in achieving that victory. Moreover, he left out references to Asa's disease in the feet and to his consultation with physicians rather than with God.[8] In similar fashion, Stephen Langton's (d. 1228) commentary on Chronicles set out to harmonize the differences between Chronicles and Samuel-Kings,[9] and Prideaux's history made frequent use of the same technique.[10] Jahn was convinced that harmonization was a legitimate method in historical research and set forth in his introduction a rationale for its practice.

> As the books of Samuel and Kings contain the same history as the books of Chronicles, the two works should be continually compared not merely in order to become the more thoroughly acquainted with the history, but also for the purpose of applying the one to illustrate or correct what may be obscure or erroneous in the other.[11]

---

[6]Cf. Thomas W. Franxman, *Genesis and the "Jewish Antiquities" of Flavius Josephus* (BibOr 35; Rome: Biblical Institute, 1979) 5.

[7]Josephus, *Contra Apionem* I 15 . The translation is Thackeray's from The Loeb Classical Library.

[8]Josephus, *Antiquitates Judaicae* VIII 292-97.

[9]Stephen Langton, *Commentary on the Book of Chronicles* (ed. Avrom Saltman; Ramat-Gan: Bar-Ilan University, 1978) 26-29.

[10]For example, Prideaux harmonized the two accounts of Josiah's reign. He wrote that Josiah undertook a religious reform in the eighth year of his reign, continued the reform in his twelfth year of rule, and finally, instituted the repair of the temple in the eighteenth year of his reign, during which time the Book of the Law was found. *History of the Jews*, 88-89.

[11]J. Jahn, *An Introduction to the Old Testament* (New York: G. & C. Carvill, 1827) 271.

Jahn's reference to the "erroneous" should not be taken to mean that he believed that the authors of Scripture had deliberately altered their sources or made mistakes in their compositions. On the contrary, the contradictions or differences between Chronicles and Samuel-Kings are either of little consequence, in Jahn's estimation, or can be explained as textual corruptions or by the author's choices to omit or add bits of information, either contained or omitted in the parallel history, or by the recognition of later interpolations.[12]

Because of the high esteem that many writers had for the Books of Chronicles in the period before 1800, some of the descriptions in the Chronicler's account were sometimes even preferred to those of Samuel-Kings. This was the case with Josephus who preferred the Chronicler's position that King Joash was denied burial in the royal tombs because of his wickedness over the position of Kings that Joash was buried with his fathers in Jerusalem.[13] Prideaux also followed Chronicles in this regard noting that it was the custom "of the Jews to lay this mark of infamy upon those that reigned wickedly over them."[14]

In spite of the confidence that most writers who dealt with Chronicles had in the books, a tendency to view Chronicles with a bit of suspicion is occasionally evident. The talmudic authorities (Lev. R. i.3; cf. Meg. 13a), for example, regarded Chronicles with suspicion and saw its chief value to be for homiletical purposes. Moreover, it is clear from its position in the third division of the Hebrew canon that Chronicles did not enjoy in Jewish circles a status equal to that of the books of Samuel and Kings.[15] At a later time, Spinoza revealed a considerable distrust for the Books of Chronicles.

> As to their actual writer, their authority, utility, and doctrine, I come to no conclusion. I have always been astonished that they have been included in the Bible by men who shut out from the canon the books of Wisdom, Tobit, and the others styled apocryphal. I do not aim at disparaging their authority, but as they are universally received, I will leave them as they are.[16]

---

[12]*Ibid.*, 269.

[13]Josephus, *Antiquitates Judaicae* IX 161-72.

[14]Prideaux, *History of the Jews*, 70.

[15]Emil J. Hirsch, "Books of Chronicles," *JE* 4 (1903) 60. The targum on Chronicles, whose written form may not have been fixed until the seventh century, is of little use to indicate the role of the books in historical reconstruction. Cf. R. Le Déaut and J. Robert, *Targum des Chroniques* (AnBib 51; Rome: Biblical Institute, 1971); Willi, *Chronik als Auslegung*, 17-18.

[16]Cited in R. H. M. Elwes, *The Chief Works of Benedict de Spinoza* (London: George Bell & Sons, 1883) 146. Moreover, Spinoza dated Chronicles to the Maccabean period. *Ibid.*

Some Christian scholars shared Spinoza's misgivings. Hugh of St. Cher, for example, thought that the Jews were too generous in allowing Chronicles even admission to the Kethubim. He believed that its place was in the Apocrypha.[17] Eichhorn also had some misgivings about information in Chronicles, but he attributed the discrepancies between Samuel-Kings and Chronicles to errors that crept into the source material that was used by both the authors of Samuel-Kings and Chronicles.[18] Jahn, too, saw textual corruption as the cause for many of the differences between the parallel texts.[19]

The matters of the authorship, date, and sources of Chronicles were not treated extensively in the earliest commentaries and histories which used Chronicles, but by the time of Simon, Eichhorn, and Jahn these matters had become important. In the discussions of these issues it was often affirmed that Ezra wrote Chronicles and that he drew upon reliable sources for his information. Simon defended the author of Chronicles from charges of error which might arise from a comparison of the books with Samuel-Kings, and he did this by pointing out that the current text of the Hebrew Bible had been corrupted by copyists' errors.[20] Eichhorn believed that some of Ezra's sources for Chronicles were "original" (e.g., "the words of Samuel"), viz., they were written by contemporaries of the events described, and others were "derived" (e.g., the "Midrash of the Book of the Kings"), viz., they were written by people who depended on written sources for their descriptions of events. He further held that the first two-thirds of the work derived from an ancient *"Lebensbeschreibung"* which Ezra reproduced with some additions. Since the same work also lay behind Samuel-Kings, Eichhorn thought that the discrepancies between the parallel histories were due to errors that slipped into the document before Ezra received it. Generally, Eichhorn held that Ezra faithfully reproduced his sources (often literally), although he sometimes made changes to accommodate the narrative to the language of the people of his own day. Eichhorn appears to have been the first to deal extensively with the issue of the Chronicler's sources.[21] Finally, Jahn was also concerned with the question of the Chronicler's sources, and he recognized that that issue was closely related to the matter of the historical reliability of 1, 2 Chronicles. Jahn began by excising the genealogy of 1 Chr 3:19-24

---

[17]Cited in Langton, *Commentary*, 12.

[18]Eichhorn, *Einleitung*, 3.587.

[19]Jahn, *Introduction*, 269.

[20]Richard Simon, *Histoire critique du Vieux Testament* (new ed.; Rotterdam: Reinier Leers, 1685-93) 1.23-28. Cf. Willi, *Chronik als Auslegung*, 30.

[21]Eichhorn, *Einleitung*, 587-600.

from consideration, arguing that it was a later addition to the work.[22] According to Jahn, the Chronicler's source citations indicate that he used many different writings in composing his work, and the references themselves, as well as the similarities between Samuel-Kings and Chronicles, indicate that the authors of the two works used many of the same sources. The references to the writings of prophets in Chronicles indicate that from Samuel on various prophets wrote the histories of their times and that these were incorporated into the royal annals. Some of these writings by the prophets, however, were not incorporated into the royal annals, as is indicated by the source citations which separate the two. Since the Chronicler sometimes carefully omitted information in Samuel, that is necessary for understanding Chronicles, it is therefore clear that the Chronicler assumed that his readers were acquainted with the Books of Samuel.[23] In addition to his observations on the sources used in the composition of Chronicles, Jahn offers eight reasons to support the reliability of the books as a historical source. (1) The Chronicler's sources were written by people who were contemporaries with the events that they described. (2) The Chronicler showed his fidelity by pointing his readers to his sources of information. (3) The first readers of Chronicles who were able to compare Chronicles with other ancient sources evidently chose to preserve Chronicles but to allow the other ancient writings to pass out of existence. Thus, the worth and reliability of Chronicles were affirmed. (4) The Chronicler adhered closely to his sources and retained their wording. This is evident from the stylistic variations within Chronicles which coincide with the use of different sources. (5) Many expressions do not fit the Chronicler's own period and so have apparently been retained from sources contemporary with the ancient events that are reported (cf. 1 Kg 8:22 with 2 Chr 6:12). (6) Many of the reports in Chronicles discredit Judah, and the speeches in Chronicles fit their speakers and situations more convincingly than one would expect of fictitious or altered compositions. (7) The entire course of history in Chronicles is confirmed by the witness of other contemporary authors (e.g., the psalmists and prophets), whose reports of the various periods agree with Chronicles. (8) The differences between Samuel-Kings and Chronicles indicate that the latter did not use the former as a source and that the former was not altered to agree with the latter.[24]

Before 1800, there had been various figures, who had had a measure of distrust for the historical reliability of 1, 2 Chronicles (e.g.,

---

[22]Jahn believed that the author of Chronicles was anonymous and that differences in style and manner of narration separated the composers of Ezra and Chronicles. *Introduction*, 261-62.

[23]*Ibid.*, 263-64.

[24]*Ibid.*, 266-70.

Hugh of St. Cher and Spinoza), but the general and prevalent opinion was that the books were reliable sources for historical information about the pre-exilic period. While the historical critical method was being applied more and more in the investigation of Chronicles, it was not being applied rigorously. There was an eagerness to supplement Samuel-Kings and Chronicles with one another and harmonize their accounts, and textual criticism was a further tool for relieving the author of Chronicles of responsibility for errors in the MT. Various writers suggested source theories, but they did not rigorously defend them and show how the author of Chronicles could have derived his information from reliable sources. Finally, in the period before 1800, most of the writers still held to some form of the view that the Pentateuch, and therefore the cultus presupposed by Chronicles, derived from Moses. Even scholars who separated the Pentateuch into various sources had no idea of the influence that the source criticism of the Pentateuch would eventually exert on the question of the Chronicler's historical reliability.

CHAPTER II

THE FIRST CHALLENGE TO THE CREDIBILITY OF CHRONICLES AND ITS CONSEQUENCES FOR THE RECONSTRUCTION OF ISRAELITE HISTORY

A. THE CHALLENGE: DE WETTE, GESENIUS, AND GRAMBERG

Before 1806, the commentaries, histories, and other works that dealt with Chronicles in terms of its historical credibility generally reflected the opinion that the books could be used with confidence for historical reconstruction. The publication of de Wette's *Beiträge* in 1806, however, changed all this by challenging forcefully and systematically the reliability of Chronicles as a witness to the pre-exilic period of Israel's history. Works by Gesenius and Gramberg soon followed, and they presented additional arguments that undercut the credibility of Chronicles' historical testimony. These criticisms of Chronicles did not pass unanswered. Bertholdt and Dahler responded to de Wette's arguments before 1820, and the 1830s witnessed the publication of four additional works that defended the trustworthiness of Chronicles as a historical source (Herbst, Keil, Movers, and Hävernick). The consequences of this debate over Chronicles' reliability became evident in the histories and other literature that evaluated the reliability of the books as historical sources. Ewald's history was the most significant work in this regard prior to Wellhausen's *Prolegomena*. The histories of Israel before Ewald were only mildly critical, and those after him but before Wellhausen were influenced greatly by Ewald's cautious acceptance of Chronicles as a reputable historical source. During the first two-thirds or three-fourths of the nineteenth century, therefore, the attitude of Old Testament scholarship towards Chronicles as a historical witness to the monarchical period may be outlined as follows. The century began with a confidence in Chronicles, which was shortly challenged by de Wette and a few others. This, in turn, was followed by a series of writings that reasserted the basic trustworthiness of Chronicles, and the end of the period saw the dominance of Ewald's view that—with

the exception of various exaggerations and embellishments—
Chronicles was a generally reliable source of information about the
pre-exilic period.

1. DE WETTE

a. De Wette and his Approach

W. M. L. de Wette (1780-1849) was born near Weimar and attended gymnasium there, where he met Herder as examiner and
preacher. In 1799, he went to the University of Jena and studied under the rationalists Gabler and Paulus and under the Kantian
philosopher J. F. Fries.[1] Subsequently, he moved to Heidelberg,
where he taught from 1807 until 1810. Smend calls this the "Jena and
Heidelberg Period" of de Wette's life,[2] and it was during this time
that his first major publication, *Dissertatio critico-exegetica, qua
Deuteronomium a prioribus Pentateuchi libris diversum, alius cuiusdam re-
centioris auctoris opus esse monstratur*, appeared (1805). In it de Wette
argued that Deuteronomy was written by a different person and at a
later time than the rest of the Pentateuch. Moreover, he concluded
that the date of the composition of Deuteronomy could be assigned to
the time shortly before Josiah's reform of 621 B. C. E. This position
proved to be crucial for later work on the Pentateuch, since it provided a specific date for a previously isolated major Pentateuchal
stratum, making it possible to relate other strata to this material and
its dating. Moreover, the assignment of a seventh-century date to
Deuteronomy demonstrated that the Pentateuch as a whole was late
and that the "Mosaic" institutions and pre-settlement traditions in the
Pentateuch could not be accepted at face value as historical.[3]

In 1806, de Wette's work on Chronicles appeared: *Kritischer
Versuch über die Glaubwürdigkeit der Bücher der Chronik mit Hinsicht auf
die Geschichte der Mosaischen Bücher und Gesetzgebung*. In this work de

---

[1]T. K. Cheyne, *Founders of Old Testament Criticism* (London: Methuen, 1893) 31-
32. See also Friedrich Lücke, "Zur freundschaftlichen Erinnerung an D. Wilhelm
Martin Leberecht de Wette," *TSK* (1850) 497-535; and John Rogerson, *Old
Testament Criticism in the Nineteenth Century: England and Germany* (Philadelphia:
Fortress, 1985) 28-49.

[2]Rudolf Smend, "De Wette und das Verhältniss zwischen historischer
Bibelkritik und philosophischem System im 19. Jahrhundert," *ThZ* 14 (1958) 107-
8.

[3]J. F. L. George (*Die älteren Jüdischen Feste mit einer Kritik der Gesetzgebung des
Pentateuch* [Berlin: E. H. Schroeder, 1835] 10ff.) argued against de Wette that
Leviticus, Numbers, and parts of Exodus were later than Deuteronomy, because
the religious rituals in the former were more highly developed and similar to
Judaism than the rituals in Deuteronomy. Consequently, the former must be
dated after Deuteronomy, which George regarded as Josiah's lawbook. Rogerson,
Criticism, 64.

Wette analyzed 1, 2 Chronicles and concluded that the books are worthless for the historical reconstruction of the periods that they treat. A second section of this publication dealt with the consequences of this conclusion for the study of the Pentateuch.

In 1807, the second half of de Wette's *Beiträge zur Einleitung in das Alte Testament* appeared. While the first part dealt with Chronicles, the second was concerned with Israelite history as it is presented in the Pentateuch and was entitled, *Kritik der Israelitischen Geschichte*. In this work de Wette defined the criteria for evaluating historical sources with regard to their credibility and usefulness for historical reconstruction, and as he moved through the Pentateuch, he found little of historical value.

A third significant work from this period of de Wette's career was his commentary *Die Psalmen* (1811). In it he anticipated in several respects the later form-critical work of Gunkel in that he classified the various psalms into six categories according to their content: hymns (in which Yahweh is praised), national (*volksthümliche*) psalms (containing references to Israel's ancient history and to the people's relationship to God), Zion and temple psalms, royal psalms, psalms of lament, and religious and moral psalms.

This earliest period of de Wette's scholarly career is often recognized as important, because it produced his greatest and most lasting contributions to Old Testament research. T. K. Cheyne, for instance, wrote,

> Criticism was his strong point, and he would have done well to concentrate himself more upon this. For I must, however unwillingly, admit that De Wette as a critic never quite realized the promise of his early years.[4]

Similarly, Wellhausen relied heavily upon de Wette's earlier work but commented, "What De Wette has written elsewhere is less important."[5]

The second major period in de Wette's career began in 1811 and lasted until 1818/19. This was the time of his stay at the University of Berlin. The school had only recently been established (in 1810), and Schleiermacher had been responsible for de Wette's call to teach there. During these years, de Wette published works on Christian dogmatics, Hebrew-Jewish *"Archäologie"* (in the sense of antiquities), religion and theology, and an Old Testament introduction. De Wette's career at Berlin came to an abrupt end because of his involvement in a political fiasco. K. L. Sand, a young liberal student, as-

---

[4]Cheyne, *Founders*, 49-50.

[5]J. Wellhausen, *Geschichte Israels*, 1, 4, f.n.1 (omitted in following editions), cited by Rudolf Smend, *Wilhelm Martin Leberecht de Wettes Arbeit am alten und am neuen Testament* (Basel: Helbing & Lichtenhahn, 1958) 109.

sassinated the Russian dramatist Kotzebue, since he regarded the latter as a threat to freedom. The act created a great outcry against liberal students and their professors, among whom were Schleiermacher and de Wette. The latter wrote a letter to Sand's mother, in which he stated, "Only according to his faith is each man judged. Committed as this deed has been by a pure-minded, pious youth, it is a beautiful sign of the time...." The secret police obtained the letter and de Wette was dismissed from his chair at Berlin.[6]

The "Basel Period," lasting from 1818 until 1849, was the final segment of de Wette's career. After leaving Berlin and staying for a brief time in Weimar, de Wette assumed a professorial chair in Basel in 1822. In the years that followed, he published a work on Christian ethics (1819, 1823), a novel (1822), five volumes of Luther's letters and other papers (1825-1828), a New Testament introduction (1826), a second didactic story (1829), an exegetical handbook to the New Testament (1836-1848), and five volumes of sermons (1825-1849).[7]

b. Influences on de Wette

Scholars have sought to determine the major influences which shaped the career and contributions of de Wette. A significant influence recognized by all interpreters was the philosopher Jakob Friedrich Fries. When Smend discusses the development of de Wette's career and writings, he assigns the influence of Fries to the second or "Berlin Period" and concludes that Fries' influence on de Wette began to wane with the beginning of the "Basel Period."[8] Moreover, Smend characterizes the writings from the first period of de Wette's career as "negative," while those from the last two periods are considered more "positive."[9] Rogerson argues convincingly that both of these observations about de Wette are a bit misleading.[10] First of all, the influence of Fries on de Wette probably began as early as 1801, when the latter attended lectures by Fries at Jena. During this time, de Wette wrote an essay entitled *Eine Idee über das Studium der Theologie*, which was later edited by A. Stieren and published in Leipzig in 1850. This work already clearly reflects the thinking and language of Fries.[11] Secondly, while de Wette's earlier works may have appeared "negative," because they challenged the traditional

---

[6]Cheyne, *Founders*, 43-45; Smend, "De Wette," 108. The chair that de Wette vacated was not filled until 1828, when Hengstenberg was appointed to it. Rogerson, *Criticism*, 87.

[7]Smend, 108-9.

[8]*Ibid.*, 109-10.

[9]*Ibid.*, 107-8.

[10]Rogerson, *Criticism*, 36-44.

[11]Adelbert Wiegand, *W. M. L. de Wette. Eine Säkularschrift* (Erfurt: A. Stenger, 1879) 11-12. Rogerson, *Criticism*, 28, 36-44.

ideas of the unity and date of certain biblical materials, these publications by de Wette in fact had a "positive" aim. De Wette, following Fries, argued that the human personality, through the faculty of premonition, could sense and grasp eternal ideas. The Old Testament, according to de Wette, was a book of religion, produced by people who sensed eternal ideas and then gave their sensations expression in various literary ways (e.g., myth and poetry). Since some religious and literary forms are more adequate expressions of eternal ideas than others, the critic must investigate the history of Israel's religion in order to sketch its development and to uncover those expressions which best embody the premonition and intuition of eternal ideas. Therefore, the purpose of biblical criticism is ultimately the study of religion, a positive aim.[12] Finally, when these goals of his work are recognized, de Wette's career emerges with a bit more homogeneity. At the beginning he published theses that were both novel and creative, and the rest of his career was spent in refining, elucidating, and extending them. Nevertheless, in de Wette's later years biographers usually find a growing attachment to "old-Lutheran orthodoxy."

> Does he become henceforth virtually "orthodox"? It is a common opinion, but it is one which needs some rectification. It is certainly true that De Wette took alarm at many expressions of the newer rationalism; true, that he attached more and more weight to many of the church-formulae;.... But it is also true... that he only advocated old-Lutheran orthodoxy "conditionally and from the stand-point of his philosophical mode of thinking".... It must never be forgotten that as a critic De Wette remained fundamentally true to himself, and that even in those old, free days at Jena he expressed strong attachment to the Augsburg Confession.[13]

---

[12]A review of Fries' philosophy is presented by A. P. D. Mourelatos in "Fries, Jakob Friedrich," *The Encyclopedia of Philosophy* 3 (1967) 253-55. Cf. de Wette, *Eine Idee über das Studium der Theologie* (ed. A. Stieren; Leipzig: 1850) 23; *Auffoderung zum Studium der Hebräischen Sprache und Litteratur* (Jena: 1805) 26-27. Cf. also Rudolf Otto's *The Philosophy of Religion* (London: Williams & Norgate, 1931), pp. 151-215, where he treats de Wette's theology as an example of a theological application of Fries' philosophy. Rogerson, *Criticism*, 36-44.

[13]Cheyne, *Founders*, 48-49. These observations about de Wette's thinking in general hold true specifically with regard to his views on Chronicles: he never renounced the substance of his earlier position on Chronicles. In the fourth edition of his Old Testament introduction, he wrote that "against the Chronicler emerges the reproach of imprecision, error and even intentional falsification" and that the Chronicler's reports were "highly suspicious." (W. M. L. de Wette, *Lehrbuch der historisch-kritischen Einleitung in die kanonischen und apokryphischen Bücher des Alten Testamentes* [4th ed.; Berlin: G. Reimer, 1833] 239-40, 241-42.) Moreover, in the fifth edition of the same work de Wette wrote in the preface, "The works of Keil and Movers, in defense of the Chronicles, have not led me to any essential alteration of my former views." (De Wette, *A Critical Introduction to*

In addition to Fries, and according to de Wette's own testimony, Herder must be singled out as one of the greatest influences on his life and work. On the one hundredth birthday celebration of Herder, de Wette wrote that Herder was the one

> who had so much influence on my general and theological education through his writings, who appeared to me on the barren steppe of theological criticism and rationalism as an inspired seer and indicated to me the eternally green pasture, saturated by the water of life, whom I had always observed as the forerunner of a rejuvenated, inspired and inspiring theology.[14]

Herder was not one of de Wette's university professors, but he was an examiner at the gymnasium and a preacher in the city of Weimar, where de Wette grew up. Herder evidently elicited the young de Wette's admiration and affection.

Herder was part of the reaction by Romanticism against eighteenth century Rationalism, and de Wette followed him in this, offering the following critique of Rationalism.

> People have in this modern time played a foolish game with this pragmatic method, especially in the field of biblical history. People have wanted to explain everything, bring everything into connection, set everything in a row in one color. People have forgotten the regard which they should have had for history; with profane curiosity people wanted to draw away the veil which lay over so many details.[15]

In addition to the rationalist's tendency toward speculation, de Wette rejected its lack of spirit and flavor. In this, also, Herder had led the way. De Wette had Theodor, the leading character of his novel, *Theodor oder des zweiflers Weihe*, which was published in 1822, say,

> They (the rationalists) act, as the scholars of language, which, unmoved by the beauties of a poem, exert themselves with the counting and mea-

---

the *Canonical Scriptures of the Old Testament* (trans. and enlarged by Theodore Parker; 3d ed. [5th German ed.]; Boston: Rufus Leighton, 1859) 1.vii. In the seventh and final edition of the work that de Wette prepared the evaluation of Chronicles as a historical source remained virtually unchanged. De Wette, *Lehrbuch der historisch-kritischen Einleitung in die kanonischen und apokryphischen Bücher des Alten Testamentes* (7th ed.; Berlin: G. Reimer, 1852) 246.

[14]Wiegand, *De Wette*, 8.

[15]W. M. L. de Wette, *Beiträge zur Einleitung in das Alte Testament. Kritik der Israelitischen Geschichte* (Halle: Schimmelpfennig, 1807) 2.9-10. Cf. Smend, *de Wettes*, 24.

suring of syllables, with the grammatical discussion of individual words and syllables.[16]

Herder, as well as Romanticism in general, saw an organic unity in history as a whole, as well as in the history of a particular people. In this the whole man was inseparable from the various elements of his changing environment. Such a conception of history ran counter to earlier views that regarded the actions of the individual as primary and thought that the whole was simply the aggregate of its parts.[17] De Wette followed Herder in his perception of history as an organic whole.

> The narratives are individuals, but history is a whole and should be presented as such; the highest and last task of the historian is thus to set forth from the thus different and dissimilar particulars an organic whole, of one spirit and character.[18]

> With the presentation of the original reports he (the historian) can and must not be satisfied; if he would simply collect and set beside one another bare narratives, then the history would be a badly connected patchwork of broken pieces. Each individual narrative is by nature one-sided; the individual reporters have always only individual broken parts of history, presenting similarly individual scenes of the great drama. The historian, on the other hand, while he surveys the whole, will view many things in another, truer light, than the individual reporters, he will be able to uncover and correct many biases, many deceptions and errors. Moreover, here his task is to a certain degree none other than a hermeneutical one, only in a higher sense: every narrative given to him is the object of this higher hermeneutic; they are brought together and observed as a whole by the author, who is to explain them; the presentation, which issues from all of them together, is the result of this research....[19]

Herder had not always maintained the same perspective toward history. In some of his treatments of Genesis, for example, especially during the early part of his career, he appeared to have been indifferent to the question of whether the events in the book actually occurred.[20] On the other hand, Herder believed that the biblical time fell in the childhood of the human race, and consequently, one had to regard the biblical reports as childish attempts to describe the acts of God. Even though they are repeated in a childish way, one cannot surrender them as unhistorical. On the contrary, in some ways they

---

[16]*Ibid.*, 25.
[17]A. O. Lovejoy, "The Meaning of Romanticism for the Historian of Ideas," *Journal of the History of Ideas* 2 (1942) 272-73.
[18]De Wette, *Beiträge*, 2.4.
[19]*Ibid.*, 2.7-8.
[20]Smend, *De Wettes*, 28-29.

were the best kind of historical reports, since they simply narrated what happened, without embellishment or pragmatic reflection.[21] To a certain degree, de Wette shared Herder's indifference to the matter of the historical basis for the biblical accounts.

> ...whether the Abraham, who sacrifices, for example, may be a historical or a mythical figure, still it is a valuable object of religious observation, and the treatment (also only invented) fills the reader up with devotion.[22]

What intrigued Herder more than the question of historicity was the matter of coming to an understanding of the author by empathetically submitting to him.

> Become with shepherds a shepherd, with a people of the sod a man of the land, with the ancients of the Orient an Easterner, if you wish to relish these writings in the atmosphere of their origin; and be on guard especially against all so-called artistry which our social circles force and press on those sacred archetypes of the most ancient days.[23]

De Wette's sympathy for this aspect of Herder's approach to ancient literature can be seen in statements such as the following.

> The first business of the historian is, consequently, the hermeneutical one. While we only know in history what is narrated, the historian above all things must grasp the narrative before he can take it up into the history; he must understand his reporter, enter into his presuppositions, adopt his views. The result of his correct interpretation (in so far as it is credible and useful) is the ingredient of history.[24]

In order to determine the usefulness of a source for historical reconstruction, de Wette believed that the historian must first understand that source as fully as possible. This understanding could only be achieved after the historian grasped the writer's biases, presuppositions, and aims, and this could be achieved only by the historian entering into the writer's own world and assuming his place beside and with the writer.

In spite of the numerous similarities between de Wette and Herder, one cannot understand them solely in terms of their opposition to rationalism. De Wette maintained—contrary to Herder—that natural law and the analogy of experience were unbreakable and

---

[21]*Ibid.*, 27-28. Note Herder's adamant stance supporting the historicity of the Gospels discussed in Hans W. Frei, *The Eclipse of Biblical Narrative* (New Haven: Yale, 1974) 188.

[22]De Wette, *Beiträge*, 2.407.

[23]Quoted in Frei, *Eclipse*, 185.

[24]De Wette, *Beiträge*, 2.5.

valid for all time.[25] When de Wette outlined his own historical critical method, he stated that after the historian has determined the testimony of his source, then he must give criticism her right to reject or maintain the results found. These are the questions to be raised:

> Are the things related credible? Do they contradict the general laws of nature, the analogy of experience? Are the presuppositions of the reporter correct? Has he seen and heard correctly? Has he not been deceived? Has he presented the facts without bias?[26]

Elsewhere, when he dealt with the character of the reporter in order to determine his reliability as a source for historical information, de Wette made it clear that he expected a "certain natural criticism" from him, viz., that

> he examine the facts that he transmits with regard to their credibility, whether they are possible, whether they are probable, that he accept nothing that contradicts the usual history or perhaps all historical belief.[27]

However, de Wette did not go so far as to say that the laws of nature enabled one to reconstruct and fill in the gaps which historical sources had left in our knowledge of the past. On the contrary, he believed that

> The total of our limited human experience, which we want to use as the measure, does not reach to the unending variety of history; the analogy, according to which we prepare and explain, is much too narrow and insufficient. There are many completely different (possibilities) from what we imagine! Powers lie dormant in men, which we still do not realize, which can accomplish startling miracles! From history we should learn daily that they are not determined by our presuppositions; and thus the historian should always be only the scholar and pupil of history; he researches and hears the reports of the past; he follows every trace exhibited, which appears to lead him to any discovery; but he presumes never to force his thinking and presuppositions on history, neither to fill gaps with them, neither to define the undefined, and neither to set firmly what is unsettled.[28]

There remained in de Wette a certain dissonance between two views: on the one hand, human experience in the present was to be used to test the credibility of reports about the past, but on the other hand, present knowledge was limited and the modern historian was unable to know the full range of what was possible in the past. De Wette be-

---

[25]Smend, *De Wettes*, 29.
[26]De Wette, *Beiträge*, 2.6.
[27]*Ibid.*, 2.15.
[28]*Ibid.*, 2.10.

lieved that present experience could be used to cut away from a narrative what was incredible but that it could not be used to supply what the sources omitted. De Wette wrote about his "criticism of credibility" (*Kritik der Glaubwürdigkeit*) that,

> This criticism can only always result in negative conclusions; it can only reject, not replace that which is rejected; it reveals simple falsehoods, but it cannot discover the truth. Therefore, by it history indeed is purified and cleansed, but even by that also the mass itself is diminished. With the rejection of narratives there always goes the loss of historical material, for only in narratives is it to be found.[29]

De Wette found inspiration in Herder, and he shared the latter's antipathy for the excesses of Rationalism. De Wette did not find in Herder, however, a scientific method for dealing with Scripture, and so for this he went elsewhere. Three figures were important in this regard for him. First was Johann Jakob Griesbach, who combined grammatical exegesis with historical explanation. Griesbach's personal devotion, his commitment to Scripture, and his caution were notable for their effect on de Wette. Another figure was Heinrich Eberhard Gottlob Paulus, a rationalist, who attempted to explain Jesus' miracles in rationalistic categories, while maintaining the substantial accuracy of the New Testament writers. While de Wette rejected Paulus' contortions to account for the miracles, he admired Paulus' ingenuity and sharp senses.[30] Finally, there was Johann Philip Gabler, whose explanation of the biblical way of thinking as "mythical" allowed de Wette and others to rescue something of positive value from what appeared to be unhistorical in the Bible.[31] De Wette drew from each of these men—and undoubtedly from others, as well—and found his method in the form of "thorough-going criticism" (*durchgreifende Kritik*).

> The proper critical investigations of the modern theologians have already denied to many historical sources their direct attention and credibility. However, a complete, thorough-going criticism will show that no one of the historical works of the Old Testament has historical worth, and all contain more or less myths, and that we have among all the books of the Old Testament no proper historical witness, except some prophets, but who can give little historical gain....[32]

The goal of de Wette's method was not destruction but discovery of truth. "Truth is the first great law of history, love of truth the first

---

[29]*Ibid.*, 2.3.
[30]Smend, *De Wettes*, 14-15.
[31]*Ibid.*, 18.
[32]*Ibid.*, 30.

duty of the researcher of history."[33] Moreover, de Wette declared, "I did not begin criticism," but "since it had begun its dangerous game, then it must be completed, for only what is completed in its way is good."[34]

c. De Wette's Work on Chronicles

In 1806, de Wette published the first part of his *Beiträge zur Einleitung in das alte Testament*. Its first half dealt with the credibility of 1, 2 Chronicles, and in the sections that follow his arguments and observations about Chronicles will be presented.

1) Introduction

De Wette began his treatment of Chronicles with a brief introduction (pp. 3-9), in which he presented the problem and the outlines of his solution. First he noted that Samuel-Kings and Chronicles give two different pictures of the period from David until the exile of Judah. In Chronicles the picture of Israel's worship is in accordance with that in the law of Moses, viz., the author of Chronicles assumed that the Israelite cultus in the monarchical period functioned in accordance with the pentateuchal laws, even though there were periods of neglect. Samuel-Kings, however, presents little or nothing of the levitical ceremonies. Moreover, in the latter, if the Mosaic legislation was in existence, one would have to assume that there was much more transgression of levitical laws and freedom for lay involvement in the cult.

De Wette claimed that people had failed to recognize and admit the discrepancy between 1, 2 Chronicles and Samuel-Kings for two reasons. First, it had been assumed that the Mosaic books or law were accurate, and so it followed that Chronicles, with its portrayal of Israel living in obedience to the law of Moses, was also accurate. Secondly, it had been widely claimed that the author of Samuel-Kings—in contrast to the author of Chronicles—was not interested in the history of Israel's religion and cult. De Wette maintained that the latter assumption was obviously erroneous, since there were many indications in Samuel-Kings that its author was interested in Israel's religious history, as the stories of the transfer of the ark by David and the building of the temple by Solomon show.

De Wette's key for the solution of the problem was to assume that the books of Moses are not reliable and that in the earlier times of David and Solomon the Israelite cult existed in a freer and simpler form, only to become encumbered with complicated levitical ceremonies at a later time.

---

[33] De Wette, *Beiträge*, 2.1.
[34] *Ibid.*, 2.408.

2) The Genetic Relation of the Two Narratives

The second part of de Wette's work is entitled *"Genetisches Verhältniss der beiden Relationen"* (pp. 10-41). In this section de Wette focused his attention primarily on the theories of Eichhorn, who envisioned Samuel-Kings and Chronicles as each drawing on several common sources but concluded that the author of Chronicles did not use Samuel-Kings, even though he wrote at a time long after the latter books had been composed. De Wette's purpose was to "clear away" Eichhorn's solutions in order to pave the way for his own analysis.

In the first section de Wette deals with the relationship of 2 Samuel to 1 Chronicles. Sometimes, he notes, these sources show verbatim agreement (cf. 1 Samuel 31 with 1 Chr 10:1-12 and 2 Sm 5:1-10 with 1 Chr 11:1-9), but elsewhere the sequence of passages is different (Samuel's list of David's warriors occurs toward the end of the account of David [2 Sm 22:8-39], while Chronicles presents it at the first of the treatment of David [1 Chr 11:10-41]), and there are differences in expressions, names, numbers, and in the entire manner of speaking (cf. 2 Samuel 6 with 1 Chronicles 13 and 15 and 2 Samuel 24 with 1 Chronicles 21).

Eichhorn had explained the relationship between Chronicles and 2 Samuel by positing a source, which he called a "Life of David" from which both 2 Samuel and 1 Chronicles drew their materials. More of this source's details about David's personal life were reproduced in 2 Samuel, while Chronicles supplied more details about worship.

De Wette rejected Eichhorn's proposal for six reasons. First, Eichhorn assumed the existence of such a biography only because he needed one. There are no historical traces of such a writing. Secondly, when one put together all the pieces of this "Life of David" from 2 Samuel and 1 Chronicles, large gaps appeared: there was nothing of David's genealogy, youth, personal life, enmity with Saul, reign over the single tribe of Judah, enthronement, or death. Thirdly, Eichhorn supported his hypothesis by the contention that 2 Samuel and Chronicles shared sections that were summary in nature, while what was unique to each presented more details. De Wette found the opposite to be true: there were more details presented in the materials that the two books had in common. Fourthly, if the parts of this "Life of David," which appeared in 2 Samuel and 1 Chronicles, were truly part of such a previous unity, then they should fit together with one another better than they fit with parts of other works, viz., as they exist presently in 2 Samuel and 1 Chronicles. This was not the case, though, and the natural connections of the material appeared to be with the history of David contained in the books of Samuel. Fifthly, Eichhorn's hypothesis required that the synoptic passages of 2 Samuel and 1 Chronicles agree with one another. In order to account for those instances in which the two exhibit disagreements in the synoptic passages, Eichhorn had assumed that scribes had re-edited the "Life of David" between the time it was used by the author of 2 Samuel and when the author of 1 Chronicles received it. This is only another tiresome hypothesis and has no basis in fact. *"Leere hypothese auf leere hypothese!"* Finally, Eichhorn's hypothesis, by its very nature (the author and date of the biography of David being unknown) was of no real historical value. It shed no light at all on the historical character of 1 Chronicles.

In the second section de Wette deals with the relationship of 1, 2 Kings to 2 Chronicles. In the account of Solomon's life there are agreements (1 Kg 3:4-14 and 2 Chr 1:3-13), as well as changes in sequence, striking omissions, and dissimilarities.

Eichhorn had argued for the existence of a "Life of Solomon" connected with the "Life of David," basing his theory on the agreements between Kings and Chronicles. He had assumed a later reediting of the "Life of Solomon," just as he had assumed there was a reediting of the "Life of David" in the interval between the composition of Kings and Chronicles.

De Wette thought that the hypothesis about a "Life of Solomon" was unjustified, since Eichhorn based his conclusions on his similar theory regarding the hypothetical "Life of David." Since the latter theory could not be justified, then the former falls, as well. De Wette argued that when the pieces that would have been part of such a biography are assembled, the result is hardly what one would expect to find in such a work. Moreover, the supposition of an editing stage between the writing of Kings and Chronicles hardly explains all the differences between the two. De Wette concluded that the arbitrariness of the theory is more evident with regard to the material on Solomon than David because of the nature of the differences between the parallel accounts. For De Wette, the sources used by the Chronicler to write his story remain unknown. Even when the Chronicler cites the histories of Nathan, Ahijah, and Iddo, it is not necessary to suppose that he used them as sources, and even if he did, one still could not determine their worth or reliability. Neither does one know whether the Chronicler created his narrative from them with discretion and a love for the truth. For de Wette, the Chronicler's history itself would have to establish its own worth or lack of worth.

De Wette saw agreement between Chronicles and Kings from the division of the monarchy until Israel's fall (cf. 1 Kg 12:1-19 with 2 Chronicles 10), but afterwards the harmony suffers (frequent additions about Israel occur in Kings, and this disrupts the harmony). The two accounts have different aims. Kings deals with Judah and Israel, but Chronicles deals only with the former. Everything in Kings about Judah is in Chronicles, but with expansions, different expressions, and sometimes with contradictions (cf. 1 Kg 15:14 with 2 Chr 14:2 and 1 Kg 15:16 with 2 Chr 15:19). From the fall of Israel until the fall of Judah both books treat the same subject, but they disagree strongly at times (very different viewpoints, for example, are exhibited in the two treatments of Hezekiah's reign).

In his explanation of the similarity between Kings and Chronicles for the post-Solomonic period, Eichhorn had supposed that both used a common source for this period. The author of Kings followed the full historical presentation found in this common source, while the author of Chronicles often reverted to the sources themselves, from which the full history had been compiled. According to Eichhorn, there may have been occasions in which the Chronicler utilized other sources that had not been employed to produce the common narrative utilized by both authors. The agreement of the works was based on their common source, and their disagreements were produced when the Chronicler relied upon earlier sources. Eichhorn sought to support his theory about the existence and use of such sources by noting that the author of Kings frequently made references to the "Chronicles of the Kings of Judah" and the "Chronicles of the Kings of Israel." Chronicles also cites other source material.

De Wette responded to Eichhorn that Chronicles cites four general works of history (the Midrash of the Book of Kings, the Book of the Kings of Judah and Israel, the Book of the Kings of Israel, and the Histories of the Kings of Israel) for the period between the fall of Israel and the end of Judah. Even if the last three citations refer to the same work, there were still at least two general histories available to the author of Chronicles. Moreover, de Wette contended that the "Book of the Kings of Israel and Judah," which is cited by Chronicles, is not the same as the "Chronicles of the Kings of Judah," which is cited by Kings. Neither does de Wette think that "Israel and Judah" is equivalent to "Judah" in the source citations. In addition, de Wette pointed out that in one instance, in which Chronicles (according to Eichhorn's theory) was supposed to have used the original sources, in fact the Chronicler cited the general history, which was used by both Kings and Chronicles. Eichhorn thought that when the two used the general history, they agreed with one another, but that when Chronicles employed special sources, they disagreed. The contradictions between 2 Chr 14:2, 4 and 1 Kg 15:14 and between 1 Kg 15:16 and 2 Chr 15:19, according to de Wette, make Eichhorn's theory untenable. The questions remain for de Wette: what was the aim of Chronicles; did its author show discretion; and did he have a love for the truth?

3) The Critical Relation of the Two Narratives

The third part of de Wette's treatment of Chronicles has seven parts and is entitled *"Kritisches Verhältniss der beiden Relationen"* (pp. 42-132).

The first division deals with the question of chronological priority for Samuel-Kings and Chronicles. This is an important question for de Wette, since the earlier work has a natural presumption in its favor as a historical source being closer to the circumstances reported. It is apparent that Samuel-Kings should be regarded as coming from one person, having been collected and edited at one time, since there is a single plan, predisposition, language, and style for all four books. That Chronicles comes from a later time than Samuel-Kings is evident from the following considerations. Chronicles' orthography and language are from a later period (Chronicles has דויד, for example, instead of דוד). The same is true for its manner of expression (in 1 Chr 21:1 the satan stood against Israel, but in 2 Sm 24:1 God was angry with Israel). While Kings ends with the Babylonian exile, Chronicles ends with the news that the exile lasted seventy years. While the Babylonian exile seems to be the appropriate time for the writing of Samuel-Kings, Chronicles seems to come from the time of Darius Hystaspes (522-486 B. C. E.), or more probably, long after his day. De Wette offered two reasons for his proposed dating of Chronicles. First, Chronicles refers to the use of Persian darics in David's day (1 Chr 29:7). Such a mistake by the author of Chronicles could only have been made long after darics first came into circulation. Secondly, the genealogy of Zerubbabel in 1 Chronicles 3 extends to the time of Alexander the Great. Therefore, Chronicles must be dated to the time of Alexander or later.

The second division treats the question, "Which preserves the original narrative?" Simply because Chronicles is the younger of the two works does not necessarily mean that it preserves an inferior report. It is natural to expect, however, that the later historical work is less pure, and in fact a comparison of Chronicles with Samuel-Kings demonstrates that the former contains alterations, embellishments, transpositions, and omissions in order to falsify. The narrative in Samuel-Kings, although by no means the first history of Israel, has the appearance of being more original and accurate. The following are examples of the kinds of changes that Chronicles introduced. De Wette pointed to two instances of embellishments and additions that reflect a later period: in 1 Chronicles 21, the Chronicler introduced "Satan" into the story of David's census, and in 2 Chr 8:12-13, he introduced levitical and priestly details that interested him. Examples of transpositions, abridgments, and omissions are also easily found. Chronicles places the story of David's dealings with Hiram and his war with the Philistines after the account of the transfer of the ark (1

Chronicles 14), rather than before it, as is the case in Samuel (2 Sm 5-25). A striking omission occurs in 1 Chr 20:1-8, which cuts out quite a bit of the material in 2 Samuel 11 and 12 about David's conquest of Rabbah. These observations lead to the general conclusion that whenever differences emerge between the two narratives, the narrative of Samuel-Kings is the more original.

The third section deals with the Chronicler's lack of precision, carelessness, and manner of compilation. Often in synoptic passages the designations of places are omitted (1 Chr 14:13 omits Rephaim, which occurs in the parallel passage 2 Sm 5:22; cf. 2 Sm 10:17 with 1 Chr 19:17; 1 Kg 8:21 with 2 Chr 21:9). Sometimes Chronicles omits the statements of circumstances, and since elsewhere he does not seem to aim at brevity, these omissions appear unnecessary (cf. 1 Sm 31:12 and 1 Chr 10:12, where the latter omits the reference to the Israelites burning the bodies of Saul and his company). Sometimes, Chronicles produces the original narrative, but in a distorted and disarranged state. 1 Chronicles 19:3 has set the phrases of 2 Sm 10:3 in a nonsensical order. Careless copying is evidenced in 1 Chr 18:6, which aims at reproducing 2 Sm 8:6. Sometimes an entire narrative is distorted and disarranged so that it becomes senseless (cf. 2 Kg 22:3-8 with 2 Chr 34:8-15, which deal with Josiah and the finding of the law). On other occasions, the author of Chronicles exhibits lack of skill by his changes in the *"Urschrift"* (cf. 2 Chr 9:25 with its parallel in 1 Kg 10:26). Even in the abridgments, Chronicles appears defective (cf. 2 Chr 22:9 with 2 Kg 9:15-27, which deal with the murder of Ahaziah). Still more characteristic are Chronicles' contradictions with itself (cf. 2 Chr 14:2 and 15:17 about Asa and the high places).

Section four details the marvelous elements found in Chronicles. A prominent example is the mythical elaboration of Chronicles in the account of the angel standing between heaven and earth with drawn sword over Jerusalem and the fire coming down from heaven to consume the offering (1 Chronicles 21). Such mythical additions admit the possibility that on other occasions the author brought into his text later elaborations of early myths and so erodes the reliability of Chronicles. Another example of this tendency occurs in 2 Chr 18:31, which parallels 1 Kg 22:32-33. Chronicles has Yahweh draw Jehoshaphat's foes away from him in battle, whereas Kings has the king cry out and reveal his identity, and consequently his foes turn from him to pursue Ahab, instead.

The fifth division deals with what de Wette calls *"Levitismus."* This term designates the author's preference for the tribe of Levi, which in many places corrupted his love for the truth and led him to falsification and untruth. Frequently, where the earlier narrative has nothing of the Levites, Chronicles has the Levites play a major role. Where the earlier narrative informs the reader of something to the disadvantage of the tribe of Levi, Chronicles has rescued its honor, and where the earlier account appears to go against levitical preroga- tives, Chronicles has likewise corrected the tendency on the basis of the Mosaic lawbook. Examples of this tendency occur in the list of David's officials (2 Sm 8:16-19 and 1 Chr 18:15-17), David's census (2 Samuel 24 and 1 Chronicles 21), the transfer of the ark (2 Samuel 6 and 1 Chronicles 13 and 15), and Joash's ascension (2 Kg 11:4-12 and 2 Chr 23:1-11).

The sixth section discusses Chronicles' vindication of the Judean cult. Since the author of Chronicles had such strong interests in the cult and often differed from Samuel-Kings in his portrayal of it, de Wette focused on this aspect of Chronicles in a major way. The Chronicler was not pleased with the picture of the condition of public religion painted by the books of Kings (most of the Judean kings were idol worshippers, and even pious kings, such as David and Solomon, gave little attention to Mosaic ceremonies). The whole must have been otherwise, and so Chronicles presented it otherwise. Among the attempts to provide vindications of Judah one finds Chronicles qui- etly passing over the details of Solomon's sin (1 Kings 11). Among Chronicles' elaborations is 2 Chr 8:12-13, which parallels 1 Kg 9:25.

The final division presents Chronicles' preference for Judah and his hatred for Israel. The narrative as a whole demonstrates Chronicles' bias against Israel. Whereas Kings supplies the history of Israel, as well as Judah, Chronicles omits everything that is related to Israel alone, and includes only what can be told to the detriment of Israel's reputation. Some examples of this can be found in 2 Chronicles 13, which reports Abijah's speech that asserts the privi- leges of the davidic dynasty, and in 2 Chr 19:2-3, which chastises Jehoshaphat for an alliance with "godless Israel."

From his examination of Chronicles de Wette concluded: the work comes from a relatively late date; its reconstruction of the monarchical period is not based on adequate historical sources; and the Chronicler himself was careless, ignorant, and motivated by prej- udices, all of which contributed errors to his work.

d. De Wette's Approach to Historical Research and Reconstruction

In his treatment of Chronicles as a historical source, several aspects of de Wette's historical methodology should be noted. As far as the historian's goal is concerned, he believed that "Truth is the first great law of history, love of truth the first duty of the researcher of history."[35] Consequently, when he investigated Chronicles' relia- bility as a historical source, de Wette believed that it was crucial to

---

[35]*Ibid.*, 2.1.

inquire, "with how much criticism and love of the truth did he execute this work."[36]

As a historian going about the task of seeking historical knowledge, de Wette argued that one is limited by both the extent and nature of the source materials.

> The source for understanding history is none other than the narrative; we know nothing about history besides what is narrated; what is based on historical narrative is true; only where there is narrative is there history; where there is no narrative, there is no history.[37]

These statements make it plain that de Wette believed the historian was utterly dependent on written historical sources. It was impossible for him to ply his trade without them. Later, in the same work, de Wette elaborates on this dependence of the historian.

> Even here, while proceeding with artistic freedom, he must not neglect the narratives, only *through them* and *in them*, not outside of them should he present the history; the whole, which he presents, should be completely grounded in the details given to him. The dangerous clasp of the historic art, on which already so many (indeed one might well say most) writers of history have foundered, because they abused the freedom given to them and presented more of a product of their subjective presuppositions, than the history given to them. The freedom of historical presentation also does not supercede the narrative; the latter is the never-to-be-neglected leader of the historian.[38]

Even when the historian strictly adheres to the reports of his narrative, however, he is still further limited by the fact that he can never return to investigate the events themselves, as they happened. He is forever restricted to later reports about them.

> However, what we have not seen and accepted as true, that we can only learn about from others, who have received it as true and reported it to us. In history, therefore, we do not know the details as such, as they were, or rather as they appeared, (for also with our own perceptions of truth we know nothing other than the appearances); but we know only the narratives of the details. All historical knowing cannot push further, here faith must be summoned, and whoever refuses to yield this, that one renounces history.[39]

Later he continues,

> The narrative is his source; he can create from it only what lies in it; he can receive about the things, about which he seeks instruction, only

---

[36]*Ibid.*, 1.40.
[37]*Ibid.*, 2.2.
[38]*Ibid.*, 2.4-5.
[39]*Ibid.*, 2.2.

what the report gives him; he cannot research the facts themselves, but only as they are reported.[40]

These observations explain much of de Wette's caution as a historian, as well as his antipathy for the eagerness of rationalists to fill in the gaps left by the historical sources. With the restrictions that he has proposed, de Wette is inevitably drawn to assume a minimalist position as far as historical knowledge is concerned.

In addition to discussing the historian's basic task and limitations, de Wette sets forth three duties of the historian. First is the duty of interpretation (*"Hermeneutik"*). The historian cannot accept reports as they come to him and then arrange a patchwork of historical narratives. On the contrary, he is obligated, first of all, to understand and interpret the reports transmitted to him. He is free to use only what the sources *intended* to say.

> While we only know in history what is narrated, the historian above all things must grasp the narrative, before he can accept it into the history; he must understand his reporter, enter into his presuppositions, adopt his views. ... Hermeneutic demands, with unchangeable truth, that one present the disposition, the presuppositions of the author, to find in the things said only what he wanted to say; the historian, though, can and must also want nothing else. The narrative is his source; he can create from it only what lies in it....[41]

The historian's second duty is the criticism of his sources. The historian must evaluate the results of his attempt to understand and interpret his sources and determine whether the sources appear to be reliable. Such criticism raises the following questions.

> Are the things related credible? Do they contradict the general laws of nature, the analogy of experience? Are the presuppositions of the reporter correct? Has he seen and heard correctly? Has he not been deceived? Has he presented the facts without bias?[42]

The third task of the historian is to arrange a historical presentation. This cannot be simply a patchwork compilation of his sources. The historian observes matters in relation to one another and then should present them as an organic whole. He proceeds with artistic freedom and yet with a loyalty to his sources.

> Each individual narrative is by nature one-sided; the individual reporters have always only individual broken parts of history, presenting similarly individual scenes of the great drama. The historian, on the other hand, while he surveys the whole, will view many things in another, truer light, than the individual reporters; he will be able to un-

---

[40]*Ibid.*, 2.5-6.
[41]*Ibid.*

cover and correct many biases, many deceptions and errors. Moreover, here his task is to a certain degree none other than a hermeneutical one, only in a higher sense: every narrative given to him is the object of this higher hermeneutic; they are brought together and observed as a whole by the author, who is to explain them; the presentation, which issues from all of them together, is the result of this research; it must be the *educt*, too, not the *product*. For the historian can indeed know nothing other than what is reported; what he researched for the history must be found, not invented.[43]

In order to execute the historian's second task (the criticism of his sources), de Wette proposes four rigorous criteria. The first is that the author of the narrative intended to write history *per se.*

The first requisite is still, to be sure, that a narrative be one such that according to its being and character its author wanted to narrate history as such. Only what he gives us as history can be useful for history. For he alone is the informant for it, and only by him can we learn history.[44]

Some narratives might appear to be historical on the surface, but, in reality, be wholly inadequate for historical research, since their authors had other intentions in mind. Composers of fairy tales wanted to delight and move their audiences, and other writings were intended to illustrate some philosophical or religious truth. Thus, one must determine the author's intent, because if he never intended to write history as such, then we are foolish to trust him as a historical source. If the narrator did not impose on himself the law of truth, then we have no right to do so.[45]

At this point de Wette anticipates a question. If a narrative contains a mixture of truth and embellishment, is it not legitimate for the historian to weed out the embellishment and falsehood and then proceed to use the truth for historical reconstruction? De Wette denies this endeavor to the historian.

If we possess about this history another correct historical narrative, then we could certainly distinguish the truth from the falsehood; but then that untrue narrative would serve us no purpose. And if we have no such external help, then it is simply impossible to distinguish truth from falsehood; for in the narrative itself lies no criterion of truth. The narrator gives indeed what is true and false in a single significance; he does not distinguish this from that, but places both in the same dignity beside one another; according to him, according to his intention the true is as good as the false, a vehicle of extra-historical (poetic, religious, philosophical) meaning, for him the false is even as true as the true. Here, no

---

[42]*Ibid.*, 2.6.
[43]*Ibid.*, 2.7-8.
[44]*Ibid.*, 2.11.
[45]*Ibid.*, 2.11-12.

skill of criticism can accomplish anything. We have pointed to the narrator; over this medium we do not know the way out.[46]

When the Chronicler as a source for reconstructing the history of Israel is judged by this criterion, de Wette finds him lacking. His careful examination of Chronicles reveals that its author did not intend to write history as such, but rather intended to demonstrate by his narrative certain philosophical or religious truths.

The design of the author was obviously this—to give an account of the theocratic kingdom of David, which was obviously, but only slightly, connected by genealogies and the death of Saul with the earlier history of the people of Israel,—an account of that kingdom, which at first embraced all the twelve tribes belonging to it,—the kingdom which observed the Mosaic law, and the Mosaic worship—and to show how, in all this, the true worship of God was preserved in all its perfection under pious kings, or restored by them, and how apostasy from this brought on distress and ruin. This he does in such a manner that the light far surpasses the dark side. Everything is tried by the priestly standard.[47]

In addition to the fact that the Chonicler never intended to write history as such, de Wette's comparison of Samuel-Kings with Chronicles led him to detect many inaccuracies in the latter. Therefore, since one cannot simply choose what one likes from Chronicles for historical information, one must reject the books entirely as a source for historical reconstruction.

Each narrative is a whole, and is given as a whole, and is to be accepted as a whole; we cannot arbitrarily reach in and choose for ourselves from it what pleases us.[48]

De Wette's second criterion is that the narrative be credible. Only an eyewitness is credible in the proper sense. Narratives that report matters second- or thirdhand are untrustworthy, as daily experience reveals; inaccuracies are compounded when the narrator did not understand those who reported the events to him. De Wette recognized, however, that the writing of history would be impossible, if one accepted evidence from eyewitnesses alone.

Only for a few moments of history are we so fortunate to use narratives by eyewitnesses. However, at least the reporters should not have lived too far from the details, and must have received their reports from sure informants. Indeed the farther the standpoint of the narrator from the

---

[46]*Ibid.*, 2.13.
[47]De Wette, *Introduction*, 2.315.
[48]De Wette, *Beiträge*, 2.16.

time of the details, the more doubtful the credibility of his narrative, and the greater the source of error.[49]

Once more, a comparison of de Wette's criterion with 1, 2 Chronicles reveals the latter's deficiency. The Chronicler himself was not an eyewitness to the events that he reports—de Wette dated his composition to the time of Alexander the Great[50]—and his sources are questionable. His single source that can be identified with certainty is Samuel-Kings, and it, too, fails to meet the eyewitness requirement.

> The accounts which run parallel with the books of Samuel and Kings were derived from that source. This appears from the following considerations:
> 1. The earlier accounts in Samuel and Kinqs have natural connection with those other accounts therein, but which are omitted by the Chronicler.....
> 2. From the original character of these accounts, compared with those in Chronicles....
> 3. From the certain fact that the Chronicler must have been acquainted with the previous books. The above statement is apparently confirmed by the fact that the Chronicler seeks to refer to the earlier books. The reference, in 1 Ch. xxix.29, to "the discourses (histories) of Samuel, Nathan, and Gad," applies to our books of Samuel.[51]

De Wette's third criterion concerns the character of the reporter himself:

> ...first of all impartiality is to be required of him, that he present the details purely and in an unclouded way, as he knows them, and then secondly a certain natural criticism, that he examine the facts transmitted to him with regard to their credibility, whether they are possible, whether they are probable, that he accept nothing that contradicts the usual history or perhaps all historical belief.[52]

The reporter is a poetic narrator, not a writer of history, if he reports as history things which exceed human experience and the laws of na-

---

[49]*Ibid.*, 2.14.

[50]*Ibid.*, 1.45-46. Not only was the author of Chronicles not an eyewitness to the events that he recorded, but he lived far later than de Wette's allowance of "not too far from the details."

[51]De Wette, *Einleitung*, 306-7. In his discussion of 2 Samuel and 1 Chronicles, de Wette concluded that it was more likely "that the author of Chronicles compiled those harmonizing passages from the second book of Samuel." *Beiträge*, 1.25. Later, in his discussion of the relationship of 2 Chronicles to 1, 2 Kings, de Wette rejected Eichhorn's source theory, and with regard to the citations in Chronicles of the histories of Nathan, Ahijah, and Iddo, de Wette observed, "From what sources the author of Chronicles, however, created the life of Solomon, we do not know. ...because he cites this work, it is not necessary that he used it as a source." *Ibid.*, 1.30.

[52]*Ibid.*, 2.15.

ture. Consequently, his testimony must be rejected as a whole. One has no basis for selecting only certain details from his report that suit the liking of the researcher.

> A narrator, who narrates *bona fide* things, which could not be true in themselves, which are completely impossible and unthinkable, which exceed not only experience, but also the laws of nature, and gives them as history, leads them along in the sequence of historical facts; such a person, if he has similarly the intention to narrate history, as history, is no writer of history; he does not assume the historical perspective; he is a poetic narrator (taken objectively, he is grasped in poetry). And such a narrator deserves also no faith at all. For even if other facts narrated by him appear probable and natural, still they are not to be accepted in this company; they are things from another world; they could have been invented, too, just as the other one (the impossible event) was. Each narrative is a whole, and is given as a whole, and is to be accepted as a whole; we cannot arbitrarily reach in and choose for ourselves from it what pleases us.[53]

According to this criterion, de Wette found Chronicles lacking. Its bias against Israel and in favor of Judah, the Judean cult, and the tribe of Levi disqualifies him as a trustworthy reporter of history.[54] Moreover, the Chronicler exercises no "natural criticism." He transmits all kinds of impossible happenings, and indeed one can affirm that he even has a preference for the miraculous.[55]

The final criterion that de Wette suggests is that tradition is not a reliable source for history. By "tradition" de Wette refers to material transmitted orally and to the time "before the dulling of the memory by literary record."[56] De Wette points out that the very interest itself of ancient peoples in the history of their fathers casts doubt on the credibility of the tradition, because

> The tradition is uncritical and biased, not historical, but with its patriotic-poetic *Tendenz*, the patriotic affection satisfies itself with anything which flatters the patriotic interest, indeed the more beautiful, wonderful, noble, so much the more acceptable; and where the tradition has left gaps, there likewise phantasy steps in with completions, and readily accepts the eavesdropping ear with its fictions.[57]

Since there is no inner criterion to distinguish the true from the false, one must reject the whole. Even the plainest and simplest of

---

[53]*Ibid.*, 2.15-16.
[54]De Wette, *Einleitung*, 239-42.
[55]De Wette, *Beiträge*, 1.78-80.
[56]*Ibid.*, 2.16.
[57]*Ibid.*, 2.16-17.

details could have been invented for some purpose and may have been set down in a misleading relationship with the other facts.[58]

Chronicles fails to meet this final criterion, too. At first it might seem that the criterion is irrelevant to a consideration of Chronicles, since 1, 2 Chronicles is written and not transmitted orally. However, those who might attempt to support the Chronicler's narrative by suggesting that many of its reports are reliable, because they are based on ancient and reliable oral tradition, are in error, according to de Wette, since oral tradition cannot be relied upon.

De Wette's conclusion about Chronicles as a historical source is overwhelmingly negative. Chronicles fails in every case to meet his minimum criteria for a useful, historical report. Consequently, the historian can use no part of 1, 2 Chronicles for the reconstruction of Israel's history. De Wette extended this radical criticism of Chronicles to the other books of the Old Testament. He concluded that it was impossible "to construct a history of the Hebrew nation" and that any attempt to do so was "a true *Danaidenarbeit*."[59]

e. Some Observations on de Wette's Treatment of Chronicles

1) De Wette's Treatment of Chronicles and the History of Israel's Religion

De Wette was apparently the first to see clearly the magnitude of the conflict between Samuel-Kings and Chronicles. He pointed out the many individual points of conflict between the two, but he saw patterns emerge and so went further to characterize the major differences in viewpoint between the two writings. His analysis led him to conclude that Samuel-Kings contained the more trustworthy accounts and that 1, 2 Chronicles could not be trusted as a historical source. This does not mean that de Wette viewed either Samuel or Kings as a completely reliable source, even though he did have great respect for the historical accomplishment of 1, 2 Samuel. He was struck by the paucity of myth there.[60]

---

[58]*Ibid.*, 2.17.

[59]Smend, *De Wette*, 24. While de Wette was quite pessimistic in theory about the possibility of writing a history of Israel, in fact he was confident enough to reconstruct Israel's religious history.

[60]De Wette had reservations about 1, 2 Samuel, especially such texts as 2 Samuel 24, where an angel appears. In praise of its author, de Wette wrote, "Elsewhere the narrative bears a true historical imprint, and is, where not from (in part at least) contemporary records, still created from a very living and true (only here and there cloudy and confused) oral tradition, which depends, certainly in part still, on monuments, sayings, and significant names (1 Sm 6:18; 7:12; etc.). It is so rich in living character-traits and descriptions, that in this respect it contends with the best history-writing, and is occasionally biographical; also, the natural connection of events is very satisfactory, even if not clearly set off enough." *Einleitung*, 227.

This conclusion was to have far-reaching results for the critical study of the Old Testament. The emergence of the documentary hypothesis, in which the sequence J, E, D, and P was accepted, required four prior developments. The first was that the P document be isolated, once J had been detected. The second was that D be connected with the Josianic reform. Thirdly, the historical reliability of Chronicles had to be broken down, or else P had to be assigned an early date. Finally, the pentateuchal laws had to be compared with the narrative of the historical books, and the fact be recognized that early Israel did not live as though she were acquainted with the Law of Moses.

The first step was achieved by Ilgen and the second by de Wette with his *Dissertatio* of 1805. In it de Wette presented his view that the lawbook of Josiah was not something that was rediscovered, but rather had come into being in the time of Josiah. He left open the question of a priestly fraud. The third step was taken by de Wette, too, in 1806 with the publication of the first part of his *Beiträge*. In it de Wette completely rejected the value of Chronicles as a historical source. This, of course, challenged the traditional view of the development of Israelite religion, which held that Moses gave the elaborate law of Exodus-Deuteronomy to Israel. The final step in the movement toward the Graf-Wellhausen understanding of Israelite history was taken in the second part of de Wette's 1806 *Beiträge*, though only in a preliminary way. De Wette sought to show that the historical books (aside from Chronicles) gave no evidence that the Law of Moses was observed by Israel early in her history. He laid out his own theory that the early worship of Israel was free and unaffected by the pentateuchal laws, and that the worship of Yahweh was carried on alongside the worship of idols in both Israel and Judah, and that the priests participated in both. The Mosaic law represents a form of legislation that assumed its pentateuchal shape only after a long period of time and development. De Wette held a form of the fragmentary hypothesis ("there were only several fragments of various authors"), and thus never arrived at the position that Wellhausen presented in his *Prolegomena* in 1878. Rather, he believed that "there were only several fragments of various authors."[61] The fragments of the Elohist fit together to form a whole (de Wette's Elohist source was for the most part later called "P"), but those of the Jehovistic document did not.[62] De Wette's third pentateuchal source was Deuteronomy.[63]

It is evident, therefore, that de Wette's publications of 1805 and 1806 played a monumental role in the development of the documentary hypothesis as it came to be formulated by Wellhausen and

---

[61]De Wette, *Introduction*, 2.77.
[62]*Ibid.*
[63]*Ibid.*, 2.150-51.

others. The questions raised by de Wette in his *Beiträge* of 1806 have continued to excite research and debate on Chronicles.

2) De Wette's View of the Historian's Task

One of the most radical aspects of de Wette's work is his view of the historiographical method. His rigorous criteria for judging the value of a historical source effectively excluded Chronicles (as well as the other historical books of the Old Testament) from serious use in the reconstruction of Israel's monarchical period. Wellhausen later adopted de Wette's position towards Chronicles, but he was not as negative in his opinion of the other Old Testament historical books.[64]

3) Opposition to Rationalism

Finally, one may detect in de Wette's polemics against "Pragmatism" a disdain for the excesses of rationalists, who eagerly employed human reason to supply what historical material their sources lacked. De Wette's caution and distrust of human ability to "fill in" the gaps of history prevented him from engaging in such speculation. He regarded it as an abandonment of the very ground of historical research.

2. GESENIUS

Linguistic support for de Wette's view of Chronicles was provided by Wilhelm Gesenius (1786-1842), a Protestant Old Testament scholar who was best known as a grammarian and lexicographer.[65] In his university training he was decisively influenced by rationalists, Heinrich Henke at Helmstadt and J. G. Eichhorn at Göttingen. According to Schrader, however, Gesenius was not committed to Rationalism for theological reasons; rather, he was largely indifferent to theological considerations and was motivated instead by the presuppositions of his historical method, which had little room for the miraculous.[66] Gesenius' teaching career was spent at Halle, where he was professor of theology.[67]

Gesenius was a younger contemporary of de Wette and followed many of the latter's critical conclusions. He assigned a later date to Deuteronomy than to the other books of the Pentateuch, as did de

---

[64]Cf. J. Wellhausen, *Prolegomena to the History of Israel* (1878; rep. Gloucester, Mass.: Peter Smith, 1973) 244.

[65]Redslob, "Gesenius," *ADB* 9 (1879) 89-93; Cheyne, *Founders*, 54-55; Rogerson, *Criticism*, 50-57.

[66]Wilhelm Schrader, F. Dummler, *Geschichte der Friedrichs-Universität zu Halle* (Berlin: 1894) 2.136-43.

[67]Cheyne, *Founders*, 54-55.

Wette.[68] In his study of Chronicles Gesenius found himself in further agreement with de Wette. His research on these books was published in 1815 in his work *Geschichte der hebräischen Sprache und Schrift*, which offered support on the basis of philology to de Wette's major conclusions about Chronicles. In this work Gesenius' treatment of Chronicles focused primarily on matters of the books' language and date. He assumed that Samuel-Kings was earlier than Chronicles and was probably used as a source by the author of the later history. Utilizing the linguistic differences between the two works, he was concerned with how changes in the Hebrew language could be seen in comparing the two works.[69]

Gesenius summarized his findings by listing several types of changes that the author of Chronicles had made.

1) Chronicles substituted later orthography and forms for earlier ones (e.g., 2 Chr 7:18 has מלכות for the form ממלכת in 1 Kg 9:5).[70]

2) Chronicles replaced the more archaic terms with newer ones (e.g., 1 Chr 10:12 reads גופה ("dead body") for גויה which occurs in 1 Sm 31:12).[71]

3) One also finds in Chronicles grammatical glosses, facilitations, and supposed improvements on the text of Samuel-Kings (e.g., 1 Chr 11:2 reads מביא for מבי in 2 Sm 5:2).[72]

4) Chronicles also presents exegetical glosses and clarifications of the older text (e.g., 2 Sm 5:18, 22 has ויפשטו, which 1 Chr 14:9, 13 expands with ויפשטו).[73]

5) For euphemisms in Chronicles, one may compare 2 Sm 10:4 with 1 Chr 19:4.[74]

6) Difficult or misunderstood texts (e.g., 2 Sm 6:5) have been conjecturally emended in Chronicles (cf. 1 Chr 13:8).[75]

On two occasions in this work, Gesenius indicated his substantial agreement with de Wette's conclusions regarding Chronicles. In the first, Gesenius indicated his acceptance of de Wette's historical conclusions.

---

[68]W. Gesenius, *Geschichte der hebraischen Sprache und* Schrift (Leipzig: Friedrich Christian Wilhelm Vogel, 1815) 32.

[69]*Ibid.*, 38.

[70]*Ibid.*

[71]*Ibid.*

[72]*Ibid.*, 39.

[73]*Ibid.*

[74]*Ibid.*, 40.

[75]*Ibid.*

> The character of this philological editing, with which we are dealing
> here, runs parallel with regard to the historical,...de Wette (Beytrage zur
> Einleit. in das A. T. B. 1. S. 42ff.)[76]

Gesenius' second note quoted de Wette's scathing judgment on the
Chronicler's knowledge of Hebrew and then stated his own partial
agreement.

> Already *de Wette* (Beytrage. B. 1. S. 67) would urge the judgment by
> some examples of this kind: "I would almost suppose that the author of
> Chronicles had not been well-versed in Hebrew. Surely he writes the
> simplest Hebrew, which we have. Probably at his time the language was
> already completely extinct." The examples above would partially estab-
> lish this judgment, partly modify it.[77]

The forgoing indicates that Gesenius' contributions to the study
of Chronicles were primarily linguistic. In spite of this narrow treatment of Chronicles, and in spite of the brief space devoted to the
books, Gesenius' conclusions were significant, as their frequent quotation in later studies indicates. De Wette, for his part, acknowledged
Gesenius' linguistic work and their areas of agreement in the preface
to his Old Testament introduction.

> My explanation of the Old Testament agrees for the most part with that
> of Gesenius, so far as this is known from his lexicon and from other
> sources; indeed, from the first I am happy to have been in the greatest
> possible agreement with this excellent friend.[78]

3. GRAMBERG

One of Gesenius' students who also supported de Wette's view of
Chronicles was Karl Peter Wilhelm Gramberg (1797-1830).[79] While he
completed his degree and later taught in several secondary schools,
Gramberg's desire for a university position was never realized. The
two greatest influences on his research and publications seem to have
been his teacher Gesenius and the writings of de Wette. Gramberg
was firmly committed to the use of the historical-critical method, and
he rejected many orthodox presuppositions about the historical reliability, authorship, and dating of the Old Testament. In 1823, he published *Die Chronik*, his investigation into the historical character of 1, 2

---

[76]*Ibid.*, 38.

[77]*Ibid.*, 40-41.

[78]De Wette, *Einleitung in das Alte Testament* (2d ed., 1831), cited in Cheyne,
Founders, 61.

[79]Redslob, "Gramberg, Karl Peter Wilhelm," *ADB* 9 (1879) 577; Rogerson,
Criticism, 57-63.

Chronicles. Five years later he issued *Libri Geneseos secundum fontes rite dignoscendos adumbratio nova,* a source-critical treatment of Genesis. That same year his book on Proverbs was published under the elaborate title, *Das Buch der Sprüche Salomo's neu übersetzt nach seinem Inhalte systematisch geordnet, mit erklärenden Anmerkungen und Parallelen aus dem Alten und Neuen Testamente versehen.* Gramberg's final publication was planned to be issued in four parts, but only the first two were printed, due to his untimely death in 1830. This work was his *magnum opus* and was entitled, *Kritische Geschichte der Religionsideen des alten Testaments.*[80]

Gramberg's *Die Chronik* challenged the historical reliability of 1, 2 Chronicles. Its subtitle, "newly examined according to their historical character and their credibility," points to this aim. The question that the author raises in the forward ("How far can we trust the reports of Chronicles?")[81] indicates the same concern. Gramberg set for himself the task of reinvestigating Chronicles systematically in order to substantiate the conclusions of de Wette and Gesenius and to defend them against the attacks of Dahler and others. That his goals were modest is evident from his remark, "I willingly resign myself to bringing forth little that is new, since the earlier works are available; but I would hope to contribute to the presentation of a more complete picture of the character of Chronicles."[82] He arranged his work in three chapters: I. About the Antiquity of Chronicles, II. About the Sources of Chronicles, and III. About the Historical Character of Chronicles. The burden of the research is presented in the third chapter, which occupies nearly three-fourths of the volume.

Gramberg's customary procedure is to present the conclusions of de Wette and Gesenius, accompanied by his own expansions. Then he cites the arguments of their opponents, chiefly those of Dahler. Finally, Gramberg responds to vindicate the positions of the former two scholars. An example of this approach is his treatment of 2 Chr 25:5-10. He first summarizes the biblical text. Next, he offers his own reflections on the passage, as well as de Wette's conclusions. Then he presents Dahler's position and objections to de Wette. Finally, Gramberg responds to Dahler, ending with the mildly sarcastic question, "Should such a thing require further illumination?"[83]

In the first chapter of the book Gramberg deals with the date of Chronicles. He begins by stating the opinion of de Wette and Gesenius: "Chronicles should be set in the late times of Hebrew literature." Then he gives Dahler's alternative view: one may only say

---

[80]Gesenius wrote the preface to this work. Rogerson, *Criticism,* 63. In addition, Gramberg's commentary on the Pentateuch was never completed. *Ibid.,* 577-78.

[81]C. P. W. Gramberg, *Die Chronik* (Halle: Eduard Anton, 1823) vii.

[82]*Ibid.*

[83]*Ibid.,* 223-24.

that it was composed after Samuel and Kings.[84] The remainder of the chapter deals with the arguments about the matter under two headings: external evidence (canonical considerations) and internal evidence (considerations within Chronicles itself). From the canon he argues three points: (1) the date of the canon itself is unknown; (2) Chronicles is not even part of the second division of the canon; and (3) Chronicles is set after Daniel in the canon, and so one must date it later than Daniel, i.e., after Antiochus Epiphanes.[85] In the second category of evidence, Gramberg presents eight arguments: (1) Chronicles must be post-exilic, since it uses Psalms (cf. 1 Chr 16:8-36 with Ps 105:1-15; 96; 106:1, 47, 48); (2) 2 Chr 36:22-23 is used to attach Chronicles to Ezra, which, consequently, must have already existed and been available to him; this also points to a post-exilic date; (3) Chaldaisms and other expressions argue for a late date (cf. the usage of אמר in 2 Chr 32:24 with Dan 7:16); (4) the reference to "darics" in 1Chr 29:7 requires a later date than Samuel-Kings; (5) Zerubbabel's genealogy (1 Chr 3:19-24) leads one to set Chronicles after Alexander the Great; (6) Judah's hatred for Samaria arose after the Samaritans asked Alexander to build a temple for them and Chronicles reflects this hostility; (7) fasts in the books of Samuel are motivated by sorrow, but the one in 2 Chr 20:3 arises as an appeal to God for victory; and (8) Chronicles refers to the book of Jeremiah (2 Chr 36:20-21).[86] He concludes, "The date of authorship cannot be determined with precision, yet what has been found seems to contradict Dahler's view of a relatively early date for Chronicles."[87]

Chapter two of Gramberg's work deals with the matter of the sources used in the writing of Chronicles. First, the opposing views of de Wette (supported by Gesenius' grammatical observations) and Dahler are presented, and then each source citation in Chronicles is treated. Gramberg concludes with five observations. First, one cannot demonstrate that Chronicles had authentic sources, which are now unknown to us, because he never refers to them and his citations are themselves "empty pomp." Secondly, the author of Chronicles had before him the MT of very many Old Testament historical books, perhaps even with the Qere provided. Thirdly, it is a futile and untenable hypothesis that Dahler advances, when he proposes that the copyists of Chronicles ruined the *Urtext*, or that the author of Samuel and Kings further improved a corrupt text. Fourthly, the examples from Chronicles show that the author of Chronicles edited his sources (Samuel, Kings, e.g.) with great carelessness, an evil desire, and an ignorance of geography, chronology, history, and the Hebrew lan-

---

[84]*Ibid.*, 1.
[85]*Ibid.*, 2.
[86]*Ibid.*, 3-19.
[87]*Ibid.*, 21-22.

guage. Finally, the entire history, as it is presented in Samuel-Kings, is more definite, orderly, and congruent with itself, while in Chronicles it is more confused, superficial, and contradictory.[88] Gramberg's final comments in chapter two praise Gesenius' sharp grammatical investigations and criticize Dahler for not exploring the sources and antiquity of Chronicles.[89]

The third chapter of *Die Chronik* is entitled "About the historical character of Chronicles." It begins with a brief statement of the problem, and there follows a survey of the text of Chronicles. The weight of the chapter, however, rests on Gramberg's analysis of Chronicles under five rubrics: (1) the negligence and ignorance of Chronicles, (2) Chronicles' delight in the miraculous, (3) levitism in Chronicles, (4) Chronicles' preference for the cult, and (5) Chronicles' love for Judah and hatred for Israel.[90] These are quite similar to the categories used by de Wette, a point clearly admitted by Gramberg, who believes that a presentation of the issues by means of such a grouping is far better than Dahler's chapter by chapter march through Chronicles. The latter, according to Gramberg, leads only to the further deception of the reader.[91] The differences between de Wette's rubrics and Gramberg's are explained by the latter as due to the fact that much of de Wette's material has already been discussed earlier in *Die Chronik*.[92] Gramberg's treatment of these topics is generally along the lines laid down by de Wette, except that it is longer (frequently twice as many pages devoted to the same topic) and that special attention is given to answering the objections of Dahler. An example of this may be seen in the two presentations of Chronicles' love for Judah and hatred for Israel. De Wette devotes six pages to the topic: one page of general remarks about the subject and five pages that treat individual passages (2 Chr 13; 19:2ff. and 25:7; 25:20; 20:35ff.). Gramberg, on the other hand, devotes twice the space to the topic (twelve pages), beginning with general remarks and following with discussions of individual passages (thirteen passages, which include all but one of de Wette's). As he treats each passage, he cites de Wette's position (if one has been expressed), supplies Dahler's response, and finally, responds to Dahler.[93] The overall aim of Gramberg's presentation seems to be to strengthen de Wette's position by increasing the number of examples that support his conclusions and to undercut Dahler's positions by detecting flaws in the latter's criticisms of de Wette.

---

[88]*Ibid.* 65.
[89]*Ibid.*, 65-66.
[90]*Ibid.*, 89.
[91]*Ibid.*
[92]*Ibid.*
[93]*Ibid.*, 224-25.

Gramberg ends the third chapter by summarizing the "results of the entire investigation." About the author of Chronicles he concludes,

> The methodical falsification of history, which goes through the entire book, and remains the same in its main characteristics, shows that it proceeds from only one author. He lived and wrote in the new Jewish state about the time of Antiochus IV Epiphanes, who died in 164 BC; he betrayed himself as a Jew by favoritism toward this kingdom and the hatred toward Israel; as a descendent of Levi, but not of the family of Aaron, because he exalts the holy power over the other tribes, and the Levites over the priests....[94]

Gramberg has further concluded that the author of Chronicles "neither could nor desired to write an objectively true and critical history."[95] He is ignorant, careless, and biased.[96] After briefly reviewing the positions of previous scholars with regard to Chronicles' usefulness as a historical source, Gramberg states his own conclusion:

> Chronicles does not fulfil any of the criteria, that one fairly expects of a critical, true, and reliable writer of history; therefore, he can have no historical authority at all for someone, and whatever he has not created from old canonical authors, is to be regarded as an unhistorical addition.[97]

His final comments constitute an appeal to his reader's sense of fairness and commitment to truth.[98]

Gramberg's final publication was entitled *Kritische Geschichte der Religionsideen des alten Testaments*. He planned for it to be issued in four parts. Only the first two parts were published by the time he died in 1830. The first part was entitled *Hierarchie und Cultus* and the second *Theokratie und Prophetismus*. His approach in both is the same: each volume is divided into chapters that treat matters relevant to the topic at hand, and then each chapter is divided into seven sections, each of which deals with a segment of time in Israel's history. The literature of the Old Testament is apportioned to the seven periods of Israel's history in the following way:

Period   I   Genesis, Exodus, Judges
           II   1, 2 Samuel, Ruth
           III   Isaiah, Hosea, Amos, Micah, Joel, Zephaniah
           IV   Leviticus, Numbers, Jeremiah, Ezekiel, Psalms
           V   1, 2 Kings, Deuteronomy, Joshua, Pseudo-Isaiah,

---

[94]*Ibid.*, 224.
[95]*Ibid.*
[96]*Ibid.*, 224-25.
[97]*Ibid.*, 225.
[98]*Ibid.*

Job, Jonah, Proverbs

VI   Ezra, Nehemiah, Malachi, Haggai, Zechariah, Qoheleth

VII   1, 2 Chronicles, Daniel, Esther, 1, 2 Maccabees

This work was noteworthy, because it directly tied the religious ideas of the Old Testament to the dates of composition of the various Old Testament books. Gramberg himself regarded this as an elaboration of what de Wette had already done in his *Einleitung*. Gramberg's approach in this publication preempted by nearly fifty years that of Wellhausen's *Prolegomena*.[99] It is evident that Chronicles belongs, according to Gramberg's reckoning, to the latest period of Israel's history, the period that Gramberg extends from the end of Persian rule until the death of Antiochus Epiphanes.[100] That his earlier estimation of Chronicles remained unchanged is evident from his description of it as an "arbitrary editing of the Books of Samuel and Kings, without independent, authentic sources...."[101]

Four observations may be made about Gramberg's treatment of Chronicles. First, Gramberg's approach to Chronicles was informed by the biblical criticism of Gesenius his teacher and that of de Wette. Consequently, he stood firmly opposed to the traditional method of dealing with Chronicles, and this becomes clearly evident in his responses to Dahler.

Secondly, Gramberg offered nothing that was really new for the study of Chronicles. By his own admission, however, his aims were in a different direction. His desire was to reinforce the conclusions of his mentors, Gesenius and de Wette, and to defend them against their critics, most notably Dahler. Consequently, he gave more examples to support de Wette's conclusions about Chronicles, and devoted extensive space to answering Dahler's challenges to de Wette.

Thirdly, Gramberg's *Religionsideen* served to demonstrate how one must reconstruct Israel's religious history, if one agreed with certain critical conclusions about Chronicles and other Old Testament books. It shows the author's desire to work out and state more fully the conclusions of others. This work, as well as *Die Chronik*, illustrates less creativity and brilliance of insight on the part of the author than his ability to fill in the details of a previously-advanced theory.

---

[99]The positions of de Wette and Gramberg diverged significantly in their treatments of Josiah's lawbook. While de Wette associated it with Deuteronomy, Gramberg connected it with Exodus or parts of Exodus (e.g., Ex 23:24ff.; 34:12-17). In turn, this allowed Gramberg to assign Deuteronomy a date toward the end of the exile. C. P. W. Gramberg, *Kritische Geschichte der Religionsideen des alten Testaments* (Berlin: Duncker and Humbolt, 1829) 1.xxvii, 307-8.

[100]*Ibid.*, 1.xxvi.

[101]*Ibid.*

Finally, while Gramberg's conclusions about the credibility of Chronicles are radical, they are no more so than those of de Wette.

4. SUMMARY OF THE CHALLENGE TO CHRONICLES

De Wette was the first to see the magnitude of the conflict between Chronicles and Samuel-Kings. Not only did he see the various isolated dissimilarities, but he was also able to characterize the differences between the two. Since Samuel-Kings was earlier and Chronicles seemed to be dominated to a greater degree by theological *Tendenzen*, de Wette rejected Chronicles for historical reconstruction of the pre-exilic period and argued that the historian was incapable of disentangling what may be true in Chronicles from what was false. De Wette's analysis of Chronicles was only one product of his thinking, which utilized the philosophy of Fries and a very rigorous method of historical research. While his conclusions regarding the usefulness of Chronicles for historical reconstruction were accepted by Gesenius and Gramberg, and then revitalized later by Wellhausen and others, it is evident that de Wette's philosophical system and rigorous criteria for a legitimate historical source did not enjoy such acceptance. Therefore, de Wette's criticism of Chronicles was separated from his philosophy of religion and historiography, and while the first was accepted by later scholars, who found his analysis of Chronicles convincing, his philosophy of religion and historiography were rejected.

Gesenius provided further support for de Wette's challenge to the historical reliability of Chronicles. He offered linguistic data supporting de Wette's historical conclusions, and a great number of later scholars found his arguments persuasive.

Finally, one of Gesenius' students, Gramberg, set forth a more detailed presentation of de Wette's position and defended the latter against its first detractors. Many later Old Testament scholars saw little value in Gramberg's work and were convinced that he overstepped the bounds of the evidence in order to argue his case and was unnecessarily sarcastic in dealing with his opponents.

With the publication of Gramberg's work in 1823, a serious challenge had been issued to those accepting the historical reliability of Chronicles. It was based on a critical analysis of the language and contents of Chronicles itself and on a careful comparison of Chronicles with Samuel-Kings. This research led a segment of German Old Testament scholarship to conclude that Chronicles was late post-exilic in date, dominated by theological biases, and filled with inaccurate information. This criticism of Chronicles no longer amounted to the mere listing of dissimilarities between Chronicles and the rest of Scripture, but was based on conclusions about the general theological *Tendenzen* of the work and was formulated in the context of the questions of *Einleitungswissenschaft*: date, authorship, and sources. The consequence of this was that responses to the challenge could only be effective if they presented convincing answers to the questions raised by the critical study and assessment of Chronicles.

B. THE RESPONSE: BERTHOLDT, DAHLER, HERBST, KEIL, MOVERS, AND HÄVERNICK

1. INTRODUCTION

The challenge by de Wette, Gesenius, and Gramberg of the historical trustworthiness of Chronicles was soon followed by responses from scholars upholding more traditional views. In this section the main figures who rose to defend Chronicles against its challengers will be discussed, but the primary focus will be on their arguments for the reliability of Chronicles.

The views of de Wette appeared far too radical for the majority of German scholars and pastors. Therefore, it comes as no surprise to see the strong reaction against de Wette and the other critics, who dismissed Chronicles for reconstructing the history of the pre-exilic period. One factor in this conservative reaction was the revival of Lutheran confessionalism. In the early and mid-nineteenth century there was considerable interest in the creeds of the churches, especially the Augsburg Confession. This was due in part to the impulses in Germany for the union of Lutherans and Calvinists after the defeat of Napoleon and with the approach of the three-hundredth anniversary of Luther's posting his Ninety-five Theses. In several parts of the country this union was accomplished, and the efforts in this direction focused attention on the church formularies. The latter consequence was also one of the by-products of the revival movement in Germany. By the 1840s, efforts were under way to safeguard the distinctive characteristics of Lutheranism, which some believed had been compromised by the efforts for unity with the Calvinists. A central tenet of the confessionalists during the nineteenth century became the historical trustworthiness of Scripture, and they affirmed this often at the expense of the historical critical method. This motive—to assert the accuracy of the Bible—should be seen as an important factor in the work of those who defended Chronicles against the charges of de Wette and his supporters.[102]

---

[102]M. A. Crowther, *Church Embattled: Religious Controversy in Mid-Victorian England* (Library of Politics and Society, ed. Michael Hurst; Hamden, Conn.: Archon, 1970) 44-45.

Two of the earliest scholars to respond to de Wette's *Beiträge* were Bertholdt (1813) and Dahler (1819). It was not, however, until the 1830s that the more impressive and influential responses were published: Herbst (1831), Keil (1833), Movers (1834), and Hävernick (1839). The work of each of these figures will be discussed briefly, and then their arguments in defense of Chronicles will be examined.

Leonhard Bertholdt (1774-1822) studied and later taught at the University of Erlangen, a school which subsequently became a stronghold of one segment of German theological conservatism (e.g., Franz Delitzsch taught there from 1850-1867, and J. C. K. von Hofmann from 1845 to 1877).[103] Bertholdt's views on Chronicles appeared in his *Historischkritische Einleitung in sämmtliche kanonische und apokryphische Schriften des alten und neuen Testaments* (1812-1819)).[104] While he accepted de Wette's late date for Chronicles (about the time of Antiochus Epiphanes IV),[105] he argued for a source theory nearer Eichhorn's and concluded that de Wette's charges against Chronicles' reliability had not all been established by precise and weighty evidence and that it was still possible to argue against him about the antiquity of reports in Chronicles. He maintained that chance rather than an evil will was probably responsible for much in Chronicles.[106]

Johann Georg Dahler (1760-1832) taught at Strassburg and was the first scholar to issue a major response to de Wette. He did this in his book *De librorum Paralipomenon auctoritate atque fide historica disputat* (1819). This work proceeded through 1, 2 Chronicles, treating each problem passage that de Wette had pointed out in the books. Dahler usually attempted to explain away the difficulties or harmonize the passages that conflicted with Samuel-Kings.[107] In general, Dahler simply reasserted the pre-de Wettian position.[108]

---

[103]Erdmann, "Bertholdt, Leonhard," *ADB* 2 (1875) 512-13.

[104]Bertholdt's *Einleitung* was published in six parts and was distinctive in that it grouped literature according to type (history, poetry, e.g.), rather than according to place in the canon. Consequently, the volume that treated the historical books of the Old Testament also dealt with those of the New Testament.

[105]Leonhard Bertholdt, *Historischkritische Einleitung in sämmtliche kanonische und apokryphische Schriften des alten und neuen Testaments* (6 vols.; Erlangen: Johann Jacob Palm, 1813) 3.983-86, 988.

[106]*Ibid.*, 3.965-83.

[107]After a brief introduction Dahler proceeded through 1, 2 Chronicles, treating each alleged discrepancy. He typically summarized the text in Chronicles—sometimes, though, printing it in full alongside the synoptic text from Samuel-Kings—and then defended it against the charges that de Wette had raised against it. J. G. Dahler, *De librorum Paralipomenon auctoritate atque fide historica disputat* (Argentorati: Johannis Henrici Heitz, 1819).

[108]Dahler's work did not adequately speak to the categories of challenges that de Wette had raised against Chronicles. On the contrary, he simply proceeded through the books addressing individual problems and not their cumulative force, as raised by de Wette's rubrics.

Johann Georg Herbst (1787-1836) was a Roman Catholic scholar who taught at Tübingen.[109] His contribution to the study of the historical reliability of Chronicles appeared in an eighty page article in the *Theologische Quartalschrift* entitled "Die Bücher der Chronik. Ihr Verhältniss zu den Büchern Samuels und der Könige; ihre Glaubwürdigkeit, und die Zeit ihrer Abfassung" (1831). His primary goal seems to have been to address the work of Gramberg and to point out what he considered the excesses of the latter's study of Chronicles. His means for accomplishing this was the harmonization of the differences between Chronicles and the rest of the Old Testament.[110]

In 1833, Carl Friedrich Keil (1807-1888) published *Apologetischer Versuch über die Bücher der Chronik und über die Integrität des Buches Esra.* The author set out to expose the baselessness of the attacks on Chronicles and to defend the integrity and authority of the books. He regarded the challenges to Chronicles as not only a challenge to the integrity of Chronicles but also as a threat to the faith of Christians as well.[111] Keil was among the first to attempt a refutation of de Wette's arguments in the fashion they had been advanced. He treated questions of Old Testament introduction as they related to Chronicles and addressed the categories of objections, which de Wette had arranged against the books.[112] Keil's later commentary on Chronicles (1870) reaffirmed the author's conclusions about the books, but with an even greater decisiveness and exactness.[113]

---

[109]Wolff, "Herbst," *ADB* 12 (1880) 50-51.

[110]J. G. Herbst, "Die Bücher der Chronik. Ihr Verhältniss zu den Büchern Samuels und der Könige; ihre Glaubwürdigkeit, und die Zeit ihrer Abfassung," *ThQ* 13 (1831) 201-82.

[111]Zev Garber, "Keil, C. F.," *Enc Jud* 10 (1971) 897; C. F. Keil, *Apologetischer Versuch über die Bücher der Chronik und über die Integrität des Busches Esra* (Berlin: Ludwig Oehmigke, 1833) ix.

[112]Keil believed that earlier scholars, who had reviewed and opposed de Wette's position on Chronicles, had been largely ineffective since they had not adequately addressed the questions about the age and sources of Chronicles and had not spoken to the categories of objections that de Wette had presented. *Ibid.*, 2-4.

[113]Keil's basic views on Chronicles remained the same in his *Versuch*, his commentaries on Chronicles and Kings, and in his *Einleitung* to the Old Testament. In his *Versuch*, he left the matter of authorship for Chronicles open; however, in his commentary thirty-seven years later he argued strongly for Ezra as its author. The same trend toward a greater decisiveness and certainty about matters is evident in his treatment of Joash. *Versuch*, 415-17; C. F. Keil, *The Books of the Chronicles* (Clark's Foreign Theological Library, 4th ser., vol. 35; Edinburgh: T. & T. Clark, 1878) 419. The original edition of Keil's commentary on Chronicles was *Biblischer Commentar über die nachexilische Geschichtsbücher: Chronik, Esra, Nehemia und Esther* (Biblischer Commentar über das Alte Testament, part 5; Leipzig: Dörffling & Franke, 1870).

Franz Karl Movers (1806-1856) published the most important of the early responses to de Wette and the others who had challenged the credibility of Chronicles.[114] He was among the first to argue for the unity of Chronicles and Ezra.[115] He used the LXX more extensively than earlier scholars had done in order to correlate Chronicles with Samuel-Kings and account for their dissimilarities as text-critical problems.[116] Finally, Movers offered an innovative source critical solution to the problem of the Chronicler's sources. This solution regarded the Midrash, which the Chronicler cites, as the author's primary source and recognized the references to prophetic writings in the books as citations of individual sections within the Midrash itself.[117]

Finally, Heinrich Andreas Christoph Hävernick (1811-1845), who taught at Rostock and Konigsberg, presented his contribution to the study of Chronicles in his *Handbuch der historisch-kritischen Einleitung in das Alte Testament* in the 1830s and 1840s.[118] He follows Movers in the belief that Chronicles and Ezra were written by the same author,

---

[114]Movers was a Catholic priest in Bonn, and later became professor of Old Testament at Breslau. Reusch, "Movers, Franz Karl M.," *ADB* 22 (1885) 417-18.

[115]In his discussion of the date of Chronicles Movers argued that the books were written about 400 B. C. E. by a priest or levite, who was a younger contemporary of Nehemiah. He bases his conviction that the same author wrote both Chronicles and Ezra on the relation between 2 Chr 36:22-23 and Ezra 1:1-3. *Kritische Untersuchungen über die biblische Chronik* (Bonn: T. Habicht, 1834) 11-14. Leopold Zunz had preempted Movers on the unity of Chronicles and Ezra-Nehemiah by two years. Zunz, however, also affirmed that the author of Chronicles and Ezra wrote Nehemiah, too. *Die gottesdienstlichen Vorträge der Juden* (Berlin: A. Asher, 1832) 22.

[116]Movers devoted the entire third chapter of his book to the matter of the text of Chronicles. His use of the parallel sections of Samuel-Kings and Chronicles, along with the LXX, in order to arrive at a better understanding of the texts of the two books was a real advance. Sometimes, he was able to show that what had been regarded as an addition that the author of Chronicles had made to his *Vorlage*, was present in the LXX. Movers, *Chronik*, 71. Cf. also, Thomas Willi, *Die Chronik als Auslegung* (FRLANT 106; Gottingen: Vandenhoeck & Ruprecht, 1972) 39-40.

[117]Movers' source theory may be diagrammed in the following way.

[118]The final volume of Hävernick's *Einleitung* was edited by C. F. Keil and published in 1849.

but he diverges from the latter in that he believes that Ezra was the writer and that he wrote the works at different times.[119] Considerable space in his presentation is devoted to the matter of the Chronicler's sources, and the outcome is a fairly complex source theory, which is built around the use of a Sepher or Midrash by the author of Chronicles.[120]

2. THE ARGUMENTS IN DEFENSE OF CHRONICLES

A variety of arguments were used in the works discussed above to defend Chronicles against charges of unreliability. Nine principal responses were made to the challenges of de Wette and his followers, and each will be discussed as its main advocate argued it. A name has been assigned to each argument in order to simplify the present discussion.

a. The Divine Inspiration Argument

This argument arose in Keil's study of Chronicles. On the title page of his book there is a quotation from Augustine: "If the authority of the Scriptures totters, at the same time faith totters." He believed that the challenges to the historical reliability of Chronicles also undermined the authority of the Bible and thus the Christian faith as well. One of his major assumptions was that the canon arose under divine influence, and therefore, no writing by a "bold and rational cheater" could have been included within it.[121]

b. The Moral Argument

Herbst bases this argument on his understanding of ancient morality. It is argued that the author of Chronicles did not operate with an "evil" motive (viz., with the intention of misrepresenting his

---

[119]H. A. C. Hävernick, *Handbuch der historisch-kritischen Einleitung in das Alte Testament* (3 vols.; Erlangen: Carl Heyder, 1839) 2/1.268-69, 271, 302.

[120]*Ibid.*, 2/1.177-201.

[121]Keil, *Versuch*, ix-x. In America Moses Stuart (1780-1852), who taught at Andover Seminary, argued for the historical accuracy of Scripture on similar grounds. He believed that since the Old Testament canon was already complete by the time of Jesus and the Apostles, and since they evidently accepted it as inspired and authoritative, then the charges of the modern biblical critics that there were errors and contradictions in it cannot be true. While Stuart maintained that the tools of biblical criticism were useful to help one understand the original meaning of the text, he restricted the use of these tools so that the conclusions that one reached by means of them did not contradict the conviction that the biblical documents were inspired, authoritative, and truthful. Moses Stuart, *Critical History and Defence of the Old Testament Canon* (Andover: Allen, Morrill & Wardwell, 845) 156-65.

sources and thus misleading his readers)[122] and that the books would probably never have been published in ancient times or included in the canon if they had contained as many falsehoods as de Wette claimed, presumably because ancient readers would have detected the errors and refused that writing the honor of publication or entry into the canon.[123] The assumption, of course, is that the ancient readers (if they were knowledgeable about the misrepresentation) would have felt the same horror as a modern, critical historian.

c. The Source Argument

It was assumed by all scholars that the credibility of the Chronicler could be strengthened if it could be shown that adequate and accurate sources lay behind his narratives. A variety of different theories were proposed in order to account for the connections between Chronicles and the rest of the Old Testament and to make sense of the various source citations in Chronicles. The theories fall into two major divisions: those which hold that the author of Chronicles used Samuel-Kings and those which deny it. In 1831, Herbst had affirmed that the author of Chronicles had used the books of the Old Testament canon and the annals of the two kingdoms for his sources.[124] Three years later Movers argued along the same lines, but he added that between the royal annals of the two kingdoms and the books of Chronicles, the former underwent two editions. The first edition of the royal annals was called "The Book of Kings" (not the canonical Kings), and when the latter was edited, it was called "The Midrash on the Book of Kings." Movers further believed that the author of Samuel-Kings made use of the royal annals (at least in abstracts) and "The Book of Kings." The great contribution of Movers in the treatment of the Chronicler's sources was his suggestion that the principal source behind Chronicles was the Midrash and that the numerous source citations in Chronicles (e.g., "The Chronicles of Jehu the son of Hanani" [2 Chr 20:34]) were references to various sections within the Midrash.[125]

Other scholars, however, denied that the author of Chronicles used Samuel-Kings as a source. This may have been partially due to

---

[122]Herbst, "Chronik," 236.

[123]*Ibid.*, 237.

[124]*Ibid.*, 239.

[125]Movers believed that when the narrative in Chronicles matched that of Samuel-Kings, it was an indication that the author of Chronicles had copied from the latter. However, whenever the text of Chronicles diverged from that of Samuel-Kings, this indicated that the author of Chronicles had copied from another source. *Chronik*, 163-94. The result of Movers' source critical views is that the historian should regard every narrative that is unique to Chronicles as founded upon a prior historical source.

the fact that one of the cornerstones in de Wette's position against the historical reliability of Chronicles was his conviction that Samuel-Kings was the only source behind Chronicles.[126] In addition, there is the fact that the influential Eichhorn had offered a source theory for Chronicles that did not include the use of Samuel-Kings by the author of Chronicles.[127] Bertholdt followed Eichhorn to some extent, suggesting that regnal histories were composed for David and for Solomon. Several years earlier, de Wette had argued in detail against Eichhorn's proposals.[128] Keil and Hävernick, however, did not reassert this aspect of Eichhorn's theory. On the contrary, they agreed that between the royal annals and the author of Chronicles there stood an intermediate source. Keil called it "The Book of the Kings of Israel and Judah" and Hävernick "The Sepher" or "Midrash".[129]

The influence of Movers, who characterized this intermediate source as midrash and who wrote after Keil,[130] may be detected in Hävernick's explanation. Both Keil and Hävernick also held that prophetic writings were used as sources—along with the royal annals—by the intermediate source and that various other writings were used by the author of Chronicles, independent of the intermediate source.[131]

A second aspect of the source argument concerns the way that the author of Chronicles used his sources. Movers sought to explain the use of sources in Chronicles by appeal to the assumed practices of ancient Near Eastern historiography. He believed that the ancient historians in the Near East were essentially annalists and compilers and that they generally copied their sources faithfully.[132] "History writing in the orient never arose above the simple form of annals to the pragmatic manner of presentation of the Greeks and Romans."[133] Furthermore, Movers maintained that the author of Chronicles had faithfully copied his single source for the monarchy that we still have available—Samuel-Kings—and, therefore, one must assume that he copied his other sources just as accurately.[134] These considerations led Movers to conclude that the books of Chronicles are "less an orig-

---

[126]De Wette, *Einleitung*, 242-43.

[127]Eichhorn, *Einleitung*, 3.587-600.

[128]In his treatments of the sources for Chronicles Bertholdt characteristically makes two suggestions: (1) between the royal annals or regnal histories and Chronicles, there was at least one intervening edition of the former works, and (2) priestly archives were available to the author of Chronicles for additional genealogical and historical reports. *Einleitung*, 3.945-46, 969-76.

[129]Keil, *Chronicles*, 17-21; Hävernick, *Einleitung*, 2/1.177-90, 192-201.

[130]Movers, *Chronik*, 174-75.

[131]Keil, *Chronicles*, 17-21: Hävernick, *Einleitung*, 2/1.177-90, 192-201.

[132]Movers, *Chronik*, 170-72.

[133]*Ibid.*, 95-96.

[134]*Ibid.*, 95-97.

inal work of history than remnants of earlier works, which the compilatory hand of the collector was busy to attach together into a whole"[135] and that it was to this work of collection and arrangement that the author of Chronicles restricted himself.[136] Consequently, one would be hard pressed to identify anything in Chronicles that arose from the author's own imagination or observation. Even when the author combined the reports of the two sources, he cautiously bound himself to the wording of his sources.[137] In this way, he used his second source, the Midrash, to supplement or correct his primary one, Samuel-Kings, which was already regarded as canonical in his day.[138] This, in turn, led Movers to conclude that the two sources that lay behind Chronicles were in essential agreement, and that even when the two sources disagreed, the disagreement was usually over nonessentials and was due to "the imprecision of eastern history writing in general."[139]

Hävernick offers a further suggestion in the matter of the sources behind Chronicles. He counters de Wette's charge that the author of Chronicles falsified history because of his bias in favor of the levites with the observation that while Chronicles has a great interest in levitical matters, this is the natural result of the fact that the levites were the ones who preserved the records which the author used. It is only to be expected that their records would deal in a significant way with matters of interest to levites. Hävernick concluded that the presence of levitical interests in Chronicles does not necessarily imply that the author resorted to the falsification of history.[140]

d. The Supplementary Argument

This argument seems to have been part of the earliest understanding of Chronicles. In the LXX the books were entitled *"Paralipomena"* and thought to include matters that served to supplement the account in Samuel-Kings. In his article on Chronicles Herbst used the last section to characterize Chronicles as a historical supplement to the earlier historical writings. He proposed that Chronicles arose when an educated Hebrew of the tribe of Levi decided to write a history of his people, since he had available additional documentary information not found in Kings.[141] Hävernick, also, employed this argument to defend the great attention that is given to the cult in Chronicles. The author of Chronicles had a strong

---

[135]*Ibid.*, 95.
[136]*Ibid.*, 97.
[137]*Ibid.*, 170-72.
[138]*Ibid.*
[139]*Ibid.*, 172.
[140]Hävernick, *Einleitung*, 2/1.246-48.
[141]Herbst, "Chronik," 282.

theocratic viewpoint and this led him to give a more complete account of the Judean cult than did Samuel-Kings.[142]

e. The Textual Corruption Argument

As early as Simon, it was argued that the MT of Chronicles was
defective in that copyists' errors had crept into the text and so were
responsible for many of the minor differences between Samuel-Kings
and Chronicles.[143] Dahler made extensive use of this argument to account for the dissimilarities between Chronicles and the other canonical books, especially in the cases that involved numbers. According to
2 Chr 22:2, Ahaziah was forty-two when he began to reign as king
over Judah. This contradicts 2 Kg 8:26, which reports the king's age as
twenty-two. Dahler proposed that a scribal error lay behind the
number forty-two and that originally the figure was twenty-two. The
mistake came about by the כ in כב being miscopied as מ, and so the
figure became מב, which meant forty-two.[144] Another instance of textual corruption occurred in 2 Chr 36:9, which set Jehoiachin's age at
eight years, rather than eighteen, as in 2 Kg 24:8. Dahler suggested
that עשרה had fallen out of the text.[145] Movers devoted the fourth and
fifth sections of his book to the matter of textual corruptions in
Chronicles. He concluded that several variants between Chronicles
and Samuel-Kings point to the use of a system similar to roman numerals, in which a letter represented a numeral (e.g., one, ten). If this
had been the kind of numbering system that was used in ancient
times among the people of Israel and Judah, then it would have been
a simple matter for the copyist to have corrupted a figure by one, ten,
a hundred, or a thousand (cf. 1 Chr 19:18 with 2 Sm 10:18).[146] In addition, Movers suggested that some numerical corruptions in
Chronicles are evidently due to the omission of a word, when the
numbers were written out. He did not believe that the same system
was always used for recording numbers in classical Hebrew.[147] In the
case of parallel passages reporting different names, Movers held that
most of the variants arose from a copyist (or author) changing one
name to a similar one or from the simple confusion of two letters that
were similar.[148] Other variants arose from the copying of an earlier
mistake.[149] Movers also pointed out that the LXX (of other Old
Testament books) sometimes agreed with Chronicles, and conse-

---

[142]Hävernick, *Einleitung*, 2/1.257-58.

[143]R. Simon, *Histoire critique*, 1.23-28.

[144]Dahler, *De librorum*, 107.

[145]*Ibid.*, 147.

[146]Movers, *Chronik*, 62-63.

[147]*Ibid.*, 64-65.

[148]*Ibid.*, 69-71.

[149]*Ibid.*, 69-70.

quently, the latter may preserve the correct reading.[150] A common feature of the early scholars, who defended Chronicles against the challenges of de Wette and others, was that textual corruption could easily account for many of the differences between Chronicles and Samuel-Kings.

f. The Modernization Argument

This line of reasoning seeks to account for distinctive features in Chronicles and differences with Samuel-Kings by arguing that the parallel histories were written by different authors at different times and for different audiences in different circumstances. It is further argued that one of the purposes of the author of Chronicles was to bring the ancient history of his people up to date and make it understandable to the people of his own day. Movers, for example, believed that since the historical settings of Chronicles and Samuel-Kings were so different, one should not be surprised to find substantial dissimilarities between the two works.[151] The author of Chronicles wrote his history according to the needs and tastes of his contemporaries, and he did it with a didactic purpose in mind. Nevertheless, Movers maintained that this effort by the author of Chronicles to make his history relevant to his contemporaries did not lead him to sacrifice accuracy or betray his sources.[152]

In the third major section of his treatment of Chronicles Hävernick addressed the credibility of the books and pointed out that their author was a scholar who eagerly researched ancient documents and tried to make them more comprehensible to his contemporaries. To this end, he changed the language and geographical expressions and made other changes for dogmatic reasons (e.g., substituting "Satan" for "God" in 1 Chr 21:1; cf. 2 Sm 24:1). Occasionally he offered observations on the matters that he reported and thus revealed his basic theocratic perspective (cf. 1 Chr 10:13-14), and omitted certain things, such as geographical details that were of no interest or unknown to his readers.[153]

g. The Harmonization Argument

This argument was used by all those who defended Chronicles against charges of falsification. Since the challenges by de Wette and others were based to a large extent on the identification of contradictions and discrepancies between Chronicles and Samuel-Kings, it became important for those who wanted to establish the credibility of

---

[150]*Ibid.*, 71.

[151]*Ibid.*, 8.

[152]*Ibid.*

[153]Hävernick, *Einleitung*, 2/1.207-9.

Chronicles to account for the differences between the parallel histories in a way that did not cast a bad light on either the morality or intelligence of the author of Chronicles. An example of the approach can be found in Dahler's treatment of 2 Chr 13:23, which reports that Asa reigned in peace for ten years. This disagrees with 1 Kg 15:32, which notes that there was war between Asa and Baasha of Israel throughout their reigns. Baasha began to reign in Asa's third year. Dahler defended Chronicles by suggesting that the statement in Chronicles only referred to the absence of overt warfare, while that in Kings referred to a generally hostile state of affairs between the two kingdoms, which only later erupted into overt warfare.[154]

h. The External Support Argument

This line of reasoning argues that the historical testimony of Chronicles is established by the support that it receives from the other canonical writings. Movers, for example, believed that a comparison of Chronicles with Samuel-Kings showed that the former copied the latter faithfully (and thus his other sources as well). This was established by Movers by harmonizing the parallel histories. Then he proceeded to argue that the narratives of Chronicles are supported by the canonical prophetic books and the psalter. He supported this assertion by pointing to the sections in Chronicles that claim David as the originator of the levitical divisions of singers and musicians (1 Chr 15:16-24; 25:1-8). This witness in Chronicles is upheld by references in the books of Samuel to singing and the use of musical instruments in various circumstances, which allow one to presume David's preparations (cf. 2 Sm 6:5). Furthermore, headings of psalms ("Psalm of David") and Sirach (17:9-12) point to David as the originator of levitical temple music and Am 6:5 to him as the inventor of musical instruments. Finally, no less than one hundred and twenty-eight singers returned from Babylonian exile (Ezr 2:41), well-provided with genealogical registers that documented their levitical descent from Asaph, the singer of David's time.[155] Movers adduced these arguments to show that even though Samuel-Kings did not record David's arrangements for temple music, nevertheless Samuel

---

[154]Dahler, *De librorum*, 98. Herbst used the same technique in order to reconcile 2 Chr 8:1-2 with 1 Kg 9:10-13 ("Chronik," 275-77), Keil with the treatments of Joash's reign in Chronicles and Kings (*Versuch*, 415-17), Movers with the presentations of David's census in 2 Samuel 24 and 1 Chronicles 21 (*Chronik*, 305-6), and Hävernick with the apparent discrepancy between 2 Chr 14:2-4 and 15:17 about Asa's actions involving pagan altars (*Einleitung*, 2/1.233).

[155]Movers, *Chronik*, 109-11.

and other Old Testament books testify to the accuracy of the account in Chronicles.[156]

i. The General Credibility Argument

This argument asserts that the narrative in Chronicles has a certain "inner constitution" that makes it believable[157] and that many of the excesses that de Wette and others have pointed out to discredit Chronicles exist in the other biblical books, as well, and therefore, should not be used to detract from the credibility of Chronicles.[158] In the first case, Hävernick notes that the cultic arrangements of David, which are reported in 1 Chronicles 23-26, bear an archival imprint and that there is no better period than David's for their origin.[159] In the case of the excesses that various scholars pointed out in Chronicles, Hävernick calls attention to two areas. First, he notes de Wette's criticism that the Chronicler took delight in the miraculous and in the romantic, and then he reminds his reader that the stories of Elijah and Elisha in Kings are just as marvelous and romantic as anything that can be found in Chronicles, and that the era that the author of Chronicles treats is a "marvelous period" in every respect, as the other books of the Old Testament show.[160] The second area that Hävernick treats is that of the Chronicler's love for Judah and hatred for Israel. While de Wette had charged that these feelings had led the author of Chronicles to falsify history, Hävernick defended Chronicles by noting that the author's low esteem for Israel was shared by the prophets and to some extent even by the author of Kings.[161]

3. SUMMARY OF ARGUMENTS IN DEFENSE OF CHRONICLES

The response to the challenge that de Wette, Gesenius, and Gramberg had issued to the historical credibility of Chronicles, arose from Protestant and Catholic circles alike. It came in the forms of

---

[156]On another occasion, Movers used the witness of Samuel-Kings to validate some of the cultic descriptions in Chronicles, which presume the existence of the Mosaic law before Josiah. Movers believed that the Mosaic law was not a late, exilic or post-exilic creation, because both Chronicles and Samuel-Kings assumed its existence from the beginning of the monarchy (David was the ideal in observing it, according to 1 Kg 18:6), and "if the Books of Kings assure us that the Mosaic law was present in the time before Josiah, why, then, should not the Chronicler be believed when he gives us the details of what the author of Kings assumed?" *Chronik*, 271-72.

[157]Hävernick, *Einleitung*, 2/1.210.

[158]*Ibid.*, 2/1.239-40.

[159]*Ibid.*, 2/1.211-12.

[160]*Ibid.*, 2/1.239-40.

[161]*Ibid.*, 2/1.262-63.

monograph, commentary, journal article, and Old Testament introduction. While the approaches and contributions of these works differed, all of them shared a common concern: the vindication of the
historical testimony of Chronicles. Some of those who wrote in defense of Chronicles believed that the challenge to Chronicles' credibility was at the same time a challenge to the Christian faith and to the
authority of Scripture. Therefore, the outcome of the debate about the
historical reliability of Chronicles was of great importance.

Of the nine arguments that were used to vindicate Chronicles two
were debated more often and more extensively than the rest: the
Source Argument and the Harmonization Argument. A third argument—the External Support Argument—would assume monumental
importance at a later time in the second challenge to the credibility of
Chronicles, which revolved about the history of Israel's religion and
the connections between Chronicles and P.

C. CHRONICLES AND THE RECONSTRUCTION
OF ISRAELITE HISTORY

The debate over the historical reliability of Chronicles was vigorous for the first four decades of the nineteenth century.
Consequently, some historians began to use the books with a bit more
caution than before, since they had become more aware of
Chronicles' late date of composition and theological biases.
Generally, however, the debate over Chronicles' reliability as a
historical source led these historians to adopt positions somewhere
between those of de Wette and Keil. Ewald's history is an outstanding
example of this moderating position.

1. BEFORE EWALD

In the period before the publication of Ewald's history of Israel,
four significant histories were published. In 1827, there was Russell's,
in 1829, those of Jahn and Milman, and in 1832, that of Jost. While
each of the three employed the historical critical method to some degree, none applied it to the biblical materials with the rigor of de
Wette or Gesenius. Consequently, all four historians operated on the
assumption that 1, 2 Chronicles was a reliable source for historical information about the pre-exilic period.

a. Russell

The first major history of Israel that was written in nineteenth
century England was that by Michael Russell (1781-1848), who attended the University of Glasgow and served as Bishop of Glasgow
and Galloway. He contributed volumes on Palestine and Egypt to the

Edinburgh Cabinet Library, wrote a biography of Oliver Cromwell, and in 1827 wrote *A Connection of Sacred and Profane History from the Death of Joshua to the Decline of the Kingdoms of Israel and Judah* in order to bridge the gap between Shuckford's history, which extended until the death of Joshua, and that of Prideaux, which began with the mid-eighth century B. C. E.[162] Russell's work focuses on chronological correlations between Israel and her neighbors, as well as the political and other connections between Israel and the nations around her.

Russell's attitude toward the biblical materials as a whole is that they are reliable for historical reconstruction, acceptable at face value, and this view pervades his treatment of information in Chronicles. Russell accepts the Chronicler's reports about such matters as David's preparations for the building of the Jerusalem temple by his son,[163] David's cultic arrangements,[164] the size of Shishak's army and the prophecies of Shemaiah against Rehoboam,[165] the account of Zechariah's murder at Joash's instigation,[166] Asa's battle with Zerah,[167] and the theological reason for Uzziah's leprosy.[168]

Russell's history shows a great concern with chronology and understands its primary purpose to be that of aligning the events described in the Old Testament with those of Israel described in the extra-biblical sources. The author's attention is not directed to the critical problem of carefully examining the accuracy of the Old Testament books as historical sources, and to this extent *A Connection of Sacred and Profane History* is uncritical. The approach toward and use of Chronicles as a source for historical reconstruction is pre-de Wettian.

b. Milman

The next scholar in Great Britain to write a history of Israel was Henry Hart Milman (1791-1868). He was an influential figure in the Anglican church as Dean of St. Paul's but won his greatest and most lasting recognition as the author of three histories: *The History of the Jews* (1829), *The History of Christianity under the Empire* (1840), and *The History of Latin Christianity down to the Death of Pope Nicholas V* (1855).[169]

---

[162]T. F. Henderson, "Russell, Michael," *DNB* 49 (1897) 467-68.
[163]Michael Russell, *A Connection of Sacred and Profane History* (new ed., rev. by J. T. Wheeler; 2 vols.; London: William Tegg, 1869) 2.172.
[164]*Ibid.*, 2.185.
[165]*Ibid.*, 2.358.
[166]*Ibid.*, 2.391.
[167]*Ibid.*, 2.361-62.
[168]*Ibid.*, 2.393-94.
[169]Richard Garnett, "Milman, Henry Hart," *DNB* 38 (1894) 1-4; William Edward Hartpole Lecky, "Dean Milman" in *Historical and Political Essays* (new

The first of these histories was published in three volumes beginning with Abraham and ending with the Jewish history of Milman's own day in Europe and America. Intended for the general public, it appeared in the series *Family Library* and refrained from technical discussions of historical problems. A great outcry greeted its publication, because its author treated the Bible much like any other book of ancient history or literature. Consequently, the sale of the book was halted, and the series in which it appeared came to an end.[170] Milman's son described the protests against the book in the following way.

> Heads wise or unwise had indeed been shaken. A wild storm of disapproval gathered, burst, and Sunday after Sunday Milman was denounced from University and other pulpits in most unmeasured language, in language to which we have since unhappily become too well accustomed, as holding heretical opinions, as a most dangerous and pernicious writer.[171]

In 1834, however, a second edition of the work appeared, this time in America and with a preface, which was dated 1830 and contained responses to some of the criticisms that had been raised against the work. A third edition with significant additions appeared in 1863. By this time, the attitude of the public was different and the book met with no general opposition.[172]

The outstanding accomplishment of Milman in the *History of the Jews* was his application of a moderately critical attitude to Israel's history. He appears to have been the first to produce such a work. Since Milman took it upon himself to write as a historian, rather than as a religious instructor, he gave his attention primarily to Israel's temporal, social, and political aspects.[173] This led him to look for natural connections in the events of Israel's past, and sometimes this resulted in biblical miracles being explained in terms of natural phenomena.[174] For example, Milman suggests that Sennacherib's army was not destroyed by the death angel mentioned in the Bible but by

---

ed.; London: Longmans, Green, 1910) 231-33; Vernon F. Storr, *The Development of English Theology in the Nineteenth Century 1800-1860* (London: Longmans, Green, 1913) 112-14; Rogerson, *Criticism*, 184-88.

[170]J. E. Carpenter, *The Bible in the Nineteenth Century* (London: Longmans, Green, 1903) 19-20.

[171]Arthur Milman, *Henry Hart Milman* (London: John Murray, 1900) 85-86.

[172]Garnett, "Milman," 3; Lecky, *Essays*, 234-35, 239, 246; Carpenter, *Nineteenth Century*, 19-20; Milman, *Milman*, 93-96.

[173]Lecky, *Essays*, 242.

[174]*Ibid.*, 237: cf. also the letter from Lockhart to Milman, which A. Milman cites (*Milman*, 85). "It is a splendid book (*The History of the Jews*), but some wise folks shake their heads at some passages touching miracles. A few sentences would have disarmed them, and will no doubt do so in the next edition."

the "hot and pestilential wind of the desert."[175] In spite of his tendency to rationalize biblical miracles, Milman still maintained that such rationalizations could not advance beyond conjecture, and so he often satisfied himself with simply repeating his source's account.[176] He defended his use of the critical method with an appeal to his readers' concern for religious faith and for evangelism.

> I cannot but think that the historian who labors to reconcile the Jewish history, where not declaredly supernatural, with common probability, with the concurrent facts, usages, opinions of the time and place, is not a less sincere, certainly not a less wise believer than those who, without authority, heap marvel on marvel, and so perhaps alienate minds which might otherwise acquiesce in religious belief.[177]

In this way, Milman stood with those other English scholars, who advocated freedom of inquiry and who wanted to separate "the essence of Christianity from its local and temporary setting."[178] His efforts in this regard led him to be among the first to introduce some of the findings of German biblical scholarship to the general English populace, but this use did not betray an unqualified or uncritical acceptance of these findings.[179]

The philosophy of history that lay behind *History of the Jews* was a developmental one. Milman believed that there was a law of intellectual development, which all peoples shared: societies pass "from an imaginative to a reflective state," and this forms the basis for their "intellectual progress."[180] According to this theory, a nation's childhood is an imaginative age, "when history, law, and religion are alike poetry."[181] A culture gradually passes from this stage where myth is so important to a higher one, where myth's place is taken by history.[182] Within this developmental framework lies Milman's use of divine accommodation.

---

[175] Henry Hart Milman, *The History of the Jews* (3d ed.; 3 vols.; Boston: William Veazie, 1864) 1.429.

[176] *Ibid.*, 1.20.

[177] *Ibid.*, 1.23.

[178] Storr, *Development*, 114.

[179] Stanley described Milman's work as, "...the first decisive inroad of German theology into England; the first palpable indication that the Bible could be studied like another book; that the characters and events of sacred history could be treated at once critically and reverently." Lecky, *Essays*, 237-38; cf. also Milman, *Milman*, 86-87.

[180] Duncan Forbes, *The Liberal Anglican Idea of History* (Cambridge: University Press, 1952) 34-35.

[181] Milman, *Quarterly Review* 49, p. 287, cited in Forbes, *History*, 35.

[182] "There must have been a border-land where the religious myth—the impersonation of the conception—ceased; and what we may call, in contradistinction, the poetic myth—that which aggrandized, altered and

...there must be some departure from the pure and essential spirituality of the Deity in order to communicate with the human race.... All this is in fact accommodation.[183]

This idea of accommodation allowed Milman to explain why the "unchangeable God" could command the extermination of entire cities in the Old Testament and later (in the New Testament, for example) command his people to avoid even anger at others. Thus, God accommodated his commands and expectations to his people's present stage of development.[184]

Milman's history did not represent a radical departure in the use of Chronicles from the age before de Wette. His concept of the relationship of Chronicles to Samuel-Kings source-critically is presented in only vague terms.

> During the reigns of David and Solomon the parallel histories in the books of Kings and Chronicles have seemingly drawn from the same authorities, the one at times supplying what was wanting in the other. They sometimes refer to, sometimes imply their authorities. The prophets among their various functions seem to have been the historiographers. The life of David was written by the prophets Samuel, Gad, and Nathan (1 Chron. xxix.29); that of Solomon by Nathan, Abijah, and Iddo (2 Chron. ix.29, &c.). Put after the disruption of the two kingdoms, the discrepancies become more embarrassing and irreconcilable, and the peculiar character of each history becomes more manifest.[185]

This sounds vaguely like the theory of Eichhorn, but Milman does not continue with it to account for the differences between Chronicles and Kings during the period of Rehoboam and following. It is clear that for Milman Chronicles is to be treated as a trustworthy historical source and is no less reliable in most respects than Samuel-Kings.

However, Mlilman does recognize the priestly bias of Chronicles, and he contrasts this with the political interests of Kings.

> The Book of Kings is properly so called; it dwells chiefly on the succession of kings to the two thrones, the acts of the kings, their lives and their deaths. The books of Chronicles may be rather called the books of the High Priests, more especially those of the House of Zadok, the line of Eleazar. Throughout there is a sacerdotal bias: though relating the

---

embellished real events and personages—began; where poetry and history were in some sort blended.... The myth, as it approached history, became, if we may so say, less and less mythic. It was by slow, yet dimly perceptible degrees that the haze cleared away and men began to see each other as men." Milman, in a review of Grote's *History of Greece*, vols. 1 and 2 (1846) in *Quarterly Review* 78, p. 121. Cited in Forbes, *History*, 35.

[183]*Ibid.*, 77.
[184]*Ibid.*

same events, and the same royal reigns, wherever power or influence
may be attributed to the priesthood, it comes forth in the Chronicles into
greater importance...this sacerdotalism becomes more manifest as the
history darkens to its close.[186]

In spite of the Chronicler's sacerdotal bias, Milman denies that this
necessarily means that the author of Chronicles falsified history in his
account: "This perhaps unconscious and hardly perceptible leaning
does not necessarily imply either dishonesty or untruth."[187] Milman
does, however, doubt the accuracy of certain numbers and dates in
Chronicles. The former are often higher than those in Samuel-Kings
and clearly have been inflated at times, but one finds the same thing
elsewhere in the Bible and in the writings of other ancient historians.[188] The dates of the reigns of the Judean kings present an even
greater problem for Milman, who confesses that he can see no way of
reconciling the figures of Kings with those of Chronicles.[189]

It is evident from all this that Milman freely accepts, as historically accurate, information that is unique to Chronicles (e.g., Asa's
victory over Zerah and Jehoshaphat's over Moab and Ammon).[190]
Whenever Samuel-Kings conflicts with Chronicles in matters of historical fact, sometimes Milman chooses to follow the former,[191] and
sometimes he chooses the latter.[192] In virtually every instance,
Milman's principle desire is to harmonize the accounts, and thus
establish the historical accuracy of both reports.

---

[185]Milman, *History of the Jews*, 1.374-75.

[186]*Ibid.*, 1.375.

[187]*Ibid.*

[188]"I will observe that, if accuracy in numbers is to determine the historical
credibility and value of ancient writers, there must be a vast holocaust offered on
the stern altar of historic truth. Josephus must first be thrown upon the he-
catomb, without hope of redemption. ... Niebuhr and Sir George Lewis, if they
agree in nothing else, must agree in the sacrifice of Livy. I must confess that I
have some fear about Caesar himself. At all events, there must be one wide
sweep of, I think, the whole of Oriental history. Beyond all people, indeed, the
Jews seem to have had almost a passion for large numbers. Compare Chronicles
with Kings: the later compiler almost invariably rises above the older. Josephus
soars high above both." (*Ibid.*, 1.36-37.)

[189]"Of all the discrepancies between the books of Kings and Chronicles, as
usual that of the dates is the most obstinately conflicting. I confess that I cannot
see how any exact chronology can be framed. No two writers agree." (*Ibid.*, 1.
377.)

[190]*Ibid.*, 1.384, 398-99.

[191]*Ibid.*, 1.434-35.

[192]*Ibid.*, 1.349, 410. It seems to be especially true that when Chronicles follows
the general statement of Kings with a more specific one of his own that Milman
accepted the witness of Chronicles (e.g., the matter of Joash's burial, in which 2
Kg 12:21 reported that he was buried with his fathers in the city of David, while 2
Chr 24:25 claimed that he was not buried in the royal tombs).

An evaluation of Milman's use of Chronicles is hampered by the difficulty of knowing precisely how much Milman himself knew about Old Testament studies. Since he was evidently composing a work for the general public, he would have necessarily omitted much that would not have interested his readers.[193] In the third edition of his work Milman refers to a number of the leading German scholars of his day (Eichhorn, de Wette, Gesenius, Winer, Ewald, Paulus, and Strauss), and so he seems to be acquainted with their research.[194] Ewald is mentioned more often than any other in this edition of *History of the Jews*, since Ewald himself had published an extensive history of Israel. Milman admits a certain admiration for the comprehensiveness of Ewald's work, but more often he is busy chastising the latter for dogmatism and arbitrariness.

> This dogmatism appears to me to be the inherent fault of the "Geschichte des Volkes Israel." ...the contemptuous arrogance with which Ewald insulates himself from all his learned brethren, and assumes an autocracy not in his own sphere alone, but in the whole world of religion, letters, and politics.[195]

Milman's references to Burckhardt (*Travels in Syria and the Holy Land*, 1822), Robinson (*Biblical Researches in Palestine and Adjacent Regions*, 1856), and Stanley (*Sinai and Palestine*, 1856) indicate a familiarity with their explorations and reports, as well as an eagerness to use geographical and archaeological data for the reconstruction of Israel's history.[196]

An additional difficulty for the proper evaluation of Milman's critical stance toward Israelite history arises when it is recognized that he refrained from the full and candid statement of his views in deference to popular opinion.

> Murray asked me to write the "History of the Jews" for his biographies. I blindly assented, thinking the affair very plain and straightforward; but you have no conception of the difficulty of finding a guide or authorities among the countless writers on the subject. I must confess that I think the subject has been fertile in nonsense; but, unhappily, much of the nonsense is sainted and canonized, and I suspect wise heads will be shaken at my views. Keep, therefore, my secret....[197]

---

[193]In a letter to a friend in 1829, Milman acknowledged some of his difficulties and misgivings about his *History of the Jews, Milman*, 84-88.

[194]Milman. *History of the Jews*, 1.31-32.

[195]*Ibid.*, 1.28-29.

[196]*Ibid.*, 1.39.

[197]Milman, *Milman*, 84-85. On the matter of Milman's exercise of moderation and self-restraint in his critical research, cf. E. S. Shaffer, *"Kubla Khan" and the Fall of Jerusalem* (Cambridge: University Press, 1975) 235-37.

> I am greatly mistaken if there is not a strong reaction in favour of the book. For my own part, I have reconsidered the whole subject; I have corrected the few points on which I have expressed myself somewhat too strongly; and am convinced, not merely that I am in the right, but that all reasonable persons think me so, and that the crowd will follow.[198]

In spite of his caution, however, his ecclesiastical and academic careers suffered as a consequence of his *History of the Jews*.[199]

Milman, by his use of the critical method and judgment instead of simply proceeding under the guidance of piety, performed a great service for the study of Israel's history. In his decision to adopt a critical stance that deviated from standard practice, Milman was responding to the excesses of those who created miracles, where there were none, and who wrote history, when historical records were lacking.

> As he (the historian) would not from reverence take away..., so with equal reverence he must refrain from adding to the marvellousness; he must not think it piety to accumulate, without authority, wonder upon wonder.'[200]

> (Baron Bunsen) seems to me to labor under the same too common infirmity, the passion for making history without historical materials. ... If I have nothing but poetry, I am content with poetry; I do not believe in the faculty of transforming poetry into history. ...when facts and chronicles appear only in a loose, imaginative dress, we cannot array them in the close and symmetrical habiliments of historic times.[201]

He used the historical critical method for the sake of scientific inquiry, as well as for the sake of religious instruction.[202] His pursuit of the latter aim undoubtedly helped promote in England the acceptance of the critical study of the Bible.

Three observations arise with regard to Milman's *History of the Jews* and its use of Chronicles. First, Milman never developed nor adopted from others a comprehensive theory of the sources behind Chronicles and Samuel-Kings. The theories of both Eichorn and de Wette had been written by 1829 when he published his history, and by the time of his revision in 1863, other theories were also available.

---

[198] *Ibid.*, 88.

[199] Lecky, *Essays*, 239.

[200] Milman, *History of the Jews*, 1.20.

[201] *Ibid.*, 1.30-31. Baron von Bunsen was the Prussian diplomat and scholar, who wrote *Vollständiges Bibelwerk für die Gemeinde* (9 vols.; Leipzig: Brockhaus, 1858-1870), a popular translation of the Bible and commentary.

[202] For example, Milman's history sets out to show how Israelite history is a preparation for Christianity. *Ibid.*, 1.23.

However, it must be remembered that most research into Chronicles in the early nineteenth century was being done in Germany and that few English theologians were able to keep apprised on developments in German biblical studies.[203] Moreover, Milman was a cautious historian and even in the third edition of his history expressed a certain lack of confidence in Ewald's rather conservative source analysis.[204]

Secondly, Milman did not take the dissimilarities between Samuel-Kings and Chronicles as seriously as de Wette and his followers in Germany. While Milman often recognized the biases of the biblical materials, he usually did not allow this to alter significantly his reconstruction of Israel's history. His assumption that both of the parallel texts were historical in intent evidently led him at times to superficial harmonizations.

Finally, while Milman's developmental theory of history aided him in separating the poetic and mythical writings from those with historiographical intents,[205] it also led him to give more credence to Chronicles than de Wette and some others had done. Since Milman set Chronicles late in the sequence of Hebrew literary works, he assumed that it was historiographical in intent.

Milman's *History of the Jews* was the first major history of Israel to be written by an English scholar in the nineteenth century. Its predecessors by Shuckford, Prideaux, and Russell were far more limited in extent and could not have claimed to be critical histories. Nevertheless, his history was not rigorous in its application of critical methods, and it used Chronicles in much the same way that the books had been employed before de Wette's *Beiträge*. The publication of Ewald's history in the 1840s did little to change Milman's position, and if anything, Ewald's history probably served to confirm Milman's more traditional approach to Chronicles.

---

[203]Daniel L. Pals (*The Victorian "Lives" of Jesus* [TUMSR 7; San Antonio: Trinity University, 1982] 127) writes, "British divinity then (in the 1820s) was in most quarters unaware of German developments and could hardly have attended to them with the seriousness they deserved. Theologians and leaders of opinion who had made the acquaintance of German scholarship were accustomed either to revile it or to confess that they found it frankly incomprehensible."

[204]Milman (*History of the Jews*, 1.29) wrote, "But Ewald seems to have attempted...an utter impossibility. ... But that any critical microscope, in the nineteenth century, can be so exquisite and so powerful as to dissect the whole (the Books of Moses) with perfect nicety, to decompose it, and assign each separate paragraph to its special origin in three, four, or five, or more, independent documents, each of which has contributed its part, this seems to be a task which no mastery of the Hebrew Language, with all its kindred tongues, no discernment, however fine and discriminating, can achieve."

[205]*Ibid.*, 1.30-31; cf. Forbes, *History*, 35.

c. Jahn

The third of the nineteenth century histories of Israel before Ewald was written by a Roman Catholic scholar, Johann J. Jahn. He was discussed earlier in Chapter I, primarily in regard to the views about Chronicles expressed in his *Einleitung*. Jahn's position on Chronicles, summarized in his *Einleitung,* can be seen in the use of the books in his history. He believed that the author of Chronicles used reliable historical sources for his composition and that 1, 2 Chronicles may be used with confidence by the modern historian in the reconstruction of Israelite history, the differences between the parallel histories being due to textual corruption or else capable of being harmonized adequately.[206]

Jahn's history was written in German but published in English translation in 1829 as *The History of the Hebrew Commonwealth*. The work begins with civilization before Noah's flood and continues until 70 C. E. In his narrative Jahn usually presents a retelling of the biblical account. In those places where Genesis-Kings and Chronicles overlap, there is no serious attempt to examine the biblical materials of the parallel history to determine their historical reliability; it is generally assumed.

Jahn makes regular use of 1, 2 Chronicles to supplement the narrative of Samuel-Kings. He incorporates, for example, Chronicles' information about the size of the Egyptian army under Shishak and the prophecies of Shemaiah to the Jewish king.[207] The account in Chronicles about Abijah's conflict with Jeroboam I is also accepted with few reservations,[208] as is the case with the story in Chronicles about Asa's battle with Zerah.[209] Finally, Jahn's analysis of Joash's reign has been determined by the narrative in 2 Chronicles 24.[210]

Jahn's attitude toward Chronicles reflects that of scholars in the pre-de Wettian period. It is supposed that Chronicles is no less valuable as a historical source for the pre-exilic period than Samuel-Kings. Therefore, while de Wette's work antedated Jahn's history by over twenty years, the latter does not refer to it, and it apparently had little impact on the position of the latter with regard to Chronicles.

d. Jost

Among the earliest critical histories of Israel was that of Isaac Marcus Jost (1793-1860), who attended the universities of Göttingen

---

[206]Jahn, *Introduction*, 263-64, 269.
[207]Jahn, *History*, 129.
[208]*Ibid.*
[209]*Ibid.*, 130.
[210]*Ibid.*, 138.

and Berlin and spent most of his teaching career in Jewish schools. His reputation was that of an educator and historian. He favored the Reform movement in Judaism, while opposing the extreme tendencies of some in the group.[211] Four of his publications dealt with Jewish history in an extensive way: *Geschichte der Israeliten seit der Zeit der Maccabaeer bis auf unsere Tage,* [212] *Neuere Geschichte der Israeliten,*[213] *Allgemeine Geschichte des Israelitischen Volkes,*[214] *and Geschichte des Judentums und seiner Sekten.*[215] Although his treatments of Jewish history were never translated into English or revised and later were overshadowed by Graetz's eleven-volume work, Jost was the first modern critical Jewish historian to describe his people's past.[216] His works on Jewish history were some of the earliest products of the *Wissenschaft des Judentums* movement and were published while the foundations of the movement were still being laid.[217]

Jost's description of the historian's task reveals a true appreciation for the difficulties involved.

> But the task requires both great caution and deep insight which, insofar as possible, penetrates to details. The historian must grasp precisely, not merely the general positions of the parties, which change in different periods, but also the positions held simultaneously but affected by locality and other circumstances. ... This understanding requires long preparation, highly comprehensive studies, and uncommon candor. The historical sources are scattered far and wide; in part they are already quite obscure; and often they deliver only fragments, isolated kernels. Many of them are inherently dull and vapid, worthy of attention more as evidence of their time and place than by virtue of their content. The gathering of testimony, which justice demands, wears upon one's patience because of the endless contradictions and absurdities, the expressions and references whose meaning can often only be surmised. One is confronted by an immense number of deeds, speeches, laws, affecting the lot of the Israelites. This is to say nothing of the many different places, times, and thinkers. One must consider as well human inclinations, cultural variations, historical setting, and in general the prevailing circumstances of entire nations, districts, and individuals, to say nothing of natural predispositions, emotions and intellectual movements. All

---

[211]"Jost, Isaac Marcus," *Enc Jud* 10 (1971) 298-99; Meyer, *Ideas of Jewish History,* 175-76; Salo W. Baron, "I. M. Jost the Historian," *History and Jewish Historians* (Philadelphia: Jewish Publication Society, 1964) 240-44. Baron's essay was originally read in 1928 at a meeting of the American Academy for Jewish Research.

[212]Berlin: Schlesinger, 1820.

[213]Berlin: Schlesinger, 1846-47.

[214]Berlin: C. F. Amelang, 1832.

[215]Leipzig: Dörffling und Franke, 1857-59.

[216]*Enc Jud* 298-99; Meyer, *Ideas of Jewish History,* 175-76.

[217]Meyer, *Ideas of Jewish History,* 175-76.

this is necessary to arrive at a certain historical understanding and to derive fruitful results and just evaluations.[218]

He continues his discussion on the nature of the Old Testament as a historical source in the following section.

We consider the entire collection of Hebrew sacred literature a source of history although it was not all intended to be historical and even the actual historical books do not proceed from an historical point of view. Indeed, we are relatively more justified in drawing our subject matter from this literature to the degree that the historical material is only, as it were, included by chance, but does not constitute a book's sole contents. For such sources which contain only the account of events are much sooner subject to doubt than those in which historical data appear as known and acknowledged, and are unconsciously repeated and supplemented. In the former instance, we must examine the author, his level of culture, and his intent with utmost care before we trust him. In the latter, we need only apply inner criticism in order not to misunderstand the individual datum torn from its context; the fact itself lives before our eyes and weaves itself into the life of the people, appears in all manner of forms, inspires poetry, and proves to be indisputable truth. In this sense, the Holy Scriptures of the Hebrews become wholly excellent sources of history.[219]

The difference between what the sacred books of Israel were—theology—and what they could be used for—history—was an important distinction for Jost. He believed that theology and history were two separate areas for investigation and that he was committed in his histories to the latter. In accordance with these views, he set out to describe primarily the political movements in Jewish history, and so omitted, to a large degree, the history of Israel's religion and religious institutions.

Theology solves questions which history does not pose or must leave unanswered. If it derives data from history, it seeks not merely to disclose in them the causes and effects suggested by historical research, but rather the revelations of divine judgment and divine providence.[220]

One may further observe that Jost's view of the historian's task is basically that of the rationalist. His concern is to describe the events of the past in terms of cause and effect and in accordance with the "laws of nature."

History, on the other hand, limits itself to representing what has occurred in accordance with the causes which disclose themselves to the

---

[218]*Ibid.*, 182-83. These quotations of Jost come from the introduction to his *Allgemeine Geschichte des Israelitischen Volkes*, volume one. The translation is Meyer's.
[219]*Ibid.*, 184.

observant eye and with the consequences that develop from them according to the laws of nature. Where it lacks the means to construct a great and conclusive chain of events, it may employ conjectures to fill in the missing links, but it must justify and support them. If, however, this proves impossible and theology therefore finds occasion to take over such facts—or miracles—which history has left aside as enigmatic and to connect them with the higher world order which is revealed to it, then we shall leave this lack of agreement inviolate on account of its beneficial influence: we are not in a position adequately to solve all the enigmas of antiquity.[221]

The foregoing statements indicate that while Jost is himself in many ways a rationalist and strives to see how the events described in the Bible can be harmonized with natural law, he sees a danger in this process and will consequently avoid the practice of rationalizing each miracle that is encountered in his sources.[222] Jost believed that genuine faith was served best by the exercise of historical criticism and that the two should be allowed to operate independently of one another.

> But religious belief, as all previous attempts attest, does cast the historian in chains, and thus there must be some arrangement from the start to free him from either relating facts which he cannot justify because he all too obediently follows the text, or breaking with faith. An accommodation is achieved through sound criticism, which faith must allow the scholar. It is the critical method which must guide the historian through the realm of history, and although he continually follows particular authorities, it must nevertheless stand by his side, advising, warning, and showing him the way. True faith, which is located in the mind, is not threatened by the transformed appearances of externals; it cannot be true if it shrinks from criticism of historical data. Criticism no more does harm to religion than a closer examination of the laws of nature and their variability threatens to shatter belief in the Creator. ... The results of this criticism must prepare the way for the historian and light his path.[223]

Jost's *Allgemeine Geschichte der Israeliten* consists of two volumes: the first treats the period from the beginnings with Abram to the

---

[220]*Ibid.*, 183.

[221]*Ibid.*, 184.

[222]Meyer (*ibid.*, 175) says that Jost had a sober, practical view of the world and was closer to eighteenth century Enlightenment rationalism than to the German romanticism around him. Jost's treatment of the Israelite crossing of the sea in their escape from Egypt is instructive. He asserts that the event was a historical certainty, but his description of it as a time when a great storm drained a shallow spot in the sea for the Israelites to cross hints at the author's rationalism and desire to have the biblical events conform to natural law. *Allgemeine Geschichte*, 1.90-91.

[223]Meyer, *Ideas of Jewish History*, 185-86.

Maccabean war of liberation; and the second the time from John Hyrcanus to the French Revolution of 1830. While Jost began the first volume appropriately enough with a general discussion of the historian's task, he gives no general statement about Chronicles to indicate his view of its date and historical value. His historical reconstructions, though, make it clear that he believed that the books of Chronicles were a good source for historical information about the pre-exilic period. He accepted, for example, the Chronicler's accounts of Zerah's attack on Asa and that of the Moabite coalition against Jehoshaphat, two battles that are reported only in 2 Chronicles.[224] Moreover, he accepted the Chronicler's narratives about David's cultic arrangements and preparations for the building of the temple, both absent from Samuel.[225]

Whenever Chronicles offers additional information to what one finds in Samuel-Kings, Jost usually proceeds to combine the two accounts and use one to supplement the other. He is not, however, averse to recognizing contradictions between the two and choosing the testimony of one source over another. For example, he calls the account of David's mighty men in 1 Chr 11:10ff. "probably more correct" than the lists in 2 Sm 20:17ff. and 23:20ff. This treatment of Chronicles is possible for Jost, since he believes that older, reliable sources lay at hand to the Chronicler.[226]

It is unclear how well acquainted Jost was with Old Testament research relevant to the use of Chronicles as a historical source. His references to the secondary literature are a bit sparse, but he does refer to Gramberg's work on Chronicles, admiring his mental acuteness[227] and notes Gesenius' commentary on Isaiah.[228] There are no references to de Wette or Keil. In spite of his reading Gramberg and Jost's own conviction that the historian should cautiously examine the credibility of his sources, Jost's work shows little appreciation for the issues involved in using the Chronicler's history. His confidence in Chronicles places him closer to Movers and Keil than to de Wette and Gramberg.

Jost's use of Chronicles is basically harmonistic. Since he regards both Chronicles and Samuel-Kings as reliable witnesses, he sets out to tell the story of Israel's past by bringing these two primary witnesses together to tell a more coherent and complete story.

---

[224]Jost, *Allgemeine Geschichte*, 1.321, 336.

[225]*Ibid.*, 1.257, 274.

[226]*Ibid.*, 1.241, 257.

[227]*Ibid.*, 1.199, 238.

[228]*Ibid.*, 1.348, 361, 369.

e. Summary of Histories before Ewald

It is clear that in spite of the challenges issued to the historical credibility of Chronicles by de Wette and the others, the histories of Russell, Milman, Jahn, and Jost assumed what amounted to a pre-de Wettian attitude toward the books. Each historian was more or less critical, but nevertheless, each proceeded on the assumption that Chronicles was a trustworthy source for historical information. The 1840s and the publication of Ewald's *Geschichte des Volkes Israel* would change this to some degree.

2. EWALD

a. General

The most influential history of Israel in the first part of the nineteenth century was written by Heinrich Ewald (1803-1875), who studied at Göttingen under Eichhorn and after the latter's death assumed his position there. Ewald spent the remainder of his career at Göttingen, except for a ten-year period at Tübingen, which was occasioned by his dismissal from the University of Göttingen for his outspoken criticism of the government. In addition to his history of Israel, Ewald's publications included an analysis of the sources in Genesis, a work on the Old Testament prophets, a treatment of the "poetic books" of the Old Testament, and a theology of the Old and New Testaments.[229]

During Ewald's ten years in Tübingen the first three volumes of his *Geschichte des Volkes Israel* appeared (1843, 1845, 1847), and the final four came out between 1852 and 1859. The second, enlarged edition of volumes one, two, and three were issued in 1851 and 1853. The entire history underwent a third edition between 1864 and 1869, and it was this edition that was translated into English. A supplementary volume, *Alterthümer Israels*, was published in 1848 to help the readers of volume two of the history understand the development of pentateuchal laws, which Ewald presupposed in his discussions.

---

[229]J. S. Black, "Ewald, Heinrich Georg August von," *Enc Brit* 8 (9th ed.; 1889) 773-74; Cheyne, *Founders*, 67-107; Julius Wellhausen, "Heinrich Ewald," *Grundrisse zum Alten Testament* (Theologische Bucherei 27; Munich: Chr. Kaiser, 1965) 122; Kraus, *Geschichte*, 199-204; A. Dillmann, "Ewald, Georg Heinrich August," *ADB* 6 (1877) 438-442; T. Witton Davies, *Heinrich Ewald, Orientalist and Theologian* (London: T. Fischer Unwin, 1903); Rogerson, *Criticism*, 91-103.

b. History of Israel

Ewald's *Geschichte des Volkes Israel* was the first truly critical history of Israel to come out of Germany. It had been preceded by many developments in historical-critical research, and undoubtedly Ewald was indebted to them for many of his views of both the methodology and philosophy of history. While one may not always be able to pinpoint the sources for the various ideas and methods that are found in Ewald's history, nevertheless, it is clear that Ewald utilized many of the philosophical concepts and historical methods that were current in his day. Herder, Niebuhr, and Ranke (as well as Hegel and others) influenced these concepts and methods, and there are several obvious parallels between the thinking and works of these men and Ewald.

Ewald was probably influenced most heavily by his teacher at Göttingen, Eichhorn. The Romantic movement was especially strong at Göttingen, and several of his colleagues, who were members of the *"Göttinger Sieben,"* were prominent figures in the movement: Dahlmann, Gervinus, and the Grimm brothers.[230] Ewald believed that by critical and objective investigation, one could arrive at an understanding of "the truths of history" that influenced the life and development of Israel. Since Israel's history had come to an end long ago, the historian could investigate the matter with greater objectivity and the public would be more receptive to the instruction that it offered.

> The case is entirely different with those portions of history which not only lie before us completely finished and irreversibly sentenced, but have no immediate bearing on our country and people, on our constitution and religion. There every passion and strife is for ever hushed for us; we are not fellow-actors on that stage...but we stand afar off as mere spectators, and tranquilly let the whole great drama pass before us.... There the manifest results of the once varied and complicated play have long ago written down its great moral, in generally intelligible and eternal characters, which no one can refuse to study; so that, though the successful investigation of histories thus remote may cost more trouble than the writing of the history of our own time, its utility for the present may be so much the greater. For though the study of these remote histories is in the first instance only an exercise of the eye and the judgment, which strengthens the better disposed, and directs others to surprising truths which they will not see in the present; yet this silent influence will go deeper, and affect decisions and acts also—and the past, with its struggles and its lessons, will not have been in vain for us. The most

---

230Alfred G. Pundt, "The Rise of Romanticism," *The Development of Historiography* (eds. M. A. Fitzsimons, A. G. Pundt, and C. E. Nowell; Harrisburg: Stackpole, 1954) 175, 188; G. P. Gooch, *History and Historians in the Nineteenth Century* (2d ed.; London: Longmans, Green, 1952) 24, 77-79.

evident and certain truths of history are found here in abundance, and above all dispute.[231]

It is clear that Ewald believed that Israel's history with the historical truths that it taught had relevance for people of the modern era. In light of Ewald's ongoing involvement in German politics, his history may be regarded as another expression of his scholarly commitment to relevancy. Kraus has described him as one who viewed himself as something of a contemporary Old Testament prophet.[232] At any rate, one should expect to find in *Geschichte des Volkes Israel* something in the way of historical lessons that Ewald believed were relevant to his own day.

There are three emphases of Ewald's history that are worth noting at the outset. First, there is the historian's task:

> To describe this history, therefore, as far as it can be known in all its discoverable remains and traces, is the design of this work; and its best commendation will be, that it describes it with the greatest fidelity as it really was (*wie sie wirklich* war). It needs no embellishment or exaggeration: its subject is sublime enough in itself....[233]

This understanding of the historian's task sets Ewald squarely within the tradition launched by Ranke in his preface to *Geschichten der romanischen und germanischen Völker*, where he affirmed that the historian's task was to discover and state the facts of history *wie es eigentlich gewesen*.[234] Such an accurate description of the past is only possible if the historian is committed to objectivity:

> To examine a proposed historical theme without any foolish fear, but with a hearty love of the subject, and the single assumption that everything, when correctly understood, has its reason and its value; with no inflexible ulterior preconceptions, but a generous appreciation and joyful welcome for all true and great results—this is the universal law of every historian.[235]

Ewald was apparently confident of his ability to attain this kind of objectivity, and he showed little awareness of the danger that his own political views and philosophy of history could distort his description of Israel's past.

---

[231]Ewald, *The History of Israel* (3 vols.; 3d ed.; London: Longmans, Green, 1876) 1.1-2.

[232]Kraus, *Geschichte*, 199.

[233]Ewald, *History*, 1.7.

[234]Leopold Ranke, *Geschichte der romanischen und germanischen Völker* (2d ed.; Leipzig: Duncker & Humbolt, 1874) vii.

[235]Ewald, *History*, 1.7.

A second feature in Ewald's work is his consideration of historical sources. At an earlier time, Niebuhr had used the source critical methods of Wolf for reconstructing ancient Roman history and insisted that source criticism precede historical reconstruction.[236] Ranke, a pioneer in the development of modern critical historiography,[237] continued Niebuhr's focus on the importance of historical criticism. He maintained two important principles relating to the use of historical sources: only original documents and archives were the proper grist for history writing, and sources should be analyzed in terms of their author's temperment, affiliations, and access to accurate information.[238] It is clear from the outset that Ewald had adopted these principles for himself, since the first two hundred pages of his history discuss the sources available for historical reconstruction, and he justifies this procedure in the following way:

> ...nevertheless a large portion of this work will necessarily consist of investigation into the sources. But such enquiries are most advantageously interwoven where an attempt is made to reconstruct a whole province of history by a correct valuation of the sources....[239]

Moreover, Ewald assumed Ranke's principles of historiography in his lengthy discussion of "tradition" (Sage).

> It is by the accurate discrimination of tradition and history, first of all, and then by the distinct appreciation of the relation which the historical books of the Old Testament bear to both, that we must gain the first step towards and sure treatment of a great portion of the history itself. ... One of the primary duties of all historical enquiry, and of every historical composition springing therefrom, is to distinguish the story from its foundation, or from that which has occasioned it, and thus to discover the truth of what actually occurred. Our ultimate aim is the knowledge of what really happened—not what was only related and handed down by tradition, but what was actual fact.[240]

In this way, Ewald drew an important distinction between the events of history and the description of those events in the written sources available to the historian. Ewald's clear differentiation between the two represents a major step in the treatment of Israel's history. In spite of his recognition of this difference, however, Ewald was more optimistic than some other scholars (e.g., de Wette) about the historian's ability to derive useful historical information from the biblical materials. In this regard, however, Ewald was not at all alone, since B.

---

[236]Gooch, *Historians*, 18-19.
[237]Pundt, "Romanticism," 188.
[238]*Ibid.*; Gooch, *Historians*, 101-102.
[239]Ewald, *History*, 1.10.
[240]*Ibid.*, 1.13.

G. Niebuhr found data in the classical legends for reconstructing the history of Rome,[241] as did K. O. Müller in the myths of Greece.[242] Therefore, there were worthy precedents in classical scholarship for Ewald's treatment of Israel's history and his understanding and utilization of ancient texts.

A third aspect of Ewald's work is his developmental concept of history. There are two elements of Ewald's thinking on this point. First, there is the idea that some divine plan is being worked out in human history.

> The ultimate attainment of perfect true religion was at once the highest and noblest aspiration of antiquity...and this one people alone, at the end of a two-thousand years' struggle, actually attained it. But as this mark seemed from the very first to be held out by Divine predetermination as the noblest aim to the whole of antiquity, and yet was attainable only by a single path; so the history of this people, so far as it had this aim from the first, and coming gradually nearer, ultimately attained it, always seems to proceed in a straight line through the whole of antiquity....[243]

This concept is as ancient as the Bible itself, and it had been held by many of Ewald's predecessors in the modern era, among whom was Herder, whose picture was one of the two that hung in Ewald's study.[244]

The second aspect is the idea that each nation, which contributed something worthwhile to humanity as a whole, chose a single aim and pursued it vigorously.

> ...every nation that pursued a lofty career in the arena of such aspirations, chose one special high aim, to which everything else was subordinated, and which, even under frequent intercourse with foreigners, was never relinquished.[245]

---

[241]B. G. Niebuhr, *The History of Rome* (Philadelphia: Thomas Wardle, 1835) 1.167-82. Niebuhr's conviction about the historical bases for legends is apparent in his comparison of the ancient poetic epics with mythology.

[242]Karl Otfried Müller, *Prolegomena zu einer wissenschaftlichen Mythologie* (Göttingen: Vandenhoeck & Ruprecht, 1825).

[243]Ewald, *History,* 1.6.

[244]Cheyne, *Founders,* 71.

[245]*Ibid.,* 1.3. Ranke believed that nations were living organisms and voiced views very similar to those of Ewald, writing, "all states that count in the world and make themselves felt are motivated by special tendencies of their own" and "the state is a living being, which by its nature incessantly grows and irresistibly progresses." "Dialogue on Politics," in Theodore von Laue's *Leopold Ranke: The Formative Years* (Princeton Studies in History, 4; Princeton: Princeton University, 1950) 168-69.

Israel's aim, according to Ewald, was the attainment of true and perfect religion. While many other nations set out to achieve the same goal and failed, Israel distinguished herself from all of them by attaining it. The quest began in earnest with Moses and found its fulfillment in Christ.

> This aim is Perfect Religion—a good which all aspiring nations of antiquity made a commencement, and an attempt, to attain; ...but which this people alone clearly discerned from the beginning, and then pursued for many centuries...until they attained it, so far as, among men and in ancient times, attainment was possible. The beginning and the end of the history of this people turn on this one high aim....[246]

> ...the true commencement of this history, which comes to its close with Christ, begins with Moses.... What precedes the sojourn in Egypt, as being foreign to this domain, belongs to the preliminary history of the nation, and might be called its primitive history....[247]

> And when a religion is really the highest and most perfect possible—as is Christianity.... But when a religion although true is yet defective, as was the case with Jahveism....[248]

This concept of each nation having a single national aim is probably rooted in Vico, Herder, and others. Herder held that each society had different ideals and conceptions of what brought happiness, and that each culture had its own spirit. This is part of the Romantic Movement's assertion of national and cultural differences and can be regarded as a rejection of the Enlightenment and Rationalism's focus on timeless laws and rules that united all peoples in a certain kind of uniformity.[249] Such ideas of cultural difference led to an appreciation of each culture for its own particular configuration of social and religious elements. Mixtures or imitation of cultures, however, was rarely viewed by Herder as advantageous to humanity. As each culture was born, matured, and died, humanity as a whole was enriched. According to his musical analogy, the various cultures form the infinite number of variations on the theme of humankind.[250] Similarly, Ewald believed peoples—at least "original" ones—were each inherently unique.

> For it will always be instructive to discern how polity, laws, poetry, literature, and similar intellectual possessions, have developed themselves

---

[246]Ewald, *History*, 1.4.

[247]*Ibid.*, 1.10.

[248]Ewald, *Antiquities*, 5.

[249]Isaiah Berlin, *Vico & Herder* (New York: Viking Press, 1976) 149-50; Frank E. Manuel, "Editor's Introduction" in Johann Gottfried von Herder, *Reflections on the Philosophy of the History of Mankind* (Chicago: University of Chicago Press, 1968) xvi-xvii; Black, "Ewald," 775.

in a nation, when they spring from no idle imitation and half-repetition, but from inherent impulses and powers, and therefore with all freshness and energy. ... Now ancient nations are generally distinguished by a greater restriction as to space and place, by a narrow attachment to their own sanctuary and country, by a shy fear of what is strange, and a scrupulous separation according to religions, customs, and ideas.... One consequence of this excessive self-enclosure of each nation with its inherited possessions and its favourite views, was that each more easily took up some characteristic aim and activity of its own.[251]

Ewald also believed that contacts between various nations were potentially disruptive to their respective pursuits of national aims, and so contamination of one culture by another could prevent the former from reaching its potential accomplishments.

So the history of this people...ultimately attained it (true and perfect religion), ...though distracted by constant contact with other and highly civilized nations.[252]

This history is, moreover, that of an original people, ...which, though constantly in close contact with many other peoples, followed out, with the strictest independence and the noblest effort a peculiar problem of the human mind to its highest point....[253]

Ewald's developmental schema and his conviction that Israel had a single national purpose led him to idealize certain periods in the nation's history. His comments about David make this clear.

In David, a king sprung from its own flesh and blood, the whole nation feels that it attains to a nobler and royal existence. Moreover, through all the sufferings and changes of life, he found only more and more strength in Him "who redeemed him out of all distress;" and so a new and higher spirit passes from him alike into the nation and the individual, and his influence in this respect is rendered more permanent by means of his nervous eloquence and the grandeur of his imperishable hymns, which had secured for him a home in the hearts of the people.[254]

Ewald's idealizations of various periods in Israel's history usually coincide with those which the Old Testament itself idealized.

---

[250]Martineau, "Preface," in Ewald's *History*, 1.xiv.
[251]Ewald, *History*, 1.6.
[252]*Ibid.*, 1.2.
[253]*Ibid.*, 1.2-3.
[254]*Ibid.*, 3.201-2.

c. Chronicles

Ewald separates himself from some earlier historians, such as Milman, by operating with comprehensive source theories for the biblical materials. One aspect of this is his understanding of Chronicles. He believed 1, 2 Chronicles to be part of a larger work that included Ezra and Nehemiah, which was written about the time of the death of Alexander the Great.[255] Whereas Samuel-Kings tells Israel's history from a prophetic perspective and could even be called the "History of the Prophets," Chronicles-Ezra-Nehemiah deals primarily with the religious activities of Israel and so could be called the "Chronicle of Jerusalem" or "history of the Priesthood."[256] The focus on the levitical musicians leads one to believe that a levitical musician wrote this large work that incorporates Chronicles.[257] The Chronicler's work consisted of three parts: (1) a primeval history to David's time (1 Chronicles 1-10), (2) a history of Jerusalem from David until the Babylonian captivity of Judah (1 Chronicles 11-2 Chronicles 36), and (3) a history of the new Jerusalem after the captivity (Ezra and Nehemiah).[258] The author's sources for the presentations in Chronicles were three: (1) a compilation from the state annals and other sources, which antedated the composition of the narrative ending with 2 Kings, (2) the canonical books of Samuel and Kings, and (3) a larger and later work entitled "Midrash on the Book of the Kings."[259] While the Chronicler undoubtedly embellished and slanted his history in order to advance his own purposes, nevertheless he had available in his sources and faithfully presented a great deal of information that is historically accurate and extant only in his work.[260] It is evident from this analysis that Ewald is prepared to accept much of what is unique to Chronicles, but he is also prepared to reject items that appear to be embellishments arising from the Chronicler's own religious viewpoint.

---

[255]Ewald claims to have arrived at this conclusion regarding unity independently of Zunz and bases it on connections between 2 Chronicles, Ezra, and Nehemiah, as well as on the uniformity of language in the three books. *History* 1.170, 188. The date is established primarily on two factors: (1) genealogical registers bring one down to five or six generations (therefore, 150-200 years) after Zerubbabel, and (2) the references to the Persian kings are of such a nature to lead one to believe that they are no more ruling over the Jewish nation, but the Greeks have not yet ruled long enough for much to be said about them. Ewald, *History*, 1.171-73.

[256]*Ibid.*, 1.174-75.

[257]*Ibid.*, 1.175-77.

[258]*Ibid.*, 1.179-81.

[259]*Ibid.*, 1.187.

[260]*Ibid.*, 1.177, 182.

Ewald's confidence in Chronicles was not hindered by the similarities between it and P, since he assigned P to the time of Solomon,
the earliest date for any of his pentateuchal sources.[261] This was in
spite of Vatke's suggestion a decade earlier that P was the latest of the
pentateuchal sources rather than the earliest. The judgments of later
scholars on Ewald's views about the Pentateuch were, therefore, in
many cases very harsh.

> ...he (Ewald) has been...the great restrainer, who by his authoritative
> influence had the effect of preventing from being carried through the
> accurate insight, which was already attained before him, into the move-
> ment of Israelite history.[262]

> Ewald impressed this general outline (of the pentateuchal sources) on
> an entire generation of students.[263]

> Thus this excellent philologian, but bad historian and worse theologian,
> was able to retard by his authority the healthy advance of biblical criti-
> cism for a whole generation.[264]

The use that he makes of Chronicles for historical reconstruction
arises from Ewald's own conclusion that the Chronicler had three
ancient sources available. Therefore, even when Ewald writes that
"the writer assumes great historical licence in his endeavor to revivify
many periods, especially of the history of the ancient Jerusalem...,"[265]
he can still maintain that the Chronicler "restrains himself within
certain bounds" [266] and that

> ...by accurately observing what is the author's own in thought, word,
> and description, and what he must have derived at all events in its ulti-
> mate basis from his authorities, and thus distinguishing the fundamen-
> tal elements of the work, we shall be enabled to use it confidently and
> with much advantage even for the earlier history, and glean from it
> many important and genuine accounts, which we should elsewhere
> seek in vain; indeed we may discover surprising relics of the earliest his-
> torical works, preserved in it through the medium of later books, which
> are here quoted literally.[267]

This means that whenever Ewald finds additional information in
Chronicles which neither violates statements elsewhere in historical
sources nor violates Ewald's own sense of what is historically possi-

---

[261]*Ibid.*, 1.76-77.
[262]Wellhausen, "Ewald," 131-32.
[263]Carpenter, *Nineteenth Century*, 123-25.
[264]Pfleiderer, *Development*, 256-57.
[265]Ewald, *History*, 1.194.
[266]*Ibid.*
[267]*Ibid.*

ble and reasonable, he is willing to accept these contributions to the historian's store of data. An example of this use of Chronicles is found in the list of Rehoboam's fortifications (2 Chr 11:5-12). Ewald accepts them without question and incorporates them into his presentation of Rehoboam's reign.[268]

Things are a bit more difficult in cases where the Chronicler's information conflicts with other historical testimony—the narratives in Kings, for example. In these instances, Ewald's approach varies. Sometimes he simply passes over the disagreement and mentions the testimony of neither source. For instance, Chronicles denies a burial in the royal tombs to both Joash and Ahaz, while Kings indicates that both were buried in the royal tombs.[269] Ewald omits any reference to the burial of either king, While he mentions the nature of the burials of the priest Jehoiada and King Asa.[270]

In other cases, Ewald harmonizes the reports, as is the case with his description of David's census. While 2 Samuel 24 says that David ordered Joab to count all of his subjects, who were able to go to war, and that Joab complied, 1 Chronicles 21 insists that Joab did not count the tribes of Levi and Benjamin. Ewald asserts that the author of Kings himself understood that Levi was omitted from the census, and Benjamin is understood (by the Chronicler) "simply as the tribe of Jerusalem, according to Deut. xxxiii.12."[271]

Ewald's statements about the Syro-Ephraimitic war come very close to rejecting the testimony of Chronicles, because the latter contradicts the report found in Kings.

> The Chronicler (2 Chron. xxviii.20-23) supposes 1) that the Assyrian king had come to Judah to oppress Ahaz: this is contrary to the older and more exact reminiscence; 2) that Ahaz had further been so foolish in this distress as to sacrifice to the gods of Damascus; but, according to the older narrative, it was only a strange altar with the appearance of which Ahaz had, foolishly enough, been pleased. Similarly, the Chronicler represents (ver. 24 sq.) in his own way what is otherwise related in 2 Kings xvi.17 sq.; hence the supposition that Ahaz finally shut up the temple altogether is not strictly historical.[272]

This rejection of Chronicles is rather unusual in Ewald's history. Most of the instances in which Ewald dismisses the testimony of

---

[268]*Ibid.*, 4.45.

[269]For Joash, cf. 2 Chr 24:25 and 2 Kg 12:21, and for Ahaz, cf. 2 Chr 28:27 and 2 Kg 16:20.

[270]Ewald, *History*, 4.53, 141.

[271]*Ibid.*, 3.162.

[272]*Ibid.*, 3.171. Another example is with regard to Jehoshaphat's shipping. *Ibid.*, 4.56.

Chronicles are cases which he labels "exaggeration."[273] What is unusual about Ewald's reasoning is that instead of regarding such exaggeration as a cause for doubting other things that the Chronicler reports, he draws the opposite conclusion: the Chronicler's exaggeration is further reason to believe that the events he describes actually happened.

> But this (exaggeration) renders it all the more certain that the Chronicler must have derived his information of the actual occurrence of the campaign...from some ancient source....[274]

There are two more areas of Ewald's treatment of Chronicles that merit consideration. The first is that of speeches that the Chronicler attributes to such ancient figures as the kings and prophets. In most cases, it is unclear whether Ewald believes that the speech was actually delivered—even if only in a form distantly similar to what is reported in Chronicles. It is, however, usually plain that Ewald thinks that the speeches unique to the Chronicler are strongly colored by the Chronicler's own linguistic usage. Some examples will illustrate Ewald's lack of clarity.

> (the Chronicler) seizes this opportunity to make Abijah deliver a long address....[275]

> The vague nature of the numerical statements proves how freely the whole account is here rendered.[276]

> Every word and every idea in the speech 2 Chron. xiii. 4-13 bears the peculiar colouring of the Chronicler....[277]

> ...but their (Azariah and Hanani's) names are certainly derived from ancient sources, and only the colouring of the speeches which are here put in their mouths at some length, is from the hand of the Chronicler.[278]

> This account (2 Chr 16:7-10)...is evidently derived from an ancient source; but the particular style of the prophet's words is peculiar to the Chronicler, and has been added by him.[279]

> In the speeches and exhortations, indeed, a slight acquaintance with the peculiarities of the writer will allow us to see nothing more than the his-

---

[273] An example of this is the assertion in 2 Chr 14:9 that Zerah led an army of one million men. *Ibid.*, 4.51.

[274] *Ibid.*

[275] *Ibid.*, 4.48.

[276] *Ibid.*, 4.49.

[277] *Ibid.*, 4.48.

[278] *Ibid.*, 4.49.

[279] *Ibid.*, 4.52.

torical license with which he endeavours wherever possible to reanimate David's age.[280]

The second area for consideration is that of miracles. It may be said from the outset that Ewald views the miracles reported in Chronicles no differently from those reported in Samuel-Kings. Sometimes, he simply reports the miracle as the biblical books recorded it,[281] but in the case of Uzziah's leprosy, which the Chronicler counts as God's punishment for the king's brazenness in worship, Ewald adds,

> The colouring of the narrative in this instance is entirely that of the Chroncler, and it is to be regretted that we possess no older account of all these circumstances....[282]

In other cases, Ewald exhibits a strong tendency to rationalize the miracles. Jehoshaphat's victory over the alliance of Moab, Ammon, and Mt. Seir is one such case.

> It is not surprising that in Jehoshaphat's army this victory was ascribed to evil spirits, which were sent by Jahveh to perplex the different forces of the enemy, and precipitate them into mutual slaughter; and in like manner the Chronicler avails himself of this example to show what sort of preparations a pious but warlike king like Jehoshaphat ought to make for battle, and how heavenly powers may help him to victory. [283]

d. Summary of Ewald

Ewald's history met with a favorable reaction in both Germany and England and was recognized as a milestone in Old Testament scholarship.[284] It made three major contributions to the study of Israel's history. First, his was the first great critical history of Israel that had come out of Germany.[285] Even when one acknowledges Milman's earlier work in the field, Ewald's *History* is still exceptional. It has often been noted that Ewald did for the study of Israel's history what Niebuhr did for the history of Rome.[286] He brought the method of historical criticism, which had been developed by Niebuhr, Ranke, and others, to bear on the study of Israel's past.

Ewald's second major contribution is related to the first: he had a talent for working with the smallest details of history, and at the

---

[280]*Ibid.*, 1.195.

[281]E.g., the ravens feeding of Elijah, according to Kings. *Ibid.*, 4.105-6.

[282]*Ibid.*, 4.145-46.

[283]*Ibid.*, 4.55; cf. 2.73 regarding the exodus.

[284]Cf. Gooch, *Historians,* 523.

[285]Kraus, *Geschichte,* 199.

[286]Black, "Ewald," 774; Carpenter, *Nineteenth Century,* 123-25.

same time, he was a great synthesizer of data. His history exhibits both talents, as he dealt in the footnotes with the details of his reconstruction, while at the same time he maintained a developmental philosophy of Israel's history, which incorporated the individual facts of her history into a grand scheme of religious development over a two thousand year period.[287] Ewald's originality emerges especially in his historical reconstruction, and it characterizes his *History* as a whole. Much of this is probably due to Ewald's intense determination to work with the primary sources of history, rather than focusing his attention on the secondary literature.[288] Ewald's reconstruction of Israel's history and the developments of her institutions and language exhibit his own "undeniable historical sense."[289]

The third contribution is Ewald's attention to source-critical matters. Ewald was the first historian of Israel to preface his discussion of Israel's past with such an extensive examination of the sources available.[290] Moreover, his investigation of the sources was sophisticated by the standards of his day, and his separation of tradition (Sage, the telling of past events by one's source) from the actual events of history, which tradition describes, is another crucial aspect of his historical method.

On the negative side, Ewald appeared overly confident to many of his readers, as he set out to reconstruct Israel's past with a minimum of data. His confidence is evident in the introduction to his *History*.

> ...so too the historian must exercise the art of correctly arranging, and laying in their proper sequence, all the infinitely scattered and various traditions...and then proceed to form further deductions from a few certain traces and testimonies, so as to piece together again the scattered and decayed members of the ruined whole in greater completeness and distinctness.[291]

In the later editions of Milman's history the author singles out Ewald's confidence in his own ability to reconstruct accurately Israel's past as a major fault of the latter's *History*: "This dogmatism appears to me to be the inherent fault of the *Geschichte des Volkes Israel*.[292] Milman's attitude in this regard was shared by other scholars in the English-speaking world, as Martineau's preface to Ewald's

---

[287]Kraus, *Geschichte*, 199.
[288]Cheyne, *Founders*, 104.
[289]Wellhausen, "Ewald," 131.
[290]Kraus, *Geschichte*, 200.
[291]Ewald, *History*, 1.9.
[292]Milman, *History of the Jews*, 1.28-29.

history indicated, "...(Ewald's) critical analysis, which to most English readers savours of arbitrary dogmatism...."[293]

One may conclude that Ewald represented both the end of one era and the beginning of another. He ignored, to a large extent, the serious criticisms and doubts that had been raised with regard to the Chronicler's value for historical reconstruction of the pre-exilic period, and he adopted to a large extent the theological perspective of his sources. Later histories would go beyond Ewald in these regards. Ewald did, however, begin a new period of research into Israel's history with his attention to primary sources and insistence that the methods of historical criticism be used in the investigation of Israel's past. Therefore, in spite of his shortcomings, Ewald's history forms an important stage in the development of the reconstruction of Israel's history.

Ewald's approach to Chronicles was a bit more critical than most of his predecessors, but it did not approach the rigorous criticism of de Wette. Ewald was inclined to accept information in Chronicles, unless it contradicted other historical sources or his own historical sensibilities. Consequently, Ewald generally accepted as reliable reports that were unique to Chronicles, and even when Chronicles contradicted the other canonical books, Ewald frequently resorted to harmonization in order to salvage elements—if not the whole—of both accounts. One reason for Ewald's confidence in the historical reliability of Chronicles was his source theory, which held that the Chronicler had ancient and credible sources for his composition. At some points (e.g., his treatment of the speeches in Chronicles) Ewald appeared to be less confident in the trustworthiness of the Chronicler's reports, but he often avoided saying so explicitly. Instead he resorted to vagueness and so allowed his readers to believe what they wanted. Therefore, Ewald's history constituted a kind of compromise between the positions of de Wette and Keil on the historical reliability of Chronicles. In the years that followed—at least until the publication of Wellhausen's *Prolegomena*—Ewald's moderating position dominated research into Israel's history.

3. AFTER EWALD

a. Germany

By the middle of the nineteenth century German biblical research as a whole had advanced far beyond what was being done elsewhere in Europe and the United States. Ewald's history represented the most notable attempt so far to combine detailed source-critical and philological research with a broad view of historical development. Since Ewald had won a reputation as an outstanding critical scholar

---

[293]Martineau, "Preface," 1.vi.

and his *Geschichte des Volkes Israel* was the most ambitious and scientific history of Israel to date, it is no surprise to find that Ewald's history came to dominate mid-nineteenth century research in the field. His dominance remained until the publication of Wellhausen's *Prolegomena*, which eroded the foundation of Ewald's reconstruction of the development of Israel's history.

In this section two general studies of Chronicles will be examined in order to show how the books were being treated by German *Einleitungswissenschaft* (Dillmann and Bleek), and then our attention will turn to five attempts at historical reconstruction (Bertheau, Reinke, Gerlach, Weber, and Hitzig). In each instance the primary focus will be on the view of Chronicles' usefulness as a historical source.

1) Dillmann

One of Ewald's most distinguished disciples was Christian Friedrich August Dillmann (1823-1894). He taught at Tübingen, Kiel, Giessen, and finally at Berlin, where he succeeded Hengstenberg. He was a great authority on Ethiopic and issued both a lexicon and a grammar of the language. In Old Testament studies he was known for his argument that P derived from ca. 800 B. C. E. (but need not have become written law until Ezra's day), and thus it antedated D. Consequently, Dillmann later came to oppose Wellhausen's view of the Pentateuchal sources, and he was followed somewhat in this regard by Kittel and Baudissin.[294]

Dillmann believed that one author wrote Chronicles, Ezra, and Nehemiah and that he issued them as a single work. He assigned a date of 330 B. C. E. to the work on the basis of the genealogy in 1 Chronicles 3 and the reference to Jaddua in Neh 12:10. The author was a priest, who aimed at admonishing and encouraging his people and especially wanted to stress their religious privileges and duties.[295] He further maintained that the Chronicler's sources were the Book of the Kings of Judah and Israel ("probably the general annals of both kingdoms"), census lists, and prophetic traditions. As the prophetic citations in Chronicles indicate, some prophetic material was already in the Book of the Kings of Judah and Israel. The author was surely familiar with 1, 2 Kings, but it is unknown to what extent he used the books. Their similarities with Chronicles may indicate reliance on common sources. The differences between Chronicles and

---

[294]"Dillmann," *Enc Brit* 2 (supplement to 9th ed.; 1898) 651; "Dillmann," *Enc Jud* 6 (1971) 47-48; R. Kittel, "Dillmann," *ADB* 47 (1903) 699-702; W. Baudissin, "Dillmann, August," *RPThK* 4 (1898) 662; R. J. Thompson, *Moses and the Law*, 61.

[295]Dillmann, "Chronik," *RPThK* (2d ed.; 1854) 690-92. The article is abridged in J. H. A. Bomberger's *The Protestant Theological and Ecclesiastical Encyclopedia* (Philadelphia: Lindsay & Blakiston, 1860) 669-670.

Samuel-Kings should not lead one to suspect the credibility of
Chronicles, but can usually be explained as examples of textual corruption or the freer use of source material by the Chronicler to edify
his audience. Finally, Dillmann believed that the works of Keil,
Movers, Hävernick, and Ewald have "fully vindicated" the historical
credibility of the Chronicler.[296]

2) Bleek

A second general treatment of Chronicles in the period just following the publication of Ewald's history was that of Friedrich Bleek
(1793-1859). He had studied at Kiel and then with de Wette, Neander,
and Schleiermacher in Berlin. His teaching career was spent at Berlin
and Bonn, where he taught Old and New Testament and was respected for the thoroughness of his research and his balanced judgment. His *Einleitung* to the Bible was issued in 1860 and 1862, edited
by his son Johannes Bleek and A. Kamphausen, one of his pupils.
while his studies on the Old Testament seem to be more in line with
the critical thought of his day, he is probably best remembered for his
\work on the New Testament, where he was a bit more traditional
and vigorous in his opposition to the Tübingen school.[297]

Bleek's views on Chronicles are presented in his *Einleitung in das
Alte Testament*, which is the first part of his *Einleitung in die Heilige
Schrift*.[298] He believed that an anonymous levitical choirmaster in
Jerusalem first edited the Books of Ezra and Nehemiah so that they

---

[296]Dillmann, "Chronik," 693-94 ("Chronicles," 670).

[297]A. Kamphausen, "Bleek," *ADB* 2 (1875) 701-2; F. Crombie, "Bleek,
Friedrich," *Enc Brit* 3 (1889) 823-24; Zev Garber, "Bleek, Friedrich," *Enc Jud* 4
(1971) 1080; A. Kamphausen, "Bleek, Friedrich," *RE* 3 (1897) 254-57; Cheyne,
Founders, 142-48; R. Smend, "Friedrich Bleek, 1793-1859, " in *150 Jahre Rheinische
Friedrich-Wilhelms Universität zu Bonn 1818-1968* (Bonn: Bouvier, 1968) 3-41; W .
Elliger, *150 Jahre Theologische Fakultät Berlin. Eine Darstellung ihrer Geschichte von
1810 bis 1960 als Beitrag zu ihrem Jubilaum* (Berlin, 1960) 30; Rogerson, *Criticism*,
130-31. In 1818, Bleek became Repetent at Berlin, but when de Wette was
dismissed from the university in 1819, he suffered as well, since he was a friend
of de Wette's and the authorities confused him with a Baueleven Blech, whom
they thought was involved in the scandal of which de Wette was a part. When
the matter was straightened out, however, Bleek was reappointed to teach in
Berlin.

[298]Bleek's *Einleitung* was published in 1860, one year after Bleek's own death,
and it was edited by Kamphausen and Bleek's son. They wrote in the preface that
they had attempted to produce Bleek's work in its most complete and final form.
(Friedrich Bleek, *Einleitung in das Alte Testament*. Volume 1 of *Einleitung in die
Heilige Schrift* [eds. J. F. Bleek and A . Kamphausen; Berlin: Georg Reimer, 1860]
x.) The fourth, fifth, and sixth editions of the work were edited by Wellhausen,
but the latter never changed Bleek's treatment of Chronicles. In the fifth edition
Wellhausen withdrew many of his additions to the fourth edition and reinstated
Bleek's original sections.

would continue the narrative of 2 Kings. Later, the same editor wrote 1, 2 Chronicles and borrowed the beginning section of Ezra to conclude 2 Chronicles.[299] The author worked near the close of the Persian or at the beginning of the Greek period,[300] and his purpose in writing was to give a brief historical review of Jewish affairs by collecting and supplementing what was in the historical books which already had public authority. For example, to the brief account of Asa's reign in 1 Kings, he added reports about a war with Zerah and dealings between Asa and the prophets Azariah and Hanani. He addressed his work especially to the inhabitants of Jerusalem and also to Judah, and took pains throughout the work to deal with the relationship of each ancient king of Judah to the Law of Moses and the levitical cult.[301]

The Chronicler's main source was Samuel-Kings, but he also used other ancient works about Judah. His "Book of the Kings of Israel and Judah" was the same work that the author of Kings called "Book of the Chronicles of the Kings of Judah and Israel."[302] A comparison of Chronicles with Samuel-Kings reveals that while the two often agree literally, many of the differences seem to be the Chronicler's attempt to emend the orthography or geographical names of his source. Thus, the Chronicler tried to make the history more understandable to his contemporaries, and this sometimes led him to change the wording better to suit current tastes (for example, in 1 Chr 21:1 he has Satan, instead of God [2 Sm 24:1], provoke David to begin a census). Some of the Chronicler's attempts to modify his source for greater precision, however, ended in failure (cf. the "ships of Tarshish" in 2 Chr 9:21 and 1 Kg 10:22).[303]

Since the Chronicler often appears to be imprecise, and since he wrote after Samuel-Kings and used the latter as one of his sources (along with other works, which had probably also been used by the author of Samuel-Kings), one is usually justified in following the text of Samuel-Kings when the Chronicler conflicts with it. An additional

---

[299]Friedrich Bleek, *An Introduction to the Old Testament* (eds. Johannes Bleek & Adolf Kamphausen; trans. of 2d Ger. ed. by G. H. Venables; ed. E. Venables; 2 vols.; London: Pell & Daldy, 1869) 1.442-44.

[300]Bleek argued for dating the Chronicler about the time of the transition from the Persian to the Greek period for five reasons: (1) the end of 2 Chronicles demands a date after the end of the Babylonian exile; (2) Chronicles' position as the last work in the Hebrew canon argues for a time after Nehemiah; (3) 1 Chr 29:7 refers to "darics" and so indicates that the coins were currently used in Palestine at the time Chronicles was written; (4) 1 Chr 3:19-24, the genealogy of Zerubbabel, takes the reader down to the end of the Persian Period, if not into the Greek; and (5) the mention of Hattush (1 Chr 3:22) may take one down to 400 B. C. E. at least, if this is the Hattush of Ezra 8:2. *Ibid.*, 1.436-37.

[301]*Ibid.*, 1.439.

[302]*Ibid.*, 1.438-39.

[303]*Ibid.*, 1.440-41.

reason for proceding in this fashion is that the Chronicler's viewpoint has influenced the way he thought about and described the history of his people. He probably composed the speeches in Chronicles himself and has projected certain later cultic practices into earlier times.[304] Nevertheless, the following need to be kept in mind.

> We must not, however, assume that everything which Chronicles contains over and above these books (Samuel-Kings) must be unhistorical and untrustworthy, or that the alterations or additions are purely arbitrary.[305]

> But in this (composition of speeches and projecting later cultic practices back in time) we must not forget that ancient authors generally used greater freedom in reporting the speeches of others than modern historians do, and that therefore no ground can be derived from thence for suspecting the historical truth of Chronicles in general.[306]

Finally, Bleek concludes that the Books of Chronicles are a valuable supplement to the work of Samuel-Kings and that the former provides the historian with many important details.[307] With this conclusion, Bleek opposed de Wette and Gramberg but did not completely endorse their more extreme opponents (e.g., Dahler and Keil).[308]

Bleek represents essentially a moderate position with regard to Chronicles, and this generally coincides with his reputation in Old Testament studies as a whole. He chose a date for Chronicles between the extremes of Ezra's day, on the one hand, and the Maccabean Period, on the other. Moreover, with regard to sources he believes that the Chronicler used Samuel-Kings and other ancient sources as well. This sets him between those who claim that the Chronicler used only Samuel-Kings (e.g., de Wette) and those who claimed that he used other sources instead of Samuel-Kings (e.g., Keil). In the matter of the trustworthiness of the Chronicler, Bleek maintains that while one cannot trust every detail in the work, since the author composed speeches and projected later cultic details into his people's past, as a whole, Chronicles can be relied upon as a source for many genuine bits of information about Israel's pre-exilic history. This, of course, places him somewhere between de Wette and Keil.

Bleek, therefore, holds that 1, 2 Chronicles is useful for reconstructing Israel's pre-exilic history, in spite of the inaccuracies that have been detected in its account. The Chronicler's mistakes are

---

[304]*Ibid.*, 1.441-42. Bleek still held to an early date for the Elohist (P)—sometime in the reign of Saul—and believed that it was the groundwork of the Hexateuch and was revised by J during the reign of David. *Ibid.*, 1.292, 300-301.

[305]*Ibid.*

[306]*Ibid.*

[307]*Ibid.*

[308]*Ibid.*, 1.435-36.

viewed by Bleek as the kinds of errors that the historian finds in other ancient documents, but which do not prevent the use of those works in historical reconstruction. He further maintains that de Wette and Gramberg have failed to show that the Chronicler composed his work arbitrarily or with the intention of falsifying history.

Since Bleek still assigned P an early date—Graf's work that assigned it a late date came out the year after Bleek's death—there was little reason for him seriously to dispute many of the cultic details that the Chronicler reported for the pre-exilic period. Had he lived to write an introduction ten years later, his assessment of Chronicles may have been much different.

3) Bertheau

Ernst Bertheau (1812-1888) was another of Ewald's pupils. He first studied at Berlin and then at Göttingen, where he was taught by Ewald, Lücke, and Gieseler. He married Lücke's daughter, and when Ewald and the others of the "Göttingen Seven" left the university, Lücke and Bertheau remained. Bertheau's publications that are relevant for the study of Chronicles as a historical source include *Zur Geschichte der Israeliten* (1842) and a commentary on Chronicles (1854).[309]

Bertheau argues for Zunz' and others' position that initially 1, 2 Chronicles, Ezra, and Nehemiah formed a single work.[310] The work was probably written by an anonymous levitical musician (or gatekeeper); it was surely not by Ezra, who in Bertheau's opinion did not even write the book that bore his name.[311] The work may be dated with some confidence near the beginning of the Greek period, due among other things to the mention of Jaddua in Neh 12:10-11, 22-23.[312]

Bertheau devoted considerable attention to the question of sources that were used in the composition of Chronicles. The following diagram illustrates the basic outline of his source theory.[313]

---

[309]Carl Bertheau, "Bertheau, Ernst," *RE* 2 (1897) 645-48; "Bertheau, Ernst," *ADB* 46 (1902) 441-43.

[310]Ernst Bertheau, *Die Bücher der Chronik* (Kurzgefasstes exegetisches Handbuch zum Alten Testament 15; 2d ed.; Leipzig: S. Hirzel, 1873) xxi.

[311] *Ibid.*, xlvii.

[312]*Ibid.*, xlv–xlvi.

[313]*Ibid.*, xl.

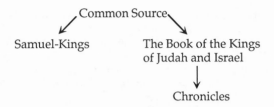

Bertheau's theory is far more complicated than the diagram would lead one to believe, and there are numerous source-critical issues, on which he remained undecided. He divides the treatment of Chronicles' sources into two parts: the sources for the genealogical section (1 Chronicles 1-9) and the sources for the rest (1 Chronicles 10-2 Chronicles 36). He suggests that the Chronicler composed the first nine chapters of his work with the help of Genesis, other Old Testament books, and extracanonical documents that have since been lost. Finally, the patronymics in some of the lists may have been supplied by the Chronicler's own knowledge of families and officials in his day.[314]

The matter of 1 Chronicles 10-2 Chronicles 36 is much more complex. Bertheau's point of departure, however, is firmly tied to the text of the books. Since 1, 2 Chronicles refers so frequently to "The Book of the Kings of Judah and Israel," although several variations of this title are used, Bertheau concludes that this must have been the author's primary source.[315] Furthermore, he argues that the references to prophetic writings in Chronicles merely note the various sections of "The History of the Kings of Judah and Israel."[316] While he acknowledges that it is possible that the citations by the Chronicler of a "Midrash" could simply be a variant title for the major historical work that the author used, Bertheau believes it to be more likely that the "Midrash" was a separate work, a kind of commentary on the "Book of the Kings of Israel and Judah."[317] In addition to this main source, the author of Chronicles also used material from other sources. The list of David's heroes in 1 Chr 11:10-47, which is more extensive than the parallel list in 2 Sm 23:8-39, and the divisions of priests and singers in 1 Chronicles 23-26 probably derived from the same source that was used for some of the genealogies in 1 Chronicles 1-9.[318] "The Book of the Kings of Judah and Israel" was composed after Samuel-Kings, and it adopted the general plan and

---

[314]*Ibid.*, xxvi.
[315]*Ibid.*, xxxvi-xxxvii.
[316]*Ibid.*, xxxi-xxxiv.
[317]*Ibid.*, xxx-xxxi, xxxiv.
[318]*Ibid.*, xxxv-xxxvi.

even the specific judgments on the various kings from the latter work.[319]

Bertheau characterizes the author of Chronicles as a basically trustworthy source for information. He was by no means the falsifier of history that de Wette and Gramberg saw. He often treated his sources with a certain amount of freedom and edited them into his work according to his own purposes, linguistic usage, historical views, and judgments.[320] There were times, however, when he seems to have created, without the use of a historical source, at least parts of speeches (e.g., 1 Chr 29:1-5, 10-19) and perhaps some descriptions of feasts and festivals (1 Chr 15:5-11, 17-24).[321] In spite of such occurrences, Bertheau maintains that the Chronicler regularly used his sources carefully and that whenever one finds material that is unique to Chronicles, it should be assumed that the author derived it from a source. Consequently, he believes that Chronicles supplies the modern historian with a wealth of important information about the pre-exilic period.[322]

Such confidence in Chronicles as a historical source was evident in Bertheau's "*Die Bewohner Palästinas,*" in which he affirms that "one should not doubt" the story in Chronicles about Manasseh's captivity and return. He explains that the author of 2 Kings omitted the account, since his aim was to give "only a general judgment about his behavior" with regard to religion and nothing more. With the aid of Ezra 4:2, Manasseh's captivity is related to Esarhaddon.[323] In addition, Bertheau supports the Chronicler's report about Zerah's attack on Asa, but he writes in a footnote that it is unknown whether Zerah was king of Ethiopia or a general and that no one has yet been able to identify him with a figure mentioned in the Egyptian records.[324] In this work Bertheau's references to Chronicles are frequent and support the ancient work's credibility.

In the second edition of his commentary on Chronicles, Bertheau continues to affirm the historicity of Manasseh's captivity[325] and of Zerah's attack, although on the latter point he is able to identify Zerah with the Egyptian Osorkhon and refers his reader to Thenius' commentary on Kings for further explanation.[326] In these and many other instances, Bertheau demonstrates in his commentary his basic

---

[319]*Ibid.*, xliv-xlv.

[320]*Ibid.*, xli.

[321]*Ibid.*, xlii-xliii.

[322]*Ibid.*, xlii.

[323]Ernst Bertheau, "Die Bewohner Palästina's seit den ältesten Zeiten bis auf die Zerstörung Jerusalem's durch die Römer," in *Zur Geschichte der Israeliten* (Göttingen: Vandenhoeck & Ruprecht, 1842) 373.

[324]*Ibid.*, 356.

[325]Bertheau, *Chronik*, 400.

[326]*Ibid.*, 308.

confidence in the Chronicler's truthfulness and credibility. Consequently, one can see that from his work of 1842 until that of 1873, Bertheau maintained that Chronicles was an essentially reliable historical source.

Bertheau shows acquaintance with the important studies that had been done on Chronicles until his day, and when he traces the development in these studies, he shows great sympathy for aspects of Keil's work and often finds himself in agreement with Ewald and Hitzig, to whom he points as evidence of the great importance that Chronicles holds for the reconstruction of Israel's history.[327] On the other hand, he is quite opposed to the conclusions of de Wette, Gramberg, and Graf and is quick to claim that de Wette softened some of his earlier conclusions about Chronicles in the later editions of his Old Testament introduction and that Graf had written Bertheau in a letter in 1866, conceding that there was always some doubt about whether information in Chronicles arose from the author's own opinion or could be traced back to the Midrash that he used as a source.[328]

Bertheau bases his confidence in Chronicles as a reliable historical witness on the source theory that he proposes. Just as Ewald had given great attention to the matter of analyzing the sources for his history and attempting to determine their sources of information, so his pupil now devotes the greater part of his introduction to Chronicles to the matter of the Chronicler's sources and their impact on his credibility. By offering a common source for the histories in Samuel-Kings and Chronicles and by interposing another source between the common source and Chronicles, Bertheau provides explanations for both the similarities and differences between the two biblical histories. Bertheau proceeds cautiously in the construction of this theory, and his conclusions generally appear well-founded.[329] He realizes, however, the difficulty in drawing concusions about information in Chronicles from assumptions about sources which are no longer extant (e.g., the assignment of material in Chronicles to one source or the other with regard to its origin). In only a few instances, though, is Bertheau willing to allow that the Chronicler invented a report without adequate documentation, and even then he sometimes admits the possibility that a source was available.

In spite of his strong insistence that the Chronicler derived his information (almost) entirely from his sources, Bertheau also admits

---

[327]*Ibid.*, ix.

[328]*Ibid.*, viii.

[329]An exception to this statement concerns the citation of two sources found in 2 Chr 33:18-19, which Bertheau interprets as duplicate references to a single source. This is an unlikely explanation and is motivated by the requirements of the author's source theory for Chronicles.

that the author of Chronicles was motivated by strong theological concerns. The latter point led Bertheau to reject—or at least strongly suspect—several of the Chronicler's reports, even though he generally maintained that the historian should accept the statements in Chronicles as truthful. The differences in language between Samuel-Kings and Chronicles, their different choices of material to include, and their different philosophies of history are all to be explained by the fact that the Chronicler (and presumably the author of Samuel-Kings, too) edited his material in accordance with his own purposes and in accordance with the language and outlook of his day. In spite of these post-exilic influences on the composition of Israel's pre-exilic history in Chronicles, Bertheau is usually reluctant to admit historical errors in the Chronicler's work.

In his commentary Bertheau's response to instances of conflict between the texts of Chronicles and Samuel-Kings is harmonization. This is the case when 1 Chronicles 21 asserts that Benjamin and Levi were omitted from David's census, while 2 Samuel 24 declares that the entire land was covered by the census.[330] The same is true when Kings records a burial for a king "with his fathers," viz., in the royal tombs, while Chronicles denies the king a burial in the royal tombs.[331]

Therefore, Bertheau stands in the tradition of Keil and Ewald as one who affirms the credibility of Chronicles and reconciles its text with other biblical reports by harmonization. However, unlike Keil and more like Ewald, he allows for the Chronicler's theology to have led to distortions of the history in a few instances.

4) Reinke

The usefulness of Chronicles for historical reconstruction was also addressed in Laurenz Reinke's (1797-1879) four volume collection of essays entitled *Beiträge zur Erklärung des alten Testamentes* between 1851 and 1855. The essays deal with various sections of the Old Testament, but it is a part of volume one that is of special interest for the study of Chronicles: "Die Schwierigkeiten und Widersprüche mancher Zahlangaben in den Büchern des altes Testamentes und deren Entstehung und Lösung." The parts of the essay that deal with Chronicles usually address the numbers of troops or amounts of money. An example of the author's approach is his treatment of 2 Chr 17:14-18, which gives the size of Jehoshaphat's army as 1,160,000 men. Reinke thinks that a land's army would be twenty or twenty-five percent of its total population. Therefore, the population of Judah would have been 4,640,000 or 5,800,000 people. This would, in turn, mean that the total population of Palestine at the time would have

---

[330]Bertheau, *Chronik*, 179.
[331]*Ibid.*, 357-58.

been thirteen to seventeen million, and this is clearly too many people to inhabit 465 square miles of land. Therefore, Reinke concludes that the numbers in Chronicles are far too large, and he suggests that the errors arose in transcription, whereby the Hebrew letters, which were used for numerals, were confused with one another. At any rate, he maintains that the numbers in ancient Hebrew writing were unclear, and the Chronicler would not have wanted to inflate the size of Jehoshaphat's army.[332] A similar method is followed by Reinke in his treatment of other troop notices and the large amounts of money mentioned in Chronicles. In the latter case, the weight and value of the shekal provide a fertile ground for discussion.[333]

Reinke's approach to Chronicles, therefore, is based on the assumption that the original edition of the work was correct. So, while he recognizes certain numerical inaccuracies in the present text of the books, he accounts for them in terms of textual corruption in the course of transmission. In this respect, therefore, Reinke is similar to Keil and the others who argued for the historical reliability of Chronicles.

5) Gerlach

Ernst Gerlach (1838-1909) of Berlin wrote an article in *Theologische Studien und Kritiken* in 1861 entitled "Die Gefangenschaft und Bekehrung Manasse's" which attacked an earlier article by Graf (1859) in the same journal.[334] Whereas Graf had concluded that the Chronicler's account of Manasseh's captivity and repentance had no historical basis in fact, Gerlach maintained that Graf's conclusions were based on hypotheses rather than reasons and that "the historicity of the report about Manasseh's imprisonment and repentance stand completely established in all points."[335]

Gerlach set out to prove the credibility of 2 Chr 33:10-13 by showing that the accounts of Manasseh's reign in 2 Kings and 2 Chronicles do not contradict one another and that the omission of the Chronicler's story about the king's captivity by the author of 2 Kings does not necessarily argue against the story's credibility.[336] Then Gerlach proceeds from the historical difficulties with the Manasseh story, that Graf and Movers had raised, to some positive reasons that argue for the credibility of the Chronicler's account.

---

[332]Laur. Reinke, *Beiträge zur Erklärung des alten Testamentes* (4 vols.; Munster: Coppenrath, 1851) 1.197-200.

[333]*Ibid.*, 1.187-97.

[334]K. H. Graf, "Die Gefangenschaft und Bekehrung Manasse's, 2 Chr. 33," *ThStKr* 32 (1859) 467-94.

[335]E. Gerlach, "Die Gefangenschaft und Bekehrung Manasse's," *ThStKr* 34 (1861) 523-24.

[336]*Ibid.*, 505.

First, Gerlach argues that a survey of Assyrian history shows that Esarhaddon and Manasseh's reigns overlapped and that while Nineveh was the Assyrian capital, Esarhaddon resided in Babylon after he had conquered it. Therefore, the Chronicler's report that the Jewish king was taken captive by Assyrian soldiers to Babylon rather than to Nineveh demonstrates precise historical knowledge.[337]

Secondly, an Assyrian inscription that Rawlinson found read "Esarhaddon conqueror of Misraim and Cush." This indicates that the Assyrian king marched against and conquered Egypt, and therefore, Eusebius' "report of the conquest of Coele-syria (by Esarhaddon)...is entirely certain."[338]

On this basis, Gerlach proposes the following historical reconstruction of Manasseh's captivity and release. In the twenty-second year of Manasseh's reign the Assyrian army brought a colony of foreigners to Samaria to settle there. For some reason, the Assyrian troops launched a raid into Judah and took Manasseh prisoner.[339] The motive for the later Assyrian release of the Judean king was the rising strength of Egypt. Manasseh was freed and immediately began to fortify Jerusalem's western side and to garrison other fortresses in Judah.[340]

A final bit of evidence that Gerlach offers to support his reconstruction comes from the prophecies of Nahum: they frequently refer to Assyria and should be set in the reign of Manasseh, since the prophet indicates that Assyria posed a threat to Judah, and since the prophecies cannot be set against the backdrop of Hezekiah's struggles with Assyria—Nahum made use of the earlier prophecies of Isaiah. Therefore, the Book of Nahum establishes the credibility of the Chronicler's account of an Assyrian attack on Judah.[341]

Gerlach's study had little influence on the subsequent discussion of the historicity of the Chronicler's report of Manasseh's captivity and release for two reasons. First, while he used several of the more important studies of Chronicles, such as those of Gramberg, Keil, Movers, Ewald, Hävernick, Bertheau, and Graf, the real impetus for his article came from the new discoveries of ancient Assyrian documents. The latter, though, also proved to be the Achilles' heel of his reconstruction. His study was soon rendered obsolete by the discovery of Assyrian texts which specifically mentioned Manasseh's dealings with both Esarhaddon and Ashurbanipal, and this provided at least two other historical settings in which one could set the Chronicler's story about Manasseh's captivity. Therefore, Gerlach's

---

[337]*Ibid.*, 512-17.

[338]*Ibid.*, 517.

[339]*Ibid.*, 517-19.

[340]*Ibid.*, 520-21.

[341]*Ibid.*, 522-23.

misfortune was in writing too soon—at the dawn of Assyriology—
rather than a bit later, when there was more evidence, and there had
been more time to analyze it.

A second weakness in Gerlach's arguments was less important. It
concerned his attempt to relate the prophecies of Nahum to
Manasseh. The prophet of Judah could have spoken to his people
anytime between 663 B. C. E. (the conquest of Thebes by Assyria, Nah
3:8-13) and 612 B. C. E. (the fall of Nineveh). This left about three
decades after Manasseh's reign, when Nahum could have spoken his
prophecies.

Gerlach's article represents one of the first attempts in Germany
to use archaeology in order to vindicate the historical reliability of
Chronicles. The author concludes in his study that the Chronicler had
precise information about Manasseh's captivity and release and that
his narrative could be completely established. Such confidence in the
historical accuracy of Chronicles places the author firmly on the side
of Keil in the debate over the credibility of Chronicles.

6) Weber

The influence of Ewald on the reconstruction of Israel's history
may also be seen in the work of Georg Weber (1808-1888), who was
professor and *Schuldirector* at Heidelberg. He wrote *Das Volk Israel*,
the first volume of a two volume work entitled *Geschichte des Volkes
Israel* (1867). The first volume treated the time from the patriarchs
until the Babylonian exile and the return. The second volume by
Holtzmann continued with the Greek period and carried the narrative into the times of the Apostle Paul. These two volumes are regarded by Weber as a further extension of his larger *Allgemeiner
Weltgeschichte* (1857-1880).[342]

Throughout the work one detects the influence of Ewald, and
Weber acknowledges his debt in this regard in the first part of his
book. In his list of his secondary sources, special praise is offered to
Ewald for his great contributions to the understanding of Israel's ancient history. [343] Later, in his discussion of the pentateuchal sources
Weber presents his readers with Ewald's conclusions.[344] The same is
true in his treatment of the date and sources of the Chronicler.[345]

Weber shows some caution about using everything that is found
in Chronicles, observing that "Where Chronicles diverges or narrates
in more detail, the author has a special religious or hierarchical pur-

---

[342]Georg Weber, *Das Volk Israel in der alttestamentlichen Zeit* in *Geschichte des
Volkes Israel und der Entstehung des Christenthums* (2 vols.; Leipzig: Wilhelm
Engelmann, 1867) 1.iii.

[343]*Ibid.*, 1.xxxvi.

[344]*Ibid.*, 1.410-11.

[345]*Ibid.*, 1.416.

pose."[346] Weber evidently does not, however, believe that the Chronicler's "religious or hierarchical" aims led him to seriously distort or fabricate the events of history, because *Das Volk Israel* regularly incorporates the Chronicler's reports. For example, Weber relates the Chronicler's enumeration of Shishak's forces, which attacked Judah, but whose numbers Kings fails to record.[347] He also accepts the testimony unique to Chronicles that Asa raised a large army from Judah and Benjamin and that he defeated a large enemy force in the valley of Zephathah.[348] In short, Weber exhibits a great deal of confidence in the Chronicler as a reliable historical witness for the pre-exilic period.

Weber seems to have been greatly influenced by Ewald, and there is some truth in the statement that his discussion of the Pentateuch and of Chronicles, as well, is little more than the presentation of Ewald's positions. As far as his use of Chronicles is concerned, Weber is much like Ewald. He is aware of the Chronicler's interests, but at the same time he is quite trusting and confident that the Chronicler's prejudices have not led the latter to invent reports. Consequently, Weber's history is interesting as an abbreviated version of Ewald's approach to Israelite history, and it demonstrates the power of the latter's influence over the field in mid-nineteenth century German scholarship.

7) Hitzig

The final scholar to be treated in this survey—Ferdinand H. Hitzig (1807-1875)—was a student of both Gesenius and Ewald. He studied under the rationalist Paulus at Heidelberg, under Gesenius at Halle, and under Ewald at Göttingen. He taught at Zurich for twenty-eight years and at Heidelberg for the last fourteen years of his life. He was reknown as a philologist and for his commentaries on the books of the Old Testament, the most important of which was probably his work on Isaiah (*Übersetzung und Auslegung des Propheten Jesaias*, 1833). These works demonstrated his exegetical creativity and gained him a reputation for original—though sometimes eccentric—hypotheses.[349]

Hitzig's *Geschichte des Volkes Israel* (1869) had two parts: the first surveyed Israel's history from the patriarchs to the end of the Persian rule, and the second covered the time until the fall of Massada. The author noted from the outset that the ancient writers were not critics, and therefore, one finds in their writings "false apologetic, exaggera-

---

[346]*Ibid.*, 1.417.

[347]*Ibid.*, 1.221.

[348]*Ibid.*, 1.222.

[349]Redslob, "Hitzig, Ferdinand H.," *ADB* 12 (1880) 507-9; "Hitzig, Ferdinand," *Enc Brit* 12 (1889) 27-28; Cheyne, *Founders*, 119-126; Kneucker, J. J. (ed.), *Dr. Ferdinand Hitzigs* Vorlesungen ueber Biblische Theologie und Messianische Weissagungen des Alten Testaments (Karlsruhe, 1880); Rogerson, *Criticism*, 134-36.

tion, and hatred for their enemies."[350] This led Hitzig to affirm his own intention to build his history on the results of source criticism and a critical examination of the ancient sources.[351]

Hitzig's view of Chronicles is more difficult to determine than Ewald's, since the former did not begin his presentation with a comprehensive statement about the sources, as his teacher did. It is evident, however, that Hitzig maintained a general confidence in the testimony of Chronicles, since he accepted the Chronicler's reports of Rehoboam's fortifications, Zerah's attack on Asa, Jehoshaphat's victory over the Moabite alliance, and Manasseh's captivity.[352] However, in the case of Manasseh's captivity, he rejected the Chronicler's report that Manasseh became a pious follower of Yahweh after his release; instead, Hitzig believed that the Judean king was always an opponent of the Yahweh cult, and the Chronicler's account of his captivity probably referred to actions by Esarhaddon's general on the way to Egypt.[353] In addition, on several occasions Hitzig referred his readers to Movers' treatment of Chronicles.[354]

It seems, therefore, that in Hitzig's use of Chronicles he did not advance beyond Ewald but that he maintained the same general attitude toward the books that his teacher had. Moreover, his history as a whole did not win anything like the popular and scholarly acceptance that Ewald's did.[355]

8) Summary of Chronicles in German Scholarship after Ewald

In the three decades following the publication of Ewald's history of ancient Israel considerable confidence was accorded the Chronicler. In the works that we have surveyed thus far there was a general consensus in three areas. First, Chronicles was assigned a date around the time of Alexander the Great and the beginning of the Greek period. Secondly, it was believed that the Chronicler had adequate sources available for his composition. Most scholars believed that he used some of the same sources that had been used by the author of Samuel-Kings. There were differences of opinion, however, on the question of whether or to what extent the Chronicler used the books of Samuel-Kings themselves. Finally, it was generally concluded that 1, 2 Chronicles was a reliable source for the reconstruction of Israel's history. While some scholars, such as Dillmann, Reinke, and Gerlach, had a great deal of confidence in the historical accuracy of Chronicles, others believed that there were occasional ex-

---

[350]Ferdinand Hitzig, *Geschichte des Volkes Israel* (Leipzig: S. Hirzel, 1869) 4.
[351]*Ibid.*, 4-5.
[352]*Ibid.*, 196-97, 165-66, 197, 199, 230.
[353]*Ibid.*, 230-31.
[354]*Ibid.*, 160, 165, 171, 201.
[355]Cheyne, *Founders*, 122.

aggerations, inaccuracies, and even inventions in Chronicles (Bleek, e.g.). None of them held de Wette's view that the Chronicler set out deliberately to falsify history. Therefore, in Germany after Ewald's history there was a cautious acceptance of Chronicles as a credible source for historical reconstruction.

b. England

While German biblical studies were not widely known in England at the beginning of the nineteenth century, by mid-century they had become more familiar to the English. T. and T. Clark's *Foreign Theological Library*, which began translating German theological works in the 1850s, was partially responsible for this new awareness in England. However, the German works, that were chosen for translation by Clark, were only the more moderate or conservative ones (e.g., Hengstenberg, Delitzsch, and Keil). Consequently, English biblical scholarship remained largely ignorant of the work of some of the more important figures in German biblical studies (e.g., de Wette and Gesenius).[356] In this section we will examine the views of Francis Newman, Samuel Davidson, and A. P. Stanley toward Chronicles. While Ewald's history did not influence the views of Newman and Davidson toward Chronicles, it exercised a great influence on Stanley's work.

1) Newman

One of the relatively few English scholars to show much familiarity with the biblical criticism of Germany was Francis Newman (1805-1897), the brother of Cardinal John Newman. He studied classics at Oxford and later taught at Bristol, Manchester, and London. His refusal to subscribe to the "Thirty-nine Articles of Religion" prevented him from receiving his M. A. at Oxford. This difficulty with Anglican articles of faith brought him face to face early in his career with the issue of whether church dogma should be allowed to dictate the results of biblical research.[357]

> If the Hebrew history has hitherto been nearly as a sealed book to us, it is because all the academical and clerical teachers of it are compelled to sign Thirty-nine Articles of Religion before assuming their office. ... Until the laity strike off these fetters from the clergy, it is mere hypocrisy in them to defer to a clergyman's authority in any theological

---

[356]Glover, *Evangelical Nonconformists*, 41-43; Rogerson, *Criticism*, 158-179.

[357]"Francis Newman," *London Times* (Oct. 6, 1897) 4; "Mr. F. W. Newman," *The Athenaeum* 3650 (Oct. 9, 1897) 489-90; Alexander Gordon, "Newman, Francis William," *DNB Supplement* 3 (1901) 221-22; J. R. Mozley, "Francis William Newman," *The Hibbert Journal* 23 (1925) 345-60; William Robbins, *The Newman Brothers* (London: Heinemann, 1966); Kenneth N. Ross, "Francis William

question of first-rate importance. We dictate to the clergy from their
early youth what they are to believe, and thereby deprive them of the
power of bearing independent testimony to it in their mature years.
...the Biblical critic is perpetually driven to the learned Germans for
aid.[358]

Newman believed that if such constraints had been applied to the
study of the Greek and Roman classics, the modern advances in those
areas would never have occurred.

It is not easy to conceive how little we might know of Greek history, if,
from the revival of Greek studies, test-articles had been imposed with a
view to perpetuate the ideas of it current in the fifteenth century; but it
is *very* easy to assure ourselves that neither Thirlwall nor Grote could
have produced their valuable works under such a restriction.[359]

This conviction of Newman's that dogmatics should not dictate historical reconstruction is apparent throughout his own history and
was shared by the German critics whom he cites in his work (de
Wette, Gesenius, and Ewald), as well as by some English scholars
(e.g., Milman), who preceded him. Moreover, it is clear that Newman
had accepted several other important tenets of historical criticism.
First, he recognized the historian's responsibility to work critically
with the sources available.[360] Secondly, he insisted that the biblical
historian must use fully "those laws of thought and of reasoning,
which in all the sciences have now received currency." Here he is
referring to the principle of analogy, according to which one attempted to understand the past in terms analogous to present experience.[361] Thirdly, he used the principle of cause and effect, and thus he
tried to offer rational and natural explanations for the events in
Israel's past.[362] These aspects of Newman's historical method set him
squarely in the mainstream of nineteenth century historical criticism,
typified by Niebuhr's study of Rome and Ranke's studies of Rome
and Germany. It is only reasonable that Newman would have been
exposed to the writings of these two historians since his education
was in the classics, and this conclusion is borne out by Newman's
own references to Thirlwall, Arnold, and others.[363]

Newman," *Church Quarterly Review* 118 (1934) 231-44; G. Sieveking, *Memoir and
Letters of Francis W. Newman* (London: Kegan, Paul, Trench, Trubner, 1909).

[358]Francis Newman, *A History of the Hebrew Monarchy* (London: John
Chapman, 1849) vi.

[359]*Ibid.*

[360]*Ibid.*, iii, v.

[361]*Ibid.*, iii, iv.

[362]*Ibid.*, iv.

[363]*Ibid.*, 170, 237.

It is difficult to define precisely the extent of Newman's acquaintance with Old Testament scholarship. His classicist training is evident in the frequent allusions to Latin and Greek works and in his citations of the secondary literature in the field of classical studies.[364] He cites Milman's *History of the Jews* infrequently but the writings of several German scholars more often: Ewald, Hitzig, and de Wette most of all, but Gesenius and Winer are also mentioned. Ewald's works on the Psalms and Prophets are used heavily by Newman, but there is no indication that Newman was acquainted with Ewald's history, the first three volumes of which had been available since 1847.[365] Since Hitzig's history did not appear for another two decades, Newman's references to this pupil of Ewald draw on his earlier studies on the Old Testament prophets.[366] Finally, Newman uses de Wette's translations of various parts of the Old Testament but nothing from de Wette's examination of Chronicles and its usefulness for historical reconstruction.[367]

Newman's history dealt only with the period of the monarchy (from Samuel and Saul to the Babylonian captivity of Judah). Aside from a brief essay at the beginning that treats primarily geographical setting and social institutions for Israel, the book moves through Israel's history chronologically. Newman never discusses the sources of his history in a comprehensive way. Consequently, one must pick up bits of information here and there. Apparently, Newman dated Chronicles long after the Books of Kings (which he dated to the Babylonian exile).[368] A reference later in the book may indicate that Newman thought that Chronicles arose during the time of Nehemiah.[369]

In his use of Chronicles, one tenet is extremely important for Newman: the earlier source is to be preferred over the later one. This means that, aside from possible complicating circumstances, the testimony of Samuel-Kings is to be accepted over that of Chronicles.[370] The following examples illustrate this principle. The burial notices in Chronicles for the kings of Judah usually deny to wicked kings an interment in the royal tombs, while Kings affirms that the kings in question "slept with their fathers." In the cases of Jehoram and Joash, for example, Newman notes this conflict and rejects the witness of Chronicles in favor of that of Kings.[371] In the matter of Ahaziah's

---

364*Ibid.*, 170, 237, 271, 286, 289, 300, 315, 318, 323, 324, 363, 368.
365*Ibid.*, 32, 80, 95, 97, 99, 102, 116.
366*Ibid.*, 235, 246, 260, 264, 274, 279, 282, 287, 301, 305.
367*Ibid.*, 8, 32, 155, 235, 257, 264, 287, 301, 305.
368*Ibid.*, v.
369*Ibid.*, 114.
370*Ibid.*, v.
371*Ibid.*, 202, 230.

death there is another contradiction between the two books: Chronicles says that he died in Samaria, but Kings says that he died in Megiddo.[372] Newman favors the latter, and so again asserts his initial observation.

> Account must be taken of all such facts in balancing authorities; and when we find a wide difference of spirit between the two historians in treating the same subject,—a difference conformable to the different aereas (sic) in which they write,—the great caution with which the later authority must be used will become evident.[373]

The foregoing should not be interpreted to mean that Newman accepted the historical witness of Kings without question. On the contrary, he also rejected the testimony of Kings on occasions, when that testimony violated aspects of his historical judgment. For instance, Newman asserts that the account in Kings of Jehoram has been distorted by the author's prejudice against the king because of the latter's relations with Ahab.[374] Moreover, Newman's judgment on Kings' account of the careers of Elijah and Elisha is that

> (their) adventures and exploits have come down to us in such a halo of romance, not unmingled with poetry of a high genius, that it is impossible to disentangle the truth. ...but as their deeds are nearly all prodigies, attested to us only by a writing compiled three centuries after the facts, and having no bearing that can be traced on the real course of the history, we are forced to pass them over very slightly.[375]

A second aspect of Newman's historical method is his argument that the historian should be sensitive to the ways in which the circumstances, biases, and aims of the author may have influenced his account. This led Newman to discount the Chronicler's information at times, when it conflicted with that of Samuel-Kings, and even at times when the Chronicler reported information supplementary to what one finds in Kings. Several examples illustrate this. Newman rejects the Chronicler's explanation that King Uzziah's leprosy was God's punishment for his usurpation of priestly prerogatives. Newman believes that the earlier kings of Judah exercised certain privileges that at a later time were restricted to priests. The Chronicler writes at a later time, and so imposes his own beliefs on an earlier era.[376] Since the Chronicler also aimed at edifying his contemporaries, he was eager to sketch earlier times in an idealistic way. This led him to inflate numbers and to describe both the piety and

---

[372]*Ibid.*, 207.
[373]*Ibid.*, v.
[374]*Ibid.*, 202.
[375]*Ibid.*, 180.
[376]*Ibid.*, 133, 233.

evil of various kings in extreme ways.[377] One of the Chronicler's tools in this regard was the setting of speeches in the mouths of various kings, priests, and prophets. Newman often regards these as fabrications by the Chronicler.[378] Finally, the Chronicler uses his history as an occasion to assert his understanding of theodicy. Newman points to several examples of how the Chronicler invented a sin to account for a tragedy in a king's reign: Shishak's attack as a consequence of Rehoboam's unfaithfulness to God,[379] Amaziah's defeat by Jehoash as God's punishment for Amaziah's worshipping Edomite gods,[380] and Uzziah's leprosy as God's penalty for Uzziah's brazen action in the cult.[381]

A third aspect of Newman's critical method is his use of archaeology and comparative materials for illuminating Israel's history. He uses Josephus for most of his description of the land and the people in the first section of his book, but at several points in the history he refers to excavations and various archaeological remains in the East.[382] In addition, Newman's background in the Greek and Latin classics led him to adduce parallels from the West to practices and institutions of ancient Israel.[383]

Finally, Newman argues that current theories about the historical accuracy of the Old Testament are exploded by the Chronicler's clear distortions of fact.

> It is inevitable that many English readers will feel distressed at what appears the only just inference from these transactions. Those who wish to take a fair view of the case must remember that the often-proved inconsistency, improbability and unfairness of the books of Chronicles alone suffices to shatter in pieces current notions as to the immaculate character of the entire and indivisible "Old Testament;" as if it were a book defined and guaranteed to us by God himself.[384]

There are three pertinent observations to be made with regard to Newman's treatment of Chronicles. First, Newman did not work out a comprehensive view of Chronicles and its sources. While de Wette and Gramberg challenged the notion that the author of Chronicles had reliable sources for his contributions to the pool of information about Israel's history, and while Movers and Ewald worked out source theories to account for the new information in Chronicles,

---

[377]*Ibid.*, 126, 160, 114, 117.
[378]*Ibid.*, 163, 170.
[379]*Ibid.*, 153.
[380]*Ibid.*, 234.
[381]*Ibid.*, 241.
[382]*Ibid.*, 162, 250, 277, 314.
[383]*Ibid.*, 17, 170, 237, 271.
[384]*Ibid.*, 330.

Newman did neither with clarity. His position on the question of Chronicles' sources appears, however, to have been nearer de Wette than Movers since he believed that the purposes of the book led its author to fabricate stories or supply information that Kings lacked.

Secondly, Newman was fully committed to the historical critical method and stood well within the mainstream of the science, as it had developed in Germany. Moreover, he advocated the historical method as an essential tool in alleviating the ignorance of the Old Testament in the English universities. He used the method more rigorously than Milman did, but he did not arrive at the radical conclusions with regard to Chronicles that de Wette and Gramberg reached. This may indicate that Newman held a more moderate view of Chronicles and employed the historical critical method less rigorously, or it may only mean that Newman had no access to the detailed studies of the Germans. At any rate, Newman was not a biblical scholar either by training or profession.

Finally, if Newman did indeed work without having access to the views of de Wette, Gramberg, Movers, and the other Germans, he accomplished a remarkable feat. He produced a history far more consistent with the principles of historical criticism than Milman or others before him in England.

2) Davidson

Another major figure in English biblical studies who published his views of Chronicles was Samuel Davidson (1806-1898), who was outstanding among nineteenth century British Old Testament scholars because of his pioneering role in the introduction of Old Testament critical studies in England. He had an extensive knowledge of German Old Testament research at a time when it was largely unknown among his colleagues. After the publication of his Old Testament introductory volume *The Text of the Old Testament* in 1856, Davidson was accused of denying the plenary inspiration of Scripture and of holding "unsound" views. Since his rebuttal to the charges was rejected in 1857, Davidson resigned his position at the Lancashire Independent College, Manchester.[385]

Davidson believed that Chronicles was originally part of a larger work that included Ezra and Nehemiah and should be dated ca. 330 B. C. E. because of the reference to Jaddua in Neh 12:11. Moreover, he believed that the work was composed by an unknown levite, who used genealogical, topographical, and statistical lists, as well as "The Book of the Kings of Judah and Israel," which was a large historical

---

[385]Ronald Bayne, "Davidson, Samuel," *DNB Supplement* 2 (1901) 115-16; "Davidson, Samuel," *Enc Brit* 7 (11th ed.; 1910) 864; see, also, the work edited by Davidson's daughter, *The Autobiography and Diary of Samuel Davidson* (Edinburgh: Clark, 1899); Rogerson, *Criticism*, 197-208.

work that treated both kingdoms. Davidson denied that the author of Chronicles used Samuel-Kings in his composition, since there are so many differences between the parallel histories. In these introductory matters Davidson is in substantial agreement with Keil.[386]

When he addressed the topic of the Chronicler's credibility as a historical source, Davidson took a position near—but not identical with—that of Keil.

> On the whole, we believe that the Chronicles are inferior to the books of Samuel and Kings in regard to historical details. Hence, when the accounts clash with one another, the latter are commonly preferable. But this fact does not take away their value, which is inestimable for the Hebrew history. The result of a former comparison between the parallel accounts is highly favourable to the general credibility of the Chronicles; if doctrinal prejudices be suppressed on the part of the reader. ... The historical character of the books, in the historical accounts which are peculiar to them, is equally credible and true.[387]

While he believed that Chronicles was generally reliable and based on adequate historical sources, Davidson acknowledged that some of the Chronicler's sources were more accurate than others (2 Chronicles 29-31 and 34, for example, were based on less reliable sources), and sometimes one finds in Chronicles instances of exaggeration, vagueness (e.g., cf. 1 Chr 21:25 with 2 Sm 24:24), and projection of later practices into earlier periods (e.g., 1 Chronicles 16 attributes to David a psalm, which had been composed of bits and pieces of various later psalms).[388] However, Davidson did not agree with de Wette and Gramberg, whom he termed "rationalists" and charged with failing to understand the purposes of the Chronicler.[389] He maintained that Movers, Hävernick, and Keil had adequately responded to de Wette and the other early challengers of Chronicles' accuracy.[390]

Davidson's view of the historical reliability of Chronicles is a moderate one and has many similarities with that of Keil. He detects historical errors in Chronicles, but he denies that the Chronicler set out to deliberately falsify the historical record. It appears, therefore, that Davidson's views on Chronicles were near those of Stanley and other moderate critics.

---

[386]Samuel Davidson, , *The Text of the Old Testament Considered* (2d ed.; London: Longman, Brown, Green, Longmans & Roberts, 1859) 680-83. Davidson also wrote about Keil, "We could only wish that the critic had not carried his apologetic tone and attempt to an unwarranted extent, nor resorted to arbitrary expedients. For it cannot be denied that real contradictions exist between the Chronicles and the earlier books in a variety of passages." *Ibid.*, 686.

[387]*Ibid.*, 686-87.

[388]*Ibid.*, 685.

[389]*Ibid.*, 684-85.

[390]*Ibid.*, 687.

3) Stanley

The second major history of Israel that emerged from England during this period was by Arthur Penrhyn Stanley (1815-1881). He had studied at Rugby under Thomas Arnold and later went to Oxford. He is best remembered as professor of church history at Oxford and as Dean of Westminster. Throughout his career Stanley was deeply involved in theological controversy in England. He was an advocate of liberal views and religious tolerance. Since he allied himself with neither the High Church party nor with the evangelicals, he aroused the anger and suspicions of both. He was regarded by many of his contemporaries as the greatest liberal English theologian of his time.[391]

Stanley's *Lectures on the History of the Jewish Church* was published in three volumes in 1863, 1865, and 1876. The work originated in his Oxford lectures and treats the period from the Jewish patriarchs to John the Baptist. The *Lectures* had been preceded and informed by the author's two earlier trips to Egypt and Palestine (1852/53 and 1862). He had used Robinson's *Biblical Researches in Palestine* for his travels there.

> (I read them) now riding on the back of a camel in the desert, now travelling on horseback through the hills of Palestine, now under the shadow of my tent, when I came in weary from the day's journey. They are among the very few books of modern literature of which I may truly say that I have read every word.[392]

Stanley did not presume to be an Old Testament scholar. On the contrary, he was careful and generous to point out that the primary sources for his history had been Ewald, Milman, Pusey, and Smith's *Dictionary of the Bible*.[393] To some extent, the statement that Stanley "popularized most of Ewald's work" is correct.[394] His aim was not that of submitting original and creative reconstructions of Israelite history; rather, he aimed at dispelling the haze that clouded the view of early Jewish history.

> Till within the present century, the characters and institutions of those two great countries (Greece and Rome) were so veiled from view in the conventional haze with which the enchantment of distance had invested them, that when the more graphic and critical historians of our time broke through this reserve, a kind of shock was felt through all the educated classes of the country. The same change was in a still higher de-

---

[391]G. Granville Bradley, "Stanley, Arthur Penrhyn," *Enc Brit* 22 (1889) 451-53; R. E. Prothero, "Stanley, Arthur Penrhyn," *DNB* 54 (1898) 46-48.

[392]R. E. Prothero and G. G. Bradley, *The Life and Correspondence of Arthur Penrhyn Stanley* (2 vols; 3d ed.; London: John Murray, 1894) 1.450.

[393]A. P. Stanley, *Lectures on the History of the Jewish Church* (3 vols.; new ed.; New York: Charles Scribner's Sons, 1892) 2.15.

gree needed with regard to the history of the Jews. Its sacred character had deepened the difficulty already occasioned by its extreme antiquity.[395]

Later he wrote that he would have attained his goal if he could "persuade anyone to look on the History of the Jewish Church as it really is."[396] Stanley's goal in this regard was that of other nineteenth century historians, who aimed at portraying the events of the past as they really happened and so to end the popular conception of Israelite history as somehow so holy that it defied description in ordinary historical terms.[397] As he approached the task of treating Israel's history, though, Stanley attempted to avoid the errors that he had detected in other English writers, whose researches had created debate and confusion in the church. His main criticism of Colenso had been

> But..., most of all, what I thought I had urged again and again, both in conversation and letters, is, that I regard the whole plan of your book as a mistake. ... To fix the public attention on the mere defects of structure and detail is to my mind to lead off the public mind on a false scent and to a false issue.[398]

> (What is beneficial in your publications is not) at all commensurate with the amount of alarm and misapprehension which they produce.[399]

Therefore, Stanley claimed for himself a more edifying task.

> My object for twenty years, and my object in my forthcoming book, is to draw forth the inestimable treasures of the Old Testament, both historically, geographically, morally, and spiritually.[400]

Stanley regarded Chronicles and Ezra-Nehemiah as a single work, which dated from the Greek period. While its author remains unknown, its priestly interest and nature are evident.[401] Even though it dates from long after the Books of Kings, its historical trustworthiness is not to be doubted. Its frequent citations of sources—like those in Samuel-Kings—"furnish a guarantee for the general truthfulness of the narrative."[402] The last statement hints at two aspects of Stanley's

---

[394] Carpenter, *Nineteenth Century*, 127-28.

[395]Stanley, *History* (1891), 1.20.

[396]*Ibid.*, 1.26.

[397]Carpenter, *Nineteenth Century*, 127-28.

[398]Prothero and Bradley, *Life*, 2.103-4.

[399]*Ibid.*, 2.104.

[400]*Ibid.*, 2.104-5.

[401]Stanley, *Lectures on the History of the Jewish Church* (3 vols.; New York: Scribner, Armstrong, 1877) 3.273.

[402]Stanley, *History*, 2.16.

view of Chronicles: (1) he believes that Chronicles is a source for reliable historical information about the Israelite monarchy, and (2) he believes that the Chronicler is generally—but not completely—reliable. The following examples illustrate Stanley's handling of Chronicles in his historical reconstruction.

Stanley is reluctant to choose Samuel-Kings over Chronicles (or vice versa) when the two contradict one another. For example, while 2 Kg 12:13 declares that King Joash's collection was not used for temple vessels, 2 Chr 24:12-14 says that it was. Stanley designates this a "contradiction," but that is all he says about it. He makes no attempt to argue for one account over the other.[403] This is his usual method of treating conflicts between these two sources, and it is consistent with his statement in the preface to the second volume of the history.

> Others again, especially where we have the advantage of comparing the parallel narratives of the Books of Kings and of Chronicles, exhibit diversities which cannot be surmounted, except by an arbitrary process of excision, which we are hardly justified in adopting and which would obliterate the value of the separate records.[404]

This means, of course, that Stanley has no reservations about accepting information that is unique to Chronicles, such as the Chronicler's accounts of Rehoboam's fortresses,[405] Zerah's attack on Asa,[406] and Jehoshaphat's victory over the alliance of Moab, Ammon, and Mt. Seir.[407] It is evident, however, that Stanley is uncomfortable with the numerous speeches by prophets, kings, and others in Chronicles, since he usually chooses to ignore them in his accounts.[408] He seems equally uncomfortable with miracles, and so usually chooses to refer to them in ways that allow the reader complete freedom to accept or reject them as true historical occurrences. His treatment of Jehoshaphat's victory over the Moabite alliance is instructive.

> The whole scene of the wild confusion of those vast multitudes in the solitude of the desert hills, their tumultuous flight, as though before a stroke of that Divine judgment of which the name of the victorious king was a pledge....[409]

403*Ibid.*, 2.344.
404*Ibid.*, 2.16.
405*Ibid.*, 2.329.
406*Ibid.*, 2.331.
407*Ibid.*, 2.333-34.
408*Ibid.*, 2.331, 333.
409*Ibid.*, 2.333.

Stanley treats the crossing of the Red Sea and the fall of Jericho similarly. In the case of the latter, there is the suggestion that volcanic activity caused the city walls to fall.[410]

On the positive side, Stanley's history should be credited with influencing the understanding of Old Testament history in England. This was due, in part, to the author's own fame. In addition, Stanley's descriptive abilities were considerable, and this, no doubt, aided the success of his history. *History of the Jewish Church* was also important for the development in England of research into Israel's history, because it served to spread the views of Ewald and German criticism. At the time, there was a great deal of distrust on the part of the English toward German biblical scholarship. Stanley's use of the results of German research could not help but counter the English distrust.

On the negative side, it must be noted that Stanley's history was not original or creative in its treatment of the details of Israel's history. Furthermore, the author made no real advance in his use of the historical critical method. The volume stands generally in line with Milman's work, deviating from it in Stanley's partial acceptance of Ewald's conclusions, although neither Milman nor Stanley followed Ewald completely.[411] Stanley believes that the Chronicler's account is based on ancient sources and that Chronicles has as much claim to the scholar's confidence as Samuel-Kings. While Stanley recognizes the priestly interest of the Chronicler, he makes no effort to use this interest to explain the Chronicler's specific contributions. Evidently, he does not believe that the Chronicler's theology distorted his historical reports.

4) Summary of Chronicles in English Scholarship after Ewald

The middle of the nineteenth century was a time when German Old Testament studies began to exert more and more influence on British scholars. Francis Newman, Samuel Davidson, and A. P. Stanley were all acquainted with advances in German critical studies. The latter two were more moderate than the first-named in their views of Chronicles as a historical source. All three recognized the presence of exaggerations and inaccuracies in Chronicles, but

---

[410]*Ibid.*, 1.208-9.

[411]In the preface to the third volume of his history (p. x), Stanley recollects his first meeting with Ewald. "It is now more than thirty years ago since I, with a dear friend, sought him out, and introduced ourselves to him as young Oxford students, in an inn at Dresden; and it is impossible to forget the effect produced upon us by finding the keen interest which this secluded scholar, as we had supposed, took in the moral and social condition of our country; the noble enthusiasm with which this dangerous heretic, as he was regarded in England, grasped the small Greek Testament which he had in his hand as we entered, and said: "In this little book is contained all the wisdom of the world.""

Newman went beyond this to claim that the Chronicler invented speeches and historical narratives in order to advance his theological aims. As a whole, though, Ewald's history with its moderate criticism and comforting tone received a warm acceptance among English critics and exerted a profound influence on their histories of Israel.

c. Jewish Scholarship

Jews in Germany had been struggling for emancipation and full German citizenship since before the nineteenth century. While some headway had been made, most Jews were not satisfied, and there arose a group of Jewish intellectuals who believed that emancipation could only be won by the acculturation of Jews to European ways. This required that Jews sacrifice aspects of life that were offensive to the gentiles around them. The means for acculturation and modernization of Jewish thought and life came to be called *Wissenschaft des Judentums*.[412] One aspect of this movement was the scientific attempt to understand the history and nature of the Jewish people, and as it was practiced by members of the Reform, it served to view aspects of Jewish life, which were different or considered odious to their neighbors, as the product of history and unnecessary for continued Jewish observance. Jost and Geiger were two influential figures in the movement.[413] The resurgent German anti-Semitism of the 1840s gave new impetus to the Reform's struggle to make Judaism palatable to gentile society, but this in turn inflamed the orthodox and more traditional elements of Judaism, who believed that accommodation by the Reform constituted a betrayal of Judaism. It was in the context of this struggle that Graetz, Sachs, Zunz, Frankel, and others used the scientific methods of *Wissenschaft des Judentums* to oppose the Reform.[414] In the section which follows two approaches to the use of Chronicles in the reconstruction of Israel's history by Jewish scholars will be examined: those of Geiger and Graetz. The former viewed Chronicles with a good deal of suspicion, while the latter was more confident in the historical accuracy of the work.

1) Geiger

Abraham Geiger (1810-1874) studied at Heidelberg and Bonn and was a leader in the Jewish Reform and the *Wissenschaft des Judentums*

---

[412]Ismar Schorsch further points out three aspects of the *Wissenschaft des Judentums* movement: (1) the critical study of the Jewish past—even the Hebrew Bible, (2) the secularization of the Jewish sacred history (viz., to rewrite it in terms of the naturalistic idiom), and (3) a concept of history deriving from German idealism. *H. Graetz: The Structure of Jewish History and Other Essays* (New York: The Jewish Theological Seminary of America, 1975) 2-9.

[413]*Ibid.*, 1-3, 8-9, 18.

[414]*Ibid.*, 19-21, 30-31.

movement.[415] He favored the social and political assimilation of Jews to their European culture and believed that Judaism should be only a religious community. In a letter to J. Derenbourg in 1836, Geiger revealed his private aim of abolishing every Jewish institution in its present form and erecting a new edifice on the ruins of the old. His research into the history of Judaism had as one of its goals the advancement of these religious reforms and civic emancipation.[416]

Geiger's chief work was his *Urschrift und Übersetzungen der Bible in ihrer Abhängigkeit von der Innern Entwicklung des Judentums,* which first appeared in 1857 and in a second edition in 1928. The work aimed at correlating the history of biblical translations with the history of Jewish sects (especially those of the Pharisees and Saducees).[417] The work has three parts: (1) history of the Bible from the return from exile to the time of the Maccabees (ca. 160 B. C. E.), (2) history of the Bible from the Maccabees to the time of Hadrian, and (3) the origins and reasons for the divergent textual recensions.

In the first section Geiger deals with Chronicles as part of his discussion of the Hagiographa (pp. 38-71). He maintains that while the writings in the third division of the Hebrew canon were composed after the Babylonian exile and so are to be assigned late dates, this does not mean that all the materials, which made up these compositions, are also to be dated after the exile. Some of these books are undoubtedly collections of earlier materials.[418] Since the writings are frequently without many references to the times of their compositions, the scholar can often only "put himself in the soul of the people" and so use his intuition and sympathy with their struggles to arrive at their date of writing.[419]

Geiger takes the Jewish struggle with the problem of marriages with the Ammonites and Moabites and follows it through the books of Ezra, Nehemiah, and Chronicles. In the process he interprets the Chronicler's treatments of Solomon, Jehoshaphat, and Joash as reflections of this issue in the Chronicler's own day. Israel's problems with Moab and Ammon during the time of the conquest are related by 2 Chronicles 20 to the attack of the Moabite coalition on Jehoshaphat, an event that is not mentioned in 2 Kings.[420] While 1 Kings tells about Solomon's many foreign wives, the Chronicler

[415]Jacob S. Levinger, "Geiger, Abraham," *Enc Jud* 7 (1971) 357-58; Meyer, *Ideas of Jewish History,* 217; Max Wiener, *Abraham Geiger and Liberal Judaism: The Challenge of the Nineteenth Century* (Philadelphia: Jewish Publication Society of America, 1962).

[416]Levinger, "Geiger," 358.

[417]*Ibid.,* 359.

[418]Geiger, *Urschrift und Übersetzungen der Bibel* (2d ed.; Frankfurt: Madda, 1928) 40-41.

[419]*Ibid.,* 41-42.

[420]*Ibid.,* 46-47.

mentions his marriage to Pharaoh's daughter (with a significant change) but omits direct references to his other foreign (including Moabite and Ammonite) wives. The Chronicler does, however, note in 2 Chr 12:13 that Rehoboam's mother was an Ammonitess and so indicates Solomon's marriage to a woman from Ammon. The Chronicler does this, though, only in the verse before his comment that Rehoboam "did evil," and so he connects Rehoboam's foreign mother with his evil reign.[421]

While the author of 2 Kings only gives the names of Joash's two assassins and the names of a parent for each of them (2 Kg 12:21), Geiger points out that the Chronicler has added that the mother of one was a Moabitess and the other an Ammonitess (2 Chr 24:26), and he concludes that for the Chronicler, "Only sons of such mothers could execute such a deed!"[422]

Geiger was clearly devoted to the critical investigation of the Hebrew Bible, and one might even add that his aims at social and political reforms in Judaism required it. His treatment of Chronicles proceeds from this critical perspective, and his efforts at linking the Chronicler's reports about ancient Israel to the circumstances of the post-exilic community set Geiger himself squarely in the critical tradition. He appears to be more willing than Ewald to discount certain details of Chronicles' account and attribute their origin to the Chronicler's desire to address the circumstances of his own day. However, Geiger is not as rigorous as de Wette in his application of the historical method to the sources for Israel's history, nor was he as pessimistic as de Wette in his view of the historian's ability to reconstruct history from partially defective documents. Geiger apparently believed that the historian could sift out useful historical reports about the pre-exilic period from the Chronicler's later and often biased accounts.

2) Graetz

The most influential history of Israel that was written by a Jewish scholar was that by Heinrich Graetz (1817-1891). He was tutored for three years by S. R. Hirsch at Oldenburg, attended the University of Breslau, and finally received his doctorate at Jena for the dissertation "Gnosticismus und Judentums" (1845). He spent most of his teaching career at the new Jewish seminary in Breslau.[423]

Many in the Reform viewed Jewish history teleologically and believed that Judaism had been gradually evolving into a higher form of religion. This meant that some movements in the history of

---

[421]*Ibid.*, 47-48.

[422]*Ibid.*, 49.

[423] Samuel Ettinger, "Graetz, Heinrich," *Enc Jud* 7 (1972) 845-46; Meyer, *Ideas of Jewish History*, 217.

Judaism could be disregarded as irrelevant to the present, higher form of the religion, and some Jewish religious practices could also be discarded as useless baggage from the past. Graetz, however, used the analogy of a plant to set forth his view of Jewish history. Just as the entire development of the plant was present in the seed, so also the various manifestations of Judaism in history were present from the beginning. This meant that each sect or movement in Judaism was important as an expression of the essence of Judaism, and that Jewish history was the story of the growth, flowering, and withering—repeated over and over again—of Judaism.[424]

Moreover, Graetz believed that the Jewish nation had a divine purpose to fulfil. God's will for the Jews was that they be holy and that their holiness be an example for the gentiles around them.[425] This was their mission. Graetz believed that the Jewish people were not capable of comprehending or fulfilling this expectation of God's in their infancy.[426] On the contrary, it was only through their struggles in history and development as a people that they were able to understand and then fulfil what God desired from them. The prophets and psalmists were the first to reveal God's aim for his people and so enable them to fulfil it.[427] The history of the Jews can be divided into three segments, through which one can trace the developing consciousness of the people. First, there is the period from Joshua to the Babylonian exile, in which the political-social dimension of Judaism predominated. Secondly, there was the time from the exile to the fall

---

[424]Heinrich Graetz, "The Structure of Jewish History" in Schorsch's *H. Graetz*, 65, 124; cf. also 39, 44-45. Meyer (*Ideas of Jewish History*, 218) traces Graetz's idea of Jewish history as successive cycles of growth, blooming, and decaying to Nahman Krochmal.

[425]"The highest purpose of Judaism is, therefore, the teaching of the philosophic truths about God, such as the necessity of His existence, His unity, omniscience, and omnipotence, His absolute will, His eternity, and then, the scrupulous discarding of all views about God which are inappropriate to the concept of God." Graetz, "Structure," 117. "The task of the nation of Israel was directed toward working on itself...in one word: to become holy." Graetz, "Introduction to Volume One of the *History of the Jews*" in Schorsch's *Graetz*, 176. "But this nation did not only possess that teaching, it was also fully conscious that it survives only for its sake, that the nation itself is merely a means and instrument for the teaching, that its significance derives solely from its vocation, to disseminate that teaching as a sacred truth, ...by the example of its own practice...." *Ibid.*, 186. Cf. Schorsch, *Graetz*, 55-56.

[426]"However, this religion or teaching of holiness was too lofty to be grasped by the entire people in its youth. The ideal...remained for the longest time an enigma. The prophets had first to unravel the enigma for the people. (Afterwards)...the people became the guardian of the teaching...and built a temple for it in its heart, ... The people itself had achieved a full understanding of its character and vocation." Graetz, "Introduction," 185.

[427]*Ibid.*, 188.

of Jerusalem in 70 C. E., in which the religious aspect of Judaism was dominant. Finally, from 70 C. E. to the present the theoretical-philosophic dimension of Judaism has been strongest.[428] The influence of German Idealism on Graetz is evident in the fact that Graetz saw the crucial continuum in Jewish history to be the developing consciousness of the Jewish people.[429] While the three-fold division of Jewish history in Graetz's plan was not unusual, the significance that he assigned to the third period was novel.[430]

Graetz's *Geschichte der Juden* was published in eleven volumes from 1853 to 1876. The first two volumes, which dealt with Jewish history from its beginning until the Hasmonean revolt, were the last to be published, since the author was unwilling to write them until he could visit Palestine for himself.[431] The work underwent many editions and translations into foreign languages. It was abridged and published from 1887 to 1889 as *Volkstümliche Geschichte der Juden*. This became one of the most widely read Jewish books in Germany. In 1891 an English translation in five volumes appeared. It was a form of the eleven volume work, compacted by the omission of footnotes and excursuses. While the original German edition took Jewish history down to 1848, the English translation extended to 1870.[432]

Graetz offers no comprehensive account of Chronicles as a historical source, but his frequent use of the Chronicler's history indicates that he regarded it as a reliable source for historical information about the pre-exilic period. While Graetz does not seem to assume that Chronicles is inferior to Samuel-Kings, nevertheless, he relies on the latter as his *Grundlage* for the monarchical period and uses Chronicles for supplementary information. When the two writings conflict, Graetz sometimes chooses to pass over the problem without even noting it.[433] On other occasions, he simply notes the contradiction in a footnote and chooses one account over the other.[434] In the

---

[428]Graetz, "Structure," 72-74, 123-24.

[429]*Ibid.*, 123.

[430]Schorsch, *Graetz*, 41-43.

[431]The land of Palestine was of particular significance to Graetz: "The concrete expression for these abstractions is the revealed Law—the Torah—and the Holy Land. The attention of the people is directed to these two possessions. The Law is the soul, the Holy Land the body of this unique political organism. Graetz, "Structure," 71.

[432]Ettinger, "Graetz," 846-47.

[433]With regard to the Davidic census, Graetz passes over the fact that 2 Samuel 24 says that all the tribes were counted, while 2 Chronicles 21 says that Levi and Benjamin were omitted from the count. Graetz, *Geschichte der Israeliten* in *Geschichte der Juden* (Leipzig: Oskar Leiner, 1874) 1.269-73.

[434]With regard to the fact that 2 Samuel 24 says that David's census obtained a total of 1,300,000 and the Chronicler offers a figure of 1,570,000, Graetz merely

case of information that is unique to Chronicles, Graetz usually accepts it,[435] but occasionally he will reject the Chronicler's contribution.[436]

His reasons for these different ways of handling materials in Chronicles are often unclear. For example, Graetz accepts the Chronicler's report about Zerah leading an Egyptian army against Asa because of "the precise fixing of the localities" in the Chronicler's account, but he rejects the Chronicler's story about a Moabite coalition attacking Jehoshaphat, even though the Chronicler supplies here, as well, information regarding the coalition's geographical location (2 Chr 20:2, 16, 20, 24, 26).[437]

As a member of the *Wissenschaft des Judentums* movement, Graetz operates as a critical historian. He does not simply repeat the stories and historical narratives of the Bible. He is concerned about cause and effect relationships and is willing to rearrange the sequence of events in the biblical history and draw connections between them in order to arrive at a reasonable account of Israel's past. Moreover, Graetz sometimes denies the historicity of events described in the Bible and frequently rationalizes the miracles reported by his sources. On the other hand, it seems that Graetz occasionally becomes enamored with romantic notions of the past and does not adequately establish his historical reconstructions in the available evidence. Thompson's criticisms of Graetz in this regard are not uncommon.

> But his *History of the Jews* is full of prejudice, and glaring inaccuracies of scholarship. He was ignorant of the immense progress made in biblical studies of either the Old or the New Testament. What can be thought of a writer with any pretensions to history who began his work with the words: It was on a sunny spring day that some pastoral tribes passed across the Jordan? Or a writer on ancient Hebrew history who omits any mention of the works of Jost, Bleek, Graf, Nöldeke, Schrader, Reusch, Delitzsch, Kuenen, Wellhausen, and Stade? Graetz' wise and good men

---

notes that the two differ and without further explanation incorporates the figure from 2 Samuel into his text. Graetz, *Geschichte*, 1.271.

[435]Graetz accepts the Chronicler's account of the Egyptian attack under Zerah against Judah (*Geschichte*, 2.18), the Chronicler's account of Uzziah's leprosy deriving from his cultic boldness (*Geschichte*, 2.102), and the story of Manasseh's captivity in 2 Chronicles 33 (*Geschichte* 2.283-84).

[436]Graetz rejects the Chronicler's stories about Jehoshaphat's appointment of judges and an attack against Jehoshaphat's Judah by a coalition of Moabites and others (*Geschichte*, 2.38). Moreover, he rejects the Chronicler's claims that Abijah took Bethel from Israel and that Abijah had twenty-two sons and sixteen daughters (*Geschichte*, 2.16-17).

[437]*Ibid.*, 2.18, 38.

in history are almost constantly Jews, his weak and foolish men as constantly Christians.[438]

Hirsch, to whom Graetz dedicated an earlier work on Gnosticism, said of him: "What does Graetz know? What can he know?" Geiger condemned him as ignorant of philology, comparative religion, the anthropology of the ancient peoples of the Orient, and even of history.[439]

In fairness to Graetz, however, it should be noted that the last two Jewish scholars (Hirsch and Geiger), whom Thompson cites to support his own evaluation of Graetz, were bitter enemies of Graetz and could hardly be regarded as unbiased critics of the latter's work.[440] Moreover, the recent appraisal of Graetz by R. E. Clements aims at showing the former as a man of his time but also a scholar who made great contributions to advancement in the study of Jewish history.

...it is also clear in retrospect that all the great figures who laid the foundations of biblical historiography in the nineteenth century were men of their time. Their particular aims and methods and the inevitable limitations that go with these must all now be seen in the particular context of culture and scholarship that found its major focus in the Historicist movement in Germany. ... What is clear, however, is that the work of Heinrich Graetz appears to have been quite peculiarly and unfairly ignored by Christian scholars, and not taken into account in the effort to attain some balanced assessment of the gains and losses of the historical movement in the study of the biblical history.[441]

As far as the method of Graetz' treatment of Chronicles is concerned, one can see little that is new. While Graetz evidently regards the books as sources for reliable historical information about the preexilic period, he is not bound to support the historicity of all that the Chronicler reports. In this respect, Graetz' handling of Chronicles is similar to Ewald's and represents a compromise between the views of de Wette and Keil. It is unfortunate that Graetz did not include in his history a programmatic statement on the usefulness of Chronicles as a historical witness or address the positions of those who produced the major studies on Chronicles up to his day (e.g., de Wette and Movers).

3) Summary of Chronicles in Jewish Scholarship after Ewald

Both Geiger and Graetz refused to accept everything that was found in Chronicles. They assumed positions between the extremes

---

[438]Thompson, *History*, 587-88.

[439]*Ibid.*

[440]Schorsch, *Graetz*, 34.

[441]R. E. Clements, "Heinrich Graetz as Biblical Historian and Religious Apologist," in *Interpreting the Hebrew Bible*, J. A. Emerton and Stefan C. Reif, eds. (Cambridge: University Press, 1982) 53.

of de Wette and Keil. They both believed that there were inaccuracies and even some fabrications in the Chronicler's history. However, Geiger tended to a more rigorous application of the critical method to the books than Graetz, and he operated with a greater awareness of the ways that the Chronicler's own circumstances may have led him to alter information from his sources and even to compose new reports. It is not evident that Ewald's history had a great impact on either of these two Jewish scholars.

d. Summary of Chronicles in Scholarship after Ewald

In spite of de Wette's vigorous challenge to the historical reliability of Chronicles, none of the histories of Israel in the first three-quarters of the nineteenth century followed de Wette's view that Chronicles was worthless for the historical reconstruction of the pre-exilic period. The question for these historians was not, "Is Chronicles ever useful?" but "In which of its accounts and to what extent is Chronicles a trustworthy historical source?"

Most of the historians in this period rejected not only de Wette's conclusions, but also those of Keil and chose the *via media*. Many of them believed that Chronicles was composed at a relatively late date—in the Persian if not the Greek period—and that the author was relatively biased in favor of the (levitical) temple personnel. It was also maintained, however, that the author had adequate sources of information available for his composition and that he did not set out to falsify history deliberately. Therefore, it was concluded that the historian should reject the obvious exaggerations and embellishments in Chronicles, and when Chronicles contradicted Samuel-Kings, the preference should usually be given to the latter.

To this extent, therefore, the work of those who defended Chronicles against the challenges of de Wette, Gesenius, and Gramberg may be regarded as partially successful, but certainly not a complete victory, since the extreme positions of Dahler and Keil did not prevail. Ewald's history represented this compromise between de Wette and Keil, and it remained the dominant position until the next challenge to Chronicles, which was issued with such force by Graf, Wellhausen, and others who, in arguing for a late dating of P, were to undercut the foundations upon which the acceptance of the historical value of Chronicles had rested.

CHAPTER III

THE SECOND CHALLENGE TO THE CREDIBILITY OF CHRONICLES AND ITS CONSEQUENCES FOR THE RECONSTRUCTION OF ISRAELITE HISTORY

A. INTRODUCTION

The second challenge to the credibility of Chronicles as a historical source for the pre-exilic period came with the proposal that the
Priestly Code be assigned an exilic or post-exilic date. Such a proposal required that P have been the latest of the pentateuchal sources
rather than among the first. The discussion in this chapter is divided
into two parts: (1) the proposal of a late P by scholars in the 1830s and
the representation of the proposal in the 1860s and 1870s, and (2) the
consequences that the debate over a late P had for the utilization of
Chronicles in the reconstruction of Israel's pre-exilic history.

B. REDATING THE PRIESTLY DOCUMENT

1. INTRODUCTION

The second third of the nineteenth century saw a new development in the investigation of the Priestly Code. In the 1830s, it was
proposed in classes by Reuss and in print by Vatke that this segment
of the Pentateuch (or at least parts of it) should be viewed as the latest pentateuchal source, rather than the earliest. Their ideas were
largely ignored until Graf, a pupil of Reuss, presented them again in
1866.

Within about a dozen years the works of Kuenen, Colenso, and
Wellhausen followed, offering their support to the substance of
Graf's theory. This development in pentateuchal studies had monumental consequences for the study of Chronicles: the assignment of
a late date to P and the challenge to P's credibility led to a reevalua-
tion of Chronicles and a challenge to its credibility, as well, because
the two works shared ideas and presented the pre-exilic cult in simi-

lar ways.[1] The works of Reuss and Vatke will be treated first as "Early Developments" and then those of Graf, Kuenen, Colenso, and Wellhausen as "Later Developments."

2. EARLY DEVELOPMENTS

a. Introduction

De Wette and other scholars in the first third of the nineteenth century had believed that the Priestly Code was composed before Deuteronomy, but the lectures of Reuss and the works of Vatke and George signaled a change.[2] The latter three scholars came to believe that the Priestly Document (or at least material that was eventually assigned to P) should be dated after Deuteronomy and so represented the end, rather than the beginning or middle, of the development of the Pentateuch. This conclusion would ultimately be of great significance for the study of Chronicles, because the portrayal of the cult in P and in Chronicles was so similar that when the former's historical reliability was challenged, that of the latter was also called into question. In the remainder of this section we will examine the views of Reuss and Vatke about the Priestly Code and the consequences of their views for the question of Chronicles' credibility.

b. Reuss

1) General

The first scholar to suggest that P was the latest of the pentateuchal sources was Eduard Reuss (1804-1891), a native of Strassburg.

---

[1]For example, 2 Kg 15:5 relates that King Uzziah was a leper, but 2 Chr 26:16-21 attributes his leprosy to his sin and says that God smote him with leprosy for offering incense in the temple. Such a story reflects the conviction of the Priestly Code (Ex 30:1-10; Num 16:40; 18:1-7) that only the descendants of Aaron were allowed to perform the sacred act of offering incense. Note also the substitution of levites for priests in 2 Chr 5:4 (cf. 2 Kg 8:3) in accordance with the legislation of P in Num 3:31 and 4:15.

[2]Johann Friedrich Leopold George (1811-1873) wrote *Die älteren Jüdischen Feste mit einer Kritik der Gesetzgebung des Pentateuch* (Berlin: E. H. Schroeder, 1835), and in it dealt with the Pentateuch in terms of the fragmentary hypothesis. He concluded that Leviticus, Numbers, and part of Exodus should be dated in the post-exilic period. This meant that this material, which generally was considered to constitute the Priestly Code, was composed after Genesis, the rest of Exodus, and Deuteronomy. George's conclusions grew out of his conviction that the cult in Leviticus, Numbers, and part of Exodus was more highly developed or complex than that in Deuteronomy.

He received his education at Strassburg, Göttingen, Halle, and Paris, and finally, he returned to Strassburg from Paris as lecturer in 1829.[3]

Reuss' greatest contribution to Old Testament studies is usually seen in his suggestion to Graf that P was later than the other pentateuchal sources.[4] He came to this conclusion as early as 1833, and wrote later, "In more than one point my system was indeed originally...a product of intuition."[5] He explained further that his aim had been to account for the greatest miracle in the Old Testament: the beginning of the religious education of Israel with the completed levitical arrangement of the cult, and the ignorance of it that was shown by Israel's greatest prophets (Samuel and Elijah).[6] Reuss said that he directed his attention to the legal data of the Old Testament

> and hoped to find in the study of this the Ariadnic thread, which would lead out of the labyrinth of the rubbish of hypotheses about the origin, both of the Mosaic and of the rest of the books in the Old Testament, to the daylight of an also psychologically comprehensible process of development of the Israelite people.[7]

When he arrived at a solution to the problem of Israel's religious development in 1833, he proposed twelve theses.

> (1) The historical element of the Pentateuch can and should be examined apart from and not be confused with the legal element.

> (2) Both have been able to exist without written edition. The mention, among ancient writers, of certain patriarchal or Mosaic traditions does not prove the existence of the Pentateuch, and a nation can have a customary law without a written code.

> (3) The national traditions of the Israelites remain earlier than the laws of the Pentateuch and the edition of the former is after that of the latter.

> (4) The historian's principal interest should carry to the date of the laws, because on this terrain there is a greater chance of arriving at certain results. It is therefore necessary to proceed to the interrogation of the witnesses.

> (5) The history reported in the books of the Judges and Samuel, and even in that part included in the books of Kings, is in contradiction with the laws spoken by Moses; therefore, these were unknown in the epoch

---

[3]Cheyne, *Founders*, 175-76; E. Kutsch, "Reuss, Eduard," *RGG* 5 (3d ed.; 1957) 1076; Rudolf Smend, "Reuss, Eduard," *Enc Jud* 14 (1971) 111-12.

[4]"The prophets were older than the law, and the Psalms younger than both." Eduard Reuss, *Die Geschichte der Heiligen Schriften Alten Testaments* (1st ed.; Braunschweig: C. A. Schwetschke & Son, 1881) vii.

[5]*Ibid.*

[6]*Ibid.*, viii.

[7]*Ibid.*

of the writing of these books, so they did not exist in the times which they describe.

(6) The prophets of the eighth and seventh centuries knew nothing of the Mosaic code.

(7) Jeremiah is the first prophet, who knew a written law and his citations relate to Deuteronomy.

(8) Deuteronomy (chapters 4:45-28:69) is the book which the priests pretended to have found in the temple, at the time of King Josiah. This code is the more ancient part of the legislation drawn up in the Pentateuch.

(9) The history of the Israelites, in so far as it is a matter of national development determined by the written laws, is divided into two periods, before and after Josiah.

(10) Ezekiel is before the writing of the ritual code and the laws which have precisely organized the hierarchy.

(11) The book of Joshua is not by any means the more recent part of the entire work.

(12) The editor of the Pentateuch is distinguished clearly from the ancient prophet Moses.[8]

Reuss was not willing, however, to publish his conclusions and to present systematically the evidence for them, because they were so contrary to the dominant scholarly opinion. Instead, he only hinted at his views in his articles in *Ersch und Gruber's Encyklopädie* and presented them in classroom lectures. Two students who heard his ideas about the Priestly Document in the summer semester of 1834 were K. H. Graf and August Kayser, and each later published works that presented Reuss' conclusion about the late date of P: Graf's work was entitled *Die geschichtlichen Bücher des Alten Testaments* (1866) and Kayser's was *Das vorexilische Buch der Urgeschichte Israels* (1874). These publications and those of Kuenen gave Reuss the impetus to publish his conclusions about P.[9] In 1879, therefore, Reuss presented his views for the first time in a systematic way in the introduction to his commentary on Genesis-Joshua, *L'histoire sainte et la loi*. First, he treated the traditional view of the composition of these books, and then he set forth his own position, concluding that P should be dated

---

[8]Eduard Reuss, *L'histoire sainte et la loi* (Paris: Libraire Sandoz et Fischbacher, 1879) 1.23-24.

[9]Reuss, *Geschichte*, viii-ix.

after Deuteronomy.[10] Reuss' second work, *Die Geschichte der Heiligen Schriften*, treated the entire Old Testament by setting the books in chronological order and explaining their respective historical settings.

2) Chronicles

In *Die Geschichte der Heiligen Schriften*[11] Reuss assigned the biblical literature to four periods: the time of heroes (the patriarchs to Saul), the time of prophets (David until the fall of Jerusalem to Babylon), the time of priests (from the Babylonian exile to the Maccabees), and the time of scribes (from the Maccabees until Jerusalem's fall to Rome in 70 C. E.). It was in the third period that Reuss set Chronicles.

Reuss thought that 1, 2 Chronicles was part of a larger work that included Ezra and Nehemiah and that while Ezra did not compose this work, the author was a member of the "levitical cast."[12] The work should be dated in the fourth century, sometime near the beginning of the Greek period.[13] The Chronicler's primary source for his writing was the Midrash (2 Chr 24:27), and the many references to various works that one finds in 1, 2 Chronicles were only citations of various parts of the Midrash.[14] The similarities between 1, 2 Chronicles and Samuel-Kings can be explained by the fact that Samuel-Kings and the Midrash used some of the same sources. Therefore, one should not conclude that the Chronicler copied from Samuel-Kings. Moreover, when the Chronicler composed his work, only the Pentateuch was regarded as canonical and so contradictions between his writing and Samuel-Kings would not have greatly concerned him.[15] Finally, Reuss believed that the Chronicler's history was *"eine kirchliche Chronik von Jerusalem,"*[16] since he also maintained that the political element of the national history faded into the background and that the levitical element took its place in the forefront of matters.[17]

Reuss thought that a great number of the differences between Samuel-Kings and Chronicles were theologically motivated: the Chronicler's additions about David organizing the cultic personnel and gathering the materials for the building of the temple, the moving of the ark to Jerusalem, and the reforms of Asa, Jehoshaphat, Hezekiah, and Josiah. Such additions should be traced to the spirit of

---

[10]Reuss advocated the order of the four pentateuchal sources: E J D P. *L'histoire*, 267-70.

[11]Reuss exhibited a thorough acquaintance with the secondary literature on Chronicles, referring to the works of de Wette, Gramberg, Keil, Movers, and others.

[12]Reuss, *Geschichte* (2d ed.; 1890) 550.

[13]*Ibid.*, 549-51.

[14]*Ibid.*, 547-48.

[15]*Ibid.*

[16]*Ibid.*, 541.

[17]*Ibid.*, 543.

the narrative as a whole, according to Reuss, rather than to sources that the author used.[18] In the Chronicler's own day the Pentateuch was regarded as canonical and as the law that derived from Moses himself. Therefore, since the law was given by Moses, its contents must have been the "unbreakable rule" throughout Israel's history. Consequently, the Chronicler set out to rewrite Israel's history in light of the Pentateuch. Since the Priestly Document reflected the institutions and convictions of the Chronicler's own day, the Chronicler was, in effect, revising Israel's history in light of fourth century beliefs and institutions: "The Chronicler narrated the history precisely as people in his time assumed it."[19] Reuss stopped short of rejecting everything that is found only in Chronicles, however, since he believed that not all of the additions in Chronicles were theologically motivated.[20] "...Exactly what interests us the least," he wrote, "the lists of families and the statistical material, especially also that in the books of Ezra and Nehemiah, probably derives from official documents of the time of the restoration."[21]

3) Summary

Reuss' evaluation of Chronicles as a historical source depended on two things: (1) his conviction that Chronicles was composed only after the Priestly Code had been written and came to prominence in the post-exilic Jewish community, and (2) the large number of contradictions between Samuel-Kings and Chronicles. The latter fact raised questions about Chronicles' reliability as a historical witness, and the former point provided the answer. While Reuss agreed almost entirely with Graf, Kuenen, and Wellhausen in their view of Chronicles, he was apparently unwilling to exclude from consideration in historical reconstruction everything in Chronicles that was not found in Samuel-Kings. Nevertheless, Reuss had serious reservations about the Chronicler's reports of the pre-exilic age, since the author's information was second- or third-hand, at best.[22]

c. Vatke

1) General

A second scholar who proposed the late dating of P in the 1830s was Wilhelm Vatke (1806-1882), who began his university training at Halle in 1824, where he studied oriental languages under Gesenius. Two years later Gesenius sent him to Göttingen to continue his oriental studies under Ewald, admonishing him not to forget the

---

[18]*Ibid.*, 545.
[19]*Ibid.*, 546.
[20]*Ibid.*, 546-48.
[21]*Ibid.*, 544-45.
[22]*Ibid.*, 545.

things that he had learned so thoroughly from de Wette. Later Vatke moved on to the University of Berlin, where he became an ardent disciple of Hegel.[23]

In 1835, Vatke published *Die biblische Theologie*, which was important as the first publication to assign the Priestly Code to the post-exilic period.[24] He had lectured from the manuscript for the book a year earlier, and it was only one year before that that Reuss had set forth similar conclusions about P in his lectures at Strassburg. Reuss' initial reaction to Vatke's book illustrates the reception that it received among many scholars at the time.

> On the appearance of the book, the table of contents, with its Hegelian formulae, of itself terrified me to such an extent that I remained at the time unacquainted with it. A speculative treatment of history I trust no further than I can see. Since then indeed I have seen that theory and formula in this book were really only an addition which might be dispensed with and that my inquiries might have been materially assisted if I had not let myself be deterred by them.[25]

Therefore, because of the heavy Hegelian introduction and the Hegelian terminology that appeared elsewhere in the book, Vatke's work was read by few scholars for nearly a generation. Finally, when Graf published conclusions similar to Vatke's in 1866, the latter's book was rediscovered and met with considerably more interest than formerly. Later, Wellhausen would write that he was indebted to Vatke for "the most and best" of his own work.[26]

In the years following 1849, Vatke's attitude toward Hegel's philosophy began to change, and he came to see less value in it. This change may, in turn, be responsible for the changes in Vatke's views on the Pentateuch. Four years after his death, Vatke's lectures were gathered, edited, and issued as *Historisch-kritische Einleitung in das Alte Testament*. In this volume it was apparent that the author's views about the Pentateuch had undergone significant changes since the publication of *Die biblische Theologie* in 1835. According to his *Einleitung*, Vatke dated the Priestly Code in the last years of

---

[23]In 1830, Vatke graduated as *Privatdocent* in theology, and in 1837, he was promoted to *ausserordentlicher Professor* at Berlin. Heinze, "Vatke, Johann Karl Wilhelm," *ADR* 39 (1895) 508-10; Cheyne, *Founders*, 131-42; Menahem Haran, "Vatke, Wilhelm," *Enc Jud* 16 (1971) 79-80; H. Benecke, *Wilhelm Vatke in seinem Leben und seinen Schriften* (Bonn: Emil Strauss, 1883); M. Brömse, "Studien zur 'Biblischen Theologie' Wilhelm Vatkes," Kiel dissertation, 1973; Rogerson, *Criticism*, 69-78.

[24]This was the same year that J. F. L. George issued his work (*Die älteren Jüdischen Feste*), which also argued for a late date for the levitical laws.

[25]Cited by Otto Pfleiderer, *The Development of Theology in Germany since Kant, and its Progress in Great Britain since 1825* (New York: Macmillan, 1890) 252-53.

[26]Heinze, "Vatke," 508-10; Cheyne, *Founders*, 133-40; Haran, "Vatke," 79-80.

Hezekiah, before both J and D. He assigned Leviticus 17-20, 26 and Num 33:52-56 to a priestly supplementer of the Priestly Code and dated this writer to the time just after the composition of J, perhaps in the middle of the seventh century B. C. E.[27] The conception of Old Testament religion that Vatke presented in his biblical theology contained, first of all, certain historical observations about Israel's past, and secondly, an Hegelian philosophy of history. The latter was undoubtedly derived from the three years that Vatke spent studying under Hegel in Berlin. The former, however, did not proceed from Hegel, but seems to have been built on the conclusions found in de Wette's early critical works.[28] Therefore, Cheyne's observation is probably correct.

> It is true that his insight into the development of the higher religion of Israel was quickened by his Hegelianism, but his conclusions were not philosophical but historical, and could to a large extent have been justified without the help of an abstruse philosophizing.[29]

Vatke believed that Israel's religion should be understood in terms of an Hegelian dialectic between opposing forces and that it was through this conflict that religion gradually moved to higher levels.

> The entire history of Old Testament religion is, so far, a constant battle and victory of thought over what is natural....[30]

In Moses' day the opposition was between the people's nature religion and Moses' law, which was a higher principle and began the ideal process (Israel's religious history).[31] The second major stage in Israel's history involved the prophets and was characterized by a greater moral consciousness. The prophets became the chief agents for the "idea" and opposed the people's idea of Yahweh as a national God with their own concept of him as a universal God.[32] The Babylonian exile did not destroy Judah's spirit but gave a new form and direction to it so that "the ideal principle" found its fulfilment in the exile.[33]

---

[27]Wilhelm Vatke, *Historisch-kritische Einleitung in das Alte Testament* (H. G. S. Preiss, ed.; Bonn: Emil Strauss, 1886) 388-89, 402.

[28]Lothar Perlitt, *Vatke und Wellhausen* (BZAW 94; Berlin: Alfred Töpelmann, 1965) 92.

[29]Cheyne, *Founders*, 137.

[30]Wilhelm Vatke, *Die biblische Theologie* (Berlin: G. Bethge, 1835) 231.

[31]*Ibid.*, 251; Perlitt, *Vatke und Wellhausen*, 119.

[32]Vatke, *Theologie*, 467, 480; Perlitt, *Vatke und Wellhausen*, 119.

[33]Vatke (*Theologie*, 552) held that the earlier opposition between the external cult and the free, prophetic instruction attained after the fall of Jerusalem the form of devotion to the letter of the levitical law and to the free contemplation

2) Chronicles

Vatke's attitude toward Chronicles changed little in the time between 1835 and his death. In his biblical theology he presented 1, 2 Chronicles, Ezra, and Nehemiah as a single work, written by one author in the first half of the third century B. C. E. There is a pronounced levitical bias throughout.[34] Consequently, Vatke dismissed the Chronicler's report of Jehoshaphat sending out levites to teach the people (2 Chr 17:7-9) as a reflection of a post-exilic practice leading to the formation of the synagogue,[35] and he rejected the report of David's regulations regarding priests and levites (1 Chronicles 23-26) as derivations of practices from the "first colony" that returned from Babylonian captivity.[36] The story about priests, levites, and other faithful people fleeing out of Israel into Judah in the days of Jeroboam and Rehoboam (2 Chr 11:13-17)[37] and the Chronicler's account of Jehoshaphat's judicial reforms (2 Chr 19:8-11)[38] were also disallowed by Vatke for use in the historical reconstruction of the pre-exilic period. He concluded, much as de Wette had earlier, that 1, 2 Chronicles was worth little to the student of Israel's pre-exilic period and that the modern apologists, who tried to harmonize Chronicles with the other Old Testament historical books, were doomed to failure.

> ...generally no true picture of the older times lies behind the author's presentation, or behind the oral or written *Sage* from which he worked. These books carry back into the davidic-solomonic (sic) age the later, even post-exilic cult, just as the Pentateuch takes back all of the priestly legislation into the mosaic period; the first operation was based on the correctness of the second and accordingly falls with it.[39]

The latter part of the quotation is instructive. In it Vatke linked what the Pentateuch did (projecting post-exilic practices into the pre-exilic period) with what Chronicles had done. Consequently, the testimony of the Chronicler about the pre-exilic period should be rejected, or at best, used only to reconstruct the events and institutions in the Chronicler's day after the exile.[40]

---

which even spread over particularism. In this way there was achieved lyrical inspiration, and both opposing segments were reconciled to one another. Cf. Perlitt, *Vatke und Wellhausen*, 120-25.

[34]Vatke cites Zunz for this conclusion about the extent of the Chronicler's work. *Theologie*, 553, 560.

[35]*Ibid.*, 561.

[36]*Ibid.*, 568.

[37]*Ibid.*, 399.

[38]*Ibid.*, 414.

[39]*Ibid.*, 290-91.

[40]Vatke explained the connection between Chronicles and the Pentateuch in the following way. "The book (Chronicles) proceeds, therefore, not from a true

In his Old Testament introduction of 1873, Vatke repeated the judgment of Zunz that the Chronicler's work should be dated in the middle of the third century, ca. 260 B. C. E.[41] He further pointed out seven characteristics of Chronicles:

(1) the Chronicler inflated the numbers in his sources, especially those of people and troops (cf. 1 Chr 21:5);

(2) he omitted reports in Samuel-Kings, which would not have edified his readers (e.g., the sins of David and Solomon);

(3) he projected later ideas back into the narratives of an earlier time (e.g., Satan incited David according to 1 Chr 21:1, instead of God having incited the king, as was the case according to 2 Sm 24:1);

(4) the narratives in Chronicles exhibit hatred for Israel but love for Judah (the Chronicler only reported the history of Judah);

(5) in order to edify his readers, the Chronicler instituted a biased pragmatism, by which he showed that good kings met with success, while evil kings were punished;

(6) while he omitted the stories about Elijah and Elisha, he gave extended treatments to priests and Levites and made some of the famous people in Israel's history (e.g., Samuel) into Levites; and

(7) he had a special fondness for the history of the cult and erroneously projected later cultic practices into earlier times (cf. 1 Chr 15:25).[42]

When he addressed the matter of Chronicles' sources, Vatke proposed that there had been three: the canonical books of Samuel and Kings, old tax lists or genealogical registers, and the midrash on the Annals of the Kings of Israel and Judah, the last of which had been the author's main source and had also been used in an unedited form by the author of 1, 2 Kings. The citations of prophetic works in Chronicles only referred to various sections in the midrash. The Chronicler, therefore, cannot be believed when he contradicted the older narratives in the Old Testament for three reasons: (1) the Chronicler did not have access to sources that were more ancient than those of Samuel-Kings; (2) since the author of Chronicles composed his work long after the publication of Samuel-Kings, it was even more difficult for him to understand the pre-exilic period correctly; and (3) the Chronicler was more interested in the edification of his readers than in the accurate portrayal of his people's history.[43]

Vatke's own evaluation of Chronicles as a historical source is evident in his discussion of the history of research into the books. He

---

historical need; rather the levitical author wanted to present the value of the Mosaic law and of the levites in the sense of the Elohim source, as well as other younger institutions, for the purpose of edification...." *Einleitung*, 480.

[41]*Ibid.*, 480-81.

[42]*Ibid.*, 474-78.

[43]*Ibid.*, 478-80.

praised de Wette for overturning the earlier view that 1, 2 Chronicles had proven that the Law of Moses had been observed since the time of David. De Wette had accomplished this, Vatke explained, by completing Vater's criticism of the Pentateuch and showing that Chronicles was from a late date and often supplied false information in the course of pursuing its aim to edify the reader.[44] The clash between Gramberg and Keil over the Chronicler's credibility constituted the next stage in the discussion of the books. Vatke believed that Gramberg—in spite of his intentions to the contrary—had damaged de Wette's position by his "frivolous spitting." On the other hand, Vatke characterized Keil's *Apologetischen Versuch* as a work "entirely according to Hengstenberg." Many saw a resolution to this conflict in the mediating position of Movers, who admitted that the Chronicler pursued the aim of edifying his readers, but nevertheless tried to rescue from criticism as many of the Chronicler's narratives as possible. Finally, Vatke noted that Graf's role in the history of Chronicles research was to oppose Ewald's hypothesis that the Chronicler relied on an ancient source for his material and to set before his readers the proper view of Chronicles.[45]

3) Summary

Vatke stood firmly on the side of de Wette in his conviction that Chronicles was a thoroughly unreliable source for the historical reconstruction of the pre-exilic period. De Wette's *Beiträge* of 1806 with its delineation of Chronicles' theological biases had convinced him of the correctness of this position. An additional factor that eroded the Chronicler's credibility in his eyes concerned the dating of P. Vatke believed that the Priestly Code had arisen long after David and Solomon's day and that it projected later cultic practices and ideas into the past. Since many of these cultic practices and ideas were similar to those in Chronicles, and since the Chronicler also projected them into the past, Vatke concluded that the Chronicler was an unreliable guide to the events of pre-exilic history. Finally, in the matter of sources Vatke did not adhere to the position of de Wette that the Chronicler had only one major source available: Samuel-Kings. Rather, he accepted the arguments of Movers that the Chronicler's primary source was a midrash on the royal annals. He did not, however, draw the same conclusion from this that Movers drew, namely that the Chronicler's narrative could be trusted on the basis of accurate historical information from the midrash. On the contrary, Movers' source theory did not divert Vatke from the

---

[44]Vater had proposed a form of the fragmentary hypothesis to explain the composition of the Pentateuch. De Wette came to hold a similar theory of pentateuchal origins.

[45]*Ibid.*, 481-82.

essentials of de Wette's earlier conclusion that the Chronicler could not be trusted. The positive value that Vatke saw for Chronicles was its usefulness as a witness to the beliefs and practices of the post-exilic period, the time in which its anonymous, levitical author lived.

d. Summary of Early Developments in the Late Dating of P

Reuss and Vatke did not agree completely in their analyses of Chronicles. While Reuss did not believe that the author of Chronicles copied from Samuel-Kings, Vatke did, and while Reuss dated the work of the Chronicler near the beginning of the Greek period, Vatke assigned it a date ca. 260 B. C. E. Nevertheless, both men were agreed that Chronicles was not a useful source of information for re-constructing Israel's history in the pre-exilic period. Moreover, their bases for this conclusion were the same: (1) the substantial differences between Chronicles and Samuel-Kings that were shown as early as 1806 by de Wette, and (2) the substantial similarities between Chronicles and the Priestly Code, both of which should be assigned relatively late dates in the history of Israel's religious development.

Therefore, a new position in the history of research into Chronicles began in the mid-1830s with the proposal by Reuss and Vatke that the Priestly Code was written after Deuteronomy and not before it. However, this proposal did not exert its full influence on the study of the Pentateuch or Chronicles until Graf issued his study in 1866, *Die geschichtlichen Bücher des alten Testaments.*

3. LATER DEVELOPMENTS

a. Introduction

A period of approximately thirty years elapsed between the suggestion by Reuss and Vatke that P material should be assigned a later date than Deuteronomy and the resurrection of the theory by Graf in 1866. The 1850s and 1870s, however, witnessed the publica-tion of several books, which advanced the theory in some form and won a widespread acceptance for it. The works of Graf, Kuenen, Colenso, and Wellhausen are four of the most important of these publications that argued for assigning P a late date, and it is to them that we now turn to see the effects that an exilic or post-exilic P had for the investigation of Chronicles' reliability.

b. Graf

1) General

Karl Heinrich Graf (1815-1869) was the first to represent the the-ory—originally suggested by Reuss and Vatke—that P material was among the latest in the Pentateuch. He had attended the University of Strassburg, where he was greatly influenced by Reuss. It was from the latter's lectures in the summer of 1834 that Graf first heard the idea that the pentateuchal cultic laws of P were late. This was to be decisive for Graf's later work.[46]

Prior to Graf's day various scholars had identified sources in the Pentateuch, but the Elohist or P source was generally assigned a pre-exilic date and usually set before Deuteronomy. Graf's contribution was that he set forth the thesis that P material was composed after Deuteronomy. In his lectures of 1834, Reuss had suggested that instead of the laws in the P source having been the earliest of the pentateuchal materials, as was commonly thought at the time, they should be regarded as the latest of the pentateuchal materials. The heart of Reuss' contribution was preserved in his statement, "The prophets are older than the law, and the psalms younger than both."[47] This struck a sympathetic chord in Graf, and in 1866, he published *Die geschichtlichen Bücher des Alten Testaments*. As far as the Pentateuch was concerned, the book advocated a late date for the legal materials in the Elohist (P) source.[48] The publication of this conclusion helped stimulate Wellhausen, who heard of Graf's view in 1867, to set forth the sequence J, E, D, P in his *Prolegomena* (1878) in the clearest and most compelling way to date.[49] The major defect in Graf's work was that he divided the P material into two parts: legal and narrative. He gave the former a late date but the latter an early one. This meant that the legal material of P was written five hundred years after the narrative segments of P, in spite of the fact that they shared the same language and conceptual world. Graf divided the P material as he did in order to maintain his narrative *Grundschrift*, to which later materials were added. The weakness in Graf's proposal, however, was quickly attacked by his opponents, and Graf himself saw the deficiency in his position when Kuenen pointed it out to him. Consequently, in 1869 Graf published an essay, *"Die sogenannte Grundschrift des Pentateuchs,"* that made the necessary adjustments in his hypothesis of 1866, so that all the P material was dated after Deuteronomy.[50]

---

[46]Graf finished his studies at Strassburg and taught in Paris and finally in Leipzig, where he was a pupil of the orientalist Fleischer. He received his degree at Leipzig in 1846 and then began teaching at the *Landesschule* in Meissen. In 1864 the University of Giessen granted him an honorary doctorate in theology. Redslob, "Karl Heinrich G. Graf," *ADB* 9 (1879) 549-50; Pfleiderer, *Development*, 258.

[47]Cited by Kraus, *Geschichte*, 246.

[48]Karl Heinrich Graf, *Die geschichtlichen Bücher des Alten Testaments* (Leipzig: T. O. Weigel, 1866) 2-3; Pfleiderer, *Development*, 258.

[49]Julius Wellhausen, *Prolegomena to the History of Ancient Israel* (reprint of the translation of the 2d ed. of 1883; Gloucester, Mass.: Peter Smith, 1973) 3.

[50]This essay was included in the 1869 edition of Graf's *Die geschichtlichen Bücher des Alten Testaments*. Pfleiderer, *Development*, 258; Kraus, *Geschichte*, 247.

2) CHRONICLES

Graf believed that the Elohistic (P source) legislation—in 1869, he included all of P—and Chronicles derived from the post-exilic era. The Priestly Code dated from Ezra's day, according to Graf, and the Chronicler's history from the last half of the fourth century. Both attempted to read the practices of post-exilic Judaism into the earlier periods, and unless the scholar was aware of their dates of composition and purposes, the pre-exilic history of Israel would be misunderstood.

> The author of Chronicles stands over against the institutions of his day having to do with the Jerusalem temple, as the catholic ecclesiastical writer of the middle ages or modern times stands over against the institutions of his own church; the latter traces back his institutions (developed as they are) to Jesus and the apostles—not according to his own arbitrary idea, but according to the view of his church, a view regarded as truth from oral and written information—just as all of the law and all that was in practice was traced back to Moses, so also all institutions, as they stood in his own day; those not being traced back to Moses, were ascribed to David as the originator and founder of the temple.[51]

Graf's opinion that P should be dated late guided him, therefore, to discount much of what the Chronicler wrote about the pre-exilic cult.[52] This conclusion about the Chronicler's credibility as a historian was further supported by Graf's use of the historical method in the evaluation of the Chronicler's narratives about non-cultic matters. While de Wette had compared Chronicles with Samuel-Kings to illuminate the interests and biases of the former, and thus had eroded scholarly confidence in Chronicles as a reliable historical witness, Graf continued the process of undermining confidence in the Chronicler by suggesting that many of Chronicles' cultic details were historically unlikely or impossible. Therefore, while de Wette found the Chronicler deficient as a credible historian on the basis of Chronicles' conflicts with Samuel-Kings and what these showed about the Chronicler's prejudices and *Tendenz*, Graf found the Chronicler deficient, too, but for an additional reason: the Chronicler's description of the pre-exilic cult conflicted with the historian's understanding of that cult.

> So then, the picture of the older history, which the Chronicler sketched, is even the picture as it is mirrored in the spirit of a levite of the fourth century, and therefore, the whole sketch of this picture cannot belong to

---

[51]Graf, *geschichtlichen Bücher*, 122-23.
[52]*Ibid.*, 247.

an earlier time, even if a few features derive from older pictures and are edited with more or less skill.[53]

As early as 1859, Graf had already taken a stand with de Wette and Gramberg about the Chronicler's reliability. In that year he published a study of Chronicles' account of Manasseh's captivity and imprisonment, and he concluded that the report in 2 Chronicles 33 was historically unreliable. His work displays an acquaintance with the major figures in Chronicles research up to that time (de Wette, Gramberg, Keil, and Movers), and it is evident that his mistrust for Chronicles on this issue was only one example of his scepticism toward Chronicles as a whole.[54]

Graf's study of Chronicles in 1866 was the second of two parts in a larger work. The first part dealt with the earlier historical books, just as was the case about sixty years earlier, when de Wette's research into Chronicles was published as the second part of a work, whose first part dealt with the Pentateuch. Graf's aim was not to gather the individual peculiarities of Chronicles and group similar ones together, as de Wette and Gramberg had done. Rather, he decided to move through 1, 2 Chronicles section by section and identify the changes that the author had made to his source (Samuel-Kings) and then draw general conclusions. He began with 2 Chronicles, since it was there that Chronicles' relation to its main source—Samuel-Kings—was clearest.[55]

Graf believed that the Chronicler's primary aim had been to edify his readers. This meant that the Chronicler did not operate as a critical historian—a point that Graf thought his contemporaries needed to remember.

> The Chronicler's purpose was not that of historical research, but rather essentially that of edification. Hence one measures all earlier writers of history with a false standard, if one assumes with them the sense of historical research that belongs to the nineteenth century. This historical sense was entirely foreign to the Jews especially.[56]

> Our sharp distinction between historical writing and epic poetry was not observed then. The Chronicler wrote his narrative—his church history—as it streamed back from the fourth century B. C.[57]

The Chronicler, therefore, pursued his aim by the selection and editing of relevant materials.

---

[53]*Ibid.*, 121.

[54]K. H. Graf, "Die Gefangenschaft und Bekehrung Manasse's, 2 Chr. 33," *ThStKr* 32 (1859) 483-88.

[55]Graf, *geschichtlichen Bücher*, 124.

[56]*Ibid.*, 122.

[57]*Ibid.*, 246-47.

We see in the narratives of the Chronicler generally the influence and activity of the idealizing, embellishing, reforming, explaining *Sage*, which usually wipes away every shadow from the picture of the good ruler, but tints the evil so much the darker, which strives to let the just punishment always go to the wicked one and the just reward to the good one, and thus to bring experience into better agreement with divine justice than it appears to happen in history, which accordingly represents the delivering and punishing hand of God in general more often and quicker, and lets it intervene in wonderful ways, and seeks to make this working so much the more obvious by brighter colors and stronger contrasts. The Chronicler acts in the spirit of his own time, according to the didactic purpose of his work, when he uses and raises what is useful for bringing into view Yahweh's justice, which governs his people, punishes and rewards them to present the relationship between compliance with God and happiness and forgetting God and unhappiness, thereby to admonish people to the unwavering hold onto the divine commandments, to the true observance of the use of the temple worship, to the rejection of every apostasy from Yahweh in a striking way, and one must only not forget that this purpose, which he had in mind, was to set no unjustified critical pretensions on him.[58]

The Chronicler made great use of speeches in his work in order to advance his purpose of edifying his readers. While Graf did not deny the possibility that the speeches may have been derived from some source used by the Chronicler, he concluded that "they have been so reworded by the Chronicler that it is no longer possible to find a historical kernal. As such they are unhistorical."[59]

Graf's view of the Chronicler's sources was similar to Movers'. The former believed that the Chronicler used Samuel-Kings for his *Grundlage* and that he made use of the Pentateuch in its completed form.[60] Chronicles' second major source, however, was entitled "Midrash on the Book of Kings."[61] This work included both the royal annals of Judah and those of Israel, as well as additional stories and information that had grown up and been collected over the years. The annals of the two kingdoms had been utilized as separate works by the author of Samuel-Kings, but they were only available to the Chronicler in a later, edited form.[62] It is likely, also, that other historical works were written after 1, 2 Kings had been composed, and it may well have been that the Chronicler used them to some degree. Graf maintained, though, that there was no evidence to indicate that any of the Chronicler's sources antedated 1, 2 Kings.[63]

---

[58]*Ibid.*, 121.
[59]*Ibid.*, 187.
[60]*Ibid.*, 189, 193, 123, 217-18.
[61]*Ibid.*, 194.
[62]*Ibid.*, 191-93.
[63]*Ibid.*, 193.

The following chart sets forth Graf's understanding of Chronicles' sources.[64]

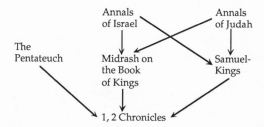

The main differences between Graf and Movers with regard to the Chronicler's sources were: (1) while Movers saw the Chronicler as a compiler and so one who wrote only what he copied from his sources (he never invented new material), Graf saw the Chronicler as both compiler and composer,[65] and (2) while Movers believed that the Chronicler's sources were both ancient and reliable historically, Graf believed that the Chronicler's sources were by and large late and of questionable value for historical reconstruction. Therefore, while Graf rejected much of the information in 1, 2 Chronicles and did not regard it as useful for reconstructing the history of pre-exilic Israel and Judah, he accepted it as useful for reconstructing the practices and thinking of post-exilic Judaism.

> If Chronicles thereby suffers loss of almost any worth as a documentary source for the ancient history, then it, on the other hand, is a so much more important document about the spirit and character of the fourth century, a period so unknown to us otherwise.[66]

---

[64]Graf divided the material in 1, 2 Chronicles into three parts for source analysis. First there was 1 Chr 1-9, 23-27, which derived from the canonical books of the Old Testament and from other sources, such as tax rolls or other public documents, which were only available to the Chronicler in later, edited forms. (*Ibid.*, 217-18.) The second block of material was 1 Chr 10-29 (excepting 23-27), which drew on the canonical books of Samuel. Much material in this section, however, arose with the Chronicler himself, and so could not make any claim to primitiveness (e.g., 1 Chr 15:2-24, David's levitical appointments). (*Ibid.*, 216-17.) Finally, the entire book of 2 Chronicles drew on the Books of Kings and on the Midrash on the Book of Kings. This latter source was written by combining and setting in chronological order the royal annals of the two kingdoms and by expanding this body of material with other stories and information that were available. The various prophetic designations for sources in Chronicles simply pointed to various parts in the Midrash on the Book of Kings. *Ibid.*, 191-93.

[65]*Ibid.*, 115.

[66]*Ibid.*, 247.

3) Summary

Graf helped launch a second challenge to the historical credibility of Chronicles by his proposal that the Priestly Code was the latest of the pentateuchal sources. He pointed out the similarities between P and Chronicles in their views of the cult and concluded that both had projected post-exilic ideas and practices into their accounts of the pre-exilic period. In this way, Graf undercut the historical reliability of both P and Chronicles. Graf's treatment of the Chronicler's sources also served to erode the work's credibility. While he adopted to a large extent Movers' source theory, Graf was unwilling to assume with Movers that the source material was ancient and historically reliable. On the contrary, he maintained that the Chronicler's use of a source for his information did not in any way answer the question of historical credibility and accuracy—it only pushed the question back another stage, and posed it for the Chronicler's source, rather than to the Chronicler himself. In addition, Graf diverged from Movers by pointing to substantial changes that the Chronicler had made to his source material in the process of his composition and to lengthy additions that the Chronicler himself had composed (e.g., the speeches). It was not, however, until the publication of Wellhausen's *Prolegomena* a dozen years later that the full impact of Graf's critique of the Pentateuch and Chronicles was felt.

c. Kuenen

1) General

Abraham Kuenen (1828-1891) was educated at the University of Leiden, where he studied under the Arabist Juynboll and fell under the influence of J. H. Scholten, who was the leading figure in the Modernist movement in the Netherlands and who secured for Kuenen his appointment to teach at Leiden upon graduation.[67]

Kuenen's first major work was a critical introduction to the Old Testament in three volumes, *Historisch-kritisch onderzoek naar het onstaan en de verzameling van de boeken des Ouden Verbonds* (1861-1865).[68] It assumed a relatively conservative position with regard to

---

[67]Kuenen's dissertation treated the Arabic version of the first twenty-four chapters of Genesis in the Samaritan Pentateuch. Philip H. Wicksteed, "Abraham Kuenen," *JQR* 4 (1892) 571-605; Simon J. de Vries, "Kuenen, Abraham," *Enc Jud* 10 (1971) 1284-85; de Vries, *Bible and Theology in the Netherlands* (Cahiers bijhet Nederlands Theologisch Tijdschrift, 3; Wageningen: H. Veenman & Zonen N. V., 1968) 56-63. The last work provides a clear historical setting of the theological controversy in which Kuenen found himself as a member of the Modernist movement (pp. 29-39); Cheyne, *Founders*, 185-94.

[68]In this work Kuenen offered a clear presentation of the current status of research. His position on the Pentateuch closely resembled that of Ewald. Wicksteed, "Kuenen," 587-88.

the Pentateuch, holding an early date for P, Mosaic authorship for the Decalogue and certain other pentateuchal laws, and that the Pentateuch was generally in its present form by the time of the exile.[69] Before his introduction had been completed, however, Colenso's *The Pentateuch and the Book of Joshua Critically Examined* (volume one, 1862) appeared, in which the author raised serious doubts about the historical reliability of the Pentateuch (primarily the Priestly Code).[70] Moreover, in 1865 Graf published his *Die geschichtlichen Bücher des Alten Testaments*, which proposed a late date for the legal material in P, while maintaining an early date for P's narrative sections. Kuenen saw both the logic in Graf's late dating of P's legal sections as well as Graf's mistake in separating the P material into two bodies of writings. Therefore, Kuenen wrote Graf in 1866 and proposed that all of P be assigned a late date. Graf subsequently accepted this view and published it in 1869—but without giving Kuenen credit for having suggested it.[71] By this time, one of Kuenen's students, W. H. Kosters, had written a dissertation which showed that the P narratives presupposed Deuteronomy and therefore Graf could not be correct in dating this part of P before Deuteronomy.[72]

Therefore, by the time Kuenen wrote *De godsdienst van Israel tot den ondergang van der Joodschen Staat* (1869-1870), his views about the development of Israel's religion had changed completely. This work was based on the pentateuchal sequence J E D P and was the first to combine this view with a completely naturalistic presentation of Israel's religious history. It was published in two volumes and began with the time of Amos and Hosea, since Kuenen believed that these two prophets were the first ones to proclaim a true monotheism. Before this time, e.g., during the period that J and E were written, polytheism (or at least henotheism) was the rule. The eighth century prophetic view of God represented the first stages of monotheism and was developed further by the later prophets and psalmists.[73] The publication of this work made it plain that Kuenen needed to revise drastically his earlier introduction to the Old Testament.[74]

---

[69]De Vries, *Bible and Theology*, 64-65.

[70]Cheyne, *Founders*, 192-93; Wicksteed, "Kuenen," 588; R J. Thompson, *Moses and the Law in a Century of Criticism Since Graf* (SVT 19; Leiden: E. J. Brill, 1970) 54-55.

[71]*Ibid.*, 55; Wicksteed, "Kuenen," 588-89; de Vries, *Bible and Theology*, 66.

[72]*Ibid.*, 77.

[73]This work was published in 1874-1875 in an English translation under the title, *The Religion of Israel to the Fall of the Jewish State* (3 vols.; London: Williams & Norgate).

[74]Between Kuenen's work on Israel's religion and the second edition of his Old Testament introduction, the author published three works worth noting: *The Prophets and Prophecy in Israel* (London: Longmans, Green, 1877) was originally

From 1885-1893, the second edition of Kuenen's Old Testament introduction appeared.[75] The differences between the first and second editions were great. Kuenen wrote of the earlier edition:

> The concessions I made were inevitable—but wholly inadequate. From my present position I regard them on the one hand as a tribute extorted by the power of the truth, but on the other hand as a humiliating proof of the tyranny which the opinions we have once accepted often exercise over us. When we are really called upon boldly to quit our ground and choose a new site for our edifice we too often attempt to stave off the necessity by timid and minute modifications in the plan to which we are already committed.[76]

The second edition of Kuenen's introduction presented the Pentateuch and the development of Israel's religious thinking and literature in accordance with the J E D P pattern that Wellhausen had popularized in his *Prolegomena*, which had appeared seven years before and to which Kuenen referred.

> ...but I can hardly describe the delight with which I first read it—a delight such as seldom indeed meets one on the path of learning. At one with the writer *a priori*, not only in principles but in general results, I was able to follow him from beginning to end with almost unbroken assent, and at the same time to learn more than I can say from every part of the work.[77]

Kuenen's influence on the rest of European biblical scholarship was hampered by the fact that his works were published in Dutch and therefore not available to as wide an audience as works in German. However, Kuenen was a leader in pentateuchal studies during his day.

> Kuenen, more than anyone else of his own generation, pointed the way for future inquiry. In particular, he saw, first of all, the right order in the stages of Israelitish religion, and secondly, the necessity of digging deeper foundations of criticism in archaeological research.[78]

---

published in Dutch in 1875; "Critical Method," *The Modern Review* 1 (1880) 461-88, 685-713, is a fine presentation of the historical critical method and occupies the spotlight in Kraus' treatment of Kuenen (*Geschichte*, 249-54); and *National Religions and Universal Religions* (The Hibbert Lectures, 1882; New York: Charles Scribner's Sons, 1882).

[75]This edition was translated into German as *Historisch-kritische Einleitung in die Bücher des alten Testaments hinsichtlichihrer Entstehung und Sammlung* (Leipzig: O. R. Reisland, 1890).

[76]Kuenen, *An Historico-critical Inquiry into the Origin and Composition of the Hexateuch* (London: Macmillan, 1886) xiv.

[77]*Ibid.*, xxxix.

[78]Cheyne, *Founders*, 194.

2) Chronicles

Kuenen believed that Chronicles was part of a larger work that included Ezra and Nehemiah and that the entirety was composed ca. 250 B. C. E.[79] He further thought that all of the Chronicler's source citations pointed to a single work, which was midrashic in nature.

> In so far as conclusions can be drawn from the Chronicler about the character of "the Book of the Kings of Israel and Judah," it was a free editing of the royal history in the sense and according to the needs of Judaism, and it was, therefore, quite correctly designated by the title "The Midrash of the Book of the Kings," under which it was cited (2 Chr XXIV, 27, cf. XIII, 22). Since it is, however, uncertain wherein the Chronicler is distinguished from his predecessor, who goes further than he, then our idea of the "Book of the Kings" remains necessarily incomplete and indefinite.[80]

Throughout the Chronicler's work the existence of the Priestly Code was presumed, and it can even be said that P was used as the Chronicler's key for rewriting Israel's ancient history.

> After the introduction of the priestly law and the conclusion of the Hexateuch, which followed it, such an entirely new publication of the Books of Samuel and Kings was a demand of the time. It was the indispensable complement to Ezra's law book, the application of that law book to the centuries, in which it, since one regarded it as Mosaic, must have existed and been valid, and at the same time the natural means for advancing and establishing the view of history, which is assumed in the law book, in spite of its contradiction with the older reports.[81]

Kuenen was familiar with the earlier histories of Israel and specialized studies of Chronicles. From the latter category he mentioned the works of de Wette, Dahler, Gramberg, Keil, Movers, Wellhausen, Graetz, and Graf.[82]

The positive value that Kuenen saw in Chronicles was its usefulness for reconstructing the post-exilic period.

> But however unfitted they may therefore be to increase our knowledge of Israel's earlier history, the unhistorical statements of the Chronicler are nevertheless of great value. They characterize to us the views of the author and of the circle whose ideas he represents. Nay, they do this the more faithfully, the more unhistorical they are. We will now employ them for this purpose.[83]

---

[79]Kuenen, *Religion*, 3.70.
[80]Kuenen, *Historisch-kritische Einleitung*, 1/2.160.
[81]*Ibid.*, 188.
[82]*Ibid.*, 103.
[83]Kuenen, *Religion.*, 3.71.

This meant that Chronicles was indeed useful to the historian, but hardly in the way that the Chronicler intended. Chronicles tells more, therefore, about its author's own day than it does about the pre-exilic period of Israel's history. This was substantially the view of Wellhausen, too.

On the negative side, Kuenen observed that nothing, which was found only in Chronicles, could be accepted with confidence for historical reconstruction.

> The reader of this history knows already that the Chronicler, where he stands alone or differs from his predecessors, deserves no credit. We had occasion more than once to remark that his accounts cannot be used to correct or supplement the older narratives; that it is necessary to choose between him and the earlier writers, and that in this case he can lay no claim to preference.[84]

> Where his (the Chronicler's) presentation of the events differs more or less from those of the older books, with which it is itself parallel, and on which it shows itself dependent, one cannot observe it as the more historical in even one instance, and it appears usually not to have been derived probably from a divergent tradition, as much as to misunderstanding or to the known effort to replace a picture of the past, which had become offensive, by another one, which corresponded better to the insights and needs of the post-exilic Judaism, which was ruled by the priestly legislation.[85]

As far as the first nine chapters of Chronicles was concerned, Kuenen believed that materials of differing worth were used. They are of little use in providing new information about the pre-exilic period, but they are useful in understanding the post-exilic age, especially the materials in the genealogies of Judah, Benjamin, and Levi.[86] The Chronicler's treatment of David is likewise of little value. It portrays David as the king who prepared for the building of the temple in Jerusalem and as the one who set in order the temple personnel. This should be regarded as entirely "unhistorical."[87] Finally, the reports in 2 Chronicles 10-36, which one finds only in Chronicles, should be rejected for serious consideration in the reconstruction of Israel's pre-exilic period.

> The numbers given therein are usually fabulous; where they concern the cult and the activity of the temple service, they stand almost everywhere in contradiction with what is established elsewhere about these things;

---

[84]*Ibid.*
[85]Kuenen, *Historisch-kritische Einleitung*, 1/2.135.
[86]*Ibid.*, 152.
[87]*Ibid.*, 144.

their content is often difficult to harmonize with the older historical books and already is highly improbable in and of itself.[88]

3) Summary

Kuenen's view of Chronicles did not differ significantly from that of Weilhausen. He offered no new insight into Chronicles, but this is hardly to be expected, since his interests were primarily in the Pentateuch. Kuenen was, however, important for the study of Chronicles, because he saw clearly the significance that a late date for the P narratives had for the development of Israel's religion. His letter to Graf pointed the way that Graf finally took and his two-volume history of Israel's religious development pointed to the Chronicler's role in that process.

d. Colenso

1) General

The first major English scholar to suggest a late date for P material was John W. Colenso (1814-1883). He was educated at Cambridge and began serving as Bishop of Natal in the mid-1850s. As he was translating Genesis into the Zulu language, he was repeatedly questioned about whether the things reported in the book were true. "My heart answered," he later said, "in the words of the Prophet, Shall a man speak lies in the name of the Lord? I dared not do so."[89] His critics in London later remarked jokingly how "the newly appointed bishop went to convert and was converted himself."[90]

General opposition to Colenso arose after the publication in 1862 of his book, *The Pentateuch and the Book of Joshua Critically Examined*.[91] He had begun his studies of the Pentateuch in 1861 and 1862 with the help of works by Hengstenberg, Kurtz, and Ewald, but had found them unsatisfying, writing later about Hengstenberg:

---

[88]*Ibid.*, 137.

[89]G. W. Cox, "Colenso, John William," *DNB* 11 (1887) 291-92. Cox also wrote a biography of Colenso (*The Life of John William Colenso, D. D., Bishop of Natal* [2 vols.; London: W. Ridgway, 1888]). A more recent biography of Colenso is that by Peter Hinchliff (*John William Colenso* [London: Nelson, 1964]), who focused on Colenso primarily as a representative of the "liberal" Anglican theology in the mid-nineteenth century. See, also, Rogerson, *Criticism*, 220-237.

[90]Cox, "Colenso," 291.

[91]*The Pentateuch and the Book of Joshua Critically Examined* (5 vols.; London: Longman, Green, Longman, Roberts & Green, 1862-1879) was published in seven parts between 1862 and 1879 (parts 1-3 are included in vol. 1, but each later part is a separate volume) and provoked considerable controversy in England. By 1881, it had elicited not less than three hundred published responses. Thompson, *Moses and the Law*, 54.

> For Hengstenberg's works, certainly, I do feel something like contempt, for his arguments are often dishonest—I can use no milder term—and that with a prodigious affectation of honesty and censure of others as suppressing the truth from interested motives.[92]

Friedrich Bleek's son, however, who lived in Cape Town, supplied Colenso with the additional works of de Wette, Kuenen, and F. Bleek. Apparently, Colenso found these more satisfying, and by 1879, he had produced seven parts of *The Pentateuch and the Book of Joshua Critically Examined.* In the sixth part of the work (1871) he argued that legal sections in the Priestly Code should be assigned exilic or post-exilic dates. This was an important change from his earlier conviction that P material was among the earliest in the Pentateuch. The reason for this shift, aside from the obvious influence of Graf (*Die geschichtlichen Bücher des alten Testaments,* 1866) and Kuenen (*De Godsdienst van Israel,* 1870), was Colenso's discovery of linguistic similarities between Leviticus and Ezekiel.[93] In Part Seven of the work Colenso defended his early dating of the narrative parts of P.[94]

2) Chronicles

In Part Seven of *The Pentateuch and the Book of Joshua Critically Examined* Colenso treated 1, 2 Chronicles. He believed that the books were part of a larger composition that included Ezra and Nehemiah and that the work arose sometime after 332 B. C. E. (perhaps as late as 250, if Kuenen's suggestions are accepted) at the hand of a "Levite Chorister." The Pentateuch, Samuel-Kings, and perhaps also "some even earlier written records" made up the author's collection of sources.[95]

Colenso's confidence in Chronicles as a historical source was not strengthened by his conclusions about the Chronicler's sources. On the contrary, Colenso believed that the author's sources were "composed after the Captivity."[96] Consequently, the historian could have little confidence in the Chronicler's contributions to the store of knowledge about the pre-exilic period. Several of Colenso's comments reflect this pessimism about the usefulness of Chronicles for reconstructing Israel's pre-exilic history.

---

[92]Hinchliff, *Colenso,* 90.

[93]Part 6 of Colenso's work was entitled "The Later Legislation of the Pentateuch." In it the author argued that Ezekiel probably wrote Leviticus 18-20 and 26 and that chapters 21-25 and 27 arose from the circle around him, if not from Ezekiel himself. *Pentateuch and Joshua,* 4.3-23.

[94]*Ibid.,* 5.129-39.

[95]*Ibid.,* 5.304-5.

[96]*Ibid.,* 5.305-6, 387.

...I have examined the two Books of Chronicles, and have shown that in those Books the real facts of Jewish history, as given in Samuel and Kings, have been systematically distorted and falsified in order to support the fictions of the LL (Later Legislation), and glorify the priestly and Levitical body, to which the Chronicler himself belonged.[97]

...it is impossible to acquit him (the Chronicler) of the grevous offence of falsifying for future generations the well-known facts of actual history.[98]

Very much of the contents of these Books (Chronicles), however, is manifestly fictitious, the offspring of his own imagination. In most of the rest, he has changed things to present practices of his own day as having been done in earlier times.[99]

Colenso's treatments of individual narratives in 1, 2 Chronicles further demonstrate his distrust of the books (e.g., he calls the Chronicler's account of Manasseh's captivity "an unhistorical addition").[100]

3) Summary

Colenso began his critical studies with the Pentateuch. By means of his own independent study, coupled with the help that he received from reading the works of Bleek, de Wette, Graf, and Kuenen, he concluded that certain parts (primarily the legal and cultic ones) of the Priestly Code were composed in exilic or post-exilic times. In addition, he maintained that the Chronicler's history was a late work that derived its information about the pre-exilic period from exilic or post-exilic compositions. Therefore, Colenso believed that Chronicles was not useful for the reconstruction of Israel's pre-exilic history.

e. Wellhausen

1) General

The suggestion, which arose with Reuss and Vatke and was reaffirmed by Graff and Colenso, that P was the last of the pentateuchal sources to be composed found its greatest champion in Julius Wellhausen (1844-1918), a student of Ewald's at Göttingen. Wellhausen began his teaching career at Göttingen, served at Greifswald, Halle, and Marburg, and then returned to teach at

---

[97]*Ibid.*, 5.ix.
[98]*Ibid.*, 5.x. Colenso reproduces this from his earlier book, *Lectures on the Pentateuch and the Moabite Stone* (London: Longmans, Green, 1873) 345.
[99]*Ibid.*, 5.387.
[100]*Ibid.*, 5.357.

Göttingen until his death in 1918.[101] His contributions to scholarship lay not only in the field of Old Testament, but also in New Testament and Arabic.[102] Three of his works, however, were of paramount importance for the study of Old Testament history. The first was *Die Composition des Hexateuchs und der historischen Bücher des Alten Testaments,* which appeared in 1889. Wellhausen had already reached the general conclusions of this work in 1867, when

> in the course of a casual visit in Göttingen in the summer of 1867, I learned through Ritschl that Karl Heinrich Graf placed the Law later than the Prophets, and, almost without knowing his reasons for the hypothesis, I was prepared to accept it; I readily acknowledged to myself the possibility of understanding Hebrew antiquity without the book of the Torah.[103]

The results of Wellhausen's research were published in 1876 in the article "Die Composition des Hexateuchs."[104] Wellhausen concluded that J and E were combined first and that later Dt (Deuteronomy) was

---

[101]Wellhausen became *Privatdocent* in 1870 for Old Testament history at Göttingen and then *ordentlicher Professor* in theology at Greifswald in 1872. Ten years later he resigned from the theological faculty there, because he believed that his teaching did not in fact help train students for ministry in the churches. "I became a theologian," he explained, "because the scientific treatment of the Bible interested me; only gradually did I come to understand that a Professor of Theology has also the practical task of preparing the students for service in the Protestant Church, and that am not adequate to this practical task; that instead despite all caution on my own part I make my hearers unfit for their office. Since then my theological professorship has been lying heavily on my conscience." (Excerpted from a letter in Jepsen 54 [266-67] by Rudolf Smend, "Wellhausen and his Prolegomena to the History of Israel," in *Julius Wellhausen and his Prolegomena to the History of Israel,* ed. Douglas A. Knight [Semeia, 25; Chico: Scholars Press, 1983].) Wellhausen moved to Halle, where he became *ausserordentlicher Professor* of oriental languages in the faculty of philosophy. In 1885, he became *ordentlicher professor* at Marburg and in 1892 returned to the University of Göttingen to succeed Paul Lagarde, who had taken the place of Ewald there. Otto Eissfeldt, "Wellhausen, Julius," *RGG* 6 (3d ed.; 1957) 1594-95; "Wellhausen," *Enc Brit* 28 (11th ed.; 1911) 507. One of the best early treatments of Wellhausen is that of Eduard Schwartz, "Julius Wellhausen, " in *Nachrichten von der Kgl. Gesellschaft der Wissenschaften* (Göttingen: Geschaftliche Mitteilungen, 1918) 43-70. This has been reprinted in Schwartz' *Gesammelte Schriften* (2d ed.; Berlin: Walter de Gruyter, 1963) 1.326-61. The latest treatment of Wellhausen's work at Greifswald is Rudolf Smend's "Wellhausen in Greifswald," *ZthK* 78 (1981) 141-76.

[102]Eissfeldt praised Wellhausen as a philologian, textual critic, exegete, translator, literary critic, but primarily as a historian. "Julius Wellhausen," *Kleine Schriften* (Tübingen: J. C. B. Mohr, 1962) 1.56-71.

[103]Julius Wellhausen, *Prolegomena to the History of Ancient Israel* (Gloucester, Mass.: Peter Smith, 1973) 3-4.

[104]J. Wellhausen, "Die Composition des Hexateuchs," *JDTh* (1876) 392-450, 531-602; (1877) 407-79.

attached to JE. Finally, Q[105] (later designated "P"), an independent work, was joined to JE+Dt to form the Hexateuch. Wellhausen admitted that this simple account of the Hexateuch's development concealed a complicated process, and that earlier sources (e.g., J1, J2, J3, E1, E2, E3) preceded the four main ones.[106] This ordering of the pentateuchal sources had momentous consequences for all later study of Israel's history.

In 1878, there appeared the first volume of Wellhausen's *Geschichte Israels*. Since the second volume—the actual sketch of Israel's history—was so long in appearing, the second edition of volume one was published in 1883, but its title was changed to *Prolegomena zur Geschichte Israels*. While this edition was translated into English, the German *Prolegomena* went through five more editions by 1914. The principal issue that Wellhausen addressed in the *Prolegomena* was the place of the law of Moses in Israel's history. Note his introductory paragraph.

> In the following pages it is proposed to discuss the place in history of the "law of Moses;" more precisely, the question to be considered is whether that law is the starting-point for the history of ancient Israel, or not rather for that of Judaism, i.e., of the religious communion which survived the destruction of the nation by the Assyrians and Chaldaeans.[107]

Wellhausen handled this issue in three parts. First, there was the history of worship, which outlined a historical development by examining the historical and prophetical books with regard to five categories: the place of worship, sacrifice, sacred feasts, priests and levites, and endowment of the clergy.[108] The second part of the work was devoted to the history of the tradition. It was here that Wellhausen treated Chronicles, the older historical books (Judges, Samuel, and Kings), and the narratives of the Hexateuch. He found the same kind of historical development in these three bodies of literature that he had found in his study of worship in the Hexateuch. Chronicles described Israel's history in accordance with the Priestly Code, while the older historical books sketched the history of Israel to conform to Deuteronomy. Finally, in the hexateuchal narratives, Wellhausen found a development in which the JE forms of the stories were older than the forms in P.[109] The third section of the *Prolegomena*

---

[105]Wellhausen initially called the Priestly Code "Q," since it was the source containing the four covenants (*quattuor*).

[106]J. Wellhausen, *Die Composition des Hexateuchs und der Historischen Bücher des Alten Testaments* (2d ed.; Berlin: Georg Reimer, 1889) 210.

[107]Wellhausen, *Prolegomena*, 1.

[108]*Ibid.*, 17-167.

[109]*Ibid.*, 171-362.

was entitled "Israel and Judaism" and had three parts: "Conclusion of the Criticism of the Law," "The Oral and the Written Torah," and "The Theocracy as Idea and as Institution."[110]

The third most significant of Wellhausen's publications for Old Testament history was his *Geschichte Israels*. It was distributed as a manuscript at Greifswald on Christmas of 1880. In 1881 it appeared as the article "Israel" in *Encyclopaedia Britannica*,[111] and the latter was in turn revised and published in 1884 in *Skizzen und Vorarbeiten*. Finally, 1894 witnessed Wellhausen's most complete treatment of Israel's history: *Israelitische und jüdische Geschichte*. This work went through seven editions by 1914.

On several counts Wellhausen's theories have been labeled Hegelian: (1) Vatke was unquestionably a follower of Hegel's; (2) Wellhausen adopted Vatke's late dating of P and said that he learned the most and the best from Vatke; and (3) Wellhausen outlined a developmental process for the history of Israel's religion.[112] As early as 1889, this charge was made against Wellhausen and it was repeated often since that time.[113] It has been shown, however, that Wellhausen's theories were not Hegelian. On the contrary, what Wellhausen derived from Vatke was not the latter's Hegelian language or philosophy of history, but the late dating of P. A simple comparison of the language of the *Prolegomena* with that of *Die biblische Theologie* makes this clear. Furthermore, the development that Wellhausen found in Israel's history was not one that rose ever upward to better things. On the contrary, Wellhausen held Israel's early religion (represented by J) in high esteem, but had considerably less regard for Judaism (represented by P).[114]

2) Chronicles

Wellhausen's first publication to deal with Chronicles was his dissertation, *"De gentibus et familiis Judaeis quae 1.Chr. 2.4. enumerantur"* (1870). In it he examined Judah's genealogy in 1 Chr 2:3-4:23 and found its kernel in 2:9, 25-33, 42-50a . He believed that the rest of the genealogy was the Chronicler's own composition from the post-exilic period and concluded that the pre-exilic kernel "appears to be contained only for the sake of the later additions."[115]

---

[110]*Ibid.*, 365-425.

[111]This is reproduced in the translation of the *Prolegomena* published by Peter Smith, pp. 429-548.

[112]Dietmar Mathias, *Die Geschichte der Chronikforschung im 19. Jahrhundert unter besonderer Berucksichtigung de exegetischen Behandlung der Prophetennachrichten des Geshichtswerkes* (3 vols.; Leipzig: Karl-Marx-Universität, 1977) 1.83.

[113]Wellhausen, *Prolegomena*, 171.

[114]*Ibid.*, 211, 215, 227, 171; cf. 223-24.

[115]*Ibid.*, 171-72.

In 1878, Wellhausen treated Chronicles extensively in his *Prolegomena*, but his interest there was not in Chronicles for its own sake. Rather, his attention was focused on the problem of historical development and his desire was to establish the place of Chronicles in the history of Israel's religion.

> Under the influence of the spirit of each successive age, traditions originally derived from one source were very variously apprehended and shaped; one way in the ninth and eighth centuries, another way in the seventh and sixth, and yet another in the fifth and fourth. Now, the strata of the tradition show the same arrangement as do those of the legislation. And here it makes no difference whether the tradition be legendary or historical, whether it relates to pre-historic or to historic times; the change in the prevailing ideas shows itself equally in either case. To show the truth of this in the case of the Hexateuch is of course our primary object, but we make our commencement rather with the properly historical books. For on various grounds we are here able with greater certainty to assert: Such was the aspect of history at this period and such at that; such were the influences that had the ascendency at one time, and such those which prevailed at another. We begin the inquiry where the matter is clearest—namely, with the Book of Chronicles.[116]

There are two factors that were decisive in accounting for the differences between Chronicles and Samuel-Kings and thus for the preparation of an outline of Israel's religious development. The first was the date of Chronicles, which Wellhausen set at the beginning of the Greek period—three hundred years after the composition of Samuel-Kings. Wellhausen had four reasons for suggesting such a date for Chronicles: (1) the genealogies in Chronicles and the Chronicler's use of Samuel-Kings (though mediated through the Midrash) argue for a late date; (2) Chronicles is part of a larger work that included Ezra and Nehemiah; (3) the language in Chronicles is evidently later than that in Samuel-Kings; and (4) the spirit of Chronicles is that of the post-exilic phenomenon of Judaism.[117] The second factor that helped explain the differences between Chronicles and Samuel-Kings was the fact that the additions and changes in the former were in accordance with the Priestly Code and so presupposed the completed Pentateuch.[118]

Wellhausen's subsequent treatment of Chronicles in this section of the *Prolegomena* was decisively influenced by de Wette's *Beiträge* of 1806.

De Wette's "Critical Essay on the Credibility of the Books of Chronicles" (*Beiträge*, i.; 1806), is throughout taken as the basis of the discussion: that

---

[116]*Ibid.*, 172.
[117]*Ibid.*, 173.

essay has not been improved on by Graf (*Gesch. Bücher d. A. T.* p. 114 seq.), for here the difficulty, better grappled with by the former, is not to collect the details of evidence, but so to shape the superabundant material as to convey a right total impression.[119]

Furthermore, as far as the question of Chronicles' historical reliability was concerned, Wellhausen maintained that de Wette saw matters clearly.

> ...one can only repeat what has already been said by De Wette. It may be that the Chronicler has produced this picture of old Israel, so different in outline and colour from the genuine tradition, not of his own suggestion and on his own responsibility, but on the ground of documents that lay before him. But the historical character of the work is not hereby altered in the smallest degree, it is merely shared by the so-called "sources." 2 Maccabees and a multitude of other compositions have also made use of "sources" but how does this enhance the value of their statements? That value must in the long run be estimated according to their contents, which, again, must be judged, not by means of the primary sources which have been lost, but by means of the secondary literary products which have survived. The whole question ultimately resolves itself into that of historical credibility; and to what conclusions this leads we have already seen. The alterations and additions of Chronicles are all traceable to the same fountain-head—the Judaising of the past....[120]

Therefore, the affirmation that the Chronicler used sources for his composition—instead of inventing his narratives—did not thereby establish the historical credibility of his reports. It only showed that his sources shared his views.

Wellhausen did, however, see a historical usefulness in the Chronicler's work. He believed that it was important for reconstructing the beliefs and institutions of the post-exilic Jewish community.

> Under the influence of the spirit of each successive age, traditions originally derived from one source were quite differently apprehended and shaped.... And here it makes no difference whether the tradition be legendary or historical, whether it relates to pre-historic or to historic times; the change in the prevailing ideas shows itself equally in either case.[121]

> In the picture it (Chronicles) gives the writer's own present is reflected, not antiquity. But neither is the case very different with the genealogical

---

[118]*Ibid.*, 171.
[119]*Ibid.*, 211.
[120]*Ibid.*, 223.

lists prefixed by way of introduction in I Chron. i.-ix.; they also are in the main valid only for the period at which they were drawn up— whether for its actual condition or for its conceptions of the past.[122]

The alterations and additions of Chronicles are all traceable to the same fountain-head—the Judaising of the past, in which otherwise the people of that day would have been unable to recognize their ideal. It was not because tradition gave the Law and the hierocracy and the *Deus ex machina* as sole efficient factor in the sacred narrative, but because these elements were felt to be missing, that they were thus introduced.[123]

It must be allowed that Chronicles owes its origin, not to the arbitrary caprice of an individual, but to a general tendency of its period. It is the inevitable product of the conviction that the Mosaic law is the starting-point of Israel's history, and that in it there is operative a play of sacred forces such as finds no other analogy; this conviction could not but lead to a complete transformation of the ancient tradition.[124]

While Chronicles was valuable for helping one understand the post-exilic period, Wellhausen denied that the books were of value in reconstructing the pre-exilic period. Wellhausen believed that the question of historical credibility for Chronicles must be answered in the negative. De Wette had shown this to be true, according to Wellhausen, and his opponents (Keil, Movers, e.g.) had not been able to reverse this verdict on the Chronicler's reliability. Chronicles was most basically a "Judaising of the past"—a rewriting of history so that it became congruent with the Priestly Code.[125] This meant that the historian must reject any information about the pre-exilic period that is found only in Chronicles for the reconstruction of preexilic history. This is especially the case, when the Chronicler's report advances his own agenda. While some valuable information may be lost by following such a rigorous procedure, this cannot be prevented.

With what show of justice can the Chronicler, after his statements have over and over again been shown to be incredible, be held at discretion to pass for an unimpeachable narrator? In those cases at least where its connection with his "plan" is obvious, one ought surely to exercise some scepticism in regard to his testimony; but it ought at the same time to be considered that such connections may occur much oftener than is discernible by us, or at least by the less sharp-sighted of us. It is indeed possible that occasionally a grain of good corn may occur among the

---

[121]*Ibid.*, 224. Wellhausen continued with the statement that a book such as Chronicles could even be written in the nineteenth century by someone such as Keil, if it had not already been written. *Ibid.*, 225.

[122]*Ibid.*, 211.

[123]*Ibid.*, 224.

[124]*Ibid.*

[125]*Ibid.*, 228, 293-94.

chaff, but to be conscientious one must neglect this possibility of exceptions, and give due honour to the probability of the rule.[126]

Sometimes scholars have attempted to salvage readings in Chronicles by suggesting that they were present in a better text of Samuel or Kings than in the text currently available. Wellhausen rejected this.

> In many cases it is usual to regard such additions as having had their origin in a better text of Samuel and Kings which lay before the Chronicler; and this certainly is the most likely way in which good additions could have got in. But the textual critics of the *Exegetical Handbook* are only too like-minded with the Chronicler, and are always eagerly seizing with both hands his paste pearls and the similar gifts of the Septuagint.[127]

A comparison of Wellhausen's treatment of Chronicles with his treatment of Judges, Samuel, and Kings shows that he viewed both histories as the products of historical revision. In the case of the latter work, the traditions about Israel's past were followed by the prophets, who shed new light on the stories. Then there arose the law of Deuteronomy—a law infused with the prophetic spirit. Finally, it became clear that Israel's older books of history had to be rewritten in light of the deuteronomic law, if they were to be edifying for the author's contemporaries, and thus the revision was completed during the Babylonian exile.[128] This approximates Wellhausen's idea of how Chronicles came into being centuries later. Therefore, one might expect Wellhausen to reject the historical witness of Judges, Samuel, and Kings, just as he had rejected that of Chronicles, but this was not the case. The crucial difference between the two works is that while Chronicles asserts that the older "saints" assumed and lived in accordance with the Priestly Code, the books of Judges, Samuel, and Kings acknowledged that ancient practices differed from the law. While at times the latter books did in fact remodel the history of the past, often they simply admitted past failures and condemned them.[129] The difference in this regard, therefore, between Chronicles and the older historical books is not one of kind, but one of degree— viz., the Chronicler produced a much more distorted picture of Israel's past than did the author of Judges, Samuel, and Kings.

---

[126]*Ibid.*, 294.

[127]Wellhausen, "Ewald," 131-32.

[128]Perlitt, *Vatke und Wellhausen*, 154-64.

[129]*Ibid.*; R. K. Harrison, *Introduction to the Old Testament* (Grand Rapids: Eerdmans, 1969) 21.

3) Summary

Wellhausen's view of Chronicles and the development of Israel's history was based on two things. First, he reclaimed de Wette's research into Chronicles and thus denied that Chronicles was a reliable guide to the pre-exilic history of Israel. He regarded the work of Movers and others between 1806 and 1878 as of little consequence for the evaluation of Chronicles as a historical source. Even though Movers had offered valuable suggestions about the Midrash as the Chronicler's source, Wellhausen believed that he had drawn erroneous conclusions about the value of Chronicles as a source for reconstructing Israel's history.

The second basis for Wellhausen's view of Chronicles was his reclamation of Vatke and Reuss' theory about the sequence of the hexateuchal sources (J E D P, as Graf had lately set them forth). The work of Ewald and others, who had opposed the late dating of P after Vatke's publication of the theory in 1835, was regarded by Wellhausen as a retreat into the errors of the pre-Vatke period. Wellhausen called Ewald the "great restrainer" and saw him as the one who prevented advances in Old Testament scholarship by his adherence to the early dating of P.[130]

Wellhausen's greatest accomplishment then was not in the arguments for Chronicles' unreliability or of the J E D P sequence of the pentateuchal sources, but in his efforts to synthesize the two conclusions and demonstrate the relevance that this synthesis held for the description of Israel's religious history. It was this clear and compelling portrayal of the historical development of Israel, which could account for the various legal codes in the Pentateuch and at the same time explained the basic differences between the various narrative records of Israel's past, that won him such recognition and influence in the world of Old Testament scholarship.

As far as the Chronicler's usefulness for historical reconstruction was concerned, Wellhausen believed, as had de Wette before him, that Chronicles was useful for understanding the institutions and beliefs of the post-exilic community but that it was misleading when used to reconstruct the pre-exilic period. Movers' researches did not sway Wellhausen from this conviction. However, Wellhausen was not as radical or pessimistic as de Wette had been with regard to the possibility of obtaining sufficient materials to write a history of Israel. De Wette said that neither Chronicles nor the earlier historical books were reliable historical sources. Wellhausen, though, while refusing to use Chronicles to reconstruct the pre-exilic period, believed that the older books of Samuel and Kings were adequate for describing Israel's pre-exilic history. Therefore, it is clear that Wellhausen was

---

[130]Perlitt, *Vatke und Wellhausen*, 165-67; Rudolf Smend, "Wellhausen, Julius," *Enc Jud* 16 (1971) 444.

not as rigorous or demanding as de Wette with regard to what he expected from a historical source.

f. Summary of Later Developments in the Late Dating of P

Graf's work of 1866 inaugurated a new period in the study of the Pentateuch. His suggestion that the legal material in the Priestly Code was composed after Deuteronomy met with the approval of Kuenen and Colenso. While Kuenen suggested that the narrative material in P should also be assigned a late date—and Graf agreed, as the 1869 edition of his *Die geschichtlichen Bücher des alten Testaments* showed—Colenso continued to assign different dates to the two kinds of material in P. Wellhausen heard about Graf's theory regarding P in 1867 and accepted it almost immediately. When he presented it in his *Prolegomena* in 1878, scholarly acceptance of a late P became widespread.

This development in pentateuchal studies inaugurated a new challenge to the credibility to Chronicles. Each of these figures, who accepted a late date for P, also adopted an extremely sceptical attitude toward Chronicles as a reliable historical source. In general, they reasoned that just as P rewrote the history of an earlier time in light of exilic or post-exilic practices, so Chronicles, too, revised the account in Samuel-Kings of the monarchical period so that it would be more congruent with the practices and ideals of the author's own day. While the redating of P initiated the new challenge to the credibility of Chronicles, the earlier work of de Wette was reaffirmed and used as an additional argument against the historical reliability of Chronicles.

4. SUMMARY OF DEVELOPMENTS IN THE REDATING OF P

The movement to redate the Priestly Code began with the work of Reuss and Vatke in the mid-1830s. The work of both figures was apparently ineffective in swaying scholarly opinion at the time, however. In the case of Reuss, it was due to his reluctance to publish his conclusions, and in the case of Vatke, it was due to the ponderous Hegelian language and philosophical system, with which he clothed his theory about P.

In 1866, Graf, who had been a student of Reuss' and heard the latter's proposals about P, published a work that argued that the legal materials in P were composed after Deuteronomy. This met with the approval of Kuenen in the Netherlands, Colenso in England (or South Africa), and Wellhausen in Germany, and each of the three published works that incorporated and argued for the substance of Graf's theory. Kuenen's suggestion to Graf that all of P, rather than just the legal sections in it, should be assigned a late date was accepted by Graf and reflected in the 1869 edition of his 1866 publication. Colenso rejected this change to Graf's initial theory, but remained largely alone in adhering to the earlier form of Graf's hypothesis. It was Wellhausen's *Prolegomena*, however, which was responsible for gaining scholarly acceptance for the theory.

Each of these scholars, who argued for the late date of P materials, also took a dim view of Chronicles' historical reliability. They were convinced that P had rewritten and distorted history, and the similarities between P and Chronicles led them to suspect the latter of similar distortions. When this suspicion was combined with the careful comparison of Chronicles with Samuel-Kings, Chronicles' historical credibility fell, and it seemed that de Wette's position had been firmly established.

C. THE CONSEQUENCES OF A LATE PRIESTLY CODE FOR THE RECONSTRUCTION OF ISRAEL'S HISTORY

1. INTRODUCTION

In this section of Chapter Three we will examine some of the histories of Israel, Old Testament introductions, and other literature that was produced after Graf's proposal in 1866 of a late date for material in the Priestly Code. The publications have been divided into two groups: those that followed Graf and accepted an exilic or post-exilic date for all or part of P and those that opposed Graf's position and argued for the pre-exilic composition of the Priestly Code. In the former group there are the histories of Seinecke (1876/1884), Meyer (1884-1902), Stade (1887/1888), Renan (1887-1893), Piepenbring (1898), and Guthe (1899), and finally, there is the article on Chronicles as a midrash (1892) by Budde, as well as the latter's Old Testament introduction (1906). In the category of writings about Chronicles by authors who continued to urge a pre-exilic date for P there are the histories of Köhler (1875-1893), Kittel (1888-1892), Klostermann (1896), and Oettli (1905), the Chronicles commentaries by Zöckler (1877), Kittel (1902), Neteler (1899), and Oettli (1889), and the introductory treatments of Chronicles by Nöldeke (1868) and Klostermann (1898). The two categories of writers will be treated separately and within each group the authors will be taken up in a roughly chronological order.

2. SCHOLARS WHO FAVORED A LATE DATE FOR THE PRIESTLY CODE

a. Introduction

In the group of seven scholars to be discussed who maintained that P was the last of the pentateuchal sources to be composed there was a general suspicion of Chronicles' narrative about the pre-exilic history. This was to be expected, since the (distorted) exilic or post-exilic picture of the cult that one found in P also appeared in Chronicles. It will be seen that the majority of these scholars rejected virtually all of 1, 2 Chronicles for the historical reconstruction of the pre-exilic period. First, Seinecke's history from the 1870s will be treated. Then three authors who wrote histories in the 1880s will be examined: Meyer, Stade, and Renan. Finally, three authors from the 1890s will be surveyed: Piepenbring, Guthe, and Budde.

b. Seinecke

The first of the figures to be discussed who accepted a late date for P is L. Seinecke, who wrote a commentary on Isaiah and a history of Israel (*Geschichte des Volkes Israel*, 1876). In the latter work Seinecke dealt primarily with the period from the Patriarchs until Saul, devoting less than a third of his history to a discussion of the monarchical and exilic periods. He was evidently familiar with the trends in Old Testament scholarship of his day,[131] and he wrote as one who had absorbed at least some of what Graf and others had written about the post-exilic date for parts of P.[132]

Seinecke evidently read Chronicles with considerable suspicion. He believed that the Chronicler wrote arbitrarily at times and created accounts in order to make history fit his own historical prejudices. For example, Seinecke saw the Chronicler's connection of Rehoboam's defeat by Shishak with the Judean king's religious unfaithfulness as an example of the author's arbitrariness.[133] Moreover, Seinecke omitted the Chronicler's contributions to the regnal histories of Asa and Jehoshaphat and proposed that the account in Chronicles about Manasseh's captivity and repentance was the author's attempt

---

[131]In the preface to his work, Seinecke mentioned Ewald's history and defended his right to write a history of Israel in the presence of Ewald's massive work. Moreover, he also referred to the works of Kuenen and Duhm. *Geschichte des Volkes Israel* (2 vols.; Göttingen: Vandenhoeck & Ruprecht, 1876 /1884) 1.iii, v.

[132]Seinecke denied, for example, that the tabernacle existed in Moses' day; instead, he regarded the tent as the creation of minds in the post-exilic period. *Ibid.*, 1.162.

[133]*Ibid.*, 1.375-76.

to explain the king's long and peaceful reign.[134] Finally, it must be acknowledged that Seinecke did not completely reject information from Chronicles. In the case of the Chronicler's accounts of Uzziah's building activities, Seinecke allowed that they may well have been based in fact, and one finds many references to Chronicles in the footnotes of *Geschichte des Volkes Israel*.[135] On the whole, however, Seinecke observed that the Chronicler's reports were "*in den meisten Fallen nur Scheingut.*"[136]

While Seinecke's history was evidently not very influential, and the author made no attempt to arrive at new conclusions with regard to Chronicles, the history demonstrated the author's critical reading and use of Chronicles—perhaps based on de Wette and Graf—in the period just before Wellhausen's *Prolegomena*.

c. Meyer

Toward the end of the nineteenth century Eduard Meyer (1855-1930), a professor of ancient history at Breslau (and later at Halle and Berlin), issued a five-volume work entitled, *Geschichte des Alterthums* (1884-1902).[137] Only a small part of the publication treated ancient Israelite history, but the author's critical stance was evident. Meyer endorsed the basic lines of Wellhausen's pentateuchal research, including the hypothesis of a late date for the Priestly Code.[138] The extent to which Meyer was influenced by Wellhausen is clear from the numerous references to the latter's *Prolegomena* and edition of Bleek's Old Testament introduction.[139] In addition, there are frequent citations of Stade's history of Israel, as well as a few to Vatke's *Die biblische Theologie*, Reuss' *Die Geschichte der heiligen Schriften Alten Testamentes*, and to the work of Kuenen.[140]

---

[134]*Ibid.*, 1.385.

[135]*Ibid.*, 1.379.

[136]*Ibid.*, 1.375.

[137]Zev Garber, "Eduard Meyer," *Enc Jud* 11 (1971) 1462.

[138]Books four and five deal with Israelite history to some degree. Meyer, *Geschichte des Alterthums* (5 vols.; Stuttgart: J. G. Cotta, 1884) 1.311-496 (cf. especially pp. 346-379 and 389-404).

[139]Meyer's references to the first edition of Wellhausen's *Prolegomena* from the first volume of his *Geschichte des Alterthums* include pp. 359, 374, 379, 396, 437, 445, and references to Wellhausen's edition of Bleek's Old Testament introduction occur in the first volume of *Geschichte des Alterthums* on pp. 354, 357, 363.

[140]In *Geschichte des Alterthums*, volume one, Meyer refers to Stade's history of Israel on p. 396 (cf. also vol. 3, p. 14), to Reuss' work on pp. vi-vii, and to Kuenen's *De Profeten* on p. 379. There are also numerous references to British scholars (e.g., Sayce, G. Rawlinson, and G. Smith) in Meyer's treatment of Assyria, since the English had been especially productive in the study of Assyrian texts (cf. vol. 1, pp. 405-96).

Meyer's view of Chronicles was also very near that of Wellhausen's. The former grouped 1, 2 Chronicles with Ruth and Esther as "the books of legends."[141] In another place he denied that Chronicles' genealogies were useful for reconstructing pre-exilic tribal allotments, writing that "the reports in Chronicles are worthless falsifications."[142] Furthermore, a survey of Meyer's treatment of Israel's pre-exilic history reveals few, if any, references to Chronicles as a source of information for his historical reconstruction.[143] However, it should be noted that Meyer thought that Chronicles' genealogical lists were useful for information about the post-exilic period.[144]

Therefore, as far as his views on the pentateuchal sources and Chronicles are concerned, it appears that Meyer followed in a generally consistent way the conclusions that Wellhausen had presented in his *Prolegomena*. He maintained a late date for P and denied that the books of Chronicles were useful for reconstructing the history of the pre-exilic period.

d. Stade

1) General

The second history in the 1880s to presume a late date for the Priestly Code was that of Bernhard Stade (1848-1906), who had studied at Leipzig under Franz Delitzsch and at Berlin. Stade is best known for founding and editing the *Zeitschrift für die Alttestamentliche Wissenschaft* and for his *Geschichte des Volkes Israel* and *Biblische Theologie des Alten Testaments*.[145]

Stade wrote all of his two-volume history except for the last part of the second volume, which dealt with Judaism during the Hellenistic period and was written by Oskar Holtzmann. Wellhausen's understanding of Israel's history dominated the work, and Stade was careful to point out that Israel's religion was not delivered to the people in its final form at the beginning of Israel's life as a nation. On the contrary, Israel began with many of the

---

[141]Meyer, *Geschichte des Alterthums* (1901), 3.13.

[142]*Ibid.*, 1.352.

[143]A glance at Meyer's treatment of David and Solomon yields no references to Chronicles. The same appears to be the case with Meyer's presentation of the rest of the monarchical period.

[144]*Ibid.*, 3.14.

[145]From 1875 onward, Stade was *ordentlicher Professor* at Giessen. He died, however, before completing his biblical theology, and consequently A. Bertholet wrote the second volume of the work and published it in 1911. The works amounted to more of a history of Israel's religion than to what one might expect to find in a biblical theology. Kraus designated Stade as "one of the most powerful personalities at the end of the nineteenth century." Kraus, *Geschichte*, 283-88; "Stade, Bernhard," *Enc Brit* 25 (11th ed.; 1910) 247.

assumptions, which one found in nature religions, and it was only after a long period of time that she came to hold the "purely spiritual, ethical monotheism," which marked the height of her religious development and prepared for Christianity.[146] The prophets were crucial in this development toward monotheism.[147]

2) Chronicles

Stade began his work by discussing the historian's task and the sources available for its accomplishment. In this section Stade clearly indicated his lack of confidence in Chronicles as a historical source for reconstructing the pre-exilic period. His verdict on the books was substantially the same as Wellhausen's. He noted that de Wette had recognized in 1806 the proper relationship between Chronicles and Samuel-Kings, and that Graf and Wellhausen had recovered de Wette's views. All the other scholars, who had argued against de Wette since 1806, had only confused matters.[148] While the usual procedure for dealing with Chronicles by historians before Stade was to use the work to supplement the information in Samuel-Kings, Stade declared this to be improper. Information that was found only in Chronicles, or which contradicted statements in Samuel-Kings, must be rejected for historical reconstruction of the pre-exilic period.[149] While it was indeed possible that the Chronicler made use of sources that have since been lost to scholarship, these sources were probably late and of little value in understanding the pre-exilic history of Israel. The earliest and best sources were used in the composition of Samuel-Kings or were lost in the destruction and confusion of the Babylonian exile. The source citations in Chronicles did not refer to a multitude of separate works, but apparently to the various parts of a single work, the "Midrash of the Book of Kings." The latter work was a post-exilic edition of the royal history and shared the "*Geist*" of the Chronicler. Both the Midrash and Chronicles altered the pre-exilic history to conform with the ideas and institutions of post-exilic Judaism.[150] Stade believed that 1, 2 Chronicles was written ca. 300 B. C. E. as part of a larger work that

---

[146]Stade believed that he had an obligation in writing such a history to include both the political and religious developments in Israel's past. The history would have been defective if either was omitted. Bernhard Stade, *Geschichte des Volkes Israel* (2d ed.; Berlin: G. Grote, 1889) 1.8-9.

[147]In his *Biblische Theologie*, Stade separated the first volume into the pre-prophetic period and the age of prophecy. The prophets represented one stream of ideas in the eighth and seventh centuries B. C. E., which served to move the people's thinking from the traditional ways. (Tübingen: J. C. B. Mohr, 1905) 1.204-5.

[148]Stade, *Geschichte*, 1.81.

[149]*Ibid.*, 1.82-83.

[150]*Ibid.*, 1.84.

included Ezra and Nehemiah,[151] and that while it was practically useless for the reconstruction of the history of pre-exilic Israel, it was useful for reconstructing the text of Samuel-Kings. Since the latter books were read more often than the former, the text of Chronicles remained freer from intentional corruptions.[152]

Stade was consistent in his antipathy to the use of Chronicles for reconstructing the history of the pre-exilic period. When he treated Asa's reign, he mentioned the Chronicler's story about the attack by Zerah against Judah, but remarked, "That this narrative is wholly unhistorical does not need to be shown."[153] Later, in his discussion of Joash's reign in Judah, Stade omitted any reference to the conflict between the Judean king and Zechariah.[154] Finally, Stade dealt with the Chronicler's account of Manasseh's captivity and conversion at length and labeled it "an allegory," suggesting that it presented the experience of God's people in the Babylonian captivity. Stade believed, though, that the Chronicler used the story to account for the king's remarkably long reign and his apparent freedom from divine punishment.[155]

There were occasions, however, when Stade chose to accept bits of information from Chronicles. For example, he accepted the assertion of 2 Chr 22:11 that Jehosheba was the wife of the priest Jehoiada, "since all is explained by it in a most unforced way."[156] While Wellhausen allowed for the presence of isolated bits of accurate information about the pre-exilic period in Chronicles, he denied that the historian had the capability to sift them out accurately.[157] Stade appeared a bit more confident in this regard, even though he maintained Wellhausen's overall view of Chronicles.

3) Summary
Stade accepted the general lines of Wellhausen's reconstruction of the development of Israel's history—and thus a late date for P—and believed, as did Wellhausen, that a proper understanding of Israel's religious development was absolutely essential for an accurate understanding of the nation's literature and history. This led Stade, in turn, to regard Chronicles as a late, post-exilic work, which was an unreliable guide to the nation's pre-exilic history. Consequently, Chronicles could not be used with confidence by the historian for the pre-exilic period, except for special instances in which the

---

[151]*Ibid.*, 1.81-82.
[152]*Ibid.*, 1.84.
[153]*Ibid.*, 1.355.
[154]*Ibid.*, 1.566-67.
[155]*Ibid.*, 1.639-40.
[156]*Ibid.*, 1.546.
[157]Wellhausen, *Prolegomena*, 224.

Chronicler's testimony was supported by compelling reasons. This exception, which Stade exercised with caution, would prove to be a passkey, which would be used more and more by later historians, who shared Wellhausen's basic distrust for Chronicles, but who found the Chronicler's tidbits appealing.

Stade appropriated Movers' theory about the Chronicler's use of a "Midrash," just as Wellhausen did before him, but both Stade and Wellhausen denied that the existence of such a source argued in favor of Chronicles' credibility. Since the "Midrash" was also late and shared the "*Geist*" of the Chronicler, its testimony must also be discounted.

e. Renan

1) General

A history of Israel that was published in France and accepted the Reuss-Graf hypothesis of a late P was that of Joseph Ernest Renan (1823-1892). He studied at St. Nicholas, the seminary of Issy, Saint Sulpice, the Sorbonne, and the Collège de France. He received his doctorate in 1852, but in 1860 he was barred from appointment to the chair of Hebrew and Chaldaic languages at the Collège de France because of Catholic pressure against him. Napoleon III, however, appointed him to be head of the French archaeological mission to Syria and Palestine. Two years later, his appointment to the Collège de France was confirmed, but his inaugural lecture created such a furor that his course (and so his appointment) was suspended—only to be confirmed later in 1870.[158]

Renan's most famous work was his *Vie de Jesus* (1863), which was tremendously popular but which also aroused enormous protest against its author. It was the first volume published of his Histoire des Origines du Christianisme, a series which also included the five volumes of his *Histoire du peuple d' Israel* (1887-93). The latter work dealt with the time from the Patriarchs until the Roman period.[159]

---

[158]During his education at the Collège de France, Renan learned the comparative method and began to see the effects that the historical-critical method had for the study of the Bible. In 1845, however, Renan turned from his training for the priesthood in order to pursue his oriental studies. This outward shift marked his breach with the Catholic Church and his unwillingness to follow ecclesiastical dogma at the expense of human reason. Eugen Lachenmann, "Renan, Ernst," *RE* 16 (1905) 649-55; L. Fillion, "Renan, Ernst," *DB* 5/1 (1908) 1041-43; Lewis Freeman Mott, *Ernest Renan* (New York: D. Appleton, 1921) 1-3, 26, 34-35, 207; Yohanan Cohen-Yashar, "Renan, Ernest," *Enc Jud* 14 (1971) 71-72.

[159]The English translation of *Histoire du Peuple d'Israel* was *History of the people of Israel* (Boston: Roberts Brothers, 188-95). Renan's interests were varied, and he published works not only in New Testament and Old Testament but also in philosophy. Of all his publications, his favorite appears to have been his *Corpus Inscriptionum Semiticarum*, a work on which he collaborated with other scholars

Renan's historical views were similar to those of his contemporaries in some respects. One notes, for example, his conviction that only three histories of ancient peoples were of importance for the investigation of human civilization (Greece, Israel, and Rome)[160] and his idea that Israel had a divine mission (the development of religion to Christianity).[161] Both ideas were held by Ewald and can be traced back to Herder and to others, as well. In addition, both Ewald and Renan saw the prophets of ancient Israel (Elijah, Amos, Isaiah, et al.) as of great importance to Israel's religious development. Renan believed that they signaled a return to the conception of God as a universal deity, an idea that had existed in the worship of Elohim by the Patriarchs but which had been lost in the worship of Yahweh as a nationalistic and vengeful deity around the time of David and Solomon. Therefore, for Renan the prophets from 850 B. C. E. until the end of Isaiah's ministry proclaimed a universal God and a relation between morality and religion that constituted a pinnacle of religious development, which prepared for Christianity. The later additions of Josiah, Jeremiah, and those who returned from Babylonian exile to restore the Jewish cult were little more than the establishment of a sectarian organization.[162]

In line with this view of Israel's religious development, Renan arranged the pentateuchal sources in the following way. E, the first written document, arose in North Israel,[163] and was followed by J, which was also composed in the North but by a member of Elijah's school, who wrote ca. 850 B. C. E.[164] Next there was P, which a priest issued in Jerusalem ca. 825-800 B. C. E. While it contained the Decalogue, P consisted primarily of narrative material.[165] The book of

---

to collect all known semitic inscriptions. Mott, *Renan*, 266, 299, 325, 367; Cohen-Yashar, "Renan," 14.71-72.

[160]*Ibid.*, 1.vii.

[161]*Ibid.*, 2.10.

[162]*Ibid.*, 2.ix-x. While it was evidently quite common in Renan's day to single out Greece, Rome, and Israel as the most significant nations in antiquity for research into the development of civilization, Renan went beyond this to claim that the Semitic mind was inherently monotheistic in its religious thought. Such assignments of innate abilities or attributes to various nationalities was brought down to the nineteenth century by Renan and applied to France and Germany as well. Such bold judgments with so little basis in historical fact did not commend Renan to his readers as a trustworthy and sober guide in historical matters. By more than one critic in his day Renan was severely chastised for his flights of imagination. His treatment of the Patriarchs was especially an occasion for this kind of criticism. Cf. W. R. Smith, "Renan's *Histoire du peuple d'Israel* (1887)," in *Lectures & Essays of William Robertson Smith* (eds. John Sutherland Black & George Chrystal; London: Adam & Charles Black, 1912) 608-22.

[163]*Ibid.*, 2.169, 176-77.

[164]*Ibid.*, 2.284-85, 290, 303.

[165]*Ibid.*, 2.318-20, 334.

Deuteronomy was added about the time of Josiah and Jeremiah.[166] Finally, many of the laws that precisely define aspects of the cult (e.g., Exodus 25ff.; Leviticus 1-7) grew up during the exile or afterwards and may well have been derived from the imaginations of priests.[167] In this way, Renan maintained an early P narrative but a late P legal code, and in this respect he was very near Graf's publication of 1866.

2) Chronicles

Renan believed that 1, 2 Chronicles was composed by a Levite—probably a singer—in the Jerusalem temple toward the close of the Persian period and that the books of Ezra and Nehemiah formed the conclusion of his work. As sources of information for the pre-exilic period, the Chronicler had available the books of Judges, Samuel, and Kings, and "fuller annals than we possess of the days of the kings of Judah and of Israel were not yet lost; accounts of the Prophets had also considerable material for their development."[168] This allowed Renan to admit some of the reports in Chronicles, which were not in Samuel-Kings, as containing genuine material for the reconstruction of the pre-exilic history of Israel. For example, Renan accepted the Chronicler's account of Zerah's attack on Judah during Asa's day, and on other occasions he cautiously accepted bits of information from Chronicles.[169]

Generally, however, Renan had a low opinion of the Chronicler's skill and reliability as a historical witness.

> The author of Chronicles is extremely narrow-minded; his intellectual perceptions are very poor. No writer is more reckless, more careless, in the use of his materials; none has sown more errors in the world than this obscure compiler. He does not seem to have been able to read correctly, and the manuscripts he had at hand were very defective. One can hardly imagine a poorer philologist, a poorer critic, or a man who knew less of paleography. Sometimes his errors are voluntary; sometimes he makes changes of set purpose, to serve religious zeal and national pride. Some narratives are his own invention, and show the fanaticus, the inhabitant of the Temple. He is especially severe on those who interfere with the rights of the levites. One man who has invaded levitical functions is struck at once with leprosy. ... The credulity and exaggeration of this writer pass all bounds. The character of David is entirely transformed. ... The ecclesiastical colour given to the episode of Joash is due to the writer of the Chronicles. It is levites who restore the heir of David to his throne, and attest his legitimacy; the chant of the levites leads to victory. Prophets can hardly be distinguished from the

---

[166]Ernest Renan, "History of the People of Israel," in *Studies of Religious History and Criticism* (New York: Carleton, 1864) 113.

[167]Renan, *History*, 3.45-47.

[168]*Ibid.*, 3.150.

[169]*Ibid.*, 2.203.

> priests. ... Chronicles is a work wholly levitical; its one interest is worship; it is history written by a sacristan.[170]

Because of the Chronicler's prejudices and ignorance, therefore, Renan usually disregarded his reports. His details about temple music and singing in the pre-exilic period are to be regarded as circumstances of the second Temple that have been projected back into the past.[171]

> There was but little sacred music in the old Temple. The details as to the bands of singers which David is said to have organised, the musical celebrities, such as the sons of Asaph, Jeduthun, and Heman, are fancies of the ecclesiastical chronicler of Jerusalem, who ascribed to Solomon's Temple what was true only of the second.[172]

The Chronicler's accounts of Hanani's opposition to Asa, a Moabite invasion of Judah, and the episode involving Oded and Israel are but three examples of Renan's rejection of material from 1, 2 Chronicles.[173]

3) Summary

Renan's view of the Priestly Code was substantially the same as Graf's of 1866 in that he divided the document into legal and narrative sections and assigned a later date to the former than to the latter. Graf himself had seen the problems with this theory and corrected his position nearly twenty years before Renan's history. In addition, Renan had the advantage of having Kuenen and Wellhausen's treatments of the Hexateuch available for his examination before writing his history. Therefore, while Renan's view of the pentateuchal sources reflected the results of critical research, it did not reflect the best available in his day.

Renan was obviously familiar with the critical work that had been done on Chronicles by de Wette, Gesenius, Wellhausen and others, and it is clear that he took the results of their investigations seriously. Renan did not, however, work out and present in his history a source critical theory for Chronicles, as Ewald and Wellhausen had done before him. On the contrary, he merely suggested several kinds of sources that he believed were available to the Chronicler, without systematically attempting to relate them to the Chronicler's source citations. In addition, Renan never revealed his criteria for determining the authenticity of Chronicles' reports. Therefore, while

---

170*Ibid.*, 3.151-53.
171*Ibid.*, 2.50; 3.23.
172*Ibid.*, 2.132-33.
173*Ibid.*, 2.201, 257, 430.

he was suspicious of nearly everything in Chronicles, he still could not "ignore" the Chronicler's accounts.[174]

As far as Old Testament scholarship outside France was concerned, Renan's history had little lasting impact. His reconstructions of history—especially in the patriarchal period—were regarded by many as too arbitrary, and as far as his treatment of Chronicles was concerned, he offered nothing new. If anything, his position on the Priestly Code and his use of Chronicles constituted a step backward from Graf and Wellhausen.

f. Piepenbring

In addition to Graf, another of Reuss' pupils whose publications achieved considerable recognition was Charles Piepenbring, who wrote a history of Israel and an Old Testament theology. The latter work was one of the first that assumed the validity of Wellhausen's developmental scheme and tried to present the principal topics of Old Testament religion within its framework.[175]

In his *Histoire du peuple d'Israel* Piepenbring divided Israel's past into nine periods and within each treated both its events and its literary products. It was in the final period—from Nehemiah to Antiochus Epiphanes—that he dealt with Chronicles. He believed that it had been part of a larger work that included Ezra and Nehemiah and was composed near the end of the fourth century B. C. E. Its author was a levite, who used the Midrash on the Books of Kings as his major source. The latter work, in turn, had been composed after the time of Ezra and Nehemiah and after the Priestly Code had been composed, and therefore, most of the differences between Samuel-Kings and Chronicles could be traced back to it.[176] In spite of this source that he detected behind Chronicles, Piepenbring denied that Chronicles had anything more than a "feeble historical value," because its author aimed his work at meeting the religious needs of his age, viz., he tried to make pre-exilic history conform to the legislation of the Priestly Code.[177]

It is no surprise then to find that Piepenbring rejected most of the Chronicler's contributions to the pre-exilic history of Israel. Rather than simply stating *a priori* that 1, 2 Chronicles could not be trusted, however, Piepenbring approached each case with arguments for the

---

[174]Renan, *History*, 1.359; 2.197, 257.

[175]Piepenbring's theology was entitled *Theologie de l'Ancien Testament* (Paris: Fischbacher, 1886), and it was translated into English by H. G. Mitchell as *Theology of the Old Testament* (New York: T. Y. Crowell, 1893). Cf. R. C. Dentan, *Preface to Old Testament Theology* (New York: Seabury, 1963) 53-54.

[176]C. Piepenbring, *Histoire du peuple d'Israel* (Paris: Librairie Grassart, 1898) 631-33.

[177]*Ibid.*, 629-30.

improbability of the Chronicler's reports. He rejected Chronicles' account of David's cultic preparations and reorganizations (1 Chronicles 22-26), since these activities by the king were not mentioned at all in 2 Samuel.[178] Similarly, Piepenbring dismissed the Chronicler's report of Zerah's attack on Asa (2 Chronicles 14), because: (1) the numbers in the account were unrealistic; (2) the complete extermination of the Ethiopian force was unlikely; (3) a powerful Egypt would have blocked the advance of an Ethiopian army into Palestine; and (4) if Asa had been powerful enough to defeat such a large enemy force, then why would he have called on Syria for help later against the smaller army of Israel?[179] In Jehoshaphat's reign Piepenbring discarded the Chronicler's report that the king sent out levitical teachers and the story about a Moabite coalition attacking Judah.[180] In the same way, he rejected Chronicles' account of Manasseh's captivity and release, since (1) Manasseh admired the Assyrian Empire and favored her cult; (2) his imprisonment would have been in Ninevah rather than in Babylon; (3) 2 Kings did not record these events but asserted instead that Manasseh's sin led to Jerusalem's fall; and (4) the historical events after Manasseh's death indicate that the idolatry, which he favored, continued until Josiah's reform.[181]

Therefore, Piepenbring rejected Chronicles as a reliable source of information about the pre-exilic period, because it depended on a late, post-exilic work as its primary source, and because both Chronicles and the Midrash represented the history of the monarchical period so that it would conform to the laws of the Priestly Code. In this respect, Piepenbring thought that the Chronicler wrote as other Jewish historians: each fashioned the historical account according to the ideas, institutions, and practices of his own day.[182] Thus, Piepenbring stood within the Reuss-Graf-Wellhausen tradition in his general rejection of Chronicles for the reconstruction of pre-exilic history.

g. Cornill

1) General

Another scholar who accepted the proposition of a late date for P was C. H. Cornill (1854-1920), a Protestant Old Testament scholar, who taught at Marburg, Konigsberg, Breslau, and Halle. His most influential work was his *Einleitung in das Alte Testament* (1895), which was one of the first critical introductions to the Old Testament

---

[178]*Ibid.*, 620.
[179]*Ibid.*, 625-26.
[180]*Ibid.*, 626-27.
[181]*Ibid.*, 353.
[182]*Ibid.*, 617.

that was based on the results of Wellhausen's *Prolegomena*. Cornill also wrote important works on Jeremiah (*Jeremiah und seine Zeit*, 1880), and Israelite history (*Geschichte des Volkes Israel*, 1898).[183]

2) Chronicles

In his history of Israel Cornill did not use 1, 2 Chronicles as a historical source at all for the pre-exilic period, primarily because he did not believe that the Chronicler was a reliable source for historical information for that period. The basis for his general suspicion of Chronicles was presented in his introduction to the Old Testament. There he set forth his convictions that Chronicles was originally part of a larger work that included Ezra and Nehemiah and had been written by a levitical temple musician in the first half of the third century.[184] The sources behind the treatment of the pre-exilic period were Samuel-Kings (either utilized directly or indirectly), the sources used by the author of the canonical books of Kings, the Midrash (which expounded the history of the monarchy), and possibly a work entitled "The words of the Seers" (a midrashic collection of narratives about the prophets). It is evident that Cornill's conclusions about the Chronicler's sources were a bit tentative. He was not clear about the precise relation of Chronicles to Samuel-Kings—whether the latter was immediately available to the former, or whether their connection could best be explained by the Chronicler's use of sources that, in turn, lay behind Samuel-Kings.[185] The materials in Chronicles that subserved the author's purpose and were different from what was found in Samuel-Kings were characterized as

> ...a very free treatment and exposition of old traditional material, the object of which is not so much to narrate history as to conduce to religious edification.[186]

Cornill assigned these materials as a whole to the Midrash, which the Chronicler used as a source, and he believed that the Chronicler's references to prophetic works may have simply designated sections in the Midrash.[187] The Chronicler's approach to the pre-exilic period was based on the author's recognition of the problem that had been of

---

[183]Zev Garber, "Cornill, Carl Heinrich," *Enc Jud* 5 (1971) 974.

[184]C. H. Cornill, *History of the People of Israel* (4th ed.; Chicago: Open Court, 1909). *Introduction to the Canonical Books of the Old Testament* (Theological Translation Library, 23; New York: G. P. Putnam's Sons, 1907) 228, 235, 249. Cornill's conclusion regarding the Chronicler's date is based primarily on his interpretation of 1 Chr 3:19-24.

[185]*Ibid.*, 230, 235-39.

[186]*Ibid.*, 237.

[187]*Ibid.*, 238-39.

major concern to Old Testament scholars throughout the nineteenth century.

> And in all this transformation of the tradition the Chronicler is actuated by good faith throughout: he has corrected in it what, according to his honest convictions, must have been clearly false. Some 2000 years before the "Grafian school" he rightly perceived that the old historical books and the Pentateuch are mutually exclusive. Either the representation of the historical books is correct, in which case the Pentateuch cannot be the basis of Mosaism and of the religion of Israel; or the Pentateuchal Law is Mosaic, and in that case the representation of the historical books cannot be correct. As in the Chronicler's eyes, of course, the authenticity of the Tora was placed beyond the reach of doubt, he was only able to adopt the second alternative, and consequently corrected the historical books: he has expounded the history as it must have been on the assumption that the entire Pentateuch was the basis of Mosaism, and has acted in good faith throughout....[188]

Therefore, Cornill saw the Chronicler's history as a revision of the work of Samuel-Kings according to the legislation in the Pentateuch. Consequently, the picture of the pre-exilic period in Chronicles was vastly different from that in Samuel-Kings, and the Chronicler had been led to omit materials that were found in the earlier work, as well as add supplementary narratives and notes. In both of these kinds of changes the Chronicler's aim was apparent.

> In Chron. we possess the latest and most pronounced outcome of that transformation of the history of Israel into Church History for which the way was first prepared by Deut. and the Deuteronomic writers. The favoured representatives of the national history are saints, and the history must be thoroughly edifying, and in particular exhibit the pragmatism of a righteous rule of God: must show that every misfortune is punishment for sin, and all prosperity the reward of Piety, and conversely, also, that all piety must realise its reward, and all sin its punishment. And, too, the piety and dogmas of the Chronicler are throughout those of P....[189]

The consequence of such an understanding of Chronicles was that the work could not be used with confidence as a historical source for reconstructing pre-exilic history.

> The representation of the Chronicler and that of the older historical books are mutually exclusive, and, such being the case, it is only the representation of the older historical books that can possibly be as a whole the correct one—and all the more so because we can indicate the prism which has produced the peculiar refraction that is visible in the Chronicler's work. This does not of necessity absolutely exclude the possibility that among the material exhibited by the Chronicler alone

---

[188]*Ibid.*, 233.

some one or other valid and useful detail may occur; more especially in cases where the tendency-aim is not obviously present the particular detail in question should be tested carefully and without prejudice.... But a narrator whose untrustworthiness has been demonstrated in all cases where he can be controlled, in cases where no such means of checking him exist has at least a very strong presumption against him. ...yet the whole picture drawn by the latter (the Chronicler) is and remains completely unhistorical.[190]

Therefore, simply because the Chronicler used ancient sources, his account was not vindicated. While he may be relieved from the charge of having been a falsifier of history, his history is not thereby proven correct.

...the picture drawn by the Chronicler is in no respect historical, although he does deduce it from "sources," for, assuming their existence, the sources themselves were already untrustworthy and unhistorical; but it may for many be some sort of satisfaction not to be obliged to lay the blame for what, in modern language, would be called the falsification of history in Chronicles on the author of the Biblical Book of Chronicles personally.[191]

3) Summary

Cornill's view of Chronicles was essentially that of Wellhausen: the Chronicler's picture of Israel's pre-exilic period differed significantly from that in Samuel-Kings and was so strongly dominated by the author's theological tendencies that it could not be trusted. Cornill avoided, however, Wellhausen's complete rejection of the Chronicler's narrative as a useful historical source of information for the pre-exilic age. According to Cornill, bits of accurate historical information could still be gained from Chronicles for the reconstruction of the history of the monarchical period (e.g., the genealogies and 1 Chr 11:10-47).[192]

For Cornill, as for Wellhausen, Graf, and others, the key to a proper appreciation of Chronicles was the recognition of its connection with the Priestly Code: both arose from the post-exilic period and reflected the beliefs and institutions of that time. The Chronicler himself, according to Cornill, set out to revise the pre-exilic history of Samuel-Kings in order to bring it into closer agreement with P.

---

[189]*Ibid.*, 231.
[190]*Ibid.*, 234.
[191]*Ibid.*, 239.
[192]*Ibid.*, 234.

h. Guthe

Another German scholar who wrote a history of Israel from Wellhausen's perspective of Israel's religious development was Hermann Guthe (1849-1936). He was known primarily as an archaeologist, having excavated on the temple mount in Jerusalem in 1881 for the Deutsche Palästina-Verein. His *Geschichte des Volkes Israel* (1899) was one of the first histories of Israel to be written from Wellhausen's perspective.[193]

Guthe was generally reluctant to dismiss information in Chronicles that was not found in Samuel-Kings. For example, he accepted the Chronicler's list of Rehoboam's fortified cities,[194] and he incorporated in his history the Chronicler's account of Zerah's attack on Asa, even though he acknowledged that it was difficult to decide on the reliability of the report.[195] While he saw an historical basis for many of the reports that were unique to Chronicles, he did not at the same time accept every detail in those reports. He called the Chronicler's record of Abijah's war with Jeroboam I "strongly embellished."[196] Similarly, he accepted as historical Chronicles' story about a Moabite coalition's attack on Jehoshaphat, since he believed that the precise place names (2 Chr 20:2, 16, 20, 26) argued for the historicity of the report, but he also thought that the account had been highly embellished.[197] Finally, Guthe detected an historical foundation for the Chronicler's report of Manasseh's captivity and return: after Assurbanipal had quelled the revolt by his brother, he summoned Manasseh and other vassals to him in Babylon to reaffirm their loyalty. Guthe rejected, however, the Chronicler's accretions around this kernel and asserted, "Manasseh did not change his (cultic) behavior as long as he reigned." Moreover, he charged that the Chronicler's account was only a "Sage," which was "spun" on the basis of a belief in divine retribution.[198] Therefore, he believed that the story of Manasseh's captivity, return, and reforms were built

---

[193]Guthe began teaching at Leipzig in 1884, and from 1911 until 1925 he served as director of the Deutsche Palästina-Verein and editor of *ZDPV*. His publications included *Palästina in Bild und Wort* (1883-84), *Ausgrabungen bei Jerusalem* (1883), *Bibelatlas* (1926, 2d ed.), and *Bibelwörterbuch* (1903). Michael Avi-Yonah, "Guthe, Hermann," *Enc Jud* 7 (1971) 985-86; Kraus, *Geschichte*, 275, 287, 299-300.

[194]Hermann Guthe, *Geschichte des Volkes Israel* in *Grundriss der Theologischen Wissenschaften* (Tübingen: J. C. B. Mohr, 1899) 3.133.

[195]*Ibid.*, 136-37.

[196]*Ibid.*, 134.

[197]*Ibid.*, 146-47.

[198]*Ibid.*, 208-9.

around an event, which occurred late in the king's reign, and were intended to demonstrate the punishment of God for royal sins.

Guthe provides an interesting look at how one German archae-ologist handled Chronicles at the end of the nineteenth century. His approach was thoroughly critical and he felt no need to defend the reliability of the Chronicler's history. However, he was unwilling to charge the Chronicler with inventing the reports that were unique to his history. He chose instead to suppose that some kind of historical kernel lay behind those reports, and he evidently felt confident enough about this to attempt reconstructions on its basis. Guthe's procedure in these reconstructions was to discard elements of Chronicles' reports, which appeared to be exagerated or which ap-peared to have arisen simply out of the author's *Tendenz*. Therefore, he was more confident of his ability to use the historical critical method to reconstruct history from defective sources than was de Wette or Wellhausen, for example, before him.

i. Budde

A friend of Wellhausen's, who generally supported the latter's critical views, was Karl Budde (1850-1933), a Protestant Old Testament scholar, who taught at Bonn, Strassburg, and Marburg. He was best known for his advocacy of the Kenite Hypothesis, which held that Mosaic Yahwism was derived from the Kenites, to whom Moses was related by marriage.[199]

Budde's views on Chronicles were presented most fully in his *Geschichte der althebräischen Litteratur* (1906). He treated Chronicles, as well as the books of Ruth, Ezra, Nehemiah, and Esther, in a chapter entitled, "The Narrative Midrash and the Writing of History under Its Influence."[200] He maintained that Chronicles, Ezra, and Nehemiah were originally one work, written by a levitical singer ca. 300 B. C. E.[201] These conclusions had become common in critical works at the turn of the century, and Budde produced no new arguments to support them. He believed that there were two primary influences on the Chronicler's work. First, there was the Priestly Code, which

---

[199]Budde produced detailed source-critical works on Genesis, Judges, and 1, 2 Samuel and became known to American and British audiences through his lectures ("Religion of Israel to the Exile," 1898-1899), which he delivered and published in America. James Muilenberg, "Budde, Karl Ferdinand Reinhard," *Enc Jud* 4 (1971) 1455; Kraus, *Geschichte*, 289-90; R. E. Clements, *One Hundred Years of Old Testament Interpretation* (Philadelphia: Westminster, 1976) 34.

[200]The title of this chapter in his Old Testament introduction points to Budde's general evaluation of Chronicles as a midrashic—rather than a historical—work. Budde's views in this regard were plainly set forth in his 1892 article in *ZAW*.

[201]Karl Budde, *Geschichte der althebräischen Litteratur* (2d ed.; Leipzig: C. F. Amelangs, 1909) 221, 227-28.

served as the basis for the Chronicler's understanding of the cult in his own day and as the guide for his reconstruction of the pre-exilic cult. Secondly, there was his belief in divine retribution: sin was punished by God and virtue was rewarded. In light of the latter principle the author of Chronicles rewrote the pre-exilic history of his people in order to correct the picture presented in Samuel-Kings.[202]

Budde's innovation in the study of Chronicles came in his discussion of the Chronicler's primary source, the Midrash. Budde believed that the Midrash of the Book of Kings (2 Chr 24:27) was identical with the Book of the Kings of Judah and Israel (2 Chr 16:11) and that the prophetical works cited in Chronicles (e.g., "the chronicles of Shemaiah the prophet" in 2 Chr 12:15) only referred to sections within the Midrash.[203] He further held that other sections from that great work were extant elsewhere in the Old Testament (e.g., Jonah, Ruth, and the apocryphal Prayer of Manasseh),[204] and he characterized the Midrash as "the fanciful and edifying interpretation and expansion of older tradition."[205] Therefore, while the restriction of the Chronicler's work to the nation of Judah must be attributed to the Chronicler himself, the author of the Midrash was responsible for the edifying expansions that illustrated divine retribution.[206]

Budde concluded, therefore, that the Chronicler's history had little value for the reconstruction of the history of the pre-exilic period, although it was useful for understanding the administration of the temple and its worship in the Chronicler's own day.[207]

> ...as a source for the old time undoubtedly (it has) very little (value). Among all those edifying stories of the midrash, there is not one, which we should assume as historical with confidence.[208]

> More valuable are the lists, especially as far as they concern Judah and Jerusalem, but only for the circumstances of the post-exilic time.[209]

Budde did admit, however, that isolated sections in Chronicles (e.g., the building notices for Uzziah and Jotham) may accurately reflect pre-exilic happenings. These sections are brief, scattered, and have an incidental ring to them, and may have derived from an earlier form of Samuel-Kings, since it is not improbable that the text of Samuel-

---

[202]*Ibid.*, 224-25.

[203]*Ibid.*, 227-28; Budde, "Vermutungen zum 'Midrasch des Buches der Könige'," *ZAW* 12 (1892) 37-38.

[204] *Ibid.*, 39-51.

[205]Budde, *Geschichte*, 228.

[206]*Ibid.*

[207]*Ibid.*, 228-29.

[208]*Ibid.*, 228.

[209]*Ibid.*, 229.

Kings was originally longer than it is now (the LXX of 1,2 Samuel seems to indicate this). However, one cannot be certain about this and at any rate, the expansions are of little value.'[210]

Budde stood in line with Wellhausen and Stade in his view of Chronicles. He did not believe that the Chronicler used authentic pre-exilic sources to any great extent but was dependent primarily on a post-exilic midrashic work. Therefore, the Chronicler's unique narratives that related to pre-exilic history could not be accepted with confidence. What little useful historical information about the pre-exilic period that could be found in Chronicles was to be discovered in various lists, but Budde assigned little historical usefulness to them. The Chronicler's real contributions to the reconstruction of history concerned the post-exilic community ca. 300 B. C. E., when the Chronicler composed his work. This agreed with Wellhausen's evaluation of Chronicles' usefulness. Budde's reconstruction of the Midrash and suggestion that the canonical books of Jonah and Ruth derived from it, however, did not meet with general acceptance.

j. Summary of the Treatment of Chronicles by Scholars Favoring a Late Date for P

Those scholars in the later half of the nineteenth century who held an exilic or post-exilic date for the Priestly Code tended to have a low estimation of Chronicles' value for the reconstruction of Israel's pre-exilic history. Five of the seven (Meyer, Stade, Piepenbring, Guthe, and Budde) clearly subscribed to Wellhausen's view of the order of the pentateuchal sources, while Renan was largely in agreement with Graf's work of 1866, and Seinecke's view was less clearly definable. Such an assignment of P to the exilic or post-exilic period and the attendant suspicion for its description of the pre-monarchical cult led quite naturally to the undermining of Chronicles' credibility, since the latter's description of the pre-exilic cult was so similar to that of P—and so different from that of Samuel-Kings. Consequently, five of the seven scholars (Seinecke, Meyer, Stade, Piepenbring, and Budde) generally rejected Chronicles for the reconstruction of Israel's pre-exilic history, and the other two (Renan and Guthe) advocated only a moderate—and even then a completely critical—use of the books. In the former group Stade, Piepenbring, and Budde believed that the Chronicler's primary source was the exilic or post-exilic Midrash of the Book of Kings, but in the latter group, Renan held that the Chronicler used Samuel-Kings, as well as a variety of other sources. Therefore, while the first group acknowledged that the author of Chronicles had sources for much of the information that is (presently, at least) unique to him, they still

---

[210]*Ibid.*, 228-29.

rejected it for historical reconstruction, since it derived from such a late and unreliable source. While Renan argued for a late Persian date for Chronicles, most of the others in this group of seven dated the books near the close of the fourth century B. C. E. Therefore, those scholars who held a late date for P exhibited a great reluctance to use 1, 2 Chronicles for the reconstruction of Israel's pre-exilic history.

3. SCHOLARS WHO HELD A PRE-EXILIC DATE FOR THE PRIESTLY CODE

a. Introduction

In the group of writers to be discussed who held that P had been composed before Deuteronomy, there was generally a greater degree of confidence in the historical reliability of Chronicles. The first figure to be treated is Nöldeke from the late 1860s. Then we will proceed to two scholars who produced works in the 1870s, Köhler and Zöckler, and one whose work dates from the 1880s, Kittel. Finally, we will move to three scholars who published studies in the 1890s, Klostermann, Neteler, and Oettli.

b. Nöldeke

The first of the figures to be treated in our discussion of scholars who rejected Graf's hypothesis of an exilic or post-exilic P is Theodor Nöldeke (1836-1930). Nöldeke specialized in the study of Semitic languages and in the history and civilization of Islam. From 1872 until 1906 he taught oriental languages at Strassburg.[211]

Nöldeke's views on the Pentateuch and Chronicles appeared in *Die Alttestamentliche Literatur* (1868). Since his own work dated two years after Graf's and since he mentioned the works of de Wette, Tuch, Ewald, Hupfeld, Knobel, Schrader, and Graf in pentateuchal research, it is apparent that he was aware of Graf's proposal that the legal materials in P were the latest of the pentateuchal sources. However, Nöldeke did not accept Graf's suggestion that a part of P should be assigned a date after Deuteronomy. On the contrary, Nöldeke proposed the order JE, P, D. He assigned the composition of D to the period just before Josiah's reform, JE to the tenth or early ninth century B. C. E., and P to a time shortly after them but before

---

[211]Nöldeke studied at Göttingen, Vienna, Leiden, and Berlin. His history of the Koran was his first major work and won the prize of the French Academie de Inscriptions (1859). In 1861, he began lecturing at Göttingen, but moved to Kiel in 1868, where he was made *ordentlicher Professor*. From there he moved to teach at Strassburg. He issued Syriac, Mandean, and Arabic grammars, essays for the *Encyclopaedia Britannica*, and various works on the Old Testament. "Nöldeke, Theodor," *Enc Brit* 19 (11th ed.; 1911) 734; "Nöldeke, Theodor," *Enc Jud* 12 (1971) 1202.

Joel and Amos, whom he assigned to ca. 800 B. C. E. The Priestly Code's picture of the Israelite law and state was an ideal one and never was a reality, according to Nöldeke. It was written from a purely theoretical standpoint.[212] Nöldeke's rejection of much in the Chronicler's picture of the pre-exilic Judean cult was consistent with this view of P's legislation.

Nöldeke held that the Chronicler was a levitical singer or door-keeper and composed a work that included Chronicles, Ezra, and Nehemiah ca. 200 B. C. E., if not later.[213] For the material in 1 Chronicles 1-9, the author relied on the Pentateuch and other collections of genealogies. For the remainder of 1, 2 Chronicles, the author used a great historical work entitled "The Book of the Kings of Israel and Judah," and his citations of prophetic works only designated sections within that great history. Nöldeke diagrammed his source-critical theory to account for the relations between Chronicles and Samuel-Kings in the following way.[214]

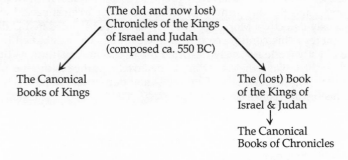

(The old and now lost)
Chronicles of the Kings
of Israel and Judah
(composed ca. 550 BC)

The Canonical
Books of Kings

The (lost) Book
of the Kings of
Israel & Judah

The Canonical
Books of Chronicles

The Chronicler's immediate source shared many of his own biases, including his dogmatic "pragmatism," which dictates that a king's misfortunes regularly pointed to his sins.[215] For this reason

---

[212]Theodor Nöldeke, *Die Alttestamentliche Literatur* (Leipzig: Quandt & Handel, 1868) 22-32.

[213]*Ibid.*, 55, 63-64.

[214]*Ibid.*, 57-59.

[215]Nöldeke traced the Chronicler's report about Manasseh's captivity back to his immediate source and proposed a rather novel idea about the way in which the story arose. He suggested first that a writer detected the problem in the text of 2 Kings: Manasseh was the worst king in the history of the Judean monarchy, and yet he reigned for fifty-five years and died peacefully. The writer's doctrine of pragmatism compelled him to believe that something had been omitted by the author of 2 Kings. Therefore, on the basis of the prediction in Isa 39:7 that Hezekiah's sons would be taken captive to Babylon, the author of the Chronicler's source proposed that the prophecy was fulfilled with Manasseh. Since the Assyrians were the dominant world power of the day, however, they had to have been Manasseh's captors. Finally, since the text said that Manasseh

and others, the Chronicler's main source was defective—even when used carefully, and the Chronicler was anything but careful. He was determined to exalt the levites, describe ancient feasts in great detail, and show that from antiquity his people had worshipped with priests and levites, just as in his own day.[216] Chronicles not only added much information that was not found in Samuel-Kings, but it also omitted much that was found in the latter work. The Chronicler dropped the history of the northern kingdom from his work, since he saw only evil there, and he omitted all reference to David's family problems, as well as to other events that would cast a shadow over things and people that were dear to him.[217] The Chronicler's inaccuracies that were due to his biases were compounded by his own carelessness and self-contradictions.[218]

It is clear that Nöldeke saw grave difficulties in the use of 1, 2 Chronicles for the reconstruction of pre-exilic history. The dissimilarities between Chronicles and Samuel-Kings had led him to believe that the Chronicler was strongly prejudiced and careless in his use of sources, and that his primary source for the monarchical period was seriously defective. Moreover, his conviction that P antedated D did not increase his confidence in Chronicles, since he maintained that the Priestly Code seriously distorted the events and institutions that it described. Nevertheless, Nöldeke believed that the historian could sift through the material in Chronicles and derive useful information for historical reconstruction.[219]

c. Köhler

One of the first histories of Israel to emerge after Graf's work of 1866 was that of August Köhler (1835-1897). Köhler was a product of Erlangen, where he had been strongly influenced by Franz Delitzsch and J. C. K. Hofmann, and spent—aside from brief periods at Jena and Bonn—most of his teaching career there, as well.[220] Köhler's

---

died in Jerusalem, the writer concluded that the king had been released and returned to Jerusalem. *Ibid.*, 59-60.

[216]*Ibid.*, 60-61.

[217]*Ibid.*, 61-62.

[218]*Ibid.*, 62.

[219]*Ibid.*, 60. Zöckler (*The Books of the Chronicles* in Lange's Commentary [New York: Scribner, Armstrong, 1877] 22) remarked that Nöldeke's treatment of Chronicles almost marked a return to the position of Gramberg. The statement by Nöldeke that prompted this evaluation was, "All great wars mentioned only in Chronicles must be very suspicious." Nöldeke, *Literatur*, 60.

[220]While Köhler did not ignore the more radical views of contemporary biblical criticism, he usually emerged from his research with a rejection of the views of modern Old Testament critics. His gifts were not those of the creative researcher, according to Sellin, but those of one who examined and evaluated the

greatest work was his *Lehrbuch der Biblischen Geschichte Alten Testamentes* (1875-93), in which he set out to write Israel's history as it was told by the documents of the Old Testament. Köhler did not approach his task as Old Testament historians had before him, because he did not believe that the historian's techniques were precise enough to get behind the books of the Old Testament in order to deal with their sources.

> Only this summons—and so often it was set up in recent times—is still not feasible without arbitrariness. For, as the contradictory results of the modern source criticism show, a severe and reliable separation of the individual components of sources of the Old Testament historical books can be accomplished only in a relatively small extent, so there is lacking a degree of certainty about the original form, kind, and *Tendenz* of the sources used by the Old Testament historical books. With this condition of the historical literature of the Old Testament, the presentation of Old Testament history must chiefly limit itself...to what has been developed in the Old Testament community itself on the basis of various and diverse reports finally as the generally admitted view of the course of its history.[221]

Köhler also pointed to the historian's presuppositions as a source for problems in the exercise of the historical critical method. Some historians saw all of life as determined by natural law, while others—like Köhler—admitted the possibility and reality of the miraculous activity and intervention of God.[222]

In his treatment of the Chronicler's contributions of information about the pre-exilic history of Israel, Köhler was reluctant to dismiss anything as clearly erroneous and the result of the author's theological *Tendenz*. He accepted the information—distinctive to Chronicles—that David organized the temple personel[223] and that David gathered materials and made preparations for the building of the Jerusalem temple.[224] In the case of the conflict between 2 Sm 24:24 and 1 Chr 21:25 over the price that David paid for the location of the future temple, Köhler proposed that textual corruption resulted in the former's figure of fifty shekels of silver and the latter's figure of six

---

positions of others. E. Sellin, "Köhler, August," *RE* 10 (1901) 615-18; Sellin, "Köhler, August," *ADB* 51 (1906) 310-11.

[221]August Köhler, *Lehrbuch der Biblischen Geschichte Alten Testamentes* (3 vols.; Erlangen: Andreas Deichert, 1875/1884/1893) 1.5-6.

[222]*Ibid.*, 1.4-5.

[223]*Ibid.*, 2.338.

[224]Köhler argued that David prepared for the building of the temple, since: (1) even 2 Samuel indicated that he had a lively interest in its construction; (2) he had plenty of stonemasons and other Canaanite laborers available; and (3) his supply of precious metals and stones would have been great from his military conquests and tribute. *Ibid.*, 2.322.

hundred shekels of gold. Originally, he thought, 2 Samuel read "fifty shekels of gold" and 1 Chronicles "six hundred shekels of silver," since the two amounts were equivalent in value.[225] Finally, Chronicles recorded immense amounts for the precious metals that were used in the building of the Solomonic temple. Köhler was doubtful that such sums were ever available to the king of Israel, and therefore, he suggested that the Chronicler's figures were in terms of the "king's shekal," which was half the weight of the usual shekal. Therefore, the amounts were halved and thus became reasonable.[226]

Köhler acknowledged in principle that the historical critical method should be used on the biblical documents, just as it had been used on nonbiblical materials, but he denied that the method was sufficiently refined to arrive at results that were not arbitrary. Consequently, he agreed with de Wette that a scientific history of Israel could not be written.

Köhler reconciled the historical witness of Chronicles with Samuel-Kings by harmonization. He assumed that the two agreed, and therefore, he saw his task to be that of discovering the reason for their present (apparent) disagreement. One very useful tool in this regard was the suggestion that textual corruption was responsible for their differences. Köhler's presumption was that the Chronicler's reports were accurate, even if they coincided with the author's *Tendenzen* and revealed information that was not recorded elsewhere. If the Chronicler's reports were at all credible, then Köhler was inclined to accept them. Therefore, Köhler's approach to Chronicles was little different from that of Keil and the other early defenders of Chronicles' historical reliability.

d. Zöckler

Another product of Erlangen and the instruction of Delitzsch and Hofmann was Otto Zöckler (1833-1906), who also studied at Giessen and Berlin. He began his teaching career at Giessen and became *ordentlicher Professor* at Greifswald in 1866. His researches were broad and extended into both the Old and New Testaments, theology, and church history. He had strong interests in history but was often eager to use his studies for apologetical purposes. He collaborated with Strack in the Kurzgefasster Kommentar, a series that Kraus called "very uncritical and conservative." As one might expect, Zöckler opposed the idea of a late P and the developmental theories of Wellhausen and accused the latter of teaching Darwinianism.[227]

---

[225]*Ibid.*, 2.330.

[226]*Ibid.*, 2.323.

[227]"Zöckler, Otto," *Enc Brit* 3 (9th ed. suppl.; 1898) 800; Victor Schultze, "Zöckler, Otto," *RE* 21 (1908) 704-8; Kraus, *Geschichte*, 290; Wellhausen, *Prolegomena*, 366.

As far as Chronicles was concerned, Zöckler maintained that it, along with Ezra and Nehemiah, were written by different authors but that they were edited by the same person. This final editor, perhaps a levitical singer or song master, was also the person who wrote 1, 2 Chronicles, and he did this at a time after Ezra and Nehemiah had already been written.[228] The date for his composition of Chronicles was the last part of the Persian or the first part of the Greek period, as the genealogy of Zerubbabel showed by tracing the generations down to about 350 B. C. E.[229] The sources for the Chronicler's work included genealogical material from Genesis and elsewhere, as well as historical sections from the Book of the Kings of Israel and Judah and from miscellaneous prophetical writings. The Book of the Kings of Israel and Judah was composed from the annals mentioned in the canonical Kings by prophets who wrote before the exile. While the prophetic writings of Jehu and Isaiah are said to have been part of the Book of the Kings of Judah and Israel, the other prophetic writings cited in Chronicles were not necessarily part of the same work (e.g., the Midrash of Iddo was surely separate).[230] Zöckler's conclusion was that,

> Where so many and so variously named sources are adduced, as in our author, it is most natural to suppose him actually to have access to a very rich field of original materials.[231]

It appeared, therefore, that Zöckler believed that the similarities between Samuel-Kings and Chronicles were best explained by their use of common sources, even though those sources only became available to the Chronicler through an intermediate writing. The differences between Chronicles and Samuel-Kings were caused by, among other things, the different intentions of the authors. Samuel-Kings was written from a prophetic standpoint and Chronicles from a levitical perspective. Moreover, the author of Samuel-Kings proceeded in an "unvarnished manner," while Chronicles' author was panegyric and apologetic in tone, and the latter author aimed at bringing out new aspects of the religious side of history.[232] Therefore, Zöckler denied that the Chronicler was a falsifier of history and that he invented materials to insert into his work.

> On the whole, a marked subjective colouring of his narrative in the direction of the priestly-Levitical standpoint may be ascribed to our author; he may be charged with having less aptitude for quiet, strictly

---

[228]Otto Zöckler, *The Books of the Chronicles,* in Lange's Commentary (New York: Scribner, Armstrong, 1877) 5-7.

[229]*Ibid.,* 8-11.

[230]*Ibid.,* 16-22.

[231]*Ibid.,* 21.

objective conception and presentation of his materials than his predecessors, the authors of the books of Samuel and Kings, and with putting
forward his didactic-moralizing been often too strongly, and not always
free from a legal externality of thought and intuition. But it appears
unwarranted to reproach him with a want of love for the truth or an
uncritical levity in dealing with facts, or to charge him with wilful
invention or falsification of history; for the solid foundation of old
original tradition gleams forth at every step of his narrative, and con-
veys, even where he goes farthest from the parallel text of the books of
Kings...the impression of the highest trustworthiness....[233]

In the body of his commentary Zöckler proceeded to accept as
historical the various unique contributions of the Chronicler (e.g., the
attack of Zerah on Asa)[234] and to harmonize statements in Chronicles
that conflicted with those in Samuel-Kings (e.g., the place of Joash's
death[235] or the cultic fidelity of Asa).[236] He also used the findings of
Mesopotamian archaeology whenever useful (e.g., using Assyrian
texts to assign Manasseh's captivity to the reign of Assurbanipal).[237]

At least one of Zöckler's aims in his commentary seems to have
been to defend Chronicles against the attacks of de Wette and the
others who attributed devious motives to the ancient writer. Consequently, Zöckler made full use of the arguments advanced by Keil,
Movers, and others in defense of the Chronicler's history. In addition
to his use of harmonization techniques to defend the credibility of
individual passages in Chronicles, Zöckler argued on the basis of his
source theory in order to vindicate the historical reliability of reports
that were unique to Chronicles. Finally, while he allowed for
differences in outlook and purpose for Chronicles and Samuel-Kings
and therefore perhaps for minor inaccuracies in Chronicles, Zöckler
was adamant that there were no major distortions in Chronicles and
that the author did not compose his work with the intent of deceiving
his readers. Therefore, Zöckler's work amounted to little more than a
continuation of the methods and arguments of Keil, Movers, and the
others who rose to defend Chronicles in the period before Graf.

e. Kittel

l) General
Of all the histories of Israel written between 1878 and 1900 in re-
sponse to Wellhausen's *Prolegomena*, the most significant was that by
Rudolf Kittel (1853-1929). The latter had studied at Tübingen in 1871

---

[232]*Ibid.*, 3-4, 24.
[233]*Ibid.*, 27.
[234]*Ibid.*, 202.
[235]*Ibid.*, 236.
[236]*Ibid.*, 201.
[237]*Ibid.*, 262.

under Johann Beck, an important figure in the *Heilsgeschichte* movement, which opposed de Wette and various other early radical critics.[238] Kittel singled out Beck and Karl Weizsacker (who taught him history) as two great influences in his education. Kittel's teaching positions were held at Tübingen, Stuttgart, Breslau, and Leipzig.[239]

Before 1903, Kittel's work was devoted primarily to studies on the Pentateuch and commentaries on the Old Testament historical books and Isaiah. His critical edition of the Hebrew text of Chronicles appeared in 1895 and his commentary on the books in 1902. His *Geschichte der Hebräer* (1888/1892) and his Old Testament theology (1899) were also published during this period. In 1903 and the years that followed, however, Kittel became increasingly involved in the study of the ancient Near Eastern background of the Old Testament and in the usefulness of archaeology for biblical studies. The beginning of this shift in his research was evident in his two publications that related to the Babel-Bible dispute in Germany.[240] In addition, there was his trip to Palestine in 1905/1906, an experience that transformed his view of the Old Testament.

> ...I came home with the resolve to see things from now on differently than before. There had begun in me a fermentation, which until today has not entirely come to rest.[241]

This trip sparked Kittel's interest in the culture and physical circumstances of ancient Israel,[242] and when he wrote the second edition to his history, he added an entire section on Palestine, which treated such matters as the pre-Israelite inhabitants of the land, the Amarna Period, and the culture and religion of Canaan before Israel's settlement. Later, in his essay "Die Zukunft der alttestamentlichen Wissenschaft" he distinguished three periods or stages in the history of Old Testament research, the last of which was a reorientation caused by various archaeological discoveries, such as the Amarna texts.[243] Two other especially significant works by Kittel during this

---

[238]Kraus, *Geschichte*, 209-15.

[239]The first to introduce Kittel to Old Testament studies was Ludwig Diestel, who published *Geschichte des Alten Testaments in der christlichen Kirche* in 1869. Rudolf Kittel, "Rudolf Kittel," in *Die Religionswissenschaft der Gegenwart in Selbstdarstellungen* (ed. E. Stange; Leipzig: Felix Meiner, 1925) 113-114, 116; Kraus, *Geschichte*, 1; Zev Garber, "Rudolf Kittel," *Enc Jud* 10 (1971) 1079-80.

[240]In 1903, Kittel wrote *Die babylonischen Ausgrabungen und die ältere biblische Geschichte* and *Der Babel-Biblestreit und die Offenbarungsfrage*.

[241]Kittel, "Kittel," 137.

[242]In 1908, Kittel published two works that indicated his archaeological interests: *Studien zur hebräischen Archäologie und Religionsgeschichte* and *Die orientalischen Ausgrabungen und die ältere biblische Geschichte* (5th ed. of *Die babylonischen Ausgrabungen*).

[243]*ZAW* 39 (1921) 84-99.

second part of his life were his new edition of the Old Testament text (*Biblia Hebraica*, 1905-) and his commentary on the Psalms (1914), which was his most prized publication.[244]

The first edition of *Geschichte der Hebräer* was published in two volumes (1888/1892) and translated into English (1895/1896). Kittel regarded it as his answer to Wellhausen.[245] After his trip to Palestine in 1905/1906, Kittel felt the need to issue a second edition of his history more strongly than ever, and in 1912 he was successful in doing so. The second volume of the history underwent little change, but the first volume received an entirely new section of over 175 pages devoted to the discussion of Israel's Palestinian surroundings and heritage. This, in turn, changed the way that Kittel viewed Israel's earliest life. The third volume of the history came out in 1927/1929.

The first major section of Kittel's history was a hundred-page discussion of the pentateuchal sources. In this part of his work, Kittel showed that he was completely committed to the historical-critical method and that he had accepted to a large degree the basic lines of Wellhausen's theory of the development of Israel's history. He diverged from Wellhausen, however, in that he dated the composition of Josiah's lawbook to the reign of Manasseh rather than to Josiah's day,[246] and he found three components in the Priestly Source: P1 was the groundwork of the Holiness Code and should be dated in the tenth or ninth centuries B. C. E.; P2 was the Priestly narrative, revised material from P1, and some newer laws and should be assigned to the eighth century—no later than Hezekiah; and P3 was a revision of the Holiness Code and ran roughly parallel in date to Deuteronomy, perhaps even as late as Jeremiah.[247]

Kittel believed that the historian's task was to relate facts to one another properly—to set them in proper chronological sequence—but also to explain

> the origin, growth, and decay of nations from the inner necessity of the forces at work in the nations themselves and from their connection with the general objects and aims of the history of the world.[248]

The essential forces at work in world history, according to Kittel, were ideas. These ideas found realization in various historical movements, and for Israel the most important ideas were religious ones.

---

[244]Kittel, "Kittel," 140.

[245]*Ibid.*, 122.

[246]Rudolf Kittel, *A History of the Hebrews* (Theological Translation Library; 2 volumes; London: Williams and Norgate, 1908/1909) 1.62-63.

[247]*Ibid.*, 1.132.

[248]*Ibid.*, 1.3.

We would rather study the external course of events in such a way as to learn from the facts the ideas they embody, believing that in every occurrence these are the really essential elements.[249]

Although the history of man's spiritual life since the beginning of our era has been largely affected by the ideas that flowed from Greece and Rome, it has received from no quarter a stronger or more lasting fertilising energy than from the small land of Judaea. But the spirit creates for itself its own forms in external life. Christianity, the embodiment of these new thoughts, has not been content with drawing into its province the faith, the mode of thought, the moral habits of the nations. It has also taken possession of their outward life, their culture and their politics, giving to these the form it would. There is hardly an event of true significance in the history of the nations touched by Christianity, the genesis and development of which can be shown to be unaffected by these fundamental facts.[250]

Religion, the most precious jewel of the Hebrew people! The State has perished. But this is the one race in which the national religion is stronger than the State, thus showing itself to be more than national. ...Israel henceforward is politically subordinate, and indeed altogether insignificant, yet her ideas conquer the world.[251]

A final aspect of Kittel's historiography was his conviction that history was teleological. While each person acted with a certain goal in mind, history as a whole also pursued a goal, and it was into this goal of all history that the goals of individuals were absorbed.

When a man acts it is because he has a single object in view. But each several event becomes a link in the chain of universal history and there alone finds its true place. So also the single object aimed at by the individual is absorbed in that more universal object, which stands above it and expresses the ultimate idea of the whole process of history. If history does not demonstrate the truth of a teleological view of the world, we, at all events, cannot understand history without carrying the latter idea in our minds. When history deals with the past it is compelled so to study the event as to find out what were the determining causes. And when it looks into the future it must point out the already existing germ of what is hereafter to be. Yet more. Out of the action and reaction it must educe the law to which all human life is subject and the goal which it seeks. And no less surely must the recognition of the purposes of the whole enrich and deepen the inquirer's comprehension of each several part.[252]

[249]*Ibid.*, 1.5.
[250]*Ibid.*, 1.1-2.
[251]*Ibid.*, 1.4.
[252]*Ibid.*, 1.4-5.

In some of these comments by Kittel about the science of historiography, he revealed his allegiance to Ranke.[253] One also finds the
influence of Hegel in his comments on the importance of ideas for
history. Generally, Kittel shared many of the concepts and assumptions about history that were held by earlier scholars, who wrote
histories of Israel, and so his historiography is nothing new.

Kittel believed that Moses proclaimed a kind of ethical monolatry
to the people of Israel and that there ensued a struggle afterwards
between two religious forces: the strict allegiance to Yahweh, as
taught by Moses and the syncretism of a Yahweh-Baal cult. The
struggle ended in victory for the former because of the preaching of
the prophets. In this way, the prophets of the eighth century were not
proclaiming something radically new; rather, they were championing
the religion of Moses. The period of Judaism which followed the exile
was a great decline, in Kittel's view, from the heights of earlier
Israelite religion.

> Judaism, so called, that is, the later or Jewish phase of the people of
> Israel, which repels us when compared with that of the Hebrew period,
> and is a caricature of true and healthy life, full of absurdity and of bad
> taste, loses its confusedness and meanness when we look at the brilliant
> goal after which it strives.[254]

As one might suspect, for Kittel Christianity represents the goal
toward which Israelite history moved.

2) Chronicles

There were three observations that Kittel made about Chronicles,
which were crucial for his use of the work as a historian. First, there
was the relatively late date of Chronicles with regard to the events of
the pre-exilic period, which it purported to describe. Kittel believed
that Chronicles, Ezra, and Nehemiah derived from a common author
and were composed sometime between 332 and 250 B. C. E.[255]
Secondly, the Chronicler used only one major source, the Midrash to
the Book of Kings.[256] Finally, the Chronicler used his source with

---

[253]*Ibid.*, 1.5.

[254]*Ibid.*, 1.4.

[255]*Ibid.*, 2.225. In his commentary Kittel specified a date ca. 300 B. C. E. on the
basis of Zerubbabel's genealogy in 1 Chronicles 3 and the mention of Jaddua in
Neh 12:22. *Die Bücher der Chronik* (Handkommentar zum Alten Testament, 6/1;
ed. W. Nowack; Göttingen: Vandenhoeck & Ruprecht, 1902) xv-xvi .

[256]*History*, 2.225-29. In his commentary, however, Kittel maintained that by
means of his source citations the Chronicler designated two works: (1) a great
Book of Kings, which had been edited on the basis of the canonical 1, 2 Kings,
and (2) a midrash, which contained still further information. All the citations of
prophetic materials in Chronicles—except for the references to Isaiah (the

considerable freedom, reshaping, omitting, and making additions in order to glorify the Jerusalem temple, the Levites, and the pious kings of Judah.[257] In light of these conclusions, the historian should exercise extreme caution in the use of Chronicles as a historical source.

> It necessarily follows from these facts that Chronicles as an historical source is to be used *only with the greatest caution*. We may say in advance that the information it gives is to be received with distrust rather than with trust, since the whole character of the book shows it to be anything but a purely documentary narrative-book.[258]

Kittel illustrated this principle in his rejection of 2 Chronicles 15, the story of an encounter between Asa and Azariah, as a "later Midrash,"[259] and in his comment about Manasseh's captivity and deliverance (2 Chr 33:10-13) that "very few serious reasons can be advanced in favour of its historicity."[260] However, Kittel stopped short of the complete, *a priori* rejection of all materials in Chronicles for the reconstruction of Israel's pre-exilic history. He believed that each datum in Chronicles should be weighed independently to determine its credibility.

> But caution and essential distrust should not lead us into the error of considering that we are relieved from the necessity of testing the actual state of matters in each individual case. Considering the defectiveness of the information given in our Biblical Book of Kings, we cannot avoid supposing it possible that Chronicles has occasionally supplied us with more detailed information based on trustworthy ancient sources. Even in the cases in which Chronicles 'has looked at and represented things entirely through the medium of Levitical priestly ideas,' it, or its authority, may quite well have drawn its facts from older narratives which are given in the Biblical Book of Kings only in the form of abstracts or epitomes. The decision on this point must depend on each individual instance; still, no one can say it is unlikely that, in the time of Alexander the Great, somewhat more was known about the older

---

canonical book of Isaiah) and Iddo (a small, independent midrash)—probably referred to sections within the great Book of Kings.

[257]*History*, 2.225-29. In his commentary Kittel wrote that the Chronicler and the authors of his two main sources held in common two beliefs: (1) a pragmatic belief in divine retribution, and (2) a commitment to the kind of worship promoted by the priestly writing of the Pentateuch. However, Kittel also believed that the Chronicler differed from his predecessors in his sympathy for the inferior members of the temple service (e.g., levitical singers, musicians, and doorkeepers). *Chronik*, xiv.

[258]*History*, 2.230.

[259]*Ibid.*, 2.248.

[260]*Ibid.*, 2.378.

Israelitish history than we are able to-day to gather from the Book of
Kings.[261]

Examples of Kittel's willingness to accept information from
Chronicles are his appropriations of the Chronicler's information
about Rehoboam's fortresses,[262] that Jehosheba was the wife of
Jehoiada,[263] and Uzziah's military successes and leprosy.[264] He left
open the matters of Zerah's attack on Asa[265] and that of the Moabite
coalition on Jehoshaphat[266]—battles reported only in Chronicles.

In these matters, Kittel qualified de Wette and Wellhausen's
radical rejection of everything in Chronicles for the reconstruction of
pre-exilic history. Stade pre-empted him in this, but Kittel stated
explicitly what Stade had only implied. The significant difference
between the two in this regard, though, is that while Stade was extremely sparing in his use of Chronicles, Kittel used the books quite
often.[267]

3) Summary

Kittel's treatment of Chronicles was thoroughly critical. His
source analysis of the books offered the most complex theory to date.
However, since he maintained relatively early dates for the material
in the Priestly Code, he was quite naturally more inclined to accept
certain cultic information from Chronicles than were Graf and
Wellhausen, for example. His position toward the historical reliability
of Chronicles in general was midway between Wellhausen's
complete rejection of the books and Keil's complete acceptance. He
concluded that each bit of information in Chronicles should be
evaluated on its own merits. Moreover, it does not appear that
Kittel's interest in archaeological matters exercised any significant
influence on his views of either P or Chronicles.

---

[261]*Ibid.*, 2.230.

[262]*Ibid.*, 2.247.

[263]*Ibid.*, 2.286.

[264]*Ibid.*, 2.331.

[265]*Ibid.*, 2.249. In his commentary Kittel wrote that one must admit that the
Chronicler's account about Asa and Zerah was strongly embellished. Kittel
himself believed that the basis for Chronicles' story was Asa's success in defeat-
ing a dangerous raid by Arabian Cushites into Judah. *Chronik*, 131-32.

[266]*History*, 2.283. Kittel notes in his commentary that the basis for the
Chronicler's account may have been the story in 2 Kings 3 about an alliance of
Jehoshaphat and Ahab against Moab. *Chronik*, 140.

[267]In his Chronicles commentary Kittel elaborated a very complex source
theory for Chronicles, which included stages behind the sources that the
Chronicler cited in his work, as well as editorial changes that were made subsequent to the Chronicler's own activity. Cf. *Chronik*, x-xv.

f. Klostermann

1) General

Along with Köhler and Zöckler, August Heinrich Klostermann (1837-1915) also studied at Erlangen, before becoming *Privatdozent* in Göttingen and finally Professor of Old Testament at Kiel, where he spent the rest of his career. He is probably known best for his "Crystallization Hypothesis," which he advanced as an alternative to the documentary hypothesis of Wellhausen and others. Klostermann maintained that the Pentateuch arose out of Israel's cultic life and that the kernel of the Pentateuch was the Sinaitic law. The remainder of the pentateuchal materials gradually "crystallized" around that law, as it was preached in the cult and "modernized" for new generations. According to his analysis, the correct order for the pentateuchal sources was J, E, P, D, with P having derived from the Solomonic period. Through his "awareness of the process of gradual agglomeration" and of the "central importance of cultic and community life," he anticipated two important insights of later traditio-historical research.[268]

2) Chronicles

Klostermann's understanding of Chronicles was most fully expressed in his article "Chronik" in Herzog's *Realencyklopädie*,[269] and his estimation of the Chronicler's value as a historical source was evident in his *Geschichte des Volkes Israel*.[270] He believed that Chronicles was initially part of a larger work that included Ezra and Nehemiah, but the only conclusions that he offered about the date and authorship of the books were contained in the following sentences.

> Modern critics conclude from doubtful indications that the author wrote in the beginning of the Greek period and, from his full description of cult and clergy, that he was a priest or a Levite. Certain it is that he

---

[268]"Klostermann, August Heinrich," *The New Schaff-Herzog Encyclopedia of Religious Knowledge* 6 (1910) 353. Klostermann's views of the Pentateuch are presented in *Der Pentateuch. Beiträge zu seinem Verständnis und seiner Entstehungsgeschichte* (Leipzig: Deichert, 1893). Cf. R J. Thompson, *Moses and the Law*, 111-12; Douglas Knight, *Rediscovering the Traditions of Israel* (SBL Dissertation Series, 9; rev. ed.; Missoula: Scholars Press, 1975) 69-70; Kraus, *Geschichte*, 375-76.

[269]Klostermann, "Chronik, die Bücher der," *PRE* 3 (3d ed.; 1898) 84-98. This article was translated into English as "Chronicles, Books of" in *The New Schaff-Herzog Encyclopedia of Religious Knowledge* 3 (1909) 68-71.

[270]Klostermann, *Geschichte des Volkes Israel* (Müchen: C. H. Beck, 1896).

wrote at a time when the memorabilia of Ezra and Nehemiah were consulted for the understanding of their time.[271]

It appears, therefore, that Klostermann wanted to separate himself from those other "modern critics" who assigned a date to Chronicles in the Greek period, but it is not clear whether Klostermann's preference was for a date in the Persian period.

The Chronicler's sources, according to Klostermann, included various canonical books of the Old Testament—Samuel-Kings and Isaiah, among others—but his primary source was "The Book of the Kings of Israel and Judah," which was composed after the restoration community had been established. Its author used compositions about David's first and last years, about Solomon and the kings of Israel and Judah, as well as a collection of Judean prophetic narratives. In addition, there were "the traditional interpretations of the schools," which gave life to dead names, and the traditions of priests, Levites, and important families. Klostermann denied that either the author of this work or the Chronicler himself acted in bad faith or invented or altered materials. On the contrary, he argued that on the basis of Ezra and Nehemiah, where the Chronicler was content to extract materials from the autobiographies of Ezra and Nehemiah and other official documents, it is clear that he faithfully copied his sources.[272] Therefore, Klostermann concluded that,

> Like all historical books, even more so, because of its origin, Chronicles demands an able and cautious examination, if one would not sin against the Biblical book, nor against the science of impartial historical investigation.[273]

Klostermann attempted to steer a middle course between the two extremes of accepting everything in Chronicles, as though the Chronicler wrote as a careful modern historian, and of rejecting everything that is unique to Chronicles, as de Wette and others had done.

In Klostermann's own history of Israel, his stance became even clearer and his confidence in Chronicles as a useful historical source for the pre-exilic period more evident. He accepted the Chronicler's reports that David organized the cult, Rehoboam built fortresses, Zerah attacked Asa and was defeated, Hannani rebuked Asa, Jehoshaphat instituted judicial and educational reforms and was attacked by a Moabite coalition, and that Joash was assassinated for his involvement in the murder of Zechariah. Finally, Klostermann reported the Chronicler's story about Manasseh's captivity, but

---

[271]Klostermann, "Chronicles," 70.
[272]*Ibid.*
[273]*Ibid.*, 71.

without arguing either for or against its historicity.[274] It appears, therefore, that Klostermann had considerable confidence in Chronicles as a reliable source for pre-exilic history.

There were at least two aspects of Klostermann's pentateuchal study that affected his work on Chronicles. First, there was the matter of his early dating of P. Since he had assigned P to the Solomonic period, and since there were many similarities between the ways that the cult was described and viewed in Chronicles and P, the Chronicler's narrative was quite naturally less suspicious to Klostermann than to those Old Testament critics, who assigned a post-exilic date to P and doubted its credibility. Therefore, Klostermann's view of P strengthened the credibility of Chronicles in his eyes.

A second matter was the MT of the Pentateuch and Chronicles. Klostermann believed that the MT of the Pentateuch was the product of considerable editorial activity—activity which continued down to the time of Ezra. In the same way, Klostermann devoted an unusually large part of his article—well over half of it—to a discussion of the text of Chronicles, and he concluded that textual corruptions and its original careless orthography and the subsequent additions, harmonizations with Samuel-Kings, and textual corruptions necessitated a thorough revision "before it may be used as a witness or its claims denied."[275] Therefore, Klostermann's view of the MT of Chronicles led him to be more reluctant than de Wette and others to point to each difference between Chronicles and Samuel-Kings as an indication of the former's theological *Tendenz*.[276]

3) Summary

Klostermann held to a very early date for P and showed a great reluctance to discard anything in Chronicles about the pre-exilic period as historically inaccurate. His presumption was in favor of the Chronicler's historical credibility, and he maintained that the scholar's inability to determine the original state of the text of 1, 2 Chronicles made it difficult to define which differences between Chronicles and Samuel-Kings derived from the Chronicler's *Tendenzen*. Therefore, while Klostermann left many matters unsettled (e.g., the date and authorship of Chronicles and the accuracy of

---

[274]Klostermann, *Geschichte*, 159-64, 202-3, 205, 208.

[275]Klostermann, "Chronicles," 70.

[276]Klostermann was not the first to recognize the serious textual problem that was involved in determining the credibility of Chronicles, but to a certain degree the importance that he attached to it anticipated the later work of Werner Lemke. Cf. Lemke's dissertation, "Synoptic Studies in the Chronicler's History" (Harvard, 1964), and his article, "The Synoptic Problem in the Chronicler's History," *HTR* 58 (1965) 349-63.

various bits of information in 1, 2 Chronicles), he showed little reluctance to use information in Chronicles for his historical reconstruction of the pre-exilic period.

g. Neteler

At the close of the nineteenth century, traditional, pre-de Wettian views of Chronicles were still popular in some circles, as Bernhard Neteler's (1821-1912) commentary on Chronicles (*Die Bücher der Chronik der Vulgata und des hebräischen Textes übersetzt und erklärt*, 1899) showed. Neteler was a Catholic scholar who argued that Ezra wrote both 1, 2 Chronicles and the book bearing his name, since the two works shared the same language and manner of presentation. He left open, however, the question of whether he wrote the works at one time or issued them separately. The genealogy in 1 Chronicles 3 that brought the generations down to a time after Ezra's day was added by a later writer.[277] Ezra's sources for the genealogical material in 1 Chronicles 1-9 included Genesis, military rolls, and priestly/levitical registers, and a variety of sources (e.g., prophetic writings, which are no longer extant) were used for 1 Chronicles 10- 2 Chronicles 36.[278] The primary usefulness of Chronicles, according to Neteler, was to be found in the supplementary information that it offered to what one found elsewhere in the Old Testament.[279]

As far as the credibility of the Chronicler's record was concerned, Neteler contended that the books set forth "true history."[280] He argued that the Jewish community had always maintained this position and that surely modern critics did not know more about Ezra's sources (e.g., the form of the Pentateuch) than Ezra himself. Furthermore, he charged that modern critical views were often characterized by subjectivity, and it had yet to be proven that the incorrect numbers in Chronicles proceeded from Ezra, rather than from his sources. On the latter point, Neteler suggested the possibility that originally the numbers were recorded and transmitted with numerals, rather than by number words, and consequently the opportunities for errors in transmission were greater.[281]

Neteler's commentary upheld the basic accuracy of the Chronicler's history, and even when there were obvious contradictions between Chronicles and Samuel-Kings (as in the case of numbers, for example), Neteler attempted to defend the Chronicler from charges of deliberate falsification or stupid carelessness. Therefore, Neteler quite naturally accepted Chronicles' reports about

---

[277]B. Neteler, *Die Bücher der Chronik* (Munster: Theissing, 1899) 4-5.
[278]*Ibid.*, 6.
[279]*Ibid.*, 5, 23.
[280]*Ibid.*, 6-7.
[281]*Ibid.*

Asa's war with Zerah (whom Neteler identified as an Ethiopian king),[282] Jehoshaphat's conflict with the Moabite coalition,[283] and finally, Manasseh's captivity.[284]

Neteler's commentary offered nothing really new to the investigation of Chronicles' historical reliability. On the contrary, it appears to represent a return to some of the positions that were popular in the pre-de Wettian period (e.g., his view that Ezra wrote 1, 2 Chronicles). Moreover, at least two of his proposals were almost certain to engender little support: (1) his excision of part of 1 Chronicles 3 in order to prevent the genealogy from extending past Ezra's day, and (2) his affirmations that the Chronicler had adequate sources and that contemporary scholarship would do better to trust the ancient writer's information rather than dispute it on the basis of modern, subjective research. Neteler's work has its chief value as an example of the more traditional views about Chronicles in Roman Catholic circles at the end of the nineteenth century.

h. Oettli

A seventh figure in the late nineteenth century who held to a pre-deuteronomic Priestly Code was Samuel Oettli (1846-1911), a professor at Greifswald. While he acknowledged the value of separating the Pentateuch into sources, he insisted that Moses was indeed Israel's chief law-giver and that even in the days of Amos and Hosea there was a Pentateuch with its priestly narrative, institutions, and law.[285]

Two of Oettli's works are useful for a consideration of his view of Chronicles' credibility: his commentary on Chronicles in *Die geschichtlichen Hagiographen und das Buch Daniel* (1889) and his *Geschichte Israels bis auf Alexander den Grossen* (1905).[286] In them Oettli

---

[282]*Ibid.*, 243-44.

[283]*Ibid.*, 267-68.

[284]Neteler's interest in relating Israel's history to discoveries in the field of ancient Near Eastern archaeology deserves mention. In his discussion of Manasseh's captivity, for example, Neteler described the revolt of Shamash-shum-ukin against Ashurbanipal and set the arrest of the Jewish king against that background. (*Ibid.*, 325.) In addition, the first part of Neteler's commentary contained a section on the connections between Egyptology and the Bible, a chronological table of Israel's history, and a discourse on the relation of Assyrian history to Israel's past.

[285]Cf. Oettli, *Das Gesetz Hammurabis und die Thora Israels* (Leipzig: Deichert, 1903) and *Amos und Hosea* (Gütersloh: C. Bertelsmann, 1901); Herbert F. Hahn, *The Old Testament and Modern Research* (Philadelphia: Fortress, 1966) 98; Thompson, *Moses and the Law*, 73.

[286]The first work was in the Kurzgefasster Kommentar series, which was edited by H. Strack and O. Zöckler. The latter scholar also wrote a commentary

set forth his conviction that Chronicles was originally part of a larger work that included Ezra and Nehemiah and that a levite of the families of singers was responsible for it. On the basis of 1 Chr 3:19-24, Oettli assigned the work to the Greek period.[287] The two main sources that the Chronicler used for his composition, according to Oettli, were the Book of the Chronicles of the Kings of Judah and Israel and a midrash on the latter work. While the author surely knew of Samuel-Kings, there is no proof that he used them. Two aspects of Chronicles that linked it with Samuel-Kings are its chronological arrangement of material and its evaluation of the various kings of Judah. Oettli believed that the former aspect was too general to establish a link between the two works, and he maintained that the Chronicler's evaluation of the kings of Judah could have been derived from some source besides Samuel-Kings. Finally, Oettli noted that the author used Genesis for the genealogies in 1 Chr 1:1-2:2 and various other extra-biblical sources, such as ancient genealogical lists, for the remainder of the genealogies.[288]

Oettli took a rather pessimistic view of the modern historian's ability to write a history of Israel according to the requirements of modern historical science.

> To write the history of Israel according to the requirements of modern historical science is an insoluable task. For the biblical sources, which are available, would probably point to the finger of God in the earthly events, but not to the pragmatic connections of events under the law of cause and effect. That first viewpoint has restricted by it both the selection and the form of the tradition's material.[289]

What the researcher of Israel's history could do, however, was to "collect the biblical reports, certify, arrange and draw lines of connection between them in order to unify them as far as possible into a complete picture of history" and also to set forth more plainly than the biblical writers did the broad background of the ancient world.[290]

As far as Chronicles' historicity was concerned, Oettli believed that it was inferior to the older historical books, "since it is dominated completely by cultic viewpoints," and so it must be used with caution

---

on Chronicles, which shared some of Oettli's confidence in the Chronicler's reliability.

[287]S. Oettli, *Die geschichtlichen Hagiographen und das Buch Daniel* (Kurzgefasster Kommentar zu den heiligen Schriften Alten und Neuen Testamentes so wie zu den Apokryphen, eds. H. Strack & O. Zöckler; Nordlingen: C. H. Beck., 1889) 4, 10.

[288]*Ibid.*, 8.7-10.

[289]S. Oettli, *Geschichte Israels bis auf Alexander den Grossen*, Part 1 of *Die Geschichte Israels* (Stuttgart: Vereinsbuchhandlung, 1905) iii.

[290]*Ibid.*

and each section be evaluated on its own merits.[291] Generally, however, Oettli was inclined to accept the reports of the Chronicler— especially those that related to the wars of the kings. He accepted, for instance, the account of Zerah's attack on Asa, arguing that the former was not Osorkon I, but was a North Arabian Cushite, whose army raided Judah. Oettli conceded, though, that the numbers of the armies that were given in Chronicles were exaggerated.[292] Similarly, he accepted the account in 2 Chr 20:1-30 about Jehoshaphat's conflict with the coalition of Moabites, Ammonites, and Meunites, although he held that the Chronicler's report was "entirely midrashic" in character and probably derived from some local tradition. Therefore, he had more serious reservations about the latter narrative than about the Asa-Zerah story.[293] Finally, Oettli also found a historical kernel in Chronicles' account of Manasseh's captivity and used the Assyrian materials to reconstruct two possible settings for the event. The first was under Esarhaddon, when the Assyrian king attacked Tirhakah and possibly moved to insure the loyalty of his Palestinain vassals. The second was the revolt of Shamash-shum-ukin against Ashurbanipal, when the anti-Assyrian party in Judah may have soiled Manasseh's reputation and led to his brief imprisonment.[294]

Oettli's observations about the difficulty in writing a scientific history of Israel were shared by Köhler, who also held an early date for the Priestly Code and tended to accept most of the Chronicler's information as historically reliable. Oettli's treatment of Chronicles, however, by no means reflects the confidence that some earlier scholars (e.g., Keil) had in the books. In general, Oettli's work represents a moderately critical approach to 1, 2 Chronicles, but it adds nothing new to its use as a historical source.

i. Summary of the Treatment of Chronicles by Scholars Favoring an Early Date for P

Among those scholars who agreed that P should be assigned a pre-exilic date, there was considerable diversity about what date should be set for the work. Klostermann believed that it derived from the Solomonic period, Nöldeke dated it shortly before 800 B. C. E., and Kittel divided the work into three parts and held that it may have been completed as late as Jeremiah's day. There was, however, with at least six of these scholars a general acceptance of information from 1, 2 Chronicles for reconstructing Israel's pre-exilic history. Neteler was the least critical of all in his use of Chronicles, and Nöldeke was

---

[291]*Ibid.*, 249.
[292]*Ibid.*, 340-41.
[293]*Ibid.*, 361.
[294]*Ibid.*, 424-25.

the most critical and urged that much of Chronicles' material be rejected for the reconstruction of the pre-exilic period. The other figures fell between these two poles, with Köhler and Zöckler nearer the position of Neteler than were Kittel, Klostermann, and Oettli. There were no consistent differences between the scholars who favored a pre-exilic P and those who opposed such as far as the date of Chronicles or the existence of sources for the books were concerned. The only figure in either group, however, who argued that Ezra wrote 1, 2 Chronicles, was Neteler. Most of the others believed that some anonymous author wrote not only Chronicles but also Ezra and Nehemiah as well.

4. SUMMARY OF THE CONSEQUENCES OF A LATE P FOR THE RECONSTRUCTION OF ISRAELITE HISTORY

The assignment of an exilic or post-exilic date for the Priestly Code had important consequences for the question of Chronicles' credibility and usefulness as a historical source. A survey of the histories of Israel, Old Testament introductions, and other literature reveals that in general those scholars who favored a pre-exilic date for P also tended to have greater confidence in Chronicles as a reliable historical source for the pre-exilic period than those who argued for an exilic or post-exilic date for P. The differences between these two views of Chronicles were not due to the different views that were held on the matters of the authorship and date of Chronicles or whether the Chronicler used Samuel-Kings or other sources. On the contrary, there was a considerable amount of agreement on these issues. The crucial factor that correlated a scholar's position on the dating of P with his view of Chronicles was that a late date for P was invariably accompanied by a rejection of the historical accuracy of much that was narrated in P. It was usually thought that a late P reflected to a large degree the ideas, institutions, and biases of the exilic and post-exilic Jewish community, and therefore, that its historical account could not be trusted. When this was combined with the recognition of the similarities between P and Chronicles in thought and description of the cult, it was usually concluded that Chronicles was also an unreliable witness to Israel's pre-exilic history. Such a conclusion was strengthened by the notation of the considerable differences between the portrayals of Israel's monarchical period in the Chronicler's history and Samuel-Kings.

D. SUMMARY OF CHAPTER THREE

The second serious challenge to the usefulness of Chronicles for the reconstruction of Israel's pre-exilic history began with the suggestion of Reuss and Vatke in the 1830s that P was the latest of the pentateuchal sources, rather than one of the earliest. The theory was largely ignored for about thirty years, until Graf presented it again in 1866 and 1869, and it was picked up in the works of Kuenen, Colenso, and Wellhausen. By the end of the nineteenth century the J E D P sequence and an exilic or post-exilic date for P comprised the most popular single theory of pentateuchal origins among Old Testament critics.

All of these scholars—Reuss, Vatke, Graf, Kuenen, Colenso, and Wellhausen—were agreed that Chronicles was generally an unreliable guide to Israel's pre-exilic history. While sometimes it was allowed that one could use isolated bits of information from Chronicles to reconstruct Israel's pre-exilic history, some (e.g., Wellhausen) denied to the historian the use of anything in Chronicles for the critical description of the pre-exilic period. Other scholars, who argued for a late P and who wrote histories of Israel, Old Testament introductions, and other works that addressed the reliability of Chronicles as a historical source, felt a similar reluctance to use material from the Chronicler's history for the reconstruction of Israel's pre-exilic history. On the other hand, those scholars who held a pre-exilic date for P used far more material from Chronicles in their treatments of Israel's pre-exilic history and displayed much more confidence in the usefulness of the Chronicler's history for reconstructing the monarchical period. Even among these scholars, however, the Chronicler's accounts were usually not accepted uncritically or without change.

The crucial element in this challenge to Chronicles' reliability was that if the credibility of P was undermined then that of 1, 2 Chronicles was eroded as well. The proposal of a late date for P and the conviction that P's narratives had been distorted by the institutions, beliefs, and prejudices of the restoration community constituted a serious challenge to the work's credibility as a historical witness to the pre-exilic period. Because of the similarities between P and Chronicles in thought and in their descriptions of the Israelite cult, and because of the striking dissimilarities between Samuel-Kings and Chronicles in their portrayals of Israel's monarchical history, scholarly confidence in Chronicles as a historical witness to the pre-exilic period was similarly shaken. The latter half of the nineteenth century, however, witnessed the growth of a movement to use archaeology to defend the historical reliability of the biblical records in general, and the credibility of Chronicles in particular.

CHAPTER IV

ARCHAEOLOGY AND THE CREDIBILITY OF CHRONICLES

A. INTRODUCTION

The archaeological investigation of the Near East began in earnest in the nineteenth century, and by the end of the century an enormous amount of ancient epigraphical and artifactual material had been recovered. These discoveries exerted a powerful influence on the interpretation of the Bible in general and on Chronicles in particular. In this chapter we will begin by surveying the progress of nineteenth century Near Eastern archaeology and then proceed to treat those figures who used the discoveries of archaeology in a major way to defend Chronicles' credibility. Finally, we will treat those who responded to this use of archaeology in defense of Chronicles' reliability.

B. NINETEENTH CENTURY ARCHAEOLOGICAL RESEARCH

1. INTRODUCTION

The attention of western Europe turned to the Near East when Napoleon led his army into Egypt in 1798 in an attempt to apply pressure on the British in India. The findings of scholars who accompanied him and the publication of their discoveries excited interest in Europe, and this interest increased throughout the century.[1] Many were particularly interested in Palestine, because they regarded it as the Holy Land, the place where their religious traditions had been born. Others, however, were impelled by the profit motive, since antiquities brought such good prices in Europe. Still others were prompted by a genuine desire to understand ancient history and

---

[1]Georg Steindorff, "Excavations in Egypt," in *Explorations in Bible Lands During the 19th Century* (ed. H. V. Hilprecht; Philadelphia: A. J. Holmman, 1903) 628; Glynn E. Daniel, *A Hundred Years of Archaeology* (London: Gerald Duckworth, 1950) 68.

cultures. Finally, European nations had strong expansionistic tendencies in the nineteenth century and were eager to push into the Near
East.[2] The Turkish government, on the other hand, controlled that
part of the Eastern Mediterranean and for the first half of the nineteenth century was reluctant to admit exploration. This reluctance
diminished, though, in the middle and latter part of the century, and
consequently, great archaeological progress was forthcoming.[3]

2. *PALESTINE*

In Palestine serious archaeological investigation began in the
nineteenth century with the explorations of travelers, who noted loca-
tions of various ancient and modern settlements and commented on
the customs of the people and aspects of the terrain. Seetzen (1805-)
and Burckhardt (1809-) were two of the earliest travelers in the
century, and they were followed by Edward Robinson and Eli Smith
(1838-), whose work laid the foundation for critical topography in
Palestine.[4] The reports of these travelers in the first half of the nineteenth century excited popular interest in Palestine, and the latter half
of the century was characterized by the formation of societies in various nations to subsidize and promote archaeological investigation. In
1865, The Palestine Exploration Fund was founded in Britain, and in
1869, it began to publish its journal. The American Palestine
Exploration Fund was founded in 1870 and modeled after the British
society, but it folded later, only to be resurrected in 1900 as the
American School of Oriental Research. The German society was
established in 1877 as the Deutsche Verein zur Forschung Palästinas,
and its journal *ZDPV* began publication the following year. The École
pratique d'Études bibliques du Convent St. Etienne was the French
counterpart to the other European societies, and it began in 1890 and
published a journal, *Revue Biblique*, from 1892 onward.

Few large excavations took place in Palestine during the nineteenth century, but there were numerous projects and discoveries
that excited public interest and laid the foundation for later archaeological investigation in the land. In 1855, the sarcophagus of
Eshmunazar, King of Sidon, was found. It contained a 990 word inscription and led to the further exploration of the Phoenician coast by
Renan and the French in 1860-1861. The work of the PEF began in
1865 with an expedition by Wilson and Anderson to map Western
Palestine; this was completed by Conder and Kitchener from 1872-
1877, and so an accurate map of western Palestine was available to
later archaeologists. In the meantime, Warren had gone to Jerusalem

---

[2]Wilbur D. Jones, *Venus and Sothis* (Chicago: Nelson-Hall, 1982) 11.
[3]Seton Lloyd, *Foundations in the Dust* (New York: Oxford University, 1947) 198.
[4]Kraus, *Geschichte*, 163-64.

for the PEF and sunk shafts at various spots in 1866, and in 1868, on the other side of the Jordan Klein found the Mesha Inscription at Diban, which was important for biblical studies, because it mentioned the relations between Moab and Israel, and in 1880, the Siloam Inscription, another exciting epigraphic discovery, was found in Jerusalem. The last two decades of the nineteenth century saw two advances in cartography in Transjordan: (1) a survey of the area was begun by the German archaeological society in 1884 by G. Schumacher, and (2) the Madaba Mosaic was found in the floor of a church in 1896. In 1890, Flinders Petrie began excavating Tell el-Hesi, and his work there demonstrated the importance of stratigraphy and ceramic dating for Palestinian archaeology. Finally, from 1894-1897 Bliss and Dickie excavated spots in Jerusalem, and in 1899-1900, Bliss undertook excavations at Tell Zakariya, Tell es-Safi, Tell ej-Judeideh, and Tell Sandahannah.

Nineteenth century archaeological work in Palestine accomplished the following: (1) Western Palestine was mapped and the maps of Transjordan were improved; (2) while nineteenth century excavations in Palestine were few and very crudely done, the foundation for further work was laid, especially by Petrie at Tell el-Hesi; (3) a few significant epigraphic and artifactual discoveries were made in Palestine, and these helped build public enthusiasm for archaeological work in the land; (4) archaeological societies were founded in Britain, United States, Germany, and France, and these helped maintain public interest and support for archaeological work in Palestine; and finally, (5) topographical, epigraphical, and cultural advances in the knowledge of ancient Palestine began to provide a firmer basis for the understanding of the ancient life and history of Palestine, and consequently, the biblical accounts were illuminated.

3. EGYPT AND MESOPOTAMIA

There were two major areas of archaeological progress in the nineteenth century investigation of the Near East: (1) excavation and the discovery of artifacts and (2) the deciphering of the ancient scripts. Napoleon's expedition into Egypt in 1798 had turned European attention to the Near East and the discovery of the Rosetta Stone in 1799 began the earnest inquiry into the languages of the area. The first period of archaeological work in the Near East during the nineteenth century was largely undertaken by explorers before 1842. C. J. Rich worked for the British and traveled through Mesopotamia. He acquired artifacts, which he sent back to Britain, and wrote two books that aroused public interest in the area. In 1811, he visited Babylon, and in 1821, he found Nineveh. Archaeological work in Egypt progressed more rapidly. The Italian Belzoni worked for the

British there, and the French and Tuscan governments sponsored Champollion and Rosellini to examine the ruins of Egypt (1828).

The work of deciphering the ancient scripts was advanced in 1802 by the work of G. Grotefend on the first column of the trilingual Behistun Inscription. He was largely successful in deciphering the Old Persian of that inscription, but the results of his investigation went largely unnoticed for decades. In 1822, Champollion deciphered Egyptian hieroglyphics by the use of the Rosetta Stone. Further work on the Old Persian of the Behistun Inscription was done by Rask, Burnouf, Lassen, H. C. Rawlinson, and J. Oppert. With the publication of Oppert's work in 1847, the decipherment of the Old Persian was complete.

The second major period of ancient Near Eastern archaeology began in 1842 with E. Botta's excavation at Kouyunjik. He met with greater success in his excavations at Khorsabad (1843-1846), however, which proved to be an ancient fortress of Sargon II. These excavations were the first great ones in Mesopotamia and began a period of intense work in ancient Assyria.[5] A. H. Layard was sent by the British to resume the French excavations deserted by Botta at Kouyunjik, ancient Nineveh. Layard worked there and at a mound named Nimrud, ancient Calah, from 1845-1847 and returned for a second time during 1849-1851. He found numerous monuments, including the Black Obelisk of Shalmaneser III, from which Hincks later read the names of Jehu of Israel and Hazael of Damascus in 1851. It was during Layard's second season (1849-1850) that he found large parts of Assurbanipal's library. This was the first of the large epigraphic finds in Mesopotamia. In Egypt, R. Lepsius undertook an expedition for the Prussian government in 1842-1846, which investigated the pyramids, private tombs, and ancient monuments along the Upper Nile.

A third period of archaeological work began about 1850. In Egypt the Frenchman A. Mariette worked from 1850 until about 1880, and during this period maintained a great control over archaeological investigation in Egypt. He undertook an excavation of the Serapeum from 1851-1855, the graves of the sacred bulls of Egypt, and later founded the Cairo Museum, which began to retard the plundering of Egyptian relics for European museums. In 1851, W. K. Loftus began archaeological work for the British on the plains of Babylon and found the tells of Nippur, Uruk, Ur, and Larsa. During the same period of time (1851-1854), J. Oppert investigated the ruins of Babylon itself for the French, and H. Rassam dug at Nineveh for the British and found more of Assurbanipal's library, including part of the

---

[5]H. V. Hilprecht, "The Resurrection of Assyria and Babylonia," in *Explorations in Bible Lands During the 19th Century* (ed. H. V. Hilprecht; Philadelphia: A. J. Holman, 1903) 216.

Gilgamesh Epic. The next twenty years saw little excavation in Mesopotamia. The Crimean War disrupted matters politically, and the European museums had plenty of artifacts and more texts than could be read.[6]

In the 1860s, however, advances were made outside Mesopotamia. In Anatolia G. Perrot's Galatian Expedition began in 1861 and returned with word of Hittite monuments, and in 1869, Schliemann went to Troy for the first time. His work there would lead to the discovery of the pre-Hellenistic culture, and the excavations in Troy and Mycenaea led to more popular enthusiasm for archaeology, than did the work in Mesopotamia.[7]

Advances in deciphering the third column of the Behistun Inscription, the Assyrian, were made by Grotefend, Löwenstern, Hincks, Rawlinson, and Oppert. In 1857, the last-named was able to translate an Assyrian text for the first time without the help of an Old Persian version. In the same year the Royal Asiatic Society of Britain undertook a test to silence the critics of Assyriology (J. A. de Gobineau, E. Renan, H. Ewald, and others), who remained skeptical of the translations proposed for the ancient Assyrian documents. The test required several linguists (H. Rawlinson, Talbot, Hincks, and Oppert) to submit their translations in sealed envelopes of a text from Tiglath-pileser I. When the envelopes were opened and the translations compared, it was clear that the decipherment of Assyrian had been successful. E. Schrader defended these early advances in Assyriology and championed the science in Germany, where little work was being done in the subject.[8]

The fourth period of archaeological work in the Near East was stimulated by Schliemann's work at Troy and by George Smith's discovery of the Mesopotamian flood story. In 1872, Smith found tablets in the British Museum from Assurbanipal's library, which described an ancient catastrophic flood, and in the same year he delivered a lecture in London which announced his discovery. The excitement over his find was tremendous, and Smith was promptly given funds to undertake a renewed search for the missing tablets of the flood story. So in 1873, Smith traveled to Kouyunjik and after only a week of exploration found the first seventeen lines of the flood story. The last quarter of the nineteenth century would see archaeological work concentrated in the south around Babylon and the turn by the French and Americans to long-term excavations at single sites. It was a time for large, methodical excavations.[9]

---

[6]Jones, *Venus*, 27; Lloyd, *Foundations*, 160-61.

[7] Daniel, *Hundred Years*, 140.

[8]Gus Van Beek, "Archaeology," *IDB* 1 (1962) 275-76.

[9]Hilprecht, "Assyria and Babylonia," 216; Lloyd, *Foundations*, 162.

The period began in earnest with the French excavations in 1877 under E. de Sarzek at Tello, which led to the discovery of the first works of Sumerian art and thousands of Sumerian documents. The site proved to be the ancient Sumerian city of Lagash, and the French expedition continued there until 1900. There was a great deal of documentary evidence found there, and H. V. Hilprecht introduced stricter scientific methods in the course of the project. Petrie began work in Egypt in 1880 and found the Merneptah Stele in 1896, the earliest mention of Israel in ancient epigraphic finds. E. Brugsch, who was working with Maspero, found a cave with the mummies of forty Egyptian Pharaohs (including those of Sethos I and Ramses II). The most important discovery in Egypt during this period, however, occurred at Tell el-Amarna in 1887, where the correspondence between Egypt and the city states of Palestine was uncovered. These tablets proved to be of great importance for the understanding of pre-Israelite Palestine.[10]

This fourth period was important as far as documentary evidence was concerned, since excavations at Tello and Nippur produced large numbers of ancient texts. Moreover, in 1890 the second column of the Behistun Inscription, the Elamite script, was deciphered by F. H. Weissbach, who benefited from the decipherment of the Assyrian column, and in 1873, F. Lenormant first outlined the language of the Sumerians. Finally, it should be noted that A. H. Sayce delivered a lecture in 1880 in London, which asserted that a Hittite Empire existed in the second millenium B. C. E.

The century closed with the Germans beginning an eighteen-year excavation at the site of ancient Babylon. This signaled a new period of investigation which focused on the careful examination of architectural remains and concern with the social setting and culture of the ancients.[11]

4. THE EFFECTS OF NINETEENTH CENTURY ARCHAEOLOGY ON BIBLICAL STUDIES IN GENERAL

One important contribution of nineteenth century archaeology to biblical studies was that it undercut the idealistic and romantic notions of Israel's history which had held that Israel's early religious beliefs were those of pagan nature religions. Archaeologists had found that the religions of the nations around Israel in the second millenium were far more developed than the primitive totemism that had been supposed. This, of course, suggested that Wellhausen's theory of Israel's religious development was seriously flawed. The Babylonian creation and flood stories with their parallels to Genesis

---

[10]Kraus, *Geschichte*, 300-1.
[11]Lloyd, *Foundations*, 198-99.

and Israel's other traditions also complicated matters and seemed to argue for lines of connection between Mesopotamia and Israel. Furthermore, the Amarna Tablets provided a much better understanding of pre-Israelite Palestine and pointed to the influence of both Egypt and Mesopotamia on the land. These texts, as well as the Assyrian royal texts, gave the Old Testament historian a much better perspective on Israel's international relations, and if anything, demonstrated that Israel was a relatively small country set midway between two powers, which far exceeded her militarily and culturally. On a more mundane level, the findings of archaeology illuminated many references in the Bible to everyday practices and items in the ancient world. In some ways, scholars such as Wellhausen and the others, who had been accustomed to comparing the culture and life of Israel with those of the pre-Islamic Arabs, were at a loss when confronted with the mass of material from Mesopotamia.[12]

While nineteenth century archaeology radically changed the view of Israel's early history, the view of the monarchical period of Israel was not dramatically changed. The Assyrian royal texts, however, filled in many details of this segment of Israel's past and enabled the historian to see how Israel's history fit into the larger picture of international diplomacy and war.

5. SUMMARY OF NINETEENTH CENTURY ARCHAEOLOGICAL RESEARCH

Archaeology in the Near East began only after Napoleon's invasion of Egypt in 1798 had stimulated European interest in the region. Travelers and explorers were followed by excavators, and there was eventually a shift from the treasure-hunter attitude toward archaeology to that of the scientific inquiry of the professional scholar. As far as the defence of the reliability of the biblical documents was concerned, it was the archaeological investigation of Egypt and Mesopotamia—rather than Palestine—that was most important. Moreover, it was the epigraphic discoveries rather than the artifactual finds that were most significant in this regard. The remainder of this chapter will examine the ways that various scholars believed archaeology impinged on the question of Chronicles' credibility.

C. Archaeology in Defense of Chronicles

1. Introduction

The first group of scholars to be treated are those who argued in defense of Chronicles' credibility on the basis of archaeological discoveries in the Near East. They held a variety of views about the Pentateuch and about the authorship, date, and sources of

---

[12]Kraus, *Geschichte*, 298-302.

Chronicles, but they were agreed that the findings of archaeology had substantially vindicated the trustworthiness of Chronicles and thus undercut Wellhausen's contention that everything unique to Chronicles should be rejected by the historian for the reconstruction of Israel's pre-exilic period. This group of scholars consists of G. Rawlinson, E. Schrader, A. H. Sayce, G. A. Smith, and J. F. McCurdy.

2. *RAWLINSON*

a. General

Among the first of those writers who defended the credibility of Chronicles by means of archaeological discoveries was George Rawlinson (1812-1902), the younger brother of Sir Henry C. Rawlinson, the British soldier who achieved a great reputation as an orientalist. George Rawlinson graduated Oxford, served as Camden Professor of Ancient History, and finally, became Canon of Canterbury.[13]

Rawlinson published a great number of works in both ancient history and biblical studies. His first major publication was a four-volume work on Herodotus (1858-1860), and it was followed by his four-volume history, *The Five Great Monarchies* (1862-1867). Other works followed, which treated the histories of Parthia, Persia, Egypt, and Phoenicia. In addition to these studies on ancient history, Rawlinson wrote commentaries on Exodus, 1, 2 Kings, 1, 2 Chronicles, Ezra, Nehemiah, Esther, and 1, 2 Maccabees, as well as several small biographical studies of various Old Testament personalities (Moses, the kings of Israel and Judah, Ezra, and Nehemiah). Another group of Rawlinson's publications concerned the relation of archaeological findings to the Bible. These works were often apologetic in nature and aimed at the general public. One of the first of these was *The Historical Evidences of the Truth of the Scripture Records*, which consisted of his eight lectures delivered at Oxford for the Bampton Lecture series of 1859.[14] These lectures offer one an initial glimpse of the author's use of archaeology to defend Chronicles' reliability as a historical source for the pre-exilic period. In the course of these lectures Rawlinson referred favorably to Keil, Hävernick, and others, who represented the positions of biblical orthodoxy, and he argued against the views of Eichhorn, de Wette, Vatke, and Strauss and regarded their works as the application of Niebuhr's historical-critical methods to the Bible.[15] As a consequence of these lectures, his

---

[13]"Rawlinson, George," *Enc Brit* 22 (11th ed.; 1910) 928; Ronald Bayne, "Rawlinson, George," *DNB* 3 (2d supplement.; 1912) 165-67.

[14]*Ibid.*

[15]George Rawlinson, *The Historical Evidences of the Truth of the Scripture Records* (London: John Murray, 1859) 113-24.

speeches for the Christian Evidence Society, and his other writings, Rawlinson won a great reputation in his day as a vigorous and learned champion of religious orthodoxy.

b. Chronicles

Rawlinson believed that 1, 2 Chronicles was written by Ezra and was his "greatest literary achievement" and that Ezra also wrote the book of Ezra as part of the same work. He based his judgment on the fact that the books shared a similar style and levitical tone; the ending of 2 Chronicles and the beginning of Ezra were the same; and many of the best scholars held that the two works were originally one.[16] He further affirmed with Keil and others that the Chronicler had authentic, historical sources for his additions to what was known of Israel's history from Samuel-Kings, and he believed that the Chronicler used the accounts of the royal history, which were written by various prophets who lived under the successive kings of Judah. Therefore, the Chronicler's sources were written by eye-witnesses of the events that they described, and 1, 2 Chronicles was independent of Samuel-Kings in its testimony regarding the monarchical period.[17]

It was apparent from Rawlinson's treatment of the various kings of Judah that he had confidence in the general reliability of Chronicles. In the case of Abijah he accepted the Chronicler's account of his victory over Jeroboam I and the speech that the Judean king made to the Israelite king. He did, however, reduce the Chronicler's figure for Israelite causalities in the war from 500,000 to 50,000, noting that the Chronicler's numbers were "in many instances exaggerated."[18] In his treatment of Asa Rawlinson accepted the Chronicler's reports about the king's war with Zerah and the speech of Azariah to Asa. He suggested that Zerah was either Osorkon II or an Ethiopian general sent by the Pharaoh of Egypt.[19] Similarly, Rawlinson reproduced the Chronicler's story about the victory of Jehoshaphat over

---

[16]G. Rawlinson, *Ezra and Nehemiah* (Men of the Bible; New York: Fleming H. Revell, 1890) 54-55.

[17]Rawlinson, *Historical Evidences*, 113-21.

[18]G. Rawlinson, *The Kings of Israel and Judah* (Men of the Bible; New York: Fleming H. Revell, 1889) 29-30. In this work the author frequently cited Ewald's (pp. 15, 33, 39) and Stanley's histories of Israel (pp. 15, 21) and acknowledged his dependence on them in the preface (pp. iii, iv), but he rejected the former's belief that miracles were unhistorical.

[19]*Ibid.*, 35-37; cf. also, G. Rawlinson, *The Testimony of History to the Truth of Scripture* (Boston: H. L. Hastings, 1885) 119-20. In the latter work Rawlinson suggested that Zerah was either Osorchon of Egypt (956-933 B. C. E.) or Azerah-Amar, who ruled Ethiopia about the time that Osorchon ruled Egypt. The variant form of the names that one finds in Chronicles resulted from the Hebrew practice of abbreviating foreign names (e.g., So, Shalman).

the Moabite coalition.[20] In several of his works Rawlinson treated Chronicles' account of Manasseh's captivity and release. He pointed out three important facets of the story that had connections with what could be known from the epigraphic evidence of Mesopotamia. First, it was unusual that Manasseh was taken to Babylon, since Nineveh was the capital of Assyria. He noted, however, that Esarhaddon built a palace at Babylon and lived there, ruling the southern part of his kingdom and entrusting the northern part to his son Assurbanipal. Therefore, it would have been only natural for an important prisoner to have been brought to him there. The mention of captivity in Babylon for Manasseh by the Chronicler, he noted, was evidence that the event occurred during Esarhaddon's reign, rather than during that of Assurbanipal, who did not reside in Babylon.[21] Secondly, Rawlinson noted that the Chronicler said that Manasseh was led with hooks and was fettered and that Mesopotamian sculptures show prisoners led to the conquering king with hooks or rings through their upper or lower lips and lines attached to the hooks or rings.[22] Finally, he pointed to the outcome of the affair: Manasseh was pardoned and released. This kind of clemency was paralleled by Esarhaddon's treatment of the son of Merodach-baladan, who revolted against Esarhaddon but was pardoned and awarded a land to rule when he submitted to the Assyrian king, and in the treatment of the chief of the Gambalu, who revolted against Esarhaddon but later submitted and was forgiven and restored to his throne.[23]

It appears, therefore, that Rawlinson believed that the Chronicler's reports were historically reliable, and that when they touched matters that were treated in the documents of Mesopotamia, they agreed with them. This general conclusion is confirmed by Rawlinson's remarks about archaeology and the Bible in general.

> The more exact the knowledge that we obtain, by discovery or critical research, of the remote past, the closer the agreement that we find between profane and Biblical history.[24]

---

[20]Rawlinson, *Kings*, 81-83.

[21]G. Rawlinson, *Egypt and Babylon from Sacred and Profane Sources* (New York: John B. Alden, 1885) 17-20; *The Five Great Monarchies of the Ancient Eastern World* (2d ed.; 3 vols.; New York: Dodd, Mead, 1881) 2.194.

[22]*Ibid*.

[23]*Ibid*. In his Bampton Lectures (1859), however, he noted that "...though no direct confirmation has as yet been found of the captivity and restoration of the Jewish monarch, yet the narrative contains an incidental allusion, which is in very remarkable harmony with the native records. *Historical Evidences*, 144-45.

[24]Rawlinson, *Testimony*, 4.

> The result seems to be, in the first place, that contradiction between the sacred and the profane scarcely occurs, unless it be in chronological statements, and that it is even there confined within narrow limits.[25]

> In the general outline of human affairs...the sacred narrative shows a remarkable agreement with the best profane sources....[26]

Rawlinson, therefore, believed that the findings of archaeology had verified certain statements in the Old Testament, and on one occasion Rawlinson spoke of the Christian apologist entering the field to use these findings for "confirming faith."[27]

Three conclusions were drawn by Rawlinson from his comparisons of the biblical records with those of the rest of the ancient Near East. First, since the Old Testament records have been confirmed by those of other nations, whenever the former could be compared with the latter, then it followed that the Old Testament reports should also be believed in those cases, in which they could not be compared with extra-biblical evidence.

> Briefly, the historic accuracy of the sacred writers in those parts of their narrative which we can test, goes far to authenticate their whole narrative.[28]

Secondly, Rawlinson concluded that the reports in the Old Testament must have "generally" been written by eye-witnesses. Since there was so much agreement between the Old Testament documents and those of the ancient Near East, the former could hardly have all been written at a very late date.[29] Finally, he concluded that scholars ought to dismiss

> ...the theory which not long ago was so popular in Germany, that the so-called historical narratives of the Old Testament are legends or myths....[30]

Finally, something should be said about Rawlinson's view of the Priestly Code, since it was so much a part of the debate about Chronicles' reliability. Rawlinson held to an early date for P, and he joined other conservative scholars in *Lex Mosaica* to argue the point. Rawlinson's contribution was to affirm four theses. First, the levitical laws are what might be expected to come from Moses, because of his

---

[25]*Ibid.*, 220.
[26]*Ibid.*, 221.
[27]*Ibid.*, 6.
[28]*Ibid.*, 224; cf. 222-23.
[29]*Ibid.*, 225.
[30]*Ibid.*, 222–23.

position and the circumstances of his day. Second, the later history of Israel assumed and required that such a law had been issued previously. Third, numerous human witnesses testified to the fact that Moses issued such a law (e.g., the author of Joshua, David, Solomon, and the prophets). Finally, Jesus also attested Mosaic authorship of the levitical law.[31] By the time that this essay was published in 1894, it was recognized that the date of the levitical legislation was crucial in the battle against Wellhausen's reconstruction of the development of Israel's religion.

c. Summary

Rawlinson believed that the Chronicler was a reliable historical witness for the pre-exilic period. He assigned it an early date and held that eye-witness accounts were available to its author. His confidence in Chronicles found additional support in his contentions that the levitical laws in P derived from Moses himself (rather than from some anonymous exilic or post-exilic author) and that the findings of archaeology confirmed the Chronicler's account.

Rawlinson's interests and training in both biblical studies and ancient history equipped him for the work of comparing the Old Testament with the history of the ancient Near East. He undertook this task, however, not simply as a scholar, but as an apologist. Consequently, he stood among the pioneers of the nineteenth century, who used the findings of archaeology to vindicate the credibility of the biblical documents. It is important to note in this regard that Rawlinson's use of archaeology to argue for the historical credibility of the Bible was directed against those advocates of historical criticism from the early and mid-nineteenth century, and that he began his labor as a Christian apologist by 1859—seven years before Graf's work on the Priestly Code and nearly two decades before Wellhausen's *Prolegomena*. It is clear then that the apologetical use of archaeology was not a direct response to the work of Graf and Wellhausen, but had already been used against the practice of historical criticism of Eichhorn, de Wette, and others.

In some respects Rawlinson's work paralleled that of Sayce. Both were ardent defenders of the historical reliability of the Old Testament, and both were critics of source criticism. Furthermore, both were confident that archaeology had confirmed the biblical record in the past and would continue to do so in the future. Finally, both were effective popularizers of their views and issued a number of small books to inform the general public about the advances of archaeology. The two differed, however, in that Rawlinson was an an-

---

[31]G. Rawlinson, "Moses the Author of the Levitical Code of Laws," in *Lex Mosaica* (ed. R. V. French; London: Eyre & Spottiswoode, 1894) 21-52.

cient historian, while Sayce was an Assyriologist. Moreover, Rawlinson began publishing his apologetical works nearly twenty-five years before Sayce.

3. SCHRADER

a. General

A prominent figure in Germany in the use of archaeology to defend the Bible's credibility was Eberhard Schrader (1836-1908), who studied under Ewald at Göttingen. Later, Schrader taught oriental languages at Zurich, Giessen, Jena, and Berlin. The first part of his career was devoted to biblical studies, but the latter part was turned to Assyriology, where his greatest contributions to scholarship were made. He was the first of the German Assyriologists, and it was largely due to his efforts that the science took root in Germany. His major works that related directly to Biblical studies included *Studien zur Kritik und Erklärung der biblischen Urgeschichte* (1863), the eighth edition of de Wette's *Einleitung* (1869), and *Die Keilinschriften und das Alten Testament* (1872).[32]

Before turning to Schrader's treatment of Chronicles, two things merit attention and both have bearing on the author's handling of Chronicles. First, it should be noted that Schrader argued for the early date of P. In his edition of de Wette's introduction he maintained that P should be dated in the early part of David's reign and that E should be assigned to the tenth century B. C. E., shortly after the division of the monarchy. Sometime between 825 and 800 B. C. E., J brought the two earlier documents together and added some of his own material. The "Deuteronomic writer" wrote just before Josiah's reform.[33] By upholding this pre-Grafian understanding of the penta-teuchal sources—especially the early date for P—it is to be expected that Schrader would also advocate the general reliability of Chronicles.

The second point worth noticing is that Schrader believed generally that the Assyrian records upheld the trustworthiness of the Old Testament. A. C. Whitehouse, who translated Schrader's book

---

[32]"Schrader, Eberhard," *Enc Brit* 24 (11th ed.; 1910) 378. A review of Schrader's book in *The Expositor* noted that he was the only Assyriologist in Germany, while the French had two (Oppert and Lenormant) and the British five (Rawlinson, Sayce, Smith, Hincks, and Norris). Editor, "Schrader's Cuneiform Inscriptions and the Old Testament," *The Expositor* 2 (3d ser.; 1885) 237-40. Schrader's *Die Keilinschriften und das Alten Testament* (Giessen: J. Ricker, 1872) was translated by O. C. Whitehouse from the second German edition as *The Cuneiform Inscriptions and the Old Testament* (2 vols.; London: Williams & Norgate, 1885/1888).

[33]De Wette, *Lehrbuch der historisch-kritischen Einleitung in die kanonischen und Apokryphischen Bücher des Alten Testaments* (ed. E. Schrader; 8th ed.; Berlin: G. Reimer, 1869) 270-325; cf. E. Schrader, *Cuneiform* Inscriptions, 1.xii-xiv.

comparing the cuneiform records with the Old Testament, made the following observations about the consequences of Schrader's work.

> ...the incidental confirmations of Old Testament narrative are so remarkable as well as instructive, that we may well hope that the new problems which have been raised will ultimately be solved in the light of fresh facts, which excavation is ever drawing forth from the soil of Aegypt and Asia Minor. One cheering indication deserves to be noted, namely that both Aegyptologists and Assyriologists have introduced a very wholesome reaction in favour of upholding the validity of Old Testament history.[34]

> This writer enters a vigorous protest against the extreme views of Stade respecting the so-called untrustworthiness of Biblical history and expressly declares his belief in the historic personality of Abraham.[35]

> Even the cursory reader of these volumes of Schrader's work cannot fail to be impressed with the constantly recurring confirmations of Old Testament records.[36]

In light of such general conclusions, one would be surprised to find Schrader arguing against the trustworthiness of the Chronicler's reports.

b. Chronicles

The Cuneiform Inscriptions and the Old Testament assumed the form of a commentary and moved through the Old Testament book-by-book, showing how the Assyrian records illuminated various passages. The section that dealt with Chronicles treated four passages. In the first Schrader found that the reference in 1 Chr 5:26 to Tiglath-pilneser was a mistake by the Chronicler or a copyist for Tiglath-pileser.[37] In the second passage (2 Chr 9:16) Schrader noted that the parallel in 1 Kg 10:17 said that Solomon had three minas of gold worked into each shield, which was placed in the House of the Forest of Lebanon, while the Chronicler set the amount at three hundred shekels of gold. He explained that while in the earlier times of Hebrew history one mina was equal to fifty shekels, in the Greek Period one mina equalled one hundred shekels.[38] The third passage Schrader noted was 2 Chr 15:18, where he found a name that also occurred in the Assyrian monuments as a woman's name, Sammuramat.[39]

---

[34]*Ibid.*, 1.xx.
[35]*Ibid.*, 1.xxi.
[36]*Ibid.*
[37]*Ibid.*, 2.52.
[38]*Ibid.*, 2.52-53.
[39]*Ibid.*, 2.53.

Finally, Schrader dealt with 2 Chr 33:11-13, which described Manasseh's captivity to Babylon. This section dominated Schrader's treatment of Chronicles, and the translator offered this as one of his two "remarkable examples" of the confirmation of the biblical records by the cuneiform texts.[40] Schrader noted the two reasons for doubting the Chronicler's account of Manasseh's captivity: (1) there was no other evidence for Assyrian supremacy in western Palestine at this time, and (2) Manasseh would have been taken to Nineveh rather than to Babylon. Schrader responded that both Esarhaddon and Assurbanipal included Manasseh's name in their records and that Esarhaddon subjected all Syria and Egypt to his control. Therefore, the first objection was met. Moreover, Schrader believed that Manasseh's captivity occurred in Assurbanipal's reign as part of the revolt led by the ruler of Babylon, Shamash-shum-ukin. There was no major revolt during Esarhaddon's reign. The second objection (Manasseh would have been taken to Nineveh, not Babylon) was turned aside when two things were recognized: (1) Assurbanipal could easily have resided in Babylon and received embassies there, after he had quelled his brother's revolt, and (2) Cyprian ambassadors were received at Babylon at an earlier time by the Assyrian king Sargon. A final aspect of the event that Schrader treated is Manasseh's release. That such a thing was indeed possible with the Assyrian kings was demonstrated by the example of the Egyptian ruler Necho I, who was bound by the Assyrians but later released.[41] Schrader concluded,

> ...there is no reason to cast any suspicion on the statement of the Chronicler (so far, of course, as facts are reported), and that what he relates can be satisfactorily accounted for from the circumstances that existed in the year 647 B. C.[42]

c. Summary

Schrader's work as an Assyrologist was that of a pioneer in mid-nineteenth century Germany, and his accomplishments in the field won him lasting recognition. From Germany he argued with the Assyrian documents what Sayce and others did from England: ancient Near Eastern archaeology validated the biblical record. While Schrader's work did not reach the extreme conclusions as some of Sayce's later works, he nevertheless believed that the Assyrian records restored a certain amount of confidence in the biblical ac-

---

[40]*Ibid.*, 1.xi-xxiii.
[41]*Ibid.*, 2.53-59.
[42]*Ibid.*, 2.59.

counts. He was not led, however, to reject the source-critical method, as Sayce did, for example.[43]

As far as Chronicles was concerned, Schrader concluded that the books offered reliable historical information about Israel's pre-exilic history. The Chronicler's account of Manasseh's captivity served as the prime example of the confirmation that archaeology could offer to the biblical text.[44] Schrader's conclusion about Chronicles' credibility was further substantiated by his conviction that the Priestly Code should be assigned a pre-exilic date.

4.SAYCE

a. General

The most prominent figure among those scholars who employed archaeology in the defense of Chronicles was Archibald Henry Sayce (1845-1933), an English Assyriologist who was educated at Bath and Oxford and became Professor of Assyriology at Oxford in 1891.[45] Cheyne described him as an Assyriologist from his youth and wrote,

> He is probably unsurpassed in his knowledge of the data of the inscriptions, and I am sure that no living scholar can excel him in his imaginative sense of history, and in his use of the imagination as the handmaid of discovery.[46]

He traveled widely in the Near East and followed the archaeological discoveries there closely. He was a member of the Old Testament Revision Company in 1874-1884, and gave the Hibbert lectures in 1887 on the topic of Babylonian religion.[47] Although he was primarily an Assyriologist, he published a number of works on the Old Testament, usually attempting to show how archaeological discoveries illuminated it.[48] In this regard he was an effective popularizer of

---

[43]In this respect, Schrader's unwillingness to surrender the source critical method was continued by his pupil McCurdy, a Canadian scholar, who wrote about the impact of archaeology on Old Testament studies.

[44]Evidently, Schrader's connection of Manasseh's captivity with Assurbanipal's reign anticipated Sayce's connection of the two, which did not occur until 1894. Schrader appears to have been one of the first to set Manasseh's captivity in Assurbanipal's reign. George Smith had already suggested that the Judean king's imprisonment should be set in Esarhaddon's reign. *The Assyrian Eponym Canon* (London: Samuel Bagster, n. d.) 67-69.

[45]"Sayce, A. H.," *Enc Brit* 24 (1910) 276. Sayce's autobiography was entitled *Reminiscences* (London: Macmillan, 1923).

[46]Cheyne, *Founders*, 231.

[47]*Enc Brit*, 24.276.

[48]*An Introduction to Ezra, Nehemiah, and Esther* (London: Religious Tract Society, 1885); *Fresh Light from the Ancient Monuments* (By-Paths of Biblical Knowledge, 2; New York: Fleming H. Revell, n.d.; the second edition of the work was published

his views and won a great reputation as one who had proven with the help of archaeology the substantial accuracy of much of the Old Testament. In the process he became a vociferous critic of "literary analysis" and the "higher critics," and while this won him considerable popularity with the masses, it earned him the disdain of many scholars who otherwise respected his great learning.[49]

b. Archaeology vs. Higher Criticism

Early in his career Sayce was open to the methods and some of the conclusions of source analysis,[50] but by 1883 and the publication of his *Fresh Light from the Ancient Monuments*, a brief work for popular reading, he had assumed the role of the champion of biblical accu-

---

in 1884); *The "Higher Criticism" and the Verdict of the Monuments* (London: SPCK, 1894); *Patriarchal Palestine* (London: SPCK, 1895); *The Egypt of the Hebrews and Herodotus* (London: Rivington, Percival, 1895); *The Early History of the Hebrews* (New York: Macmillan, 1897); *Early Israel and the Surrounding Nations* (London: Service & Paton, 1899); and *Monument Facts and Higher Critical Fancies* (New York: Fleming H. Revell, n. d.).

[49]Cheyne, *Founders*, 231-41; G.B. Gray, "Professor Sayce's 'Early History of the Hebrews'," *The Expositor* 7 (5th ser.; 1898) 404-19. John A. Wilson characterized Sayce in the following way. "This prissy but kindly man had been a great scholar. He had been a pioneer in some of the lesser-known cuneiform writings, and his great delight was the reading of a new text or the decipherment of an unknown language, as in his forays on Elamite and Vannic. To his work in 1876-79 we owe the recognition that the Hittites of Anatolia had been a powerful empire in antiquity. Yet he felt no compulsion to follow up his flights of bold insight and would drop a study after a few magisterial generalizations. A kindly critic said of him: His width of knowledge and interests was amazing, and he had little liking for the laboriousness of a specialist. ... His attitude to life was that of a fastidious ascetic, almost one might say of an austere sybarite.... He was impatient of the claims, the pride and the reticence of exact scholarship. He himself was quite accustomed to making mistakes. Around his head raged a controversy which shook Old Testament scholars and churchmen, the debate over the Higher Criticism. He blandly brushed aside the arguments of the "German" theological critics, using that national term as though it were condemnatory in itself, proclaimed himself a "champion of orthodoxy," and then did little to defend the orthodox view against attack. A distaste for continuous hard work and for the rough-and-tumble of controversy made him supple enough to escape hard and fast conclusions." *Signs & Wonders upon Pharaoh* (Chicago: University of Chicago, 1964) 100. It was rather ironic that Sayce was passed over, when the time came to appoint a successor to Pusey in Hebrew at Oxford. Driver was chosen instead of Sayce because Gladstone believed that the latter had heterodox tendencies. Sayce had acquired the reputation of a Broad Churchman, who was a leader in German critical theology and thus "unsafe" for appointment to ecclesiastical office. Cf. Barbara Zink MacHaffie, "'Monument Facts and Higher Critical Fancies': Archaeology and the Popularization of Old Testament Criticism in Nineteenth-Century Britain," CH 50 (1981) 324.

[50]Cheyne, *Founders*, 235.

racy. Sayce's procedure in the book was to move chronologically through the Bible from creation to the Persian period, relating various archaeological and inscriptional discoveries to the biblical record. His aim was essentially a historical one: to see whether present knowledge "bears out that 'old story' which has been familiar to us from our childhood."[51] Even in the preface to the work, Sayce revealed what his conclusion would be.

> The same spirit of scepticism which had rejected the early legends of Greece and Rome had laid its hands also on the Old Testament, and had determined that the sacred histories themselves were but a collection of myths and fables. But suddenly, as with the wand of a magician, the ancient Eastern world has been reawakened to life by the spade of the explorer and patient skill of the decipherer, and we now find ourselves in the presence of monuments which bear the names or recount the deeds of the heroes of Scripture.[52]

Sayce pursued the same approach in 1894 with his book *The "Higher Criticism" and the Verdict of the Monuments*. This was a much more substantial volume than his work of 1883, but the aim, tenor, and conclusions were essentially the same. Here, too, his task was to compare the Old Testament with the discoveries of archaeology in order to test the historical accuracy and reliability of the former.[53] He believed that his approach to the Old Testament was especially valid, since archaeology provided a kind of "corrective" or external control to insure the proper understanding of the ancient Near East.

> Between the scholar who has been trained in a German study and the oriental even of to-day, there is a gulf fixed which cannot easily be passed. If we are to have judgments upon ancient oriental literature based solely on the previous education and beliefs of the critic, let them be pronounced by men like Burckhardt or Sir Richard Burton, not by those whose knowledge of oriental ideas has been derived from books. But it is just men like Burckhardt and Burton who shrink from pronouncing such judgments at all.[54]

> Perhaps it is this inability to recognise the vital difference that exists between the Oriental and the European world that has been the cause of so vast an amount of wasted time and labour over the records of the Old Testament.[55]

> Oriental archaeology is a corrective of this inability to realise and therefore to understand the history of the ancient East. It speaks to us in the tones of the nineteenth century—tones which we can comprehend and

---

[51]A. H. Sayce, *Fresh Light*, 3.
[52]*Ibid.*
[53]Sayce, *Verdict* (2d ed.; 1894) 554.
[54]*Ibid.*, 557.

listen to. It sweeps away the modern romance which we have woven around the narratives of the Old Testament, and shows us that they are no theological fairy tales, but accounts of events which are alleged to have taken place in this work-a-day world.[56]

Sayce concluded his study with the observation that archaeology destroyed some of the conclusions of "higher criticism."

...we cannot fail to be struck by the fact that the evidence of oriental archaeology is on the whole distinctly unfavourable to the pretensions of the "higher criticism." The "apologist" may lose something, but the "higher critic" loses much more.[57]

Sayce's next book took a bit different form, but the technique was still the same: a comparison of archaeological discoveries with the biblical record in order to validate the latter. The work appeared in 1897 under the title *The Early History of the Hebrews*. It dealt with the periods from the Patriarchs through the reign of Solomon. While five of the chapter headings related to various historical periods (Patriarchs, Exodus, Conquest, Judges, and Monarchy), the second one dealt with "The Composition of the Pentateuch." The superficiality of the discussion in this section is illustrated in the following citation.

The huge edifice of modern Pentateuchal criticism is thus based on a theory and an assumption. The theory is that of "the literary analysis" of the Hexateuch, the assumption that a knowledge of writing in Israel was of comparatively late date.[58]

Sayce labeled his history "the first attempt to write one (a history of Israel) from a purely archaeological point of view,"[59] and he evidently believed that such a history was warranted since "during the last few years discovery after discovery has come crowding upon us from the ancient East, revolutionising all our past conceptions of early Oriental history."[60] There were two observations that Sayce made about the method of source analysis that are worth noting. The first was that the method involved "subjective assumptions," and in this regard the method was inferior to "the facts of archaeology."[61] The implication, of course, was that literary criticism was subjective and thus more prone to error than was the practice of archaeology.

---

[55]*Ibid.*, 558.
[56]*Ibid.*, 559-60.
[57]*Ibid.*, 561.
[58]Sayce, *Early History*, 105.
[59]*Ibid.*, v.
[60]*Ibid.*
[61]*Ibid.*, vi.

The second observation by Sayce was that the results of archaeology and "higher criticism" were irreconcilable, and "the latter must therefore be cleared out of the way before the archaeologist can begin his work."[62]

> In dealing with the history of the past we are thus confronted with two utterly opposed methods, one objective, the other subjective, one resting on a basis of verifiable facts, the other on the unsupported and unsupportable assumptions of the modern scholar. The one is the method of archaeology, the other of the so-called "higher criticism." Between the two the scientifically trained mind can have no hesitation in choosing.[63]

In this way, Sayce asserted that the scholar must choose between the results of the source analysis of the "higher critics" and those of his own method of "historical comparison."

Finally, Sayce's *Early Israel and the Surrounding Nations* (1899) offers another glance at the author's confidence in archaeology as the illuminator of the biblical text. This work aimed at providing the reader with an understanding of the broader context for Israel's past. In the book's introduction Sayce again praised the merits of archaeology for vindicating the biblical record.

> The discoveries of Oriental archaeology have come with a rude shock to disturb both the conclusions of this imperfectly-equipped criticism and the principles on which they rest. Discovery has followed discovery, each more marvellous than the last, and re-establishing the truth of some historical narrative in which we had been called upon to disbelieve.[64]

Sayce adduced the example of Schliemann and those who excavated ancient Troy as further evidence that archaeology could illuminate the past and destroy the theories of the literary critics.[65] Two further observations by Sayce in the introduction to this work deserve mention. First, he noted that "higher criticism" or "critical scepticism" erred because it lacked the control of "external testimony." Apparently, he regarded the findings of the archaeologist as the needed external testimony.[66] Secondly, he charged that the "higher critic" operated on the basis of dogmatism and used improper western analogies to understand the Old Testament, an oriental composition.

> Criticism, accordingly, deemed itself competent to decide dogmatically on the character and credibility of the literature and history of which it

---

[62]*Ibid*.
[63]Sayce, *Monument Facts*, 17-18.
[64]Sayce, *Early Israel*, xv.
[65]*Ibid*.

was in possession; to measure the statements of the Old Testament writings by the rules of Greek and Latin literature, and to argue from the history of Europe to that of the East.[67]

c. Chronicles

In 1885, Sayce evidently believed that Ezra wrote 1, 2 Chronicles and Ezra, but thought that the book of Nehemiah was a separate work.[68] By 1893, however, he had changed his position and held that Chronicles was part of a larger work that included both Ezra and Nehemiah.[69] Sayce further maintained that the single object of the Chronicler's attention in his narrative was the "growth and consummation of the Israelitish theocracy." In this Chronicles differed from Samuel-Kings. The latter concentrated on the history of Judah and Israel, while the former reported the history of the temple and the temple services. Moreover, Chronicles only used the civil history of Judah to point out "the moral that observance of the Levitical laws brought with it prosperity, while disaster followed upon their neglect."[70] While Sayce evidently believed that the Chronicler had worthwhile sources available, he presented no comprehensive theory to delineate them. Rather, he attempted to demonstrate the reliability of reports, which were unique to Chronicles, by adducing archaeological evidence. In this way he sought to affirm the reliability of Chronicles without having to advance a theory of sources to account for that reliability.[71]

Several examples will illustrate Sayce's approach. The report of the Chronicler that Sayce most often attempted to validate with archaeological evidence was that found in 2 Chr 33:10-13, the captivity and reinstatement of Manasseh by the Assyrians. Chronicles reported that the Assyrians carried the king of Judah away captive to Babylon, where he repented of his sin and God forgave him, and from which he was released by the Assyrians to return to rule over Judah. Since 2 Kings said nothing of such an event, many scholars had rejected it as an invention of the Chronicler or of one of the Chronicler's sources. Sayce proposed in 1883 that the report in Chronicles was adequately explained as having occurred during the reign of Esarhaddon, since: (1) the Assyrian royal record mentioned Manasseh as a tributary of Esarhaddon; (2) Esarhaddon dwelt in Babylon during half of the year to win the favor of the people there; and (3) Assurbanipal, one of

[66]*Ibid.*, xiv.
[67]*Ibid.*
[68]Sayce, *Verdict*, 537-38.
[69]Sayce, *Ezra, Nehemiah*, 28-29.
[70]*Ibid.*, 457.
[71]*Ibid.*, 457-58.

Esarhaddon's sons, imprisoned a rebellious vassal only to release him later. In addition, Sayce mentioned in this passage that the Assyrian annals also referred to Manasseh as a vassal of Assurbanipal.[72] In 1894, however, Sayce again offered support for the historicity of Manasseh's captivity, but this time he suggested that the Judean king was captured by the forces of Assurbanipal, when they put down a revolt led by Shamash-shum-ukin, the brother of the Assyrian king. In this reconstruction Manasseh was viewed as one of the rebellious kings of Syro-Palestine, who took sides with the rebel prince and who was punished with imprisonment in Babylon, which Assurbanipal visited after his enemies' defeat.[73] Finally, in 1899 Sayce again treated the matter, but was unable to decide whether it was Esarhaddon or Assurbanipal who imprisoned Manasseh. Nevertheless, he was able to conclude confidently with regard to the difficulties in the biblical text about Manasseh's captivity, "And yet the cuneiform inscriptions have smoothed away all these objections."[74]

Another instance of the Chronicler's vindication, which Sayce offered repeatedly, concerned the Siloam inscription. In 1883, Sayce proposed that the discovery of the Siloam inscription, of which Sayce himself (by his own admission) made the "first intelligible copy," vindicated the claims in 2 Chr 32:30 and 2 Kg 20:20 that Hezekiah cut a water tunnel from a spring to a pool. Isa 8:6, however, raised problems with the assignment of the inscription to Hezekiah's day, and consequently, Sayce suggested that the writing may in fact have derived from Solomon's rule. That some of the letters in the inscription appeared to be more ancient than those in the Mesha inscription also inclined him toward the earlier dating of the Siloam inscription.[75]

A third example of the Chronicler's vindication concerned his claim (2 Chr 2:3, 11) that a series of letters passed between Solomon and the king of Tyre. The following was Sayce's proof on this point.

> Archaeology has vindicated the authenticity of the letters that passed between Solomon and the Tyrian king (2 Chron. ii.3, 11); similar letters were written in Babylonia in the age of Abraham, and the tablets of Tel el-Amarna have demonstrated how frequent they were in the ancient East. As in Babylonia and Assyria, so, too, in Palestine, they would have been preserved among the archives of the royal library.[76]

G. B. Gray reviewed Sayce's book in 1898 and charged that the author's reasoning was "extraordinarily loose and illogical" and that

---

[72]Sayce, *Fresh Light*, 122.

[73]Sayce, *Verdict*, 257-61.

[74]Sayce, *Early Israel*, xvii-xviii.

[75]Sayce, *Fresh Light*, 81-84; cf. *Verdict*, 376-88.

[76]Sayce, *Early History*, 480.

> Archaeology...does not even prove that Hiram and Solomon ever wrote
> to one another; much less does it prove the authenticity of the particular
> letters recorded by the chronicler.[77]

All that Sayce had demonstrated, according to Gray, was that
hundreds of years before Solomon other kings wrote letters.

Sayce concluded from such examples of Chronicles' vindication
by archaeology that

> We have no right to reject as unhistorical a narrative which is found
> only in the Books of the Chronicles, merely because there are no traces
> of it in the Books of Kings. On the contrary, as it has been proved that
> one of these narratives is in strict accordance with historical facts, we
> may assume that in other instances also we should find the same accor-
> dance if only the monumental testimony were at hand.[78]

> This conclusion leads on to another. A narrative like that of the captivity
> of Manasseh must have been extracted from some more or less contem-
> porary document which was not used by the compiler of the Books of
> Kings. Consequently the Chronicler was not confined to the Books of
> Kings and the writings of the canonical prophets for the sources of his
> history, and we can thus accept with confidence the claim he makes to
> the employment of other means of information.[79]

> We can accordingly grant him a much higher degree of historical trust-
> worthiness than critics have of late years been disposed to allow.[80]

Therefore, Sayce believed that generally the Chronicler was a more
reliable historical source than many had thought. More specifically,
he maintained that his "proofs" of the Chronicler's credibility had
demonstrated that the Chronicler had accurate sources of historical
information available for his use. Finally, according to Sayce, one
could extend confidence in the Chronicler from the narratives, where
his testimony was supported by archaeological evidence, to others of
his narratives, which lacked such external support.

These observations should not be taken, however, to mean that
Sayce advocated the total acceptance of the Chronicler's narratives.
On the contrary, he offered the following caveats:

> But at the same time oriental archaeology makes it clear that his (the
> Chronicler's) statements are not always exact. He cannot follow him
> with the same confidence as that with which we should follow the au-
> thor of the Books of Kings. His use of the documents which lay before
> him was uncritical; the inferences he drew from his materials were not

---

[77]Gray, "Sayce," 406.
[78]Sayce, *Verdict*, 461.
[79]*Ibid*.
[80]*Ibid*.

always sound, and he makes them subserve the theory on which his
work is based.[81]

Sayce illustrated this point with the Chronicler' deduction from the
text of 2 Kings that Pul and Tiglath-pileser were two different per-
sons and with examples of inflated figures in Chronicles. Then he
concluded,

> The consistent exaggeration of numbers on the part of the Chronicler
> shows us that from a historical point of view his unsupported state-
> ments must be received with caution. But they do not justify the accu-
> sations of deliberate fraud and "fiction" which have been brought
> against him. What they prove is that he did not possess that sense of
> historical exactitude which we now demand from the historian. He
> wrote, in fact, with a didactic and now with a historical purpose. That
> he should have used the framework of history to illustrate the lessons
> he wished to draw was as much an accident as that Sir Walter Scott
> should have based certain of his novels on the facts of mediaeval his-
> tory. He cared as little for history in the modern European sense of the
> word as the Oriental of to-day, who considers himself at liberty to em-
> bellish or modify the narrative he is repeating in accordance with his
> fancy or the moral he wishes to draw from it.[82]

Therefore, according to Sayce the reader must continually bear in
mind the personal and idealistic character of the Chronicler's history
and the effect that the author's religious convictions had on his narration. In Chronicles one found the "beginnings of that transformation of history into Haggadah, which is so conspicuous in later Jewish
literature," but nevertheless, the historian should cautiously accept
the Chronicler' unsupported statements, rather than proceed by rejecting them altogether.[83]

d. Summary

Sayce vigorously opposed the source analysis of his day and
charged that it was subjective and prone to error, that it was essentially a "western" method and so was incapable of dealing with
oriental materials. He suggested instead that the proper method for
interpreting the biblical materials was that of historical comparison.
The latter was objective and served as an external control for the
reader's interpretation of the ancient texts. While Sayce did not deny
that the Pentateuch consisted of elements from various hands and
times, he did dispute the source critic's ability to divide neatly the
Pentateuch into four sources.

---

[81]*Ibid.*, 461-62.
[82]*Ibid.*, 463-64.
[83]*Ibid.*, 464-65.

"Higher critics" such as Wellhausen had argued that the historian should presume that the material that was unique to Chronicles was worthless for reconstructing Israel's pre-exilic history. Sayce argued to the contrary that the historian should presume that the reports that were unique to Chronicles were valuable for the historical reconstruction of the pre-exilic period, because archaeological evidence had proven the accuracy of several of the Chronicler's accounts. Such validations of Chronicles' credibility indicated that the author of the books had reliable sources at hand for his history. Moreover, the substantiation of these reports in Chronicles compels one to assume that the other material in Chronicles could also be verified, if the relevant archaeological data were available.[84]

While the general public often perceived Sayce as a champion of theological orthodoxy and believed that the archaeologists were on the verge of overthrowing the conclusions of "higher criticism," some scholars remained unconvinced by Sayce's writings and regarded his efforts as futile and misleading.

5. G. A. SMITH

A fourth figure among those who had considerable confidence in the historical reliability of Chronicles was George Adam Smith (1856-1942). He studied at Edinburgh under A. B. Davidson and spent summer semesters in Leipzig, Tübingen, and Berlin. His teaching career was spent at the Free Church's colleges in Aberdeen and Glasgow. Although he published works on Isaiah, Jeremiah, the Minor Prophets, Deuteronomy, and other topics, his most outstanding work was *The Historical Geography of the Holy Land* (1894), which drew on his travels in Egypt and Palestine between 1875 and 1894.[85] It is this work that allows one to see the author's view of Chronicles.

In *The Historical Geography of the Holy Land* Smith drew information from Chronicles over eighty times—often with regard to Israel's pre-exilic history. He accepted the story in 2 Chronicles 14 about Asa's victory over Zerah and that of 2 Chronicles 13 about Abijah's

---

[84]Two problems with Sayce's approach are: (1) his argument depended on there being archaeological proof for at least some of the information that is unique to Chronicles, and he was unable to produce such proof—all that he offered were possibilities; and (2) even if Sayce had been able to offer archaeological proof for some of the information that was unique to Chronicles, his conclusion (the historian should always presume that the Chronicler's offerings had factual bases) would not follow.

[85]George A. Smith replaced W. Robertson Smith at Aberdeen, after the latter had been dismissed. W. Manson, "Smith, Sir George Adam," *DBN 1941-1950* (1959) 792-94.

success against North Israel.[86] His handling of Jehoshaphat's conflict with the Moabite coalition (2 Chronicles 20) was more extensive. He rehearsed the route of the invading forces, while acknowledging that "these places are as unknown as the agents of the mysterious slaughter," and then he concluded that even though the Chronicler's narrative was obscure, the geographical characteristics of the region emerged clearly and provided a suitable setting for a surprise Bedouin ambush against the Moabite coalition. Then, he summarized his findings in the following way, "It was probably some desert tribes which thus overcame Jehoshaphat's enemies before he arrived."[87]

Therefore, while Smith did not accept the information of Chronicles about Israel's pre-exilic history at face value, he was generally confident that there was a historical foundation for the Chronicler's reports, and he made use of the knowledge that he had gained traveling in Palestine in order to reconstruct Israel's history on the basis of Chronicles.

6. MCCURDY

The impact of archaeology on biblical studies was also treated by the Canadian James Frederick McCurdy (1847-1935), professor of oriental languages at the University of Toronto, in his *magnum opus*, *History, Prophecy and the Monuments of Israel and the Nations* (1896-1901).[88]

McCurdy saw the primary importance of history in its "moral significance and influence,"[89] and he believed that the greatest gift of the Hebrew people to humanity was religious truth and freedom.[90]

---

[86]G. A. Smith, *The Historical Geography of the Holy Land* (4th ed.; New York: Hodder & Stoughton, 1896) 233, 251.

[87]Smith's reconstruction of Jehoshaphat's victory is instructive. The Chronicler reported that God set an ambush against the foreign coalition and accomplished their defeat by turning one group against the other. There was no mention of another party (of Bedouin, e.g.) attacking the allied armies. This was a bit difficult for Smith to accept, however, and since the terrain, in which the events had been set, was so rugged, he seized the term "ambush" and proposed that the Bedouin of the area attacked the coalition. While his reconstruction is possible, it violates the sense of 2 Chronicles 20 and is not required by the geography. *Ibid.*, 272-73.

[88]He also wrote a brief commentary on Haggai, translated Moll's works on the Psalms from German, and wrote a brief essay entitled "Oriental Research and the Bible" in Hilprecht's *Recent Research in Bible Lands* (1896). Cf. John S. Moir, *A History of Biblical Studies in Canada* (SBL Centennial Publications, 7; Chico: Scholars Press, 1982) 14-17. Moir dedicated his book to McCurdy, "the father of biblical studies in Canada."

[89]J. F. McCurdy, *History, Prophecy and the Monuments* (3 vols.; New York: Macmillan, 1894/1896/1901) 1.1.

[90]*Ibid.*, 1.7.

Two Aryan races (the Greeks and Romans?), however, were needed to pass these gifts on to all humanity, after the Messiah's own community had sacrificed him.[91] Of all the documents that were available to the historian for the reconstruction of Israel's history, McCurdy valued the prophetic literature most of all, since

> Prophecy demonstrates how these controlling motives of truth and freedom, and the unchangeable moral forces of the divine government, were most signally illustrated and justified in that...history. (They)...are a depository of the facts of national and social life, more complete and more pertinent to the uses of the historian than those contained in that portion of the Biblical literature usually called historical.[92]

McCurdy further contended that archaeology served to complement the Old Testament prophetic literature.

> While prophecy shows the inner divine motive of the history of Israel and its environment of nations, and reveals the moral import of its events, the monuments are the complement of both, as they exhibit the causal relations between them and amplify their lessons.[93]

Therefore, according to McCurdy, archaeological discoveries illuminated history in general, as well as the lessons that history taught. Accordingly, one should not think of archaeology as proving the Bible, but as supplementing and illustrating it.

> The great primary revelation of his (God's) dealings with men is embodied in the Hebrew literature. These Bible lands have yielded to us a secondary revelation. It is subordinate, indeed, to the first, but it is richly supplementary and illustrative. It is the province of Oriental archaeology to deal with the peoples and countries and languages of the Bible so as to bring out their true relations to Bible teaching. They were formerly regarded as the mere framework of the picture. Now we are learning that they make up its groundwork, its coloring, and its perspective. They embrace, in a word, what is material in the revelation, apart from what is spiritual and ideal. And these elements, the outward and the inward, are to us inseparable, as they were in their evolution mutually involved and interwoven.[94]

> It is now in place to use the word "illustrate" almost exclusively instead of "confirm" in describing the biblical function of the monuments. The stadium of needed vindication of the historical accuracy of the Old

---

[91] *Ibid.*

[92] *Ibid.*, 1.14.

[93] J. F. McCurdy, "Oriental Research and the Bible," in *Recent Research in Bible Lands*, 27.

[94] *Ibid.*, 4-5.

Testament is now as good as past in our progress towards the final goal of truth and knowledge.[95]

While McCurdy evidently valued archaeological discoveries as highly as Sayce, the former did not become so disenchanted with source analysis so as to reject the method *en toto*. Rather, he believed that it should be used in conjunction with archaeology to reconstruct the past.

> To test and amplify the work of excavation, it is wont to invoke the results of literary criticism, as well as of comparative sociology and politics.[96]

> ...we examine the sources (the Old Testament writings) themselves directly, in the light of contemporary monuments, and with the established methods of historical research according to the well-ascertained laws of mental and moral, political and social evolution.[97]

> It would thus appear that we have to interpret the Old Testament both as a history and as a literature. Literary criticism is an adjunct and instrument, almost a sub-department, of historical research, because (1) the literature is a product of the history; and (2) because we need the results of literary criticism to check and control our scheme of the facts of history, and sometimes even to explain the facts as ascertained.[98]

McCurdy's openness to the source-critical method was further evident in his adoption of the four-source theory of the Pentateuch (J, E, D, P) as Wellahusen had proposed it in the latter part of the century. McCurdy thought that Josiah's lawbook contained the legal part of Deuteronomy (Dt 12-26),[99] that J derived from Judah near the end of the eighth century B. C. E.,[100] that E arose in Israel about 770 B. C. E.,[101] and that the Holiness Code (Lev 17-26) was from the latter half of the Exile.[102] He designated the writings of W. R. Smith, B. Stade and Kautzsch as "the most directly instructive writings on the literary history of the Old Testament."[103]

---

[95]*Ibid.*, 28. McCurdy believed that he stood at a critical time as far as archaeology was concerned, since most of what had been known in his day from archaeological work had been uncovered in the last half of the nineteenth century, and since it could be properly appreciated and evaluated in his day to a degree that it could not have been earlier. *Ibid.*, 18, 27.

[96]*Ibid.*, 6.

[97]McCurdy, *History*, 3.22.

[98]*Ibid.*, 3.23.

[99]*Ibid.*, 3.9.

[100]*Ibid.*, 3.72.

[101]*Ibid.*, 3.69.

[102]*Ibid.*, 3.287.

[103]*Ibid.*, 3.21.

When McCurdy dealt with the Chronicler's details of Israelite history, he was confident that Chronicles' reports were generally reliable. In this regard, he believed that Wellhausen and others were wrong to reject completely the witness of Chronicles to pre-exilic history.

> There is perhaps no graver case of literary and historic injustice in the records of biblical study than the treatment accorded to the book of Chronicles, as respects its statements about Uzziah and his time by one of the dominant schools of Old Testament criticism.[104]

McCurdy cited the names of Wellhausen, Stade, Meyer, and W. R. Smith, as examples of those who disregarded Chronicles' account about Uzziah without adequate cause.[105] Therefore, it is not unexpected to find that McCurdy accepted not only the Chronicler's report about Uzziah's conquests in Philistia, but also his accounts of Zerah's attack on Asa,[106] the Moabite coalition's assault on Jehoshaphat,[107] and finally, the story about Manasseh's captivity, repentance, and return.[108]

McCurdy wrote during the same period of time that A. H. Sayce wrote at Oxford, and both were strongly interested in archaeology and the contributions which it could make to the study of the Old Testament. Furthermore, both of them believed that on the whole archaeology supported the biblical records. The two diverged from one another, however,—especially in Sayce's later days—on the value that they saw in source analysis. McCurdy saw it as a valuable tool, while Sayce came to regard it as a subjective and faulty method. Consequently, Sayce violently rejected the method and results of source analysis, but McCurdy used both the method and its results

---

[104]McCurdy, "Uzziah and the Philistines," *The Expositor* 4 (4th ser.; 1891) 388. McCurdy's article made use of Assyrian records to show how they assumed Judean hedgemony over Philistia and the occurrence of Philistinian names with Yah or Yahu components in those records, thus demonstrating the influence of Judah on Philistia. He concluded that, "...it may be safely set down as established that events such as those ascribed in Chronicles to Uzziah must necessarily have occurred, else Jewish history would have been quite different from what we know it to have been." *Ibid.*, 396. Cf. *History*, 1.312-13.

[105]*Ibid.*, 388.

[106]McCurdy believed that Zerah's attack was an Egyptian attempt to repeat Shishak's successful attack on Rehoboam. *History*, 1.259.

[107]*Ibid.*, 1.260.

[108]McCurdy believed that Manasseh was part of the revolt against Assurbanipal in which the city of Babylon was eventually destroyed. He held that Manasseh was really taken to Nineveh and that the reference to Babylon in 2 Chronicles 33 "is mentioned as...a natural mistake of the writer or perhaps of some copyist." *History*, 2.388.

(at least with regard to the Pentateuch), as it was practiced by the leading Old Testament scholars of his day.

Sayce argued fervently that archaeological discoveries had served to validate the biblical records and regarded this as a legitimate function of archaeology. McCurdy, however, disagreed and argued that archaeology should be used to "supplement" and "illustrate" the biblical writings. It may be, though, that their difference in this regard was primarily one of semantics or rhetoric and that in fact they used archaeological discoveries to the same end—to prove the accuracy of the biblical record. It is clear, however, that the tone of McCurdy's article in Hilprecht's volume and that of his *History, Prophecy and the Monuments* was much less radical and polemical than what one finds in Sayce's later writings. With regard to Chronicles, however, both scholars believed in its basic reliability and historical trustworthiness and were not at all hesitant to use the work in the reconstruction of pre-exilic history.

7. SUMMARY OF ARCHAEOLOGY'S USE
IN THE DEFENSE OF CHRONICLES

Of all the nineteenth century archaeological discoveries, the epigraphical finds and their translation had the greatest impact on the interpretation of Chronicles. Rawlinson, Schrader, Sayce, G. A. Smith, and McCurdy were agreed in their conviction that archaeology had largely—if not entirely—vindicated Chronicles against the contentions of de Wette and Wellhausen that Chronicles' testimony should be rejected for the reconstruction of Israel's pre-exilic history. These scholars were generally optimistic about the usefulness of archaeology to establish the credibility of the Bible and believed that more and more archaeological discoveries would be forthcoming and that these would further confirm the Bible's reliability. An argument that one meets in the writings of Rawlinson and Sayce is that since archaeology has established the veracity of the biblical records where archaeological data has been available, then the biblical testimony should be presumed correct in those cases where archaeological information is not accessible.

As far as the dating of P and Wellhausen's documentary hypothesis were concerned, Sayce was most radical, since he rejected the entire source critical method. Rawlinson and Schrader were a bit less extreme, since they accepted the source critical method but still argued for the pre-exilic dating of P. McCurdy stood at the opposite end of the spectrum on this issue and accepted Wellhausen's J E D P sequence of pentateuchal sources.

G. Rawlinson and A. H. Sayce were more extravagant in their claims for archaeology than the other two scholars treated in this section, and the former two figures often assumed an apologetical tone in their publications. Schrader and McCurdy, however, appeared to have been less interested in popularizing their views. This was especially clear with regard to McCurdy, who argued for the use of "illuminate" rather than "confirm" when one spoke of the service that archaeology performed for the Bible. Nevertheless, all five of these scholars believed that archaeology had by and large restored confidence in Chronicles as a historical source for reconstructing Israel's pre-exilic period.

D. Critical Response to the Apologetical Use of Archaeology

1. Introduction

The second group of scholars to be discussed in this chapter will be used to show the response that was made to Sayce and those others who thought that archaeology had vindicated Chronicles as a historical witness. W. R. Smith, S. R. Driver, W. H. Bennet, W. E. Barnes, T. K. Cheyne, and F. Brown made up this group. Smith, Driver, and Brown saw a value in archaeological research and believed, as a whole, that the science had illuminated Israel's pre-exilic history, but they were not as confident as some (e.g., Sayce) of its vindication of Chronicles' credibility. Bennet, Barnes, and Cheyne did not address the issue of the use of archaeology as extensively, but they have been included in this section, since they were contemporaries of the three foregoing scholars and dealt with Chronicles in a significant way.

2. W. R. SMITH

a. General

One of the most influential figures in the promotion of Old Testament scholarship in nineteenth century Britain was William Robertson Smith (1846-1894). Smith began his university studies at Aberdeen and later went to Edinburgh, where he studied under A. B. Davidson. During the summers of 1867 and 1869, he studied in Bonn and Göttingen.[109] His major ecclesiastical conflicts began after his appointment to teach oriental languages and Old Testament exegesis at Free Church College in Aberdeen. His articles in the *Encyclopaedia Britannica* on angels and the Bible aroused protest from the church's conservative element, and in 1881, his debates with his opponents ended with his dismissal from Aberdeen. Smith continued to argue his case by giving lectures in Edinburgh and Glasgow to large audiences on the topic of biblical criticism (1880-1882), and these lectures

---

[109]J. S. Black, "Smith, William Robertson," *DNB* 53 (1898) 160-62; A. E. Shipley, "Smith, William Robertson," *Enc Brit* 25 (11th ed.; 1911) 271-72; Cheyne, *Founders*, 212-25; T. O. Beidelman, *W. Robertson Smith and the Sociological Study of Religion* (Chicago: Univeristy of Chicago Press, 1974) 3-27.

were printed in two volumes: *The Old Testament in the Jewish Church* (1881) and *The Prophets of Israel and their Place in History* (1882).[110] The first of these volumes and Smith's article on Chronicles in *Encyclopaedia Britannica* are the primary sources for determining the author's views on Chronicles.

b. Chronicles

In his encyclopedia article on Chronicles Smith set the books with Ezra and Nehemiah as originally a single work, and he dated this publication to the time of Alexander the Great. Its author was not, therefore, Ezra, but was probably someone with a levitical bent of mind. The sources that the author used for 1, 2 Chronicles were the Pentateuch, Samuel-Kings, the Book of the Kings of Israel and Judah (no longer extant), the writings of Isaiah and Jehu, and perhaps a work called the Midrash (no longer extant). Smith concluded that the author of Chronicles copied from his sources accurately, but that he still introduced additional information according to his own theological perspective. Therefore, one should be suspicious of the Chronicler's offerings when these coincided with his purposes, but one should not accuse him of setting out deliberately to distort and falsify history. With regard to German research into these problems, Smith believed that the truth lay somewhere between Keil and Graf, and he found himself sympathetic to the works of Ewald and Bertheau. The work of Schrader, the German Assyriologist, was cited by Smith as evidence in favor of the Chronicler's treatment of Manasseh's captivity.[111] Therefore, it appears that in 1889, Smith had

---

[110]*Ibid.*, 13-22.

[111]W. R. Smith, "Chronicles," *Enc Brit* 5 (9th ed.; 1889) 706-9. Smith's willingness to accept Schrader's use of archaeology for illuminating Israelite history showed that he was not adverse to this use of archaeological materials. He was, however, adverse to those proponents of archaeology who rejected the source critical method. Conder, for example, ("The Old Testament: Ancient Monuments and Modern Critics," *Contemporary Review* 51 [1887] 376-93) attacked biblical criticism in general and Wellhausen in particular. He wrote (p. 389) of his desire "to take our critic (Wellhausen) out of his study, and set him on a camel in the wilderness, to surround him with human beings in all their primitive conditions of society and of thought, to humanize and to Orientalize the student, and to show him what men think and do in lands where they still swear by the 'Living God' and still say in their daily life 'It is from the Lord.'" Smith responded sharply to Conder ("Captain Conder and Modern Critics," *Contemporary Review* 51 [1887] 561-69), because he believed that Conder was ignorant of Old Testament studies in general and that he had set himself up as an authority, to whom the public should listen. "Does Captain Conder think that to be set on a camel in the wilderness will give a man 'an independent Knowledge of Oriental history, antiquity and thought?' Most of us have supposed that this knowledge is only to be acquired by hard study of the documents of Oriental antiquity, and it is a new doctrine that the most meritorious field-work will make a man a

assumed a stance toward Chronicles, which acknowledged the theological *Tendenz* of Chronicles and the effects that this had on its accounts, but he was unwilling to dismiss as historically worthless all reports that were unique to the books.

In the second edition of *The Old Testament in the Jewish Church*, Smith's view of Chronicles seemed a bit more like that of Graf than it did in the earlier encyclopedia article. In 1892, therefore, Smith argued for the priority of Samuel-Kings over Chronicles as a source for historical information about the pre-exilic period, since the former work was composed much earlier than the latter.

> In dealing with sources for profane history, however, we should never dream of putting books of such different age on the same footing; the Book of Kings was substantially complete before the Exile, in the early years of the sixth century B. C., while the Chronicler gives genealogies that go down at least six generations after Zerubbabel, and probably reach to contemporaries of Alexander the Great. ...it must also be remembered that the Book of Kings is largely made up of verbal extracts from much older sources, and for many purposes may be treated as having the practical value of a contemporary history. Hence, according to the ordinary laws of research, the Book of Kings is a source of the first class, and the Chronicles have a very secondary value. It is the rule of all historical study to begin with the records that stand nearest to the events recorded and are written under the living impress of the life of the time described. ... It is manifest that the Chronicler, writing at a time when the institutions of Ezra had universal currency, had no personal knowledge of the greatly different praxis of Israel before the Exile, and that the general picture which he gives of the life and worship of the Hebrews under the old monarchy cannot have the same value for us as the records of the Book of Kings.[112]

Smith further argued that the Chronicler's only genuine source for the monarchical era was Samuel-Kings.

> But for the history proper, his (the Chronicler's) one genuine source was the series of the Former Prophets, the Books of Samuel and especially of Kings.[113]

---

linguist, an epigrapher, and an historian. Even the inaccurate second-hand knowledge which, as I shall presently show, makes up the staple of Captain Conder's contributions to Biblical science, was not gathered in the field but drawn from books, and I fail to see that the German critic in his study is at a disadvantage as compared with the English amateur. Both draw from the same documents, but Professor Wellhausen reads them in the original, and Captain Conder in translations and popular manuals." (p. 562)

[112]Smith, *The Old Testament in the Jewish Church* (2d ed.; London: Adam and Charles Black, 1892) 140-41.

[113]*Ibid.*, 142.

Consequently, Smith concluded that the Chronicler's testimony was unreliable whenever he offered the reader information that was not found in Samuel-Kings: "where he (the Chronicler) adds to the narrative of Kings or departs from it, his variations are never such as to inspire confidence."[114] Smith proceeded to elaborate in detail the Chronicler's "mechanical" view of theocracy, according to which God punished sin and rewarded obedience immediately, and with regard to Manasseh in Chronicles he wrote,

> ...the wicked Manasseh is converted into a penitent to justify his long reign. All this is exactly in the style of the Jewish Midrash; it is not history but Haggada, moralising romance attaching to historical names and events. And the Chronicler himself gives the name of Midrash...to two of the sources from which he drew..., so that there is really no mystery as to the nature of his work when it departs from the old canonical histories.[115]

Smith concluded his treatment of Chronicles with the bold statement,

> I have dwelt at some length on this topic, because the practice of using the Chronicles as if they had the same historical value as the older books has done more than any other one cause to prevent a right understanding of the Old Testament and of the Old Dispensation.[116]

Therefore, the two chief differences between Smith's two discussions of Chronicles are: (1) the encyclopedia article listed a variety of different sources that the Chronicler used, while the lecture noted only Samuel-Kings; and (2) the encyclopedia article admitted some usefulness of Chronicles for reconstructing the pre-exilic history, but the lecture denied that Chronicles was useful for that purpose.

c. Summary

Smith's treatments of Chronicles offered little that was new or original, and his bibliographical notes made it clear that he was rehearsing for his readers the findings of German scholarship. Moreover, it appears that Smith's own views of Chronicles became more like those of Graf and the more radical German critics as time passed. Although he had first believed that Chronicles had some usefulness for reconstructing Israel's pre-exilic history, he later came to believe that this was not the case. He rejected the harmonizing techniques, which smoothed over the differences between Chronicles and Samuel-Kings, as well as Conder's use of nineteenth century archaeo-

---

[114]*Ibid.*
[115]*Ibid.*, 147-48.
[116]*Ibid.*, 148.

logical findings to undermine the critical views of Wellhausen and others.

3. DRIVER

a. General

The most influential figure in securing a place for critical scholarship in English Old Testament studies was Samuel Rolles Driver (1846-1914), who studied at Oxford and in 1883 became Regius Professor of Hebrew and Canon of Christ Church there. Two of his most important linguistic publications were *A Treatise on the Use of the Tenses in Hebrew* (1872) and the English version of Gesenius' Hebrew lexicon (1906), on which he collaborated with Francis Brown and Charles A. Briggs. He issued commentaries or notes on Genesis, Exodus, Deuteronomy, Samuel, Psalms, Isaiah, Jeremiah, Daniel, and the Minor Prophets, and several volumes of sermons and essays. His most influential work, however, was probably his *Introduction to the Literature of the Old Testament* (1891).[117]

Driver's career at Oxford came at a time of transition for the Anglican Church. Higher criticism had made inroads in theological education long before his day, but it was still highly suspect among many clergymen and most of the laity, and Driver served to promote the critical study of the Bible, while reassuring the more orthodox element in the church that the conclusions of higher criticism were not "in conflict either with the Christian creeds or with the articles of the Christian faith."[118] While this work was appreciated by his colleagues at the time, some of them, such as T. K. Cheyne, believed that he made too many concessions to the church's conservative element and "that he often blunts the edge of his decisions, so that the student cannot judge of their critical bearing."[119]

While Driver made no pretense at being an archaeologist, there was a great deal of interest in archaeological discoveries around the turn of the century, and some, such as A. H. Sayce, were making grand claims for the science, predicting that it would destroy the conclusions and even the method itself of the higher critic's source analysis. Driver traveled to Palestine first in 1888 and again to Palestine and Egypt in 1910. In 1908, he delivered the Schweich

---

[117]George A. Cooke, "Driver, Samuel Rolles," *DNB 1912-1921* (1927) 162-63; S. R. Driver, *The Ideals of the Prophets*, (ed. G. A. Cooke; Edinburgh: T. & T. Clark, 1915) 235-37.

[118]S. R. Driver, *An Introduction to the Literature of the Old Testament* (International Theological Library; 9th ed.; Edinburgh: T. & T. Clark, 1913) viii. The first edition of the work was issued in 1891 by T. & T. Clark in Edinburgh and Charles Scribner's Sons in New York.

[119]Cheyne, *Founders*, 252.

Lectures and published them under the title *Modern Research as Illustrating the Bible* (1909) and used the occasion to discuss archaeological findings and the Bible. He had written with a similar purpose in mind in his essay "Hebrew Authority" in the volume *Authority and Archaeology* (1899). In the latter work, as in the preface to the eighth edition of his Old Testament introduction, he opposes the claims of Sayce and asserted that while archaeology indeed served to illuminate the literature and history of ancient Israel, it had not proven higher criticism wrong about the historical credibility of any biblical text.

> The fact is, the antagonism which some writers have sought to establish between criticism and archaeology is wholly factitious and unreal. Criticism and archaeology deal with antiquity from different points of view, and mutually supplement one another. Each in turn supplies what the other lacks; and it is only by an entire misunderstanding of the scope and limits of both that they can be brought into antagonism with one another. What is called the "witness of the monuments" is often strangely misunderstood. The monuments witness to nothing which any reasonable critic has ever doubted. No one, for instance, has ever doubted that there were kings of Israel (or Judah) named Ahab and Jehu and Pekah and Ahaz and Hezekiah, or that Tiglath-pileser and Sennacherib led expeditions into Palestine; the mention of these (and such-like) persons and events in the Assyrian annals has brought to light many additional facts about them which it is an extreme satisfaction to know: but it has only "confirmed" what no critic had questioned. On the other hand, the Assyrian annals have shewn that the chronology of the Books of Kings is, in certain places, incorrect: they have thus confirmed the conclusion which critics had reached independently upon internal evidence, that the parts of these books to which the chronology belongs are of much later origin than the more strictly historical parts, and consequently do not possess equal value.[120]

> The attempt to refute the conclusions of criticism by means of archaeology has signally failed. ...they (archaeoloaical discoveries) have revealed nothing which is in conflict with the generally accepted conclusions of critics. ...the idea that the monuments furnish a refutation of the general critical position, is a pure illusion.[121]

b. Chronicles

Driver's treatment of Chronicles will be examined in three parts: general introductory matters, the speeches, and the bearing of archaeology on the books. He believed that Chronicles, Ezra, and

---

[120]S. R. Driver, "Hebrew Authority" in *Authority and Archaeology* (ed. David G. Hogarth; New York: Charles Scribner's Sons, 1899) 150-51.

[121]Driver, *Introduction*, xviii.

Nehemiah were originally a single work, written by a levite (perhaps a member of the temple choir) not before the beginning of the Greek period. The author's aim was to produce a "history of *Judah*, with specific reference to the institutions connected with the *Temple*, under the monarchy, and after the restoration."[122] The Chronicler's main sources can be understood according to the following diagram.[123]

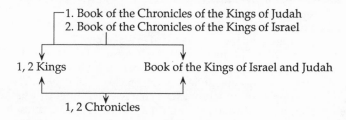

In addition to the canonical books of Old Testament history (Genesis-2 Kings), Driver maintained that the Chronicler used a work entitled Book of the Kings of Israel and Judah, which was probably a post-exilic work, incorporating statistical information and dealing with the histories of both Israel and Judah. Driver left open the possibility that the Chronicler used a work called the Midrash and various other prophetical works,[124] but he concluded that one could not, on the basis of these sources, accept all of the Chronicler's additional information "as strictly and literally historical."[125] While it is probable that a "traditional element lies at the basis of the Chronicler's reports," it is also probable that the Chronicler (or his post-exilic sources) has projected post-exilic practices and institutions back into the pre-exilic period, and so Chronicles becomes an important witness to the Jewish community ca. 300 B. C. E.[126]

In 1895, there was an exchange of three articles in *The Expositor* between Driver and Valpy French about the speeches in Chronicles. This debate grew out of French's earlier attack in *Lex Mosaica* (1894) on Driver's view of the speeches, which the latter had expressed in *Contemporary Review* (1890). Driver argued that speeches found only in Chronicles were markedly post-exilic in language and thought and so had been composed by the Chronicler. He still allowed, however, that some accurate historical information was contained in them. French, though, maintained that all the speeches and narratives in Chronicles contained a mixture of pre-exilic and post-exilic language

---

[122]*Ibid.*, 517.
[123]*Ibid.*, 532.
[124]*Ibid.*, 519-31.
[125]*Ibid.*, 532-33.
[126]*Ibid.*, 532-35.

and that there were no significant differences between the speeches which were unique to Chronicles and those which had parallels in Samuel-Kings. Driver's first article in *The Expositor* of 1895, compared the speech in 2 Samuel 7 with that in 1 Chronicles 17 and found only a few, unimportant changes by the Chronicler. Then he examined the speech in 1 Chronicles 29 and found numerous instances of post-exilc language and of a style that was characteristic of 1, 2 Chronicles.[127] French replied in the same year and argued that Driver had smoothed over the differences between 1 Chronicles 17 and 2 Samuel 7, but had exaggerated the occurrence of exilic or post-exilic idioms in 1 Chronicles 29.[128] The final article in the exchange was Driver's response to French, and in it he defended his earlier conclusions with regard to the language and style of 1 Chronicles 17 and 29, offered a few other examples of the Chronicler's characteristic linguistic usage, and concluded by citing the remarks by Keil and Delitzsch—recognized conservatives—which demonstrated that they were in agreement with Driver.[129] Therefore, while Driver found that the Chronicler was largely responsible for composing speeches and narratives that were unique to his history, he did not conclude from this that they were fictional and so worthless for historical reconstruction. On the contrary, he believed that elements of tradition lay behind them.

The premiere example of Driver's attitude toward the claim that archaeology had vindicated the historical credibility of Chronicles is found in the issue of Manasseh's captivity. Sayce had argued that the references to Manasseh in the Assyrian annals of both Esarhaddon and Assurbanipal supplied sufficient evidence to establish the reliability of the Chronicler's report that the Jewish king was imprisoned by the Assyrians and later released. Driver observed, however, that

> The inscriptions do not decide the question. They shew that what is said to have happened to Manasseh is, in the abstract, possible: they do not shew that it actually occurred. ...and the Chronicler remains still our sole positive authority for the captivity of Manasseh. The monuments shew that the statement is not, in the abstract, incredible: they do not neutralize the suspicions which arise from the non-mention of the fact in the Kings, and from its being associated in the Chronicles with the account of Manasseh's repentance, which, conflicting as it does directly

---

[127]S. R. Driver, "The Speeches in Chronicles," *The Expositor* 1 (5th ser.; 1895) 241-56.

[128]Valpy French, "The Speeches in Chronicles. A Reply," *The Expositor* 2 (5th ser.; 1895) 140-52.

[129]S. P. Driver, "The Speeches in the Chronicles," *The Expositor* 2 (5th ser.; 1895) 286-308.

with the testimony of both Jeremiah and the compiler of Kings, must certainly be exaggerated, even if it have any basis in fact at all.[130]

Therefore, Driver believed that archaeology had only provided a possible set of circumstances for the Chronicler's story—not a proof of the story's truthfulness.

c . Summary

Driver introduced nothing new into the study of Chronicles. His Old Testament introduction and other works represented a cautious acceptance of German critical research on the books. His perspective on Chronicles was similar to that of Ewald and Bertheau and consequently was a rejection of the more extreme views of both de Wette and Keil. Driver believed that the Chronicler's history was decisively biased in favor of its author's levitical interests, and that this resulted in exaggerations, significant omissions, and historically unreliable speeches and narratives. He maintained, however, that Chronicles could be profitably used to reconstruct the pre-exilic history of Israel, but that the books had to be used with caution. In this regard, Driver found himself at odds, on the one hand, with Sayce and those who supported Chronicles' historical credibility on the basis of archaeological discoveries, but on the other hand, with Wellhausen and others who favored a more radical rejection of Chronicles' testimony. Driver's work was significant for the history of research into Chronicles, however, because he opposed the excessive confidence in archaeology to decide historical-critical issues and argued for a moderate but thoroughly critical approach to Chronicles.

4. BENNET

A third British Old Testament scholar who wrote about Chronicles near the end of the nineteenth century—but one for whom archaeology did not play a dramatic role—was William Henry Bennet (1855-1920). He wrote two works that dealt with Chronicles: a commentary in The Expositor's Bible (1894) and an article on Chronicles in *The Jewish Encyclopedia* (1903). In both publications he wrote that Chronicles was originally part of a larger work that included Ezra and Nehemiah, that the author was a levite of the temple singers, and that the work should be assigned a date between 300 and 250 B. C. E.[131] Moreover, in both works Bennet took a cautious stance toward the Chronicler's credibility. He was unwilling to accept as historically accurate everything that the Chronicler

---

[130]Driver, "Authority," 15-16.

[131]W. H. Bennet, *The Books of Chronicles* (The Expositor's Bible, 4; New York: A. C. Armstrong & Sons, 1903) 3-5; "Chronicles, Books of," *The Jewish Encyclopedia* 4 (1903) 60.

wrote, but on the other hand, he certainly did not regard the author as a "falsifier of the past."[132] He believed that when Chronicles contradicted Samuel-Kings, the latter merited our confidence, and that many of the cultic details in Chronicles more closely agreed with the Chronicler's own day than with the times of the monarchy.[133] In addition, speeches and prophetic admonitions in Chronicles were also apparently the work of the Chronicler himself.[134] On the other hand, some of the material that was unique to Chronicles had a "neutral" flavor (e.g., genealogies, family histories, anecdotes, and notes on ancient life and customs, and in these cases its archaic flavor and relative unimportance argued for its authenticity.[135] In specific cases of political events that are reported only in Chronicles, Bennet appeared inclined to accept them as credible. For instance, in his commentary he accepted the Chronicler's account of Asa's battle with Zerah and the episode about Jehoshaphat's confrontation with the Moabite coalition.[136] In his encyclopedia article, he noted that while some political accounts, such as that of Abijah's victory over Israel, Asa's over Zerah, and Manasseh's captivity, were "possibly accurate," they "must be used carefully," since they came to us from Chronicles.[137] Bennet's two writings were separated by about ten years and diverged on the matter of the Chronicler's sources. In the earlier publication—the commentary—he wrote that the Chronicler's primary source was Samuel-Kings and that the Pentateuch, Joshua, Ruth, oral tradition, manuscripts of the fragmentary literature of the post-exilic period, and genealogies from public, ecclesiastical, and family archives were used to a more limited extent. The Chronicler's references to the Book of the Kings of Israel and Judah—the references to the prophetic Writings only related to sections within this larger world—were not necessarily indications that he had used or even had had direct knowledge of the work.[138] In the later encyclopedia article, however, Bennet's view had changed and set forth the belief that the Chronicler's main source was a "late, post-exilic Midrashic history of the Kings of Judah and Israel," and thus he proposed two alternative views of the Chronicler's sources.[139]

---

[132]*Ibid.*, 63; *Chronicles*, 7-12.

[133]*Ibid.*, 11-12; "Chronicles," 63.

[134]*Ibid.*

[135]Bennet, *Chronicles*, 23-24.

[136]*Ibid.* 340-41, 372-77.

[137]Bennet, "Chronicles," 63.

[138]Bennet, *Chronicles*, 14-19.

[139]Bennet, "Chronicles," 62.

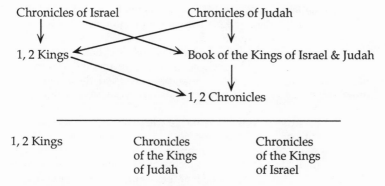

1, 2 Kings   Chronicles   Chronicles
                     of the Kings   of the Kings
                     of Judah   of Israel

The Book of the Kings of Israel & Judah

1, 2 Chronicles

This shift in Bennet's view of Chronicles' sources seems to have had no appreciable effect on his general view of the Chronicler's reliability as a historical source.

Bennet's conclusions about Chronicles were generally those of British scholarship at the end of the nineteenth century. They evidenced a recognition of the Chronicler's biases and limitations as a historical source, but at the same time they exhibited an unwillingness to label the author a "falsifier of history." Therefore, the Chronicler's errors were regarded as honest ones. In this connection Bennet urged caution in the use of information in Chronicles for reconstructing the history of the pre-exilic period, and in practice he accepted the Chronicler's battle reports, speeches, and other information, while making allowances for exaggeration and embellishment.

5. BARNES

A second English scholar who dealt with Chronicles in a significant way but who did not deal extensively with archaeological considerations was William Emery Barnes (1859-1939). He studied at Cambridge and spent his teaching career there, issuing a number of publications on Chronicles, as well as commentaries on Psalms, 1, 2 Kings, and the Minor Prophets. His greatest scholarly contributions, however, were in the field of Syriac.[140]

---

[140]J. F. Bethune-Baker, "Barnes, William Emery," *DNB 1931-1940* (1949) 42-44. Barnes also wrote the following publications that dealt with Chronicles: "The Religious Standpoint of the Chronicler," *AJSL* 13 (1896/97) 14-20; "Chronicles a Targum," *ET* 8 (1896/97) 316-19; *An Apparatus Criticus to Chronicles in the Peshitta Version* (Cambridge: University Press, 1897); "On 2 Chron. xiv.9; Job i.15; Prov.

Barnes believed that Chronicles was written as part of a larger work that included Ezra and Nehemiah by an anonymous contemporary of Nehemiah in order to advance the religious organization of those who returned from the exile. The final touches on the work (e.g., additions to genealogies), however, were made between 300 and 250 B. C. E.[141] The author's sources included the Hexateuch, Samuel-Kings, family or tribal songs or traditions (e.g., 1 Chr 2:23; 4:39-41), local traditions (e.g., 1 Chr 11:8), and prophetic or priestly writings that are no longer extant (2 Chr 9:29, e.g., refers to this prophetic work or series of works).[142]

Barnes gave considerable attention to the matter of Chronicles' historical reliability. His general conclusion was that "the substantial accuracy of the Chronicler's sketch of the history of Judah cannot reasonably be questioned,"[143] and he supported this point of view by treating a series of six narratives in Chronicles. The first was the report about Abijah's victory over Jeroboam I (2 Chr 13:3-20). He noted the various problems with the account (e.g., no parallel in Kings, inflated casualty figures for Israel, and the reference to Rehoboam at age forty-one as "young and tender-hearted"), and then he proceeded to note the various aspects of the story that were credible (e.g., 1 Kg 15:7 notes warfare between the two kings, "the story is circumstantial and consistent" in that Bethel and two other cities were the prizes for Judah's victory). His conclusion was that there is nothing incredible in the story of a victory of some king being gained by Abijah over Jeroboam.[144] The other stories from Chronicles that Barnes treated were: Asa's victory over Zerah (2 Chronicles 14) and Jehoshaphat's over the Moabite coalition (2 Chronicles 20), Uzziah's leprosy (2 Chr 26:16-20), and Manasseh's repentance (2 Chr 33:13). In each case Barnes concluded that a historical kernel lay behind the Chronicler's report, in spite of the fact that one could detect midrashic or haggadic elements in the accounts.

> ...we shall be inclined neither to reject any one of the five stories altogether, nor on the other hand to accept any one in all its details. Moreover we are led to draw a distinction between some of the stories and the rest. In three cases (the Repentance of Manasseh, the Leprosy of Uzziah, and the Victory of Abijah) the Chronicler's Tendenz is seen not merely in the details, but also in the substance of the stories. Yet even these three narratives are not thereby necessarily discredited. Events do

---

xxvii.22," *ET* 8 (1896/97) 431-32; "The David of the Book of Samuel and the David of the Book of Chronicles," *The Expositor* 7 (7th ser.; 1909) 49-59.

[141]W. E. Barnes, *The Books of Chronicles* (The Cambridge Bible for Schools and Colleges; Cambridge: University Press, 1899) x-xii.

[142]*Ibid.*, xviii-xxi.

[143]*Ibid.*, xxxiii.

sometimes happen in accordance with men's theories. ... On the other hand the details which are expressed in the Chronicler's own phraseology ought probably to be given up.[145]

On the whole it seems that, though the presence of Haggadah in Chronicles cannot be denied, the amount of it to which we can point with any confidence is small. The Chronicler may have been the first Darshan whose works have been preserved, but Chronicles has too many points of contact with history to be lightly called a Midrash "as one of the Midrashim."[146]

Barnes dealt with Chronicles critically and concluded that many of the details in the Chronicler's history could not be trusted as historically reliable. On the other hand, however, Barnes assigned a relatively early date to the substance of Chronicles by positing the work of a later redactor, and he exhibited considerable confidence in the basic historicity of the stories that were unique to Chronicles. With regard to the latter point, Barnes usually reasoned that if the Chronicler's story was at all plausible or possible, then one should assume that it had a basis in fact. Therefore, it was largely irrelevant to him whether the stories advanced the author's *Tendenz* or were filled with exaggerations or details that were unlikely. It appears, therefore, that Barnes' presumption was in favor of Chronicles' credibility and that he dealt with evidence to the contrary by acknowledging a midrashic tendency on the part of the author. Thus, Barnes tended to have more confidence in the historical reliability of Chronicles than W. R. Smith and S. R. Driver.

6. CHEYNE

a. General

Another important figure in late nineteenth century British Old Testament scholarship was Thomas Kelly Cheyne (1841-1915). He studied at Oxford and under Ewald at Göttingen, and he served as Oriel Professor of Interpretation of Scripture at Oxford from 1885-1908.[147] The publication of his commentary on Isaiah in 1880 marked

---

[144]Barnes, "The Midrashic Element in Chronicles," *The Expositor* 4 (5th ser.; 1896) 427-29.

[145]*Ibid.*, 437.

[146]*Ibid.*, 439.

[147]Cheyne served on the revision committee for the AV and wrote a great number of book reviews for the *Academy*, a journal founded by C. E. Appleton to promote biblical criticism in Britain. This journal was identified as one of the most disturbing factors for the study of the Old Testament in the Church of England in the years following Pusey's debate with H. J. Rose in the 1820s and 1830s. (W. Robertson Nicoll, "Professor Cheyne," *The Expositor* [3d ser.; 1889] 59-

a significant shift of emphasis in his work toward the mediation of the results of biblical criticism to the laity, but it did not represent the turn toward a more conservative application of the critical method, which some thought they detected at the time. Cheyne accepted Graf's theory about the Priestly Code and rejected the intrusion of dogmatic assumptions into exegesis as early as 1871, when he published his first book, and he apparently retained these positions until his death.[148]

b. Chronicles

Two of Cheyne's works are useful for understanding his views toward Chronicles. The first is a series of lectures that Cheyne delivered in America, *Jewish Religious Life After the Exile* (1898).[149] Barely three pages were devoted to the Chronicles in the work, but those pages revealed the substance of Cheyne's perspective on the books. He believed that Chronicles was originally the first part of a larger work, which included Ezra and Nehemiah, and it was written by a levitical musician ca. 250 B. C. E. The author had a strong attraction to the details of Jewish religious ritual and to a belief in divine retribution.

> I need not quote all the astounding distortions and inventions of fact into which the Chronicler's pious illusion has led him. Quite enough has been said against the Chronicler as a historian....[150]

Finally, Cheyne noted that the Chronicler was remarkable for his "tender piety," which found expression in the speeches that he created for his composition.

> Here, as at other points of his faulty historical reconstruction, the worthy Chronicler opens a window in his heart. And no attainments of intellectual wisdom are worth as much as that loving reverence for God in which he lived and moved.[151]

In a work that appeared ten years later, *The Decline and Fall of the Kingdom of Judah* (1908), Cheyne's view of Chronicles remained un-

---

61.) Cheyne also wrote articles for the ninth edition of the *Encyclopaedia Britannica* and served as co-editor for the *Encyclopaedia Biblica*.

[148] A. S. Peake, "Thomas Kelly Cheyne," *ET* 6 (1894/95) 439-44; "T. K. Cheyne," *DNB 1912-1921* (1927) 119-20; G. A. Cooke, "Thomas Kelly Cheyne," *The Expositor* (8th ser.; 1915) 445-51. Cheyne's later works were criticized for their insistence on his Jerameelite hypothesis of North Arabian influence on Israel.

[149] Cheyne, *Jewish Religious Life After the Exile* (American Lectures on the History of Religions, 3d series, 1897-98; New York: G. P. Putnam's Sons, 1898). Karl Budde delivered lectures for the series in the following year.

[150] *Ibid.*, 214.

[151] *Ibid.*, 215.

changed. The reign of Hezekiah provided the Chronicler with an opportunity to present his theory of retribution, according to Cheyne, and consequently, his account about the king could not be trusted.

> The Chronicler, however, has no scruple in exaggerating to the utmost what little he may have learned from tradition (2 Chr. xxix.3-xxxi.1). ... The Chronicler's narrative, however, is obviously not history; it is rather a development of what is related in 2 K. xviii.4a, and it serves as an explanation of the prosperity ascribed by the Chronicler to Hezekiah. Here, said this pious writer, is an opportunity of proving on a grand scale that righteousness exalteth a king as well as a nation. ... Surely there must have been some kings of the Davidic line who carried out these iconoclastic injunctions (the commands in Exodus to destroy pagan idols) and were rewarded for it. The most exemplary of these kings, according to the Chronicler, were Hezekiah and Josiah.[152]

It appears, however, that Cheyne may have had reservations about rejecting the Chronicler's account of Manasseh's captivity in Babylon. He noted the Chronicler's story and remarked, "Why this is not mentioned in 2 K. is a secret of the last redactor."[153]

Cheyne's final remarks in this section on Chronicles pointed out that while the Chronicler had indeed used his sources uncritically and distorted his accounts, nevertheless, it was likely that he had ancient sources available, and consequently, some of his facts were true.

> The Chronicler, after his manner, fills up the gap with an account of a religious movement. In the eighth year of his reign Josiah "Began to be zealous for the God of David his father," and in the twelfth to "purge Judah and Jerusalem" (2 Chr. xxxiv. 3). It so happens that...the twelfth year of king Josiah was the death-year of the last great Assyrian king.... May not the movement (of reform) really have begun in the twelfth year? This is indeed only an ingenious surmise, and may, to some, appear discredited by its connexion with the Chronicler. Still intelligent surprises are often called for, and may we not—must we not—believe that the Chronicler had access to and used, even if uncritically, older historical sources? His facts may sometimes be right, even if the setting or the colouring is wrong.[154]

c. Summary

Cheyne was among the most eager of all British scholars around the turn of the century to mediate the results of Continental scholarship to Britian. This led him to a certain impatience with men like S. R. Driver, who proceeded more cautiously and seemed more eager to

---

[152]Cheyne, *The Decline and Fall of the Kingdom of Judah* (London: Adam and Charles Black, 1908) 5.

[153]*Ibid.*

[154]*Ibid.*, 7.

make concessions to the orthodox element in the churches. In the later part of his career, Cheyne showed more consideration for the sensibilities of his British audiences, but on the other hand, his last works were marred by excessive concern for his Jerameelite theory.

While Cheyne maintained a post-exilic date for P, a third century date for Chronicles, and that the latter was theologically biased and subject to exaggeration, he did not go as far as Wellhausen and assert that 1, 2 Chronicles had no value at all for historical reconstruction. His position was more moderate and made allowances for the cautious use of Chronicles as a historical source on the basis of (1) his conviction that the author probably had ancient sources available, and (2) information in Chronicles sometimes agreed with modern historical reconstructions. In this regard, Cheyne's views were similar to those of S. R. Driver.

7. BROWN

On the other side of the Atlantic, Driver's perspective was largely shared by Francis Brown (1849-1916), who attended Dartmouth and studied under Charles A. Briggs at Union Theological Seminary. For two years after he graduated Union, Brown studied in Berlin, where he learned Assyriology from E. Schrader. He returned to Union and spent the remainder of his career there.[155]

Brown's earliest volume on Assyriology (*Assyriology: Its Use and Abuse in Old Testament Study*, 1885) illustrated the author's view of the critical method and the usefulness of nineteenth century archaeological finds for the study of the Old Testament. He listed three abuses of Assyriology: (1) *"overhaste in its employment,"* (2) *"refusal to accept its clear facts,* in the interest of some theory of interpretation,"* and (3) ignoring *"the new problems* with which it confronts the Biblical scholar." The first abuse had resulted in extravagant claims being made that Mesopotamian archaeological discoveries had proven the truthfulness of various biblical accounts. The second abuse referred to the unwillingness of some biblical scholars to accept the findings of Assyriology, when those findings contradicted a biblical statement or one of the scholar's own favorite

---

[155]Brown returned to Union in 1879 and became instructor in biblical philology. He was promoted to associate professor in 1881 and then succeeded Briggs in 1890 as Professor of Biblical Theology. In this capacity Brown taught Hebrew, Greek, Aramaic, and Accadian, and thus became the first to teach Accadian in America. He gave the Eli Lectures (1907) on the relations of Israel with Babylon and Assyria, served as director of the American School of Oriental Study and Research in Jerusalem (1907-8), was general editor of the *Hebrew and English Lexicon of the Old Testament* (1906), and finally became president of Union in 1908 "Brown, Francis," *Enc Brit* 4 (11th ed.; 1910) 658; A. C. McGiffert, "Brown, Francis," *DAB* 3 (1929) 115-16.

theories. Brown's third point was aimed at those, who eagerly used the discoveries of Assyriology to support the Bible, but who then were unwilling to acknowledge the questions that the new science raised for biblical interpretation. Brown's volume was clearly directed against some of the excesses of George Smith, George Rawlinson, and A. H. Sayce in Britain, as well as against Oppert and Lenormant in France.[156] His caution in the use of Assyriology was similar to that of Driver. On the positive side, Brown pointed out that Assyriology had given the Old Testament "a *new setting;*" it had illuminated "the *essential difference* between the Hebrews and other ancient peoples" (the spiritual superiority of the Hebrew religion); and it had offered certain "positive historical confirmations and explanations" for the biblical scholar. [157]

Brown's treatment of Chronicles appeared in the *Hastings Dictionary of the Bible* (1898). In it he determined that the books' author was an unknown levitical musician, who wrote between 300 and 250 B. C. E., and he argued for the latter on the basis of the genealogy in 1 Chronicles 3 in the MT, the appearance of Jaddua in Neh 12:11, and the lateness of the language.[158] He found that Chronicles, Ezra, and Nehemiah were initially a single work[159] and that the Chronicler used canonical as well as non-canonical works for sources. Among the latter, Brown suggested that the Chronicler's primary source for his account of the Judean monarchy was the Book of the Kings of Judah and Israel, a work "which was...based on our S and K, with additional matter of uncertain and probably varying value."[160] These source-critical conclusions, the comparison of Chronicles with Samuel-Kings, and the relatively late date of Chronicles led Brown to conclude that whenever Chronicles disagreed with Samuel-Kings, the latter must be preferred. He further observed that since the Chronicler's special interests detracted from his reliability as a transmitter of information that one found also in Samuel-Kings, it was likely that the Chronicler was equally unreliable in his accounts that were not found in parallel biblical texts.[161] On the positive side, however, Brown denied that the Chronicler was a deliberate falsifier or inventer, and he asserted that there probably was reliable data in the Chronicler's history of pre-exilic times.

It is plain that the character of Ch's testimony, when we can control it by
parallel accounts, is not such as to give us reason to depend on it with

---

[156]F. Brown, *Assyriology: Its Use and Abuse in Old Testament Study* (New York: Charles Scribner's Sons, 1885) 10-37.

[157]*Ibid.*, 40-52.

[158]F. Brown, "I and II Chronicles," *HDB 1 (1898)* 392, 396.

[159]*Ibid.*, 389.

[160]*Ibid.*, 395.

[161]*Ibid.*

security when it stands alone. Perhaps it does not enlarge our stock of historical matter beyond that given in S and K. We cannot say *absolutely* that it does not; e.g. Rehoboam's buildings, Uzziahs's buildings and wars, Hezekiah's waterworks, Manasseh's captivity, etc., may be in part, or altogether, stated accurately, and to some of them a certain degree of probability attaches (cf. Kittel), but on the unsupported evidence of Ch we cannot be sure of them. It is not certain whether his source derived them from other documents or from tradition, and we cannot tell with positiveness how far they are trustworthy. This uncertainty passes over into Ch itself. Its main value lies in another direction.[162]

Nevertheless, its value is real and great. It is, however, the value more of a sermon than of a history.[163]

Brown's treatment of Chronicles and his attitude toward the use of the findings of Assyriology were very similar to the tradition of British scholarship, exemplified by S. R. Driver. He was unwilling to reject completely the Chronicler's testimony about pre-exilic times, as Wellhausen had done, but on the other hand, he was unwilling to accord Chronicles the near-complete confidence that characterized A. H. Sayce. He chose a path between the two.

8. SUMMARY OF THE CRITICAL RESPONSE TO THE APOLOGETICAL USE OF ARCHAEOLOGY

Of the six scholars treated in this section of chapter four, two stand apart from the rest. On the one hand, W. R. Smith was the most radical of the group in that he pronounced Chronicles worthless for reconstructing Israel's pre-exilic history. He believed that Samuel-Kings was the only source that the Chronicler used which transmitted historically reliable information about the pre-exilic period. On the other hand, W. E. Barnes believed that virtually all the reports in Chronicles should be sifted by the historian for their contributions to what is known of Israel's pre-exilic history. Not only did Barnes believe that the Chronicler had authentic and reliable sources for his reports about the pre-exilic period, but he also believed that the main part of 1, 2 Chronicles was written by a contemporary of Nehemiah. This is a considerably earlier date than any of the others in this group proposed.

The others in this section held views between those of Smith and Barnes. Driver, Cheyne, and Brown were closer to Smith, and Bennet appears to have been closer to Barnes in his estimation of Chronicles' value for reconstructing the pre-exilic period. It may be said of all six

---

[162]*Ibid.*, 395-96.
[163]*Ibid.*, 396.

scholars that they held late dates for P (per the Grafian Hypothesis) and that they were keenly aware of the fact that the Chronicler's *Tendenz* led him to distort his historical account.

The three scholars in this group (Smith, Driver, and Brown), who addressed in an extensive way the bearing of archaeological discoveries on the usefulness of Chronicles for reconstructing Israel's pre-exilic period, were agreed in their opposition to A. H. Sayce. They believed that his claims were extravagant and that while archaeology had indeed suggested some possibilities for historical backgrounds of some of the Chronicler's reports (Manasseh's captivity, e.g.), it had not proven the historical accuracy of any report that was unique to Chronicles.

E. SUMMARY OF CHAPTER FOUR

In the latter half of the nineteenth century, when the epigraphical evidence from the monuments and ruins of the ancient Near East was translated and made available to historians, some scholars began to use this information in order to support their claims that Old Testament texts should be taken at face value and be regarded as historically reliable. Their arguments were directed against those scholars—especially in Germany—who had applied the historical critical method to the Bible and found the latter filled with historical inaccuracies. G. Rawlinson was one of the first major proponents of this apologetical use of archaeology, and by 1859, he was arguing against early (pre-Grafian) critics, such as Eichhorn and de Wette. A. H. Sayce, however, became the outstanding figure in the use of archaeological evidence against Old Testament critics, and his arguments were directed primarily against Graf, Wellhausen, and their followers, since in the final quarter of the nineteenth century the latter were regarded as the most prominent and dangerous foes of the view that the Bible's statements were historically accurate. Schrader in Germany, G. A. Smith in England, and J. F. McCurdy in Canada were less extravagant in their claims for archaeology. All five believed, however, that ancient Near Eastern archaeology had demonstrated that certain accounts in Chronicles—whose historical accuracy had been disputed by various critics—were useful for reconstructing Israel's pre-exilic history.

The claims of Rawlinson, Sayce, and others did not go unanswered, though. Leading Old Testament scholars, such as W. R. Smith, S. R. Driver, and F. Brown, argued that archaeology had not proven the historical accuracy of Chronicles (or of the Bible in general); it had only suggested various historical settings against which Israel's past could be seen. Their point with regard to Chronicles was that the findings of archaeology had not invalidated the historical critical conclusions of scholars, such as de Wette, Graf, and Wellhausen. The books of Chronicles remained highly suspect and could by no means be taken at face value and used to reconstruct Israel's pre-exilic history. While Smith, Driver, Cheyne, and Brown were not in agreement with Wellhausen's position that nothing in 1, 2 Chronicles could be used to reconstruct the pre-exilic period, they were even farther from the position of Keil and others, who had argued that Chronicles was a reliable witness to Israel's pre-exilic history. Other British scholars, such as Barnes and possibly Bennet, had a bit more confidence in Chronicles than W. R. Smith, but they were by no means in agreement with Rawlinson and Sayce about Chronicles.

CHAPTER V

CONCLUSIONS

This study has set out to trace the way that 1-2 Chronicles was used in the reconstruction of Israelite history in the nineteenth century. With few exceptions, these books, prior to the nineteenth century and the work of de Wette, were regarded as generally reliable sources for reconstructing Israel's history. This position was supported by the use of harmonization and textual criticism to bring the books of Chronicles into agreement with Samuel-Kings. Various source theories were proposed to account for the similarities and differences between the two histories, but none—with the possible exception of Eichhorn's—was worked out carefully and systematically. In this period before de Wette's *Beiträge* of 1806, Chronicles was viewed as a reliable source of information that the historian could use to supplement the narrative in Samuel-Kings.

In general, it may be said that the nineteenth century witnessed two serious challenges to the credibility of Chronicles as a historical source for reconstructing the pre-exilic period: (1) the application of the historical critical method to Chronicles by de Wette and others near the beginning of the century, which capitalized on the differences between the accounts of Israel's history in Chronicles and Samuel-Kings, and (2) the hypothesis of Reuss and Vatke of an exilic or post-exilic date for P, which was subsequently elaborated by Graf, Kuenen, Colenso, and Wellhausen in the 1860s and 1870s.

De Wette was the first to recognize the magnitude of the conflict between Chronicles and Samuel-Kings. While others had seen isolated dissimilarities or apprehended a general notion of the prophetic concern of Samuel-Kings and the priestly concern of Chronicles, de Wette characterized the dissimilarities between the two works more systematically. On the basis of this research, he concluded that various theological *Tendenzen* dominated Chronicles and led the author to distort the information that he derived from his sources. Thus, de Wette believed that to a large degree the differences between Samuel-Kings and Chronicles fell into various patterns, and that if the Chronicler's primary concern was to vindicate his own theological prejudices—rather than to present an accurate historical account—then the Chronicler's history was useless as a historical source for the pre-exilic period. De Wette's criteria for a useful historical source further strengthened his resolve about the uselessness of Chronicles for reconstructing Israel's pre-exilic history. The main lines of de Wette's position on Chronicles were supported by the linguistic research of Gesenius and to some degree by additional arguments advanced by Gramberg.

The challenge that was issued to Chronicles' credibility by de Wette, Gesenius, and Gramberg was answered by a number of scholars. Nine arguments have been identified, which were proposed to counter the challenge to and substantiate the veracity of the Chronicler: (1) the Divine Inspiration Argument, (2) the Moral Argument, (3) the Source Argument, (4) the Supplementary Argument, (5) the Textual Corruption Argument, (6) the Modernization Argument, (7) the Harmonization Argument, (8) the External Support Argument, and (9) the General Credibility Argument. Numbers three, seven, and eight would prove most important for later discussion in the nineteenth century of Chronicles' reliability. While some of these writers who defended the Chronicler's credibility made concessions to de Wette and acknowledged that there were incidental inaccuracies in Chronicles, these scholars were agreed that as a whole the work was a reliable guide for the reconstruction of the pre-exilic period.

Those who composed histories of Israel in the first three-quarters of the nineteenth century did not accept de Wette's position on Chronicles, but neither did most of them accept the opposite position—that of Keil. An intermediate stance was usually taken in which it was admitted that there were distortions and exaggerations in Chronicles, but in which it was also maintained that the historian was generally capable of sifting out the historically reliable information from the historically unreliable material in Chronicles. This is essentially the position that Ewald assumed in his history of Israel. Consequently, when it came to reconstructing Israelite history, the defenders of Chronicles' integrity had been somewhat successful, although de Wette's challenge to Chronicles had left its mark on the study and use of the book. No longer could the Chronicler's history simply be utilized and its statements accepted at face value for the reconstruction of the monarchical period.

The second challenge to the credibility of Chronicles came with the proposal that the Priestly Code should be assigned a late date. This was first suggested in the mid-1830s by Reuss and Vatke but did not begin to win a large following until the 1860s and 1870s, when the theory was resurrected and argued by Graf, Kuenen, Colenso, and Wellhausen. Since the picture of the Israelite cult in P was so similar to that in Chronicles, it had been assumed that the widely accepted early date for P supported the historical value of Chronicles. When

P's credibility as a historical source for the pre-exilic period had been seriously eroded, the scholars who held a late date for P rejected to a large extent the usefulness of Chronicles as a historical source for information about Israel's monarchical period. The similarities in theology and portrayal of the cult between Chronicles and P made it almost inevitable that if the historical reliability of one fell, then that of the other did as well. The effect of a late date for P on the estimation of Chronicles' value as a historical source was compounded by the reappropriation of de Wette's earlier studies and conclusions based on the striking dissimilarities between Chronicles and Samuel-Kings. Therefore, with the publication of Graf's *Die geschichtlichen Bücher des alten Testaments* (1866) and Wellhausen's *Prolegomena* in 1878, it appeared that Chronicles would find little use for the reconstruction of Israel's pre-exilic history in future histories of Israel.

Those historians and Old Testament scholars, who published works after Graf and Wellhausen and accepted the former's suggestion of a late P, were generally suspicious of Chronicles' testimony about the pre-exilic period. Consequently, Chronicles found but little use in their works. While some insisted that the Chronicler's history should be entirely ignored in the reconstruction of the pre-exilic period, others allowed the use of incidental information in Chronicles.

Among those scholars who retained a pre-exilic date for P, there was a greater willingness to appropriate material from Chronicles for historical reconstruction. The exception to this among the scholars surveyed was Nöldeke, but it was noted that he regarded even an early P as an idealized account that could not be trusted for reliable historical information about the pre-exilic period. The others in the group, however, were not interested in dismissing P's description of the cult, and therefore, the portrayal of the cult in Chronicles was more credible in their view. In general, however, the scholars in this group (with the exception of Neteler) maintained a moderately critical perspective in their dealings with Chronicles.

In the latter half of the nineteenth century there arose a movement in Old Testament scholarship that made use of archaeological discoveries in order to defend the credibility of Chronicles. The center of this movement was in England, where its chief proponents were George Rawlinson, Archibald H. Sayce, and George A. Smith. As early as the 1850s, Rawlinson began using archaeology to challenge the conclusions of Old Testament critics such as de Wette, and he continued his defense of the Chronicler's history (as well as that of the rest of the Bible) after the appearance of the arguments for a late P in the 1860s and 1870s. Eventually, however, Sayce became the champion of the movement to vindicate the credibility of the biblical records, even though he allowed that there were exaggerations and errors in the Chronicler's account. He differed from some of the others in the movement, however, by insisting that the comparative archaeological method should be used to the exclusion of source criticism. The use of archaeology to vindicate Chronicles also found representatives in Germany (Schrader) and Canada (McCurdy). Each of them set forth the story of Manasseh's imprisonment (2 Chr 33:10-13) as the premiere example of archaeology's proof of Chronicles' historical reliability. This, as well as most of the other instances of archaeology "proving the Bible," depended on the translation and use of epigraphical finds from Mesopotamia.

The claims for the usefulness of archaeology in establishing the veracity of Chronicles were disputed by several scholars (e.g., W. R. Smith, S. R. Driver, and F. Brown). Driver, for instance, wrote at the close of the nineteenth century that archaeology had not disproven a single position that critical Old Testament scholarship had taken with respect to the Bible. With regard to the Chronicler's account about Manasseh's captivity in particular, G. B. Gray argued that while the Assyrian texts supplied a possible historical setting for the story, they did not prove the historical accuracy of the Chronicler's report. These scholars, as well as several others in Britain at the time, believed that Chronicles' usefulness for historical reconstruction was limited. Some—such as W. R. Smith—believed that few, if any, of its reports could be used with confidence by the historian, but most believed that incidental reports (e.g., the list of Rehoboam's fortresses in 2 Chronicles 11) could be used with some assurance and that many other reports (such as the various battle accounts) were useful to the historian, provided that the latter sifted out the exaggerations and other unhistorical additions that had accumulated from later times.

Although not the concern of the present dissertation, one could trace the debate about Chronicles' usefulness for reconstructing Israel's pre-exilic history into the twentieth century and see that the arguments for the nineteenth century reappear in updated form. The discussion of the books' relation to Samuel-Kings had been crucial for de Wette's work at the beginning of the nineteenth century, and it continued to be important. The differences between the two works were often viewed as primary indicators of the Chronicler's *Tendenz*. Lemke's research in the mid-1960s, for example, could be taken as representative of earlier attempts to understand the *Tendenz* of Chronicles. Although he issued a warning against certain excesses in this regard and used textual criticism and philology to show that many of the differences between Chronicles and Samuel-Kings were probably not theologically motivated at all but derived from the

Chronicler's stylistic preferences or from his *Vorlage*.[1] Similarly, the controversy about whether archaeology had vindicated the Chronicler as a trustworthy witness to the pre-exilic period continued into the twentieth century. In 1938, W. F. Albright made the following general observation,

> Archaeological and inscriptional data have established the historicity of innumerable passages and statements of the Old Testament; the number of such cases is many times greater than those where the reverse has been proved or has been made probable.[2]

Later, Albright argued for the historicity or a judicial reform under Jehoshaphat, an event described only in Chronicles,[3] and for the Chronicler's report about war between Judah and Israel in Asa's thirty-sixth year.[4] Ancient Near Eastern archaeology played a prominent role in both articles. Similar arguments in favor of Chronicles' general historical credibility were advanced by Neil Richardson in 1958.[5] In 1974, however, Robert North addressed this general impression that archaeology had vindicated Chronicles as a witness to Israel's pre-exilic history and thus had proven that the Chronicler had reliable extrabiblical sources for his composition. He concluded,

> Unless we have some of our facts wrong or have interpreted them more tendentiously than is done by current consensus, it would follow as a fact that no single use of extrabiblical sources by the Chronicler has ever been proved. From this further follows not the fact but the undeniable

---

[1]Lemke, "Synoptic Problem," 349-50, 360-63. Similarly, a two-part article by J. Barton Payne ("The Validity of the Numbers in Chronicles," *BSac* 136 [1979] 109-28, 206-20) set out to defend the Chronicler against charges that he had inflated the numbers in his work.

[2]W. F. Albright, "Archaeology Confronts Biblical Criticism," *American Scholar* 7 (1938) 181.

[3]W. F. Albright, "The Judicial Reform of Jehoshaphat," in *Alexander Marx Jubilee Volume* (New York: Jewish Theological Seminary of America, 1950) 61-82. Albright argued that the Chronicler's story about Jehoshaphat's judicial reform was "substantially correct" (p. 82) on the basis of other instances in which archaeology had demonstrated the veracity of material in Chronicles and on the basis of an Egyptian stele from the temple of Amun at Karnak which described a similar judicial reform, but one carried out centuries before Jehoshaphat's reign.

[4]W. F. Albright, "A Votive Stele Erected by Ben-Hadad I of Damascus to the God Melcarth," *BASOR* 87 (1942) 23-29. Albright's argument depends on his own reconstruction of the text of the stele and adjustments to the biblical chronologies.

[5]H. Neil Richardson, "The Historical Reliability of Chronicles," *JBR* 26 (1958) 9-12. Richardson deals with three instances in which he claims that archaeology has supported the "general reliability" of Chronicles: (1) the Ben-Hadad stele supports the Chronicler's chronology for Asa; (2) a survey of the Buqe'ah valley by Cross and Milik lends support to Chronicles' description of building activity during the reign of Jehoshaphat (or Uzziah); and (3) the Babylonian Chronicle tends to support the setting that 2 Chr 35:20 gives for the death of Josiah.

possibility that any information communicated to us only by the Chronicler may be due in every case to his own legitimate theological inference or paraphrase from the canonical Scripture.[6]

These observations by North are amazingly similar to Driver's conclusions at the end of the nineteenth century[7] and further show that the issues raised in the debate over Chronicles' credibility in the nineteenth century have continued to be debated along the same lines in the twentieth century.

Finally, it should be noted that more recently in the twentieth century there has been a renewed interest in the Chronicler as a theologian. In Germany books by Thomas Willi,[8] Rudolf Mosis,[9] and Peter Welton[10] use the Chronicler's theological *Tendenzen* to account for elements in his historical presentation. In England the work of Peter Ackroyd[11] and H. G. M. Williamson[12] has gone in the same direction, as has that of Roddy Braun in the United States.[13] In each case the authors have set out to demonstrate that theology—rather than an earlier historical event or source alone—has been responsible for important parts of the Chronicler's history. Even this development was foreshadowed in many respects by de Wette's *Beiträge* with its attention to the Chronicler's *Tendenzen*.

---

[6]Robert North, "Does Archaeology Prove Chronicles Sources?" in *A Light unto My Path: Old Testament Studies in Honor of Jacob. M. Myers* (Philadelphia: Temple University, 1974) 392.

[7]*Ibid.*, p. 330-31.

[8]Thomas Willi, *Die Chronik als Auslegung* (FRLANT, 106; Göttingen: Vandenhoeck & Ruprecht, 1972).

[9]Rudolf Mosis, *Untersuchungen zur Theologie des chronistischen Geschichtswerkes* (Freiburger theologische Studien, 92; Freiburg: Herder, 1973).

[10]Peter Welten, *Geschichte und Geschichtsdarstellung in den Chronikbüchern* (WMANT, 42; Neukirchen-Verlag: Neukirchener Verlag, 1973).

[11]Peter R. Ackroyd, "History and Theology in the Writings of the Chronicler," *CTM* 38 (1967) 501-15; "The Theology of the Chronicler," *Lexington Theological Quarterly* 8 (1973) 101-16; "The Chronicler as Exegete," *JSOT* 2 (1977) 2-32.

[12]H. G. M. Williamson, "The Accession of Solomon in the Books of Chronicles," *VT* 26 (1976) 351-61; "Eschatology in Chronicles," *Tyndale Bulletin* 28 (1977) 115-154; *Israel in the Books of Chronicles* (Cambridge: University Press, 1977); *1 and 2 Chronicles* (The New Century Bible Commentary; Grand Rapids: Wm. B. Eerdmans, 1982).

[13]Roddy L. Braun, "The Significance of 1 Chr. 22, 28, & 29 for the Structure and Theology of the Work of the Chronicler." Corcordia Seminary dissertation, 1971; "The Message of Chronicles: Rally 'Round the Temple," *CTM* 22 (1971) 502-14; "Solomonic Apologetic in Chronicles," *JBL* 92 (1973) 503-16; "Solomon, the Chosen Temple Builder: the Significance of 1 Chronicles 22, 28, and 29 for the Theology of Chronicles," *JBL* 95 (1976) 581-90; "Chronicles, Ezra, and Nehemiah: Theology and Literary History," in *Studies in the Historical Books of the Old Testament* (SVT, 30; Leiden: E. J. Brill, 1979) 52-64.

It appears, therefore, that the debate over the credibility of Chronicles has continued unabated into the twentieth century and that it has largely involved the same issues that were crucial in the nineteenth century.

BIBLIOGRAPHY

Ackroyd, Peter R. "History and Theology in the Writings of the Chronicler," *Concordia Theological Monthly* 38 (1967) 501-15.

_____. "The Theology of the Chronicler," *Lexington Theological Quarterly* 8 (1973) 101-16.

_____. "The Chronicler as Exegete," *Journal for the Study of the Old Testament* 2 (1977) 2-32.

Albright, W. F. "Archaeology Confronts Biblical Criticism," *American Scholar* 7 (1938) 176-88.

_____. "The Judicial Reform of Jehoshaphat." *Alexander Marx Jubilee Volume,* pp. 61-82. New York: Jewish Theological Seminary of America, 1950.

_____. "A Votive Stele Erected by Ben-Hadad I of Damascus to the God Melcarth," *Bulletin of the American Schools of Oriental Research* 87 (1942) 23-29.

Avi-Yonah, Michael. "Guthe, Hermann," *Encyclopaedia judaica* 7 (1971) 985-86.

Barnes, W. E. "The Religious Standpoint of the Chronicler," *American Journal of Semitic Literature* 13 (1896/97) 14–20.

_____. "Chronicles a Targum," *Expository Times* 8 (1896/97) 316-19.

_____. *An Apparatus Criticus to Chronicles in the Peshitta Version.* Cambridge: University Press, 1897.

_____. "On 2 Chron. xiv.9; Job i.15; Prov. xxvii.22," *Expository Times* 8 (1896/97) 431-32.

_____. "The David of the Book of Samuel and the David of the Book of Chronicles," *The Expositor* 7 (7th ser.; 1909) 49-59.

_____. *The Books of Chronicles.* The Cambridge Bible for Schools and Colleges. Cambridge: University Press, 1899.

_____. "The Midrashic Element in Chronicles," *The Expositor* 4 (5th ser.; 1896) 427-29.

Baron, Salo W. "I. M. Jost the Historian," *History and Jewish Historians,* pp. 240-62. Philadelphia: Jewish Publication Society, 1964.

Bayne, Ronald. "Davidson, Samuel," *Dictionary of National Biography Supplement* 2 (1901) 115-16.

_____. "Rawlinson, George," *Dictionary of National Biography* 3 (2d supplement.; 1912) 165-67.

Beidelman, T. O. W. *Robertson Smith and the Sociological Study o f Religion.* Chicago: University of Chicago Press, 1974.

Benecke, H. *Wilhelm Vatke in seinem Leben und seinen Schriften.* Bonn: Emil Strauss, 1883.

Bennet, W. H. *The Books of Chronicles.* The Expositor's Bible, 4. New York: A. C. Armstrong & Sons, 1903.

_____. "Chronicles, Books of," *The Jewish Encyclopedia* 4 (1903) 59-63.

Berlin, Isaiah. *Vico & Herder.* New York: Viking Press, 1976.

Bertheau, Carl. "Bertheau, Ernst," *Realencyklopädie für protestantische Theologie und Kirche* 2 (1897) 645-48.

_____. "Bertheau, Ernst," *Allgemeine Deutsche Biographie* 46 (1902) 441-43.

Bertheau, Ernst. *Die Bücher der Chronik.* Kurzgefasstes exegetisches Handbuch zum Alten Testament, 15. 2d ed. Leipzig: S. Hirzel, 1873.

_____. "Die Bewohner Palästina's seit den ältesten Zeiten bis auf die Zerstörung Jerusalem's durch die Römer," *Zur Geschichte der Israeliten,* pp. 117-452. Göttingen: Vandenhoeck & Ruprecht, 1842.

Bertholdt, Leonhard. *Historischkritische Einleitung in sämmtliche kanonische und apokryphische Schriften des alten und neuen Testaments.* 6 vols. Erlangen: Johann Jacob Palm, 1813.

Bethune-Baker, J. F. "Barnes, William Emery," *Dictionary of National Biography 1931-1940* (1949) 42-44.

Black, J. S. "Smith, William Robertson," *Dictionary o f National Biography* 53 (1898) 160-62.

_____. "Ewald, Heinrich Georg August von," *Encyclopaedia Britannica* 8 (1889) 773-74.

Bleek, Friedrich. *Einleitung in das Alte Testament.* Vol. 1 of *Einleitung in die Heilige Schrift.* 2 vols. Eds. J. F. Bleek and A. Kamphausen. Berlin: Georg Reimer, 1860.

_____. *An Introduction to the Old Testament,* 2 vols. Eds. J. F. Bleek and A. Kamphausen. Trans. of 2d Ger. ed. Ed. E. Venables. London: Bell & Daldy, 1869.

Bradley, G. Granville. "Stanley, Arthur Penrhyn," *Encyclopaedia Britannica* 22 (1889) 451-53.

Braun, Roddy L. "The Significance of 1 Chr. 22, 28, & 29 for the Structure and Theology of the Work of the Chronicler." Corcordia Seminary dissertation, 1971.

_____. "The Message of Chronicles: Rally 'Round the Temple," *Concordia Theological Monthly* 22 (1971) 502-14.

_____. "Solomonic Apologetic in Chronicles," *Journal of Biblical Literature* 92 (1973) 503-16.

_____. "Solomon, the Chosen Temple Builder: the Significance of 1 Chronicles 22, 28, and 29 for the Theology of Chronicles," *Journal of Biblical Literature* 95 (1976) 581-90.

_____. "Chronicles, Ezra, and Nehemiah: Theology and Literary History," *Studies in the Historical Books of the Old Testament*, pp. 52-64. Supplements to Vetus Testamentum, 30. Leiden: E. J. Brill, 1979.

Bromse, M. "Studien zur 'Biblischen Theologie' Wilhelm Vatkes." Kiel dissertation, 1973.

"Brown, Francis," *Encyclopaedia Britannica* 4 (1910) 658.

Brown, F. *Assyriology: Its Use and Abuse in Old Testament Study*. New York: Charles Scribner's Sons, 1885.

_____. "The Books of Chronicles, with Especial Reference to the Books of Samuel," *Andover Review* 1 (1884) 405-26.

_____. "I and II Chronicles," *Hastings Dictionary of the Bible* 1 (1898) 389-97.

Budde, Karl. *Geschichte der althebräischen Litteratur*. 2d ed. Leipzig: C. F. Amelangs, 1909.

_____. "Vermutungen zum 'Midrasch des Buches der Könige'," *Zeitschrift für die alttestamentliche Wissenschaft* 12 (1892) 37-51.

Bunsen, Baron von. *Vollständiges Bibelwerk für die Gemeinde*. 9 vols. Leipzig: Brockhaus, 1858-1870.

Carpenter, J. E. *The Bible in the Nineteenth Century*. London: Longmans, Green, 1903.

Cheyne, Thomas Kelly. *Jewish Religious Life after the Exile*. American Lectures on the History of Religions, 3d series, 1897-98. New York: G. P. Putnam's Sons, 1898.

_____. *The Decline and Fall of the Kingdom of Judah*. London: Adam and Charles Black, 1908.

_____. *Founders of Old Testament Criticism*. London: Methuen, 1893.

Clements, Ronald E. *One Hundred Years of Old Testament Interpretation*. Philadelphia: Westminster, 1976.

_____. "Heinrich Graetz as Biblical Historian and Religious Apologist," *Interpreting the Hebrew Bible*, pp. 35-55. Eds. J. A. Emerton and Stefan C. Reif. Cambridge: University Press, 1982.

Cohen-Yashar, Yohanan. "Renan, Ernest," *Encyclopaedia judaica* 14 (1971) 71-72.

Colenso, John William. *The Pentateuch and the Book of Joshua Critically Examined*. 5 vols. London: Longman, Green, Longman, Roberts & Green, 1862-1879.

_____. *Lectures on the Pentateuch and the Moabite Stone*. London: Longmans, Green, 1873.

Conder, C. R. "The Old Testament: Ancient Monuments and Modern Critics," *Contemporary Review* 51 (1887) 376-93.

Cooke, George A. "Thomas Kelly Cheyne," *The Expositor* (8th ser.; 1915) 445-51.

_____. "Driver, Samuel Rolles," *Dictionary of National Biography 1912-1921* (1927) 162-63.

Cornill, Carl Heinrich. *History of the People of Israel*. 4th ed. Chicago: Open Court, 1909.

_____. *Introduction to the Canonical Books of the Old Testament*. Theological Translation Library, 23. New York: G. P. Putnam's Sons, 1907.

Cox, G. W. "Colenso, John William," *Dictionary of National Biography* 11 (1887) 291-2.

_____. *The Life of John William Colenso, D. D., Bishop of Natal*. 2 vols. London: W. Ridgway, 1888.

Crombie, F. "Bleek, Friedrich," *Encyclopaedia Britannica* 3 (1889) 823-24.

Crowther, M. A. *Church Embattled: Religious Controversy in Mid-Victorian England*. Library of Politics and Society. Hamden, Conn.: Archon, 1970.

Dahler, J. G. *De librorum Paralipomenon auctoritate atque fide historica disputat*. Argentorati: Johannis Henrici Heitz, 1819.

Daniel, Glynn E. *A Hundred Years of Archaeology*. London: Gerald Duckworth, 1950.

"Davidson, Samuel," *Encyclopaedia Britannica* 7 (1910) 864.

Davidson, Samuel. *The Autobiography and Diary of Samuel Davidson*. Edinburgh: Clark, 1899.

_____. *The Text of the Old Testament Considered*. 2d ed. London: Longman, Brown, Green, Longmans & Roberts, 1859.

Davies, T. Witton. *Heinrich Ewald, Orientalist and Theologian*. London: T. Fisher Unwin, 1903.

Dentan, R. C. *Preface to Old Testament Theology*. New York: Seabury, 1963.

De Vries , Simon J. *Bible and Theology in the Netherlands*. Cahiers bijhet Nederlands Theologisch Tijdschrift, 3. Wageningen: H. Veenman & Zonen N. V., 1968.

"Dillmann," *Encyclopaedia Britannica* 2 (1898) 651.

Dillmann, C. F. A. "Ewald, Georg Heinrich August," *Allgemeine Deutsche Biographie* 6 (1877) 438-442.

_____. "Chronik," *Realencyklopädie für protestantische Theologie und Kirche* 2 (1854) 690-95.

_____. "Chronicles," *The Protestant Theological and Ecclesiastical Encyclopedia* 1 (1860) 669-70.

Driver, S. R. "Hebrew Authority," *Authority and Archaeology*, pp. 1-152. Ed. David G. Hogarth. New York: Charles Scribner's Sons, 1899.

_____. *The Ideals of the Prophets*. Ed. G. A. Cooke. Edinburgh: T. & T. Clark, 1915.

_____. *An Introduction to the Literature of the Old Testament*. International Theological Library. 9th ed. Edinburgh: T. & T. Clark, 1913.

_____. "The Speeches in Chronicles," *The Expositor* 1 (5th ser.; 1895) 241-56.

_____. "The Speeches in the Chronicles," *The Expositor* 2 (5th ser.; 1895) 286-308.

Eichhorn, J. G. *Einleitung in das Alte Testament*. 3d ed. Leipzig: Weidmann, 1803.

Eissfeldt, Otto. "Julius Wellhausen," *Kleine Schriften*, vol. 1, pp. 56-71. Tübingen: J. C. B. Mohr, 1962.

_____. "Wellhausen, Julius," *Religion in Geschichte und Gegenwart* 6 (1957) 1594-95.

Elliger, W. *150 Jahre Theologische Fakultät Berlin. Eine Darstellung ihrer Geschichte von 1810 bis 1960 als Beitrag zu ihrem Jubilaum*. Berlin: De Gruyter, 1960.

Elwes, R. H. M. *The Chief Works of Benedict de Spinoza*. London: George Bell & Sons, 1883.

Erdmann. "Bertholdt, Leonhard," *Allgemeine Deutsche Biographie* 2 (1875) 512-13.

Ettinger, Samuel. "Graetz, Heinrich," *Encyclopaedia judaica* 7 (1972) 845-46.

Ewald, Heinrich. *The History of Israel*. 3 vols. 3d ed. London: Longmans, Green, 1876.

Fillion, L. "Renan, Ernst," *Dictionnaire de la Bible* 5/1 (1908) 1041-43.

Forbes, Duncan. *The Liberal Anglican Idea of History.* Cambridge: Univeristy Press, 1952.

Franxman, Thomas W. *Genesis and the "Jewish Antiquities" of Flavius Josephus.* Biblica et orientalia, 35. Rome: Biblical Institute, 1979.

Frei, Hans W. *The Eclipse of Biblical Narrative.* New Haven: Yale, 1974.

French, Valpy. "The Speeches in Chronicles. A Reply," *The Expositor* 2 (5th ser.; 1895) 140-52.

Garber, Zev. "Bleek, Friedrich," *Encyclopaedia judaica* 4 (1971) 1080.

_____. "Cornill, Carl Heinrich," *Encyclopaedia judaica* 5 (1971) 974.

_____. "Dillmann, August," *Encyclopaedia judaica* 6 (1971) 47-48.

_____. "Keil, C. F.," *Encyclopaedia judaica* 10 (1971) 897.

_____. "Kittel, Rudolf," *Encyclopaedia judaica* 10 (1971) 1079-80.

_____. "Meyer, Eduard," *Encyclopaedia judaica* 11 (1971) 1462.

Garnett, Richard. "Milman, Henry Hart," *Dictionary of National Biography* 38 (1894) 1-4.

Geiger, Abraham. *Urschrift und Übersetzungen der Bibel.* 2d ed. Frankfurt: Madda, 1928.

George, Johann Friedrich Leopold. *Die älteren Jüdischen Feste mit einer Kritik der Gesetzgebung des Pentateuch.* Berlin: E. H. Schroeder, 1835.

Gerlach, Ernst. "Die Gefangenschaft und Bekehrung Manasse's," *Theologische Studien und Kritiken* 34 (1861) 503-24.

Gesenius, Wilhelm. *Geschichte der hebräischen Sprache und Schrift.* Leipzig: Friedrich Christian Wilhelm Vogel, 1815.

Gooch, G. P. *History and Historians in the Nineteenth Century.* 2d ed. London: Longmans, Green, 1952.

Gordon, Alexander. "Newman, Francis William," *Dictionary of National Biography Supplement* 3 (1901) 221-22.

Graetz, Heinrich. *Geschichte der Israeliten.* Vols. 1-2 of *Geschichte der Juden.* 11 vols. Leipzig: Oskar Leiner, 1874-1875.

_____. *The Structure of Jewish History and Other Essays.* Ed. and trans. Ismar Schorsch. New York: The Jewish Theological Seminary of America, 1975.

Graf, K. H. "Die Gefangenschaft und Bekehrung Manasse's, 2 Chr. 33," *Theologische Studien und Kritiken* 32 (1859) 467-94.

_____. *Die geschichtlichen Bücher des Alten Testaments.* Leipzig: T. O. Weigel, 1866.

Gramberg, C. P. W. *Die Chronik.* Halle: Eduard Anton, 1823.

_____. *Kritische Geschichte der Religionsideen des alten Testaments.* Berlin: Duncker and Humbolt, 1829.

Gray, G. B. "Professor Sayce's 'Early History of the Hebrews'," *The Expositor* 7 (5th ser.; 1898) 404-19.

Guthe, Hermann. *Geschichte des Volkes Israel.* Vol. 3 of *Grundriss der Theologischen Wissenschaften.* Tübingen: J. C. B. Mohr, 1899.

Hahn, Herbert F. *The Old Testament and Modern Research.* Philadelphia: Fortress, 1966.

Haran, Menahem. "Vatke, Wilhelm," *Encyclopaedia judaica* 16 (1971) 79-80.

Harrison, R. K. *Introduction to the Old Testament.* Grand Rapids: Eerdmans, 1969.

Haym, R. *Gesenius. Eine Erinnerung für seine Freunde.* Berlin: Rudolph Gaertner, 1842.

Heinze. "Vatke, Johann Karl Wilhelm," *Allgemeine Deutsche Biographie* 39 (1895) 508-10.

Henderson, T. F. "Russell, Michael," *Dictionary of National Biography* 49 (1897) 467-68.

Herbst, J. G. "Die Bücher der Chronik. Ihr Verhältniss zu den Büchern Samuels und der Könige; ihre Glaubwürdigkeit, und die Zeit ihrer Abfassung," *Theologische Quartalschrift* 13 (1831) 201-82.

Herder, Johann Gottfried von. *Reflections on the Philosophy of the History of Mankind.* Ed. Frank E. Manuel. Chicago: University of Chicago, 1968.

Hilprecht, H. V. "The Resurrection of Assyria and Babylonia," *Explorations in Bible Lands During the 19th Century,* pp 1-578. Ed. H. V. Hilprecht. Philadelphia: A. J. Holman, 1903.

Hinchliff, Peter. *John William Colenso.* London: Nelson, 1964.

Hirsch, Emil J. "Books of Chronicles," *Jewish Encyclopaedia* 4 (1903) 59-60.

"Hitzig, Ferdinand," *Encyclopaedia Britannica* 12 (1889) 27-28.

Hitzig, Ferdinand. *Geschichte des Volkes Israel.* Leipzig: S. Hirzel, 1869.

"Jahn, Johann," *Encyclopaedia Britannica* 13 (1889) 542-43.

Jahn, Johann J. *Biblia Hebraica.* 4 vols. Vienna: F. C. Wappler & Beck, 1806.

_____. *The History of the Hebrew Commonwealth from the Earliest Times to the Destruction of Jerusalem A.D. 72.* London: Hurst, Chance, 1829.

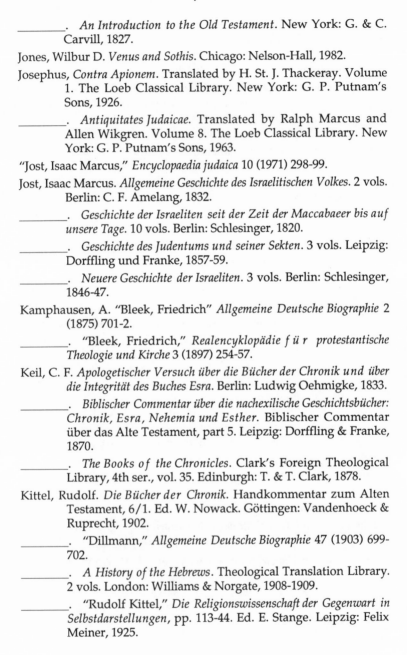

_____. *An Introduction to the Old Testament*. New York: G. & C. Carvill, 1827.

Jones, Wilbur D. *Venus and Sothis*. Chicago: Nelson-Hall, 1982.

Josephus, *Contra Apionem*. Translated by H. St. J. Thackeray. Volume 1. The Loeb Classical Library. New York: G. P. Putnam's Sons, 1926.

_____. *Antiquitates Judaicae*. Translated by Ralph Marcus and Allen Wikgren. Volume 8. The Loeb Classical Library. New York: G. P. Putnam's Sons, 1963.

"Jost, Isaac Marcus," *Encyclopaedia judaica* 10 (1971) 298-99.

Jost, Isaac Marcus. *Allgemeine Geschichte des Israelitischen Volkes*. 2 vols. Berlin: C. F. Amelang, 1832.

_____. *Geschichte der Israeliten seit der Zeit der Maccabaeer bis auf unsere Tage*. 10 vols. Berlin: Schlesinger, 1820.

_____. *Geschichte des Judentums und seiner Sekten*. 3 vols. Leipzig: Dorffling und Franke, 1857-59.

_____. *Neuere Geschichte der Israeliten*. 3 vols. Berlin: Schlesinger, 1846-47.

Kamphausen, A. "Bleek, Friedrich" *Allgemeine Deutsche Biographie* 2 (1875) 701-2.

_____. "Bleek, Friedrich," *Realencyklopädie f ü r protestantische Theologie und Kirche* 3 (1897) 254-57.

Keil, C. F. *Apologetischer Versuch über die Bücher der Chronik und über die Integrität des Buches Esra*. Berlin: Ludwig Oehmigke, 1833.

_____. *Biblischer Commentar über die nachexilische Geschichtsbücher: Chronik, Esra, Nehemia und Esther*. Biblischer Commentar über das Alte Testament, part 5. Leipzig: Dorffling & Franke, 1870.

_____. *The Books of the Chronicles*. Clark's Foreign Theological Library, 4th ser., vol. 35. Edinburgh: T. & T. Clark, 1878.

Kittel, Rudolf. *Die Bücher der Chronik*. Handkommentar zum Alten Testament, 6/1. Ed. W. Nowack. Göttingen: Vandenhoeck & Ruprecht, 1902.

_____. "Dillmann," *Allgemeine Deutsche Biographie* 47 (1903) 699-702.

_____. *A History of the Hebrews*. Theological Translation Library. 2 vols. London: Williams & Norgate, 1908-1909.

_____. "Rudolf Kittel," *Die Religionswissenschaft der Gegenwart in Selbstdarstellungen*, pp. 113-44. Ed. E. Stange. Leipzig: Felix Meiner, 1925.

_____. "Die Zukunft der alttestamentlichen Wissenschaft," *Zeitschrift für die alttestamentliche Wissenschaft* 39 (1921) 84-99.

"Klostermann, August Heinrich," *The New Schaff-Herzog Encyclopedia of Religious Knowledge* 6 (1910) 353.

Klostermann, August Heinrich. "Chronik," *Realencyklopädie für protestantische Theologie und Kirche* 3 (1898) 84-98.

_____. "Chronicles, Books of," *The New Schaff-Herzog Encyclopedia of Religious Knowledge* 3 (1909) 68-71.

_____. *Geschichte des Volkes Israel*. München: C. H. Beck, 1896.

_____. *Der Pentateuch. Beiträge zu seinem Verständnis and seiner Entstehungsgeschichte*. Leipzig: Deichert, 1893.

Kneuckcer, J. J. (ed.) *Dr. Ferdinand Hitzigs Vorlesungen ueber Biblische Theologie und Messianische Weissagungen des Alten Testaments*. Karlsruhe: H. Reuther, 1880.

Knight, Douglas. *Rediscovering the Traditions of Israel*. Society of Biblical Literature Dissertation Series, 9. Rev. ed. Missoula: Scholars Press, 1975.

Köhler, August. *Lehrbuch der Biblischen Geschichte Alten Testamentes*. 3 vols. Erlangen: Andreas Deichert, 1875/1884/1893.

Kuenen, Abraham. "Critical Method," *The Modern Review* 1 (1880) 461-88, 685-713.

_____. *An Historico-critical Inquiry into the Origin and Composition of the Hexateuch*. London: Macmillan, 1886.

_____. *Historisch-kritische Einleitung in die Bücher des alten Testaments hinsichtlich ihrer Entstehung und Sammlung*. 3 vols. in 2. Leipzig: O. R. Reisland, 1890.

_____. *National Religions and Universal Religions*. The Hibbert Lectures, 1882. New York: Charles Scribner's Sons, 1882.

_____. *The Prophets and Prophecy in Israel*. London: Longmans, Green, 1877.

_____. *The Religion of Israel to the Fall of the Jewish State*. 3 vols. London: Williams & Norgate, 1874-1875.

Kutsch, E. "Reuss, Eduard," *Religion in Geschichte und Gegenwart* 5 (1957) 1076.

Lachenmann, Eugen. "Renan, Ernst," *Realencyklopädie für protestantische Theologie und Kirche* 16 (1905) 649-55.

Langton, Stephen. *Commentary on the Book of Chronicles*. Ed. Avrom Saltman. Ramat-Gan: Bar-Ilan University, 1978.

Laue, Theodore von. *Leopold Ranke: The Formative Years*. Princeton Studies in History, 4. Princeton: Princeton University, 1950.

Lecky, William Edward Hartpole. "Dean Milman," *Historical and Political Essays*, pp. 227-50. New ed. London: Longmans, Green, 1910.

Le Déaut, R. and J. Robert. *Targum des Chroniques*. Analecta biblica 51. Rome: Biblical Institute, 1971.

Lemke, Werner. "Synoptic Studies in the Chronicler's History." Harvard dissertation, 1964.

_____. "The Synoptic Problem in the Chronicler's History," *Harvard Theological Review* 58 (1965) 349-63.

Levinger, Jacob S. "Geiger, Abraham," *Encyclopaedia judaica* 7 (1971) 357-58.

Lovejoy, A. O. "The Meaning of Romanticism for the Historian of Ideas," *Journal of the History of Ideas* 2 (1942) 257-78.

Lücke, F. "Zur freundschaftlichen Erinnerungen an D. Wilhelm Martin Leberecht de Wette," *Theologische Studien und Kritiken* (1850) 497-535.

McCurdy, J. F. *History, Prophecy and the Monuments*. 3 vols. New York: Macmillian, 1894/1896/1901.

_____. "Oriental Research and the Bible," *Recent Research in Bible Lands*, pp. 1-28. Ed. H. V. Hilprecht. Philadelphia: J. D. Wattles, 1896.

_____. "Uzziah and the Philistines," *The Expositor* 4 (4th ser.; 1891) 388-96.

McGiffert, A. C. "Brown, Francis," *Dictionary of American Biography* 3 (1929) 115-16.

MacHaffie, Barbara Zink. "'Monument Facts and Higher Critical Fancies': Archaeology and the Popularization of Old Testament Criticism in Nineteenth-Century Britain," *Church History* 50 (1981) 316-28.

Manson, W. "Smith, Sir George Adam," *Dictionary of National Biography 1941-1950* (1959) 792-94.

Mathias, Dietmar. *Die Geschichte der Chronikforschung im 19. Jahrhundert unter besonderer Berucksichtigung der exegetischen Behandlung der Prophetennachrichten des chronistischen Geschichtswerkes*. 3 vols. Leipzig: Karl-Marx-Universität, 1977.

Meyer, Eduard. *Geschichte des Alterthums*. 5 vols. Stuttgart: J. G. Cotta, 1884.

Meyer, Michael A. *Ideas of Jewish History*. Library of Jewish Studies. New York: Behrman, 1974.

Milman, Arthur. *Henry Hart Milman*. London: John Murray, 1900.

Milman, Henry Hart. *The History of the Jews.* 3d ed. 3 vols. Boston: William Veazie, 1864.

————. *Quarterly Review* 49, p. 287.

————. Review of Grote's *History of Greece,* vols. 1 and 2 (1846) in *Quarterly Review* 78, p. 121.

Moir, John S. *A History of Biblical Studies in Canada.* Society of Biblical Literature Centennial Publications, 7. Chico: Scholars Press, 1982.

Mosis, Rudolf. *Untersuchungen zur Theologie des chronistischen Geschichtswerkes.* Freiburger theologische Studien, 92. Freiburg: Herder, 1973.

Mott, Lewis Freeman. *Ernest Renan.* New York: D. Appleton, 1921.

Mourelatos, A. P. D. "Fries, Jakob Friedrich," *The Encyclopedia of Philosophy* 3 (1967) 253-55.

Movers, Franz Karl. *Kritische Untersuchungen über die biblische Chronik.* Bonn: T. Habicht, 1834.

Mozley, J. R. "Francis William Newman," *The Hibbert Journal* 23 (1925) 345-60.

Muilenberg, James. "Budde, Karl Ferdinand Reinhard," *Encyclopaedia judaica* 4 (1971) 1455.

Müller, Karl Otfried. *Prolegomena zu einer wissenschaftlichen Mythologie.* Göttingen: Vandenhoeck & Ruprecht, 1825.

Neteler, B. *Die Bücher der Chronik.* Munster: Theissing, 1899.

"Francis Newman," *London Times* (Oct. 6, 1897) 4.

"Mr. F. W. Newman," *Athenaeum* 3650 (Oct. 9, 1897) 489-90.

Newman, Francis. *A History of the Hebrew Monarchy.* London: John Chapman, 1849.

Nicoll, W. Robertson. "Professor Cheyne," *The Expositor* 9 (3d ser.; 1889) 59-61.

————. "Schrader's Cuneiform Inscriptions and the Old Testament," *The Expositor* 2 (3d ser.; 1885) 237-40.

Niebuhr, B. G. *The History of Rome.* Philadelphia: Thomas Wardle, 1835.

Nöldeke, Theodor. *Die Alttestamentliche Literatur.* Leipzig: Quandt & Handel, 1868.

"Nöldeke, Theodor," *Encyclopaedia Britannica* 19 (llth ed.; 1911) 734.

"Nöldeke, Theodor," *Encyclopaedia judaica* 12 (1971) 1202.

North, Robert. "Does Archaeology Prove Chronicles Sources?", *A Light unto My Path: Old Testament Studies in Honor of Jacob M. Meyers,* pp. 375-401. Philadelphia: Temple University, 1974.

Oettli, Samuel. *Amos und Hosea*. Gütersloh: C. Bertelsmann, 1901.

_____. *Die geschichtlichen Hagiographen und das Buch Daniel*. Kurzgefasster Kommentar zu den heiligen Schriften Alten und Neuen Testamentes so wie zu den Apokryphen. Nördlingen: C. H. Beck, 1889.

_____. *Geschichte Israels b i s a u f Alexander den Grossen D i e Geschichte Israels*. Stuttgart: Vereinsbuchhandlung, 1905.

_____. *Das Gesetz Hammurabis und d i e Thora Israels*. Leipzig: Deichert, 1903.

Otto, Rudolf. *The Philosophy of Religion*. London: Williams & Norgate, 1931.

Pals, Daniel L. *The Victorian "Lives" of Jesus*. Trinity University Monograph Series in Religion, 7. San Antonio: Trinity University, 1982.

Payne, J. Barton. "The Validity of the Numbers in Chronicles," *Bibliotheca Sacra* 136 (1979) 109-28, 206-20.

Peake, A. S. "Thomas Kelly Cheyne," *Expository Times* 6 (1894/95) 439-44.

_____. "T. K. Cheyne," *Dictionary of National Biography 1912-1921* (1927) 119-20.

Perlitt, Lothar. *Vatke und Wellhausen*. Beihefte zur Zeitschrift für die alttestamentliche Wissenschaft, 94. Berlin: Alfred Töpelmann, 1965.

Pfleiderer, Otto. *The Development of Theology in Germany since Kant, and its Progress in Great Britain since 1825*. New York: Macmillan, 1890.

Piepenbring, Charles. *Theologie de l'Ancien Testament*. Paris: Fischbacher, 1886.

_____. *Theology of the Old Testament*. New York: T. Y. Crowell, 1893.

_____. *Histoire du peuple d'Israel*. Paris: Librairie Grassart, 1898.

Prideaux, Humphrey. *The Old and New Testament Connected in the History o f the Jews, and Neighbouring Nations; fro m t h e Declension of the Kingdoms of Israel and Judah t o the Time of Christ*. 15th ed. 2 vols. New York: Harper & Bros., 1871.

Procopius. *Commentarii in Libros I,II Paralipomenon. Patrologiae Grecque in Patrologiae cursus completus*. Volume 87a. Jacques Paul Migne, editor. Paris, 1865.

Prothero, R. E. "Stanley, Arthur Penrhyn," *Dictionary of National Biography* 54 (1898) 46-48.

_____. and G. G. Bradley. *The Life and Correspondence of Arthur Penrhyn Stanley.* 2 vols. 3d ed. London: John Murray, 1894.

Pundt, Alfred G. "The Rise of Romanticism," *The Development of Historiography.* Eds. M. A. Fitzsimons, A. G. Pundt, and C. E. Nowell. Harrisburg: Stackpole, 1954.

Ranke, Leopold. *Geschichte der romanischen und germanischen Völker.* 2d ed. Leipzig: Duncker & Humbolt, 1874.

"Rawlinson, George," *Encyclopaedia Britannica* 22 (1910) 928.

Rawlinson, George. *Egypt and Babylon from Sacred and Profane Sources.* New York: John B. Alden, 1885.

_____. *Ezra and Nehemiah.* Men of the Bible. New York: Fleming H. Revell, 1890.

_____. *The Five Great Monarchies of the Ancient Eastern World.* 2d ed. 3 vols. New York: Dodd, Mead, 1881.

_____. *The Historical Evidences of the Truth of the Scripture Records.* London: John Murray, 1859.

_____. *The Kings of Israel and Judah.* Men of the Bible. New York: Fleming H. Revell, 1889.

_____. *The Testimony of History to the Truth of Scripture.* Boston: H. L. Hastings, 1885.

_____. "Moses the Author of the Levitical Code of Laws," *Lex Mosaica,* pp. 21-52. Ed. R. V. French. London: Eyre & Spottiswoode, 1894.

Redslob. "Gesenius," *Allgemeine Deutsche Biographie* 9 (1879) 89-93.

_____. "Hitzig, Ferdinand H.," *Allgemeine Deutsche Biographie* 12 (1880) 507-9.

_____. "Graf, Karl Heinrich G.," *Allgemeine Deutsche Biographie* 9 (1879) 549-50.

_____. "Gramberg, Karl Peter Wilhelm," *Allgemeine Deutsche Biographie* 9 (1879) 577.

Reinke, Laurenz. *Beiträge Zur Erklärung des alten Testamentes.* 4 vols. Munster: Coppenrath, 1851.

Renan, Ernest. *History of the People of Israel.* 3 vols. Boston: Roberts Brothers, 188-95.

_____. "History of the People of Israel," *Studies of Religious History and Criticism.* New York: Carleton, 1864.

Reusch. "Movers, Franz Karl M.," *Allgemeine Deutsche Biographie* 22 (1885) 417-18.

Reuss, Eduard. *Die Geschichte der Heiligen Schriften Alten Testaments.* 1st ed. Braunschweig: C. A. Schwetschke & Son, 1881.

_____. *L'histoire sainte et la loi*. Paris: Librairie Sandoz et Fischbacher, 1879.

Richardson, H. Neil. "The Historical Reliability of Chronicles," *Journal of Bible and Religion* 26 (1958) 9-12.

Ritschl, O. *Die evangelisch-theologische Fakultät zu Bonn in dem ersten Jahrhundert ihrer Geschichte, 1819-1919*. Bonn: A. Marcus & E. Webers Verlag, 1919.

Robbins, William. *The Newman Brothers*. London: Heineman, 1966.

Rogerson, John. *Old Testament Criticism in the Nineteenth Century*. Philadelphia: Fortress, 1985.

Ross, Kenneth N. "Francis William Newman," *Church Quarterly Review* 118 (1934) 231-44.

Russell, Michael. *A Connection of Sacred and Profane History*. New ed. Ed. J. T. Wheeler. 2 vols. London: Milliam Tegg, 1869.

"Sayce, A. H.," *Encyclopaedia Britannica* 24 (1910) 276.

Sayce, Archibald H. *The Early History of the Hebrews*. New York: Macmillian, 1897.

_____. *Early Israel and the Surrounding Nations*. London: Service & Paton, 1899.

_____. *The Egypt of the Hebrews and Herodotus*. London: Rivington, Percival, 1895.

_____. *Fresh Light from the Ancient Monuments*. By-Paths of Biblical Knowledge, 2. New York: Fleming H. Revell, n.d.

_____. *The "Higher Criticism" and the Verdict of the Monuments*. London: SPCK, 1894.

_____. *An Introduction to Ezra, Nehemiah, and Esther*. London: Religious Tract Society, 1885.

_____. *Monument Facts and Higher Critical Fancies*. New York: Fleming H. Revell, 1904.

_____. *Patriarchal Palestine*. London: SPCK, 1895.

_____. *Reminiscences*. London: Macmillan, 1923.

Schorsch, Ismar. *H. Graetz: The Structure of Jewish History and Other Essays*. New York: The Jewish Theological Seminary of America, 1975.

"Schrader, Eberhard," *Encyclopaedia Britannica* 24 (1910) 378.

Schrader, Wilhelm. *Geschichte der Friedrichs-Universität zu Halle*. Berlin: F. Dummler, 1894.

_____. *Die Keilinschriften und das Alten Testament*. 2 vols. Giessen: J. Ricker, 1872.

_____. *The Cuneiform Inscriptions and the Old Testament*. 2 vols. Trans. from the 2d German ed. London: Williams & Norgate, 1885/1888.

Schultze, Victor. "Zöckler, Otto," *Realencyklopädie für protestantische Theologie und Kirche* 21 (1908) 704-8.

Schwartz, Eduard. "Julius Wellhausen," *Nachrichten von der Kgl. Gesellschaft der Wissenschaften*, pp. 43-70. Göttingen: Geschaftliche Mitteilungen, 1918. Reprinted in Schwartz' *Gesämmelte Schriften*, vol. 1, pp. 326-61. 2d ed. Berlin: Walter de Gruyter, 1963.

Seinecke, L. *Geschichte des Volkes Israel*. 2 vols. Göttingen: Vandenhoeck & Ruprecht, 1876/1884.

Sellin, E. "Köhler, August," *Realencyklopädie für protestantische Theologie und Kirche* 10 (1901) 615-18.

_____. "Köhler, August," *Allgemeine Deutsche Biographie* 51 (1906) 310-11.

Shaffer, E. S. *"Kubla Khan" and the Fall of Jerusalem*. Cambridge: University Press, 1975.

Shipley, A. E. "Smith, William Robertson," *Encyclopaedia Britannica* 25 (1911) 271-72.

Sieveking, G. *Memoir and Letters of Francis W. Newman*. London: Kegan, Paul, Trench, Trubner, 1909.

Simon, Richard. *Histoire critique du Vieux Testament*. New ed. Rotterdam: Reinier Leers, 1685-93.

Smend, Rudolf. "De Wette und das Verhältniss zwischen historischer Bibelkritik und philosophischem System im 19. Jahrhundert," *Theologische Zeitschrift* 14 (1958) 107-19.

_____. "Friedrich Bleek, 1793-1859," *150 Jahre Reinische* Friedrich-Wilhelms-Universität zu Bonn, 1818-1968. Bonn: Bouvier, 1968. Pp. 31-41.

_____. "Reuss, Eduard," *Encyclopaedia judaica* 14 (1971) 111-12.

_____. "Wellhausen in Greifswald," *Zeitschrift für Theologie und Kirche* 78 (1981) 141-76.

_____. "Wellhausen, Julius," *Encyclopaedia judaica* 16 (1971) 444.

_____. "Wellhausen and his Prolegomena to the History of Israel," *Julius Wellhausen and his Prolegomena to the History of Israel*. Ed. Douglas A. Knight. Semeia, 25. Chico: Scholars Press, 1983. Pp. 1-20.

_____. *Wilhelm Martin Leberecht de Wettes Arbeit am alten und am neuen Testament*. Basel: Helbing & Lichtenhahn, 1958.

Smith, George. *The Assyrian Eponym Canon*. London: Samuel Bagster, n. d.

Smith, G. A. *The Historical Geography of the Holy Land*. 4th ed. New York: Hodder & Stoughton, 1896.

Smith, William Robertson. "Captain Conder and Modern Critics," *Contemporary Review* 51 (1887) 561-69.

_____. "Chronicles," *Encyclopaedia Britannica* 5 (1889) 706-9.

_____. *The Old Testament in the Jewish Church*. 2d ed. London: Adam and Charles Black, 1892.

_____. "Renan's *Histoire du peuple d'Israel* (1887)," *Lectures & Essays of William Robertson Smith*, pp. 608-22. Eds. John. Sutherland Black and George Chrystal. London: Adam & Charles Black, 1912.

"Stade, Bernhard," *Encyclopaedia Britannica* 25 (1910) 247.

Stade, Bernhard. *Biblische Theologie*. Tübingen: J. C. B. Mohr, 1905.

_____. *Geschichte des Volkes Israel*. 2d ed. Berlin: G. Grote, 1889.

Stanley, A. P. *Lectures on the History of the Jewish Church*. 3 vols. New York: Scribner, Armstrong, 1877. New ed., 1892.

Steindorff, George. "Excavations in Egypt," *Explorations in Bible Lands During the 19th Century*, pp. 623-90. Ed. H. V. Hilprecht. Philadelphia: A. J. Holman, 1903.

Storr, Vernon F. *The Development of English Theology in the Nineteenth Century, 1800-1860*. London: Longmans, Green, 1913.

Theodoret. *Quaestiones in libros Regnorum et Paralipomenon. Patrologiae grecque in Patrologiae cursus completus*. Volume 80. Jacques Paul Migne, ed. Paris, 1864.

Thompson, R. J. *Moses and the Law in a Century of Criticism Since Graf*. Supplements to Vetus Testamentum, 19. Leiden: E . J. Brill, 1970.

Van Beek, Gus. "Archaeology, " *The Interpreters Dictionary of the Bible* 1 (1962) 275-76 .

Vatke, Wilhelm. *Die biblische Theologie*. Berlin: G. Bethge, 1835.

_____. *Historisch-kritische Einleitung in das Alte Testament* . Ed . H. G. S. Preiss. Bonn: Emil Strauss, 1886.

_____. "Kuenen, Abraham, " *Encyclopaedia judaica* 10 (1971) 1248-85.

"Wellhausen, Julius." *Encyclopaedia Britannica* 28 (1911) 507.

Wellhausen, Julius. "Die Composition des Hexateuchs," *Jahrbücher für Deutsche Theologie* (1876) 392-450, 531-602; (1877) 407-79 .

_____. *Die Composition des Hexateuchs und der Historischen Bücher des Alten Testaments.* 2d ed. Berlin: George Reimer, 1889.

_____. *Prolegomena to the History of Ancient Israel.* Reprint of the translation of the 2d ed. of 1883. Gloucester, Mass.: Peter Smith, 1973.

Welten, Peter. *Geschichte und Geschichtsdarstellung in den Chronikbüchern. Wissenschaftliche Monographien zum Alten und Neuen Testament,* 42. Neukirchen-Vluyn: Neukirchener Verlag, 1973.

Werner. "Jahn, Johann J.," *Allgemeine Deutsche Biographie* 13 (1881) 665-66.

De Wette, W. M. L. *Auffoderung zum Studium der Hebräischen Sprache und Litteratur.* Jena: C. E. Gabler, 1805.

_____. *Beiträge zur Einleitung in das Alte Testament.* 2 vols. Halle: Schimmelpfennig, 1807.

_____. *A Critical Introduction to the Canonical Scriptures of the Old Testament.* 3d ed. Trans. and enlarged by Theodore Parker from the 5th German ed. Boston: Rufus Leighton, 1859.

_____. *Eine Idee über das Studium der Theologie.* Ed. A. Stieren. Leipzig: 1850.

_____. *Lehrbuch d e r historisch-kritischen Einleitung i n die kanonischen und apokryphischen Bücher des Alten Testamentes.* 4th ed. Berlin: G. Reimer, 1833. 7th ed., 1852. 8th ed., ed. E. Schrader, 1869.

Wicksteed, Philip H. "Abraham Kuenen," *Jewish Quarterly Review* 4 (1892) 571-605.

Wiegand, Adelbert. *W. M. L. de Wette. Eine Säkularschrift.* Erfurt: A. Stenger, 1879.

Wiener, Max. *Abraham Geiger and Liberal Judaism: The Challenge of the Nineteenth Century.* Philadelphia: Jewish Publication Society of America, 1962.

Willi, Thomas. *Die Chronik als Auslegung.* Forschungen zur Religion und Literatur des Alten und Neuen Testaments, 106. Göttingen: Vandenhoeck & Ruprecht, 1972.

Williamson, H. G. M. "The Accession of Solomon in the Books of Chronicles," *Vetus Testamentum* 26 (1976) 351-61.

_____. "Eschatology in Chronicles," *Tyndale Bulletin* 28 (1977) 115-54.

_____. *Israel in t h e Books of Chronicles.* Cambridge: University Press, 1977.

_____. *1 and 2 Chronicles.* The New Century Bible Commentary. Grand Rapids: Wm. B. Eerdmans, 1982.

Wilson, John A. *Signs & Wonders Upon Pharaoh.* Chicago: University of Chicago, 1964.

Wolff. "Herbst, Johann Georg" *Allgemeine Deutsche Biographie* 12 (1880) 50-51.

Zobel, Hans-Jürgen. "Eichhorn, Johann Gottfried," *Theologische Realencyklopädie* 9 (1982) 369-71.

"Zöckler, Otto," *Encyclopaedia Britannica* 3 (9th ed. supplement.; 1898) 800.

Zöckler, Otto. *The Books of Chronicles.* Lange's Commentary. New York: Scribner, Armstrong, 1877.

Zunz, Leopold. *Die gottesdienstlichen Vorträge der Juden.* Berlin: A. Asher, 1832.